THE SMART GUIDE TO

Classical Music

BY ROBERT SHERMAN
AND PHILIP SELDON

The Smart Guide To Classical Music

Published by

Smart Guide Publications, Inc.
2517 Deer Chase Drive
Norman, OK 73071
www.smartguidepublications.com

For information, address: Smart Guide Publications, Inc. 2517 Deer Creek Drive, Norman, OK 73071

SMART GUIDE and Design are registered trademarks licensed to Smart Guide Publications, Inc.

International Standard Book Number: 978-1-937636-22-7

Library of Congress Catalog Card Number:
11 12 13 14 15   10 9 8 7 6 5 4 3 2 1

Printed in the United States of America

Cover design: Lorna Llewellyn
Back cover design: Joel Friedlander, Eric Gelb, Deon Seifert
Illustrations: James Balkovek
Production: Zoë Lonergan
Indexer: Cory Emberson
V.P./Business Manager: Cathy Barker

Dear Reader,

This book will de-mystify classical music. Reading it will instantly turn you into a savvy connoisseur, and you'll sally forth into the world of Mozart, Beethoven, and company with new confidence and understanding. You'll be able to decipher the music reviews in the morning paper, make sense out of program notes at a concert, know a kettledrum when you see one boiling, and hold your own when party conversation gets around to the latest opera telecast or the hot new pianist who practiced enough to get to Carnegie Hall.

Why should you listen to fine music? For the same reason you dine at a fine restaurant: It's delicious. Music not only stimulates the senses and animates the intellect, it satisfies the soul. Classical music can soothe your fevered brow after a hard day at the office, or take you in the other direction, bouncing even the most confirmed couch potato up to rewarding attention. It can enhance a romantic evening (just remember what Ravel's "Bolero" did for Bo Derek in the movie Ten), it can be uplifting, elating, relaxing, or all of the above, depending on your mood and the music you select.

After you finish this book, you'll be able to recognize the subtle nuances of color, texture, and instrumentation that give special delight to classical music. You'll be wise in the ways of composers from Bach to Philip Glass, you'll know all about symphonies and sonatas, concertos and cantatas, operas and oratorios. You'll learn how music developed, from the chanting of monks in their cloistered abbeys to whizbang, multi-media works using state-of-the-art electronics.

We'll even give you practical advice on what to wear to a concert, and how to act so your next-seat neighbor doesn't look at you funny. We'll clue you in on ways and means to build and maintain a record collection, and how not to get ripped off when you're buying a new stereo. In fact, when you finish this book, you'll know so much about classical music that you'll probably be able to teach your friends a thing or two.

"Without music," wrote the German philosopher Nietsche, "life would be a mistake." We don't want that to happen to you, so read. Listen. Enjoy. And have a good life...

Sincerely,

Bob Sherman   Philip Seldon

TABLE OF CONTENTS

PART ONE

Overture

CHAPTER 1

 # If You Know Nothing About Classical Music, Start Here

In This Chapter

➤ What is classical music?

➤ The elements of classical music

➤ How classical music is different from other kinds of music

➤ The organization of classical music

We all know what music is. It's the tune you whistle while you work; it's what the brothers Gershwin dubbed "Fascinating Rhythm;" it's the song you sing in the shower. So how to define it? In the simplest terms, music is the organization of sound to create beauty of form and expression of emotion. Classical music is just like any other kind of music except that the sounds are organized differently, usually within a more formal structure. On the other hand, "classical" composers frequently use folk songs, pop tunes, jazz riffs, and ethnic dance rhythms, so don't get too wrapped up in academic definitions. As the saying goes, just sit back and enjoy it.

Classical music used to be called "long-hair," probably because Liszt, Paganini, and other early virtuosos were too busy making their audiences faint with ecstasy to bother about going to the barber. That worked fine until The Beatles, the Rolling Stones, and various other rock groups came on the scene, after which no self-respecting electric guitarist or band drummer would be seen without hair curling down his shoulders.

So what is classical music already? Let's find out.

Why Do I Need to Know Anything About Classical Music? I Already Enjoy It

Just as you don't need to know anything about art to enjoy a gorgeous painting, or how to follow a recipe to enjoy chocolate chip cookies, you don't need a college education to love classical music. On the other hand, the more you do know, the deeper your enjoyment will be.

Ever since some monks in the ninth century figured out that a tune might sound better if it were harmonized, music has been getting more and more complicated. And with complexity comes subtlety. Just as you'll savor a wine more when you understand its nuances, you'll enjoy music more when you are familiar with the textures and forms that give it life.

Can you tell an oboe from a saxophone, a symphony from a sonata? Sure you can. Well, why not go a step further, and learn about the theremin, the only instrument you play without touching it, or the symphonic poem, where music and the literary arts come together. Classical music is a language, and while you can get along without being a grammarian or a spelling bee champion, the more you do learn about it, the better the communication, and the greater your satisfaction.

Music Word

Symphony literally means "a sounding together." in the baroque era, the word was often used to denote an overture to an opera, or instrumental sections within a vocal work. Since Haydn wrote his 104 symphonies, the word has come to mean an orchestral work of considerable length and weight, most often in three or four movements.

A **movement** is a major, usually self-contained unit of a larger work. The name probably derives from the fact that these different sections usually have different tempo markings, indicating their speed of progression.

You'll Like It Better If You Know Something About It

Most people think French is a beautiful language. If you listen to someone speaking—or singing—in French, you may be impressed by the lyrical flow of sounds, the gentle inflections, the expressivity of voice. On the other hand, your appreciation of the sound is limited to just that: If you don't understand the language, if you can't figure out what is being said or sung, your appreciation is obviously going to be severely limited.

It's the same way with music. Even if you've never heard of Beethoven, you can be swept away by the wondrous sounds of his Sixth Symphony—the "Pastorale." But when you know that the music depicts a day in the country, complete with twittering birds and a summer thunderstorm, the music takes on an entirely new listening dimension. Long before "Man of La Mancha," Richard Strauss portrayed the adventures of Don Quixote in orchestral form, but if you don't know that the viola represents Sancho Panza, or that when the Knight goes forth to battle with the windmills, it's a solo cello vs. a wind machine (an instrument that makes a sound like the wind), you're missing half the fun. In short, the more you look into the elements of classical music, the easier it is to experience the events and emotions the composer intended.

Bet You Didn't Know

Not everybody liked the "Pastorale" Symphony. The famous English writer John Ruskin told a friend that "Beethoven always sounds to me like the upsetting of bags of nails, with here and there also a dropped hammer."

Learning About Classical Music is Going to Be a Song and Dance

Fortunately, learning about classical music does not require anything like the time, talent, or dedication it takes to play it. The purpose of this book, in other words, is not to turn you into a Pavarotti wannabee, but simply to heighten your enjoyment as a listener. For starters, let's look at some of the basic elements that go into classical music.

Rhythm is the heartbeat of music, propelling it forward. Just as there is rhythm to almost every human activity, from breathing to walking, the pulse of music often defines its character. There is the flowing measure of Gregorian chant, the precise and ordered cadences of a baroque concerto, and the syncopated beat of a Scott Joplin rag.

A melody is a succession of single notes varying in pitch and strung together to form a satisfying entity. When you leave "The King and I" whistling a happy tune, that's the melody. When a Schubert song tugs at your heartstrings, or you have an uncontrollable urge to hum along with the "Full Moon and Empty Arms" theme of the Rachmaninoff Second Piano Concerto, the composer has succeeded in creating a melody to remember.

Harmony is the simultaneous sounding of two or more notes. It enriches the sound of a melody, accentuates changing rhythmic patterns, and gives classical music its special richness and resonance. Aaron Copland said, "It represents one of the most original conceptions of the human mind."

The color of a tone, the distinctive timbre of each voice and instrument, gives music its depth and variety. It's the difference between the way Dorothy sees Kansas (in black-and-white) and the Land of Oz (in Technicolor). It's the sauce a great chef adds to the pasta, the flowing lines a master architect puts into a skyscraper. Imagine Wagner's Ring Cycle without brasses, or Beethoven's "Für Elise" played on trumpet instead of piano, and you'll realize the enormous impact color has on our appreciation of music. The combined sound of the many individual instruments within the symphonic ensemble is known as orchestral color. Sometimes the woodwinds predominate, sometimes the strings do; it's the composer's job to mix and match those separate tones until they produce the desired sonic entity.

The imaginative combination of all these ingredients is the stuff of classical music. It's up to the composer to devise these combinations, the performers to interpret them, and within each category there are endless variations, just waiting to be savored by a savvy listener. We, in other words, have the far simpler task of enjoying the fruits of their labors.

Music Word

A fancypants way of saying tone color, **timbre** is the peculiar characteristic of sound produced by different instruments or voices. It's what lets us distinguish between "Happy Birthday" played on the flute and the same tune pumped out on the trumpet.

What is Classical Music?

Think of it as a type of architecture. Classical music is organized according to certain conventions of line and form. Within this broad denomination are a number of subgroups, each with a distinctive style. The Chrysler and Empire State Buildings in New York City, for instance, exemplify art deco style. On this basis, we can compare them to each other. In a musical equivalent, we might pair Haydn and Mozart; to contrast two different styles, we might match Bach and Stravinsky.

You'll Know It When You Hear It

Even the best-trained musicians can't always distinguish Haydn from Mozart or Corelli from Vivaldi, but chances are that you'll recognize classical music after only a few notes. That's because every type of music has its own distinctive and immediately recognizable features, such as orchestral color in classical music. Press the scanning button on your car radio, and within 60 seconds, you'll know perfectly well that you've passed through a rock station, one featuring jazz, a country music station, or (ah, ecstasy!) one with a classical format.

Music Word

The combined sound of the many individual instruments within the symphonic ensemble is known as do

Give Me European Royalty and Cultural Elite

When asked for a definition of folk music, a balladeer once replied that all music is folk music—you don't hear horses singing it. (I prefer Mark Twain's witty observation: "Folk music," he said, "is music nobody ever wrote.") Way back in the Middle Ages, when those nobodys were composing "Greensleeves" and other ballads we still cherish today, a different sort of music was evolving within the castle walls that kept out the riffraff. The Kings and Queens of Europe demanded more lofty musical expressions, and imported masters of the lute, mandolin, and harpsichord to play it for them.

Soon, every monarch worth his royal salt had a couple of court composers to produce music for weddings, funerals, private parties, and all manner of other functions. Some of them were pretty good musicians themselves—Frederick the Great played the flute and Louis IX danced in courtly ballets—and the great body of what we call classical music derived from these aristocratic arbiters of culture.

Bet You Didn't Know

When he wasn't beheading wives, Henry VIII kept a court band of 79 musicians on hand for his royal entertainment. Meanwhile, his daughter, Queen Elizabeth, started the whole idea of dinner music. They say she couldn't enjoy her supper unless she was being serenaded by an orchestra of trumpets, fifes, and kettledrums.

It's All For You

Things have changed a lot since Handel wrote music for King George to go barging down the Thames. These days, classical music is for everybody. We hear it on radio and television, go to concerts, or just create our own surround-sound environment at home. Most large cities have free summer concerts with orchestras playing under the stars—a far cry from those bygone days when a concertgoer needed the keys to the castle—and every form of music, from solo recitals to the grandest of operas, is as close as your friendly neighborhood Internet site.

Who Done It?

Classical music is the creation of a composer, who determines the organization of tones and sounds. You'll not find improvisational riffs by the sax player as you will in a jazz band and the soprano singing Lucia better not interpolate scat-singing à la Ella Fitzgerald. Interpretations, of course, may vary greatly: Listen to the same symphony conducted by Herbert von Karajan and Leonard Bernstein and you may wonder whether they were working from the same manuscript. They were, of course: it's just that the variables of speed, loudness, and instrumental emphasis, keep classical music ever fresh and exhilarating.

Complex Texture and Organization

Okay, it's not all complex. There is nothing simpler than the unharmonized melody of a Gregorian chant. But when we move on to motets and madrigals, with their interweaving melodic lines, when we consider symphonies, concertos, and that mighty mishmosh known as opera, we realize how complicated a musical structure can get. This doesn't make it less enjoyable, mind you, it's just that it becomes a little harder to tell the players apart without a program.

The Kinds of Classical Music

Classical music can be instrumental, vocal, or a combination of the two. Below, you can discover the wealth of musical arrangements available in each.

Instrumental Music

I know you never would have guessed this, but an instrumental piece is written for instruments only. It can be for a single guitar or a 110-piece orchestra, but you have to check your vocal cords at the door, since there's nary a singer in sight.

> ➤ **Solo** means one. One cello. One trumpet. One kazoo. Just to be difficult, though, a solo can sometimes mean two, such as when a featured instrument has a less important partner, such as a piano accompanying a virtuoso solo on the violin.

> ➤ **Duet** means two equal partner, either at the same instrument, like two guitars, or contrasting ones, such as flute and bassoon.

> ➤ **Chamber Music** is for two or more equally important instruments, although here again, there sometimes can be an accompanying part as well. The term began as a description of the location in which this music was played—usually a small room as opposed to a large hall—but now it's used to designate any sort of small ensemble.

> ➤ Paired instrumental pieces are often called **sonatas**; **trios (3 players)**, **quartets (4 players)**, **quintets (5 players)**, etc., each add one more musician to the performing pot. A string quartet, as its name suggests, is for four strings (normally two violins, a viola and a cello); a wind quintet brings together flute, oboe, clarinet, bassoon and horn; but a piano trio or quartet doesn't mean multiple keyboards—it's just an indication that the piano shares the spotlight with the strings or winds.

> ➤ Once you get beyond an octet (eight musicians), players usually need a traffic cop (i.e., a conductor) to keep things running smoothly; anything up to thirty-five or so instrumentalists is usually called a **chamber orchestra**, since it could conceivably fit into your chamber (especially if you live at Versailles).

> ➤ With a **symphony orchestra** we're into the big time, with 60, 70, sometimes well over 100 players on stage at the same time. There are four main instrumental families in the orchestra, all of whose members make sounds in more or less the same ways.

Strings include violins, violas, cellos, double basses and, if you insist, the harp. The player either moves a bow across the strings, or plucks them with his fingers. Brasses are those loud, shiny things in the back: trumpets, horns, trombones, tubas. Woodwinds are so called because they were originally made of wood and you blew through them. Now, wind instruments have all sorts of metal parts and some, like the flute and piccolo, are made entirely of metal. The percussion section is the noisiest bunch of all, including anything that's fit to be banged, bonged, or beaten. It's sometimes called "the kitchen" because it has everything but the sink.

Music Word

A **concerto** is an extended work for one or more solo instruments and orchestra, usually in three movements. Sometimes composers use this title for solo or purely orchestral pieces, when the intended effect is to mimic the scope and focus of a genuine concerto.

Bet You Didn't Know

It was German violinist, composer, and conductor Ludwig Spohr (1784–1859) who popularized the small baton we know today, since he liked to carry it around in his pocket. Before that, conductors used everything from a violin bow (Gluck) to a cane with ivory knobs on either end (Spontini).

Vocal Music

Vocal music is any progression of musical sounds emanating from the human throat. In a way, it is the most elemental form of music making, since it proceeds from performer to listener without any intervening contraptions.

➤ **Songs**—Basically, a song is a poem set to music. During the Middle Ages, troubadours went from castle to castle singing about deeds of love, valor, and despair, not to mention tasty bits of local gossip, spilling the beans about which royal personage was doing what to whom. In France these were called chansons; in Germany they were known as lieder. A madrigal was a song in five or six parts, pretty much of a poem set to music. In Germany, songs are called lieder. Lieder were especially popular during the Romantic era, and you can follow them to the heights of emotion with works by composers like Schubert, Schumann, and Brahms.

➤ **Sacred or Church Music**—Gregorian chants were meant to echo through the high arches of a cathedral and fill the listener with the presence of God. They were monophonic and a capella; that is, they had a single voice and were unaccompanied. By the eleventh century, composers began to develop polyphony for two voices. The motet was an early example, typically a song based on Latin text and performed as part of the church service. The Mass, the rite of consecration, evolved during the Renaissance, and has since become an integral part of the classical realm. Composers from Mozart to Leonard Bernstein have composed Masses, some of which are not quite as solemn as they were once intended to be.

➤ **Chorus**—Choral music is an arrangement of voices. There are women's choruses and men's choruses, but many choruses are mixed, to incorporate the full range of voices, from soprano to bass.

➤ **Opera**—When a dramatic story unfolds in vocal music and you add an orchestral underpinning, you wind up with an opera (or if it's a Biblical story set to music, an oratorio). Operas can be funny ("The Daughter of the Regiment") or tragic ("Aida"), short ("Salome") or endless ("Götterdämmerung"), fanciful ("The Magic Flute") or realistic ("Tosca"), uplifting ("Amahl and the Night Visitors") or upsetting ("Wozzeck"). They can also be thrilling and enormously satisfying (all of the above).

Bet You Didn't Know

The French composer Jean-Baptiste Lully used to conduct his operas by banging out the rhythm on the floor with a large walking stick. One day he banged out the rhythm on his foot by mistake, and died of blood poisoning shortly afterwards.

Why Listen to Classical Music?

Listening to classical music takes us out of our workaday world, with all of its stresses and strains. New York City's Lincoln Center once had a banner proclaiming "Savage Breasts Soothed Here," and while it may seem contradictory to think of being soothed by the dissonant harmonies of Bartok or the boisterous cries of the Valkyries, it really isn't. We instinctively turn to music when we feel troubled, angry, or upset, and this is not a recent phenomenon.

Bet You Didn't Know

Early in the 16th century, Martin Luther told us that "Nothing on earth is so well suited to make the sad merry, to give courage to the despairing, to make the proud humble, to lessen envy and hate, as music."

It Provides Aesthetic Enjoyment

Think of music as Picasso or Rembrandt for the ears. You don't have to be refined, elegant, or artistic to enjoy classical music, but listening to it will elevate your mind and soul.

It's Inspiring

The German expressionist Wassily Kandinsky painted to music. Or more accurately, he painted music: his canvasses are the visual illustrations of sounds that he heard. A composer like Scriabin, on the other hand, wrote music evoking specific colors, and Sir Arthur Bliss wrote an entire "Color Symphony." These expressions, whether visual or aural, convey emotions, enhance our sense of artistic awareness, and even produce a burst of energy within us. It is no accident that Olympic skaters do all of their incredible jumps and turns to music, or that civil rights workers found new strength and confidence when they sang "We Shall Overcome."

It Sounds Beautiful

Beauty is in the eye—or ear—of the beholder. Music that is considered enchanting in one culture may be seen as ugly in another; similarly, we, as individuals, have widely varying musical judgments. One man's meat, as the saying goes. Some of us, for instance, may groan at the repetition in baroque concertos, yet Vivaldi's "The Four Seasons" is among the most popular pieces ever written. And when a Paris critic wrote that "these chromatic meows of an amorous cat will never replace an expressive tonal melody," he wasn't referring to some avant-garde symphony, but to Bizet's "Carmen." Moral: Give classical music a chance; without a doubt you'll find some form or style that will make you feel better about yourself and the world you live in.

Bet You Didn't Know

George Philipp Telemann, who was born four years before Bach, wrote 44 oratorios, 60 overtures, hundreds of chamber pieces and at least three thousand songs. "A proper composer should be able to set a placard to music," he said.

Don't Be Intimidated by All Those Scary Terms

Lots of scary terms—"heavy," "serious"—were coined by people who didn't understand classical music and were afraid to admit it. Can you imagine anything lighter than a Strauss waltz, anything less serious than Mozart's "Musical Joke"? It used to be that you could tell a classical piece from some other kind because it was written for orchestra, but even that doesn't work any more: Lots of pop musicians feel naked without a full symphonic ensemble behind them and some, such as The Moody Blues, have created their niche creating full-length works backed by classical orchestras.

In this chapter we have begun to introduce you to the terms of classical music—timbre, color, harmony, concerto, and the like. Look, we're not talking about modems, motherboards, or mice (except possibly the three blind sort). There's nothing in this book that hasn't stood the test of time. Wagner and Beethoven, not to mention Callas and Caruso, may have intimidated the conductors and impresarios they worked for, but they always enchanted their audiences. The more you know about classical music, the less threatening it becomes. In the end, it's all about rhythm and color, tunes and textures, comfortable concepts with which we're all familiar. And that's not scary at all, is it?

CHAPTER 2

Where Do You Find Classical Music?

In This Chapter

➤ Concert Halls

➤ Church

➤ Radio and TV

➤ Recordings

➤ At the Movies

You can run, but you can't hide from classical music. You know "Twinkle, Twinkle Little Star," right? Well then, congratulations: You also know the theme for a piano piece by Mozart and a whole set of variations for piano and orchestra by Dohnanyi. If you watch television, you've heard opera arias and symphonic excerpts in commercials for everything from airlines to anniversary diamonds. If your kids go to the movies, they can probably tell you all about Beethoven—not only the shaggy dog, but the famous da-da-da-dum opening of the Fifth Symphony that infiltrates the soundtrack of the film with that name, "Beethoven." It drives some folks crazy, but you'll hear symphonic bits and pieces in banks, in elevators, and in restaurants. Yes, classical music has very decidedly departed the castles of royalty to thrive on the media airwaves, in public places, and on the green lawns of summer.

Lend Us Your Ears

Concert halls have lessened their lock on the classics, but, as recently as 1938, it was a front-page shocker when Benny Goodman brought his swing band to Carnegie Hall in New York, that holy of holies for every classical musician. Playing Carnegie Hall is still the dream of classical artists in every part of the world, but the house on 57th Street (in New York City) has also been home to rock and rap, not to mention folk, funk, and a host of other styles as well.

The rigid lines of earlier eras, in other words, have melted away. Jazz pianist Chick Corea and pop vocalist Bobby McFerrin can go on a national tour playing Mozart, while classical violinist Itzhak Perlman cooked up two CDs and a TV special with a klezmer band. At the 2011 Kennedy Center Honors, jazz saxophonist Sonny Rollins, theatre and cabaret singer Barbara Cook, and pop minstrel Neil Diamond stood alongside classical cellist Yo-Yo Ma—and a grateful country paid them homage in equal measure.

We can, of course, hear music anywhere—in the car, while shopping, at the dentist—but nothing can replace the joy of experiencing great music live, in a hall designed for maximum acoustical effect. The fortissimos (loudest sounds) arrive without distortion, while the softest passages waft their way cleanly to the last row in the balcony. Especially in more recently constructed (or renovated) buildings, the seats are designed to be non-threatening to your neck or neighbor, and the sound in the peanut gallery is as good (often better) than it is front row center. If you're intent on seeing the maestro's hair flying, of course, or want to keep a closer eye on that cute concertmaster, an up-close ticket may be right for you after all.

In short, concert halls are accessible, so if you've never attended a classical program, give it a try. It can be a superb introduction to music at its most eloquent, and a wonderful way to expand your tonal horizons. Concert hall prices are usually on par or less than the cost of a Broadway play. In New York City, the cost of an orchestra seat varies from $35 to $70 for a major orchestra and range down to $15 for the balcony. Lesser known orchestras can cost as little as $10 or be entirely free. Check the music listings in your newspaper to see if there are free or low-cost performances in your area.

Be daring. Pick a program that includes some composers you haven't heard of. Try one that offers music from different centuries, including our own. You may be pleasantly surprised to find that your musical tastes are far more varied than you imagined. On the other hand, if you've formed a liking for a piece you heard on the radio or on CD, by all means graduate to the infinitely greater pleasure of hearing it live.

The Houses That Opera Built

Opera houses are just like concert halls, only more so. They're usually bigger (seating 2,000 or more) persons, fancier, more expensive, and they have much larger backstage areas where the horses can wait for their cue to join the Triumphal March in "Aida." Red drapery, gold fluting, and glittering chandeliers frequently go with the territory, although some opera houses function quite happily in more austere settings.

The operas themselves, needless to say, cover the stylistic waterfront as well. You'll find high tragedy ("Madame Butterfly"), low comedy ("Die Fledermaus"), fairy tales for children ("Hansel and Gretel"), legends definitely not for children ("Salome"), epics of ancient history ("Moses and Aron"), and pages torn from modern headlines ("Nixon in China"). You name it, opera has it. And fear not: We'll tell you lots more about it in later chapters.

Important Things to Know

There are basically two types of operas: comic operas and dramatic operas. Do we need to explain? Comic operas have stuff to laugh at, and hardly anybody dies; dramatic stageworks tend to the tragic and most everybody dies (at least the main characters).

Opera houses sometimes are used for concerts too, naturally—especially if the performer is famous enough to fill up all those seats—and when the opera is out of town, the house will frequently resound to the pitter-patter of dancing feet. Like their operatic counterparts, classical ballet companies need stages large enough to encompass extended casts, exotic scenery, and special lighting effects. Oddly enough, there doesn't seem to be any such thing as a "ballet house," but since the dancers haven't complained, let's not make a fuss about it either.

Whether the hall hosts song or dance, though, whether Carmen is vamping the toreador or the Sleeping Beauty is waltzing off with her Prince Charming, it's all happening to the glorious sounds of music by the best composers of the past three centuries and more. And tickets can be on the expensieve side (orchestra seats can cost upwards of $150, with balcony seats going for $35 or more). Well, somebody has to pay for all those sets and costumes and special lighting effects. Don't be intimidated by all the red velvet, though. Just smile nicely at the ushers, avoid the overpriced drinks in the lobby, and enjoy the performances on stage. Whatever the price, a great opera is worth the price, even if you have to save up for it.

Bet You Didn't Know

The first official radio opera broadcast did not emanate from the Met: It was a Covent Garden "The Magic Flute" transmitted from London in 1923. Less than a year later, though, New Yorkers would hear a broadcast of "Aida" from the Metropolitan.

Get Me to the Church on Time

The church is where Western classical music all began. We'll tell you lots more about this stuff in a later chapter, but just so you'll know what's coming: The monks in the Middle Ages expressed their devotion to God through chants, hymns, motets, and eventually such more extended compositions as the Mass, the principal service of the Roman Catholic Church. Composers of every era have put their own stylistic stamp on such music of faith, even to the proliferations of folk, jazz and rock, and masses.

Ritual music of the Jewish Synagogue, the Greek Orthodox Church, and other faiths followed similar paths. Some chants are still performed in forms very similar to those that moved worshippers centuries ago, while others bear the imprint of modern compositional styles.

Bet You Didn't Know

Gregorian Chants are not only named for Saint Gregory, but many of them were edited by Pope Gregory himself. The collection was put forward in final form shortly after St. Gregory's death, and was thereafter regarded as closed.

At the Movies

Have you heard Richard Strauss' "Thus Spake Zarathustra"? How about Mozart's Piano Concerto No. 21 or Giordano's "Andrea Chenier"? Two bucks says you have! All we have to do is put those pieces in cinematic context: Zarathustra helped the sun rise in *2001: A Space Odyssey*; the slow movement of the Mozart swept the lovers away in *Elvira Madigan*; and, if you saw *Philadelphia*, you'll never forget Tom Hanks' heartrending translation of the aria "La Mama Morte" as the Callas recording played on screen.

The list of movie borrowings from the classics is endless, dating back to silent days, when theater pianists swiped everything from "The William Tell Overture" to "The Ride of the Valkyries" as they scrambled to keep up with the heroes and villains on screen. Many of us learned to love "Second Hungarian Rhapsody" from our old friend Bugs Bunny (or more recently, the framed Roger Rabbit), and now that *Fantasia* has been reissued on video, a whole new generation knows that Mickey Mouse shook hands with Leopold Stokowski before doing battle with all those multiplying mops and buckets, as portrayed in Paul Dukas' "The Sorcerer's Apprentice."

In more recent years, the haunting strains of Samuel Barber's "Adagio for Strings" has been used to shockingly ironic effect in *Platoon*, accompanying scenes of horror during the Vietnam War; the music of Beethoven—authentic and synthesized—heightened the bizarre futurism of *A Clockwork Orange*, and Bo Derek could never have finished counting to *10* without Ravel's "Bolero."

Then we have all the musical biographies. Liszt, Chopin, Beethoven, Brahms, Johann Strauss, Schumann and, of course, Amadeus have all been enshrined on the silver screen—and their music appropriated for background (and frequently foreground) service. If you've been to the movies lately, or follow the golden oldies on several TV channels devoted to them, you've also had a fine fling with classical music. For some folks, this experience can be the start of a beautiful love affair. At least it ought to be enough to try going steady for a while.

Bet You Didn't Know

More than 80 years before the film (and play) *Amadeus*, Rimsky-Korsakov tackled the same subject in his opera "Mozart and Salieri."

On the Boob Tube

With the proliferation of cable channels and public television stations has come more and more programming dedicated to the arts. Televised symphonies, operas, and ballets are becoming easier to find all the time, and while most commercial networks would rather regale you with sitcoms and police dramas, even they will occasionally slip up and present an evening with the Boston Pops. The award-winning "Live from Lincoln Center" series has been presenting full productions from the Met and the New York City Opera for many years now, along with complete concerts by the New York Philharmonic and equally distinguished visiting orchestras.

In addition to these designated doses of culture, classical music wends its way into our consciousness in a number of subliminal ways. It shows up in commercials for cars and creams and other upscale items; there are dramatic programs where a character (remember Frasier Crane?) plays the piano or flips on some classical music on the hi-fi to demonstrate his high intellect and breeding, and classical pieces are often called into service as background to the on-screen comic or dramatic action.

Even if there was a time when you bought into the foreboding "long-hair" description of classical music, forget it. It's beautiful, its uplifting, and you may find yourself less intimidated. As the Beatles once said, it's "Here, There and Everywhere." Enjoy.

Same Time, Same Station

There was a time when radio meant Burns and Allen, The Shadow, and Jack Armstrong, the All-American Boy. These days, the comedy and high adventure shows are pretty well confined to TV, but radio still talks, and, perhaps above all, radio still means great music, available any time, any place. Most radio stations carry rock, rap, middle-of-the-road, country, and any other type of popular music you can think of, but even if you have to do a bit of dial-twisting to locate a classical station, keep trying, and chances are it's there waiting for you.

Public radio is an especially likely source, non-commercial stations having make their mark. Depending upon what hour you tune in, you'll find symphonic programs, opera, choral music, and such smaller enclaves within the classical circumference as art songs or guitar solos. You'll find the most familiar works of Bach, Beethoven, and Brahms followed by brand new pieces by the best and brightest of today's younger composers. You'll hear the latest CDs and vintage recordings recalling artists who flourished nearly a century ago. Whatever your particular preferences may be, the limitless world of classical music is yours to enjoy on the radio, and since stations around the world stream their broadcasts, you can catch them on your computer as well.

Under the Stars

Outdoor concerts have become popular summer events in cities large and small, from casual programs by local community groups to major performances by the greatest orchestras and opera companies in the land. When the Boston Symphony plays at Tanglewood, or the Metropolitan Opera comes to Central Park, some avid concert enthusiasts arrive hours ahead of time to stake out their claims on prime locations on the greenery—blankets, lounge chairs, and picnic baskets at the ready. Granted, the sound can't compare with that of a good concert hall. Aside from the amplification, with its uneven balances and inevitable distortions, there are the distractions from earth and sky, leading to such unexpected offerings as Bellini's "Aria for Soprano and Barking Dog," or Tchaikovsky's "Serenade for Strings and Jet Plane."

On the other hand, you can't beat the price (zero, except maybe for a bottle of wine to go with the music), the ambiance (utterly relaxed), or the atmosphere (totally non-threatening, except maybe for anything Mother Nature has in mind). You can leave your suit and dress pumps home—a pair of shorts, T-shirt, and sneakers are the outdoor costume of choice— and if perchance you nod off a bit during the slow movement, your companion need not elbow you awake. (Be a good fellow, though, and take precautions against snoring.) What a great way to make the acquaintance of classical music! It's informal, it's festive, it's fun.

Bet You Didn't Know

The great violinist Yehudi Menuin was playing the Mendelssohn Concerto at an outdoor program with the Israel Philharmonic when a drum beat shattered the serenity of the slow movement. The conductor (Zubin Mehta) looked angrily at the offending typanist, who simply pointed a blaming finger upwards: turned out a dove was enjoying the music, but decided to relieve itself directly over the orchestra.

For the Records

A whole generation of music listeners has grown up without ever encountering a long-playing record. Most folks over sixty, meanwhile, probably never ran into one of the breakable 78 r.p.m. discs that introduced their parents to great music. In the 1927 edition of Groves Dictionary, readers who wanted to know more about recordings were invited to see the entry under "Mechanical Appliances. The erudite editors of that earlier era were blissfully unaware of the major role recordings were already playing in the widening popularity of classical music.

It was in 1877 that Thomas Edison recited "Mary Had a Little Lamb" into a weird little contraption of his own design, consisting of a grooved cylinder covered with tinfoil and turned by a crank, and a tube connected to the cylinder by a sharp metal point. He called his little gadget the phonograph, little guessing the musical revolution that it would eventually inspire. By 1891, the Columbia Phonograph Company was able to issue a 10-page catalog of its musical cylinders, including 27 marches, 13 polkas, and 36 items performed by an "artistic whistler," one J.Y. Atlee.

The first major improvement came from another American inventor, Emile Berliner, who converted the cylinder into a more usable shellac disc revolving on a turntable. Since Edison owned the word "phonograph," Berliner inverted the syllables and came up with "gramophone". Your great-grandparents, in other words, exulted in their gramophone records and—after the Victor Talking Machine Company produced an inexpensive machine to play them on—their Victrolas.

Shortly after the turn of the 20th century, some of the greatest musical personalities took their turn singing or playing into the primitive recording horns. The first in a long series of records by Dame Nellie Melba was produced in 1904 (with labels printed in a delicate shade of lilac), and such other legendary singers as Adelina Patti, Enrico Caruso, and Ernestine Schumann-Heink followed along in fairly short order. Orchestral music was slower in coming to the market because of its greater complexity, but a complete recording of Beethoven's Fifth (on eight single sides) was issued in 1913. Now that many of these early recordings have been reissued, we have a unique—and enormous—legacy to cherish and explore.

Bet You Didn't Know

The first American-made recording of an orchestra came in 1917 when the 100 members of the Boston Symphony squeezed into a reconverted church and spent the better part of four sweltering days playing into the huge recording horns (primitive microphones). "Now everything is possible," said Victor Herbert, when he heard those pioneering discs.

Meanwhile, we all know about CDs, the compact discs with crisp and brilliant sound emanating from everything from portable players weighing a few ounces to massive built-in sound systems. Here's another easy and nonthreatening way to acquaint yourself with classical music: Buy or download CDs (or borrow some from your neighborhood public library) and listen in the quiet of your own home. If you don't like the Mozart, try the Chopin. Hate the Wagner? Opt for Tchaikovsky. You can skip the parts that bore you, repeat the sections that elate you, listen intently with the lights down low, or casually while you do the dishes. But listen: Take advantage of the fabulous opportunities that await the turning of a switch and the spinning of that little platter.

CHAPTER 3

How Do You Listen to Classical Music?

In This Chapter

➤ Background music

➤ Foreground music

➤ How to listen

➤ Tunes and themes

➤ Feeling the beats

It's as simple as a flick of the remote switch or a push-button on your radio dial—maybe. Few people can say they've never heard classical music, but hearing and listening are not necessarily the same thing. When it's your choice of music—not something being pushed at you through speakers in an elevator or at the supermarket—chances are you're doing some degree of active listening (paying attention to what's being played or sung). The quality of that listening, of course, and therefore the quality of your musical experience, will vary depending on whether the music is the star or merely a supporting player.

In the Background Music

We all know that it's a lot easier to pedal your exercise bike with headphones on, and all that nice music can help you make forget that, like Robert Frost, you still have miles to go before you sleep. You can choose a lively march or an upbeat aria for the main event, and a quiet serenade may be perfect for the cool down. Music can make you a little less fearful while you're cowering in the dentist's chair, and sometimes even makes it vaguely tolerable to stay on "hold" while the %@#$%! computerized phone system foils your every attempt to reach an actual human being. Music stimulates the creative part of the brain, so in workshops and offices, it just might help you to come up with clever and innovative ideas. On the other hand, classical music can be soothing, helping a reluctant child (or stressed-out adult) on the road to dreamland; and the next morning, it's certainly more civilized to wake up to Bach than a buzzer.

Important Things to Know

In each of the above scenarios, music performs an important role, but it's still not the star player. Background music is exactly that: music in the background. When we choose pieces for that purpose, we often look for something familiar, so it won't unduly distract us from the primary task at hand. Yes, we do get something from the sounds—energy, relaxation, creativity, company, whatever—but we are missing the full range and power of what the composer intended. To retrieve that, listening has to be its own point and purpose.

Bet You Didn't Know

The great pianist-comedian Victor Borge hates background music because he starts concentrating on it instead of whatever else he's supposed to be doing. "Once I went into a building," he says, "and instead of Muzak in the elevator they were playing a Brahms Quartet. I rode up and down for 24 minutes before the damn piece was over."

In the Foreground

Close your eyes, open your ears, and let your mind (and possibly body, especially if you're at home) go along with what you hear. Tap your feet to the rhythm, if you like, hum along with the main theme, but listen. Experience the full range of what the composer put into his score and the performers into their interpretation. The textures will be richer, the colors brighter, the impact more profound; in fact, the impact will be totally different, even if it's the same piece that let you go an extra mile on the bike.

Pay Attention, Children

Okay, we know that's what your music appreciation teacher told you (if you're old enough to have gone to school when music was still an important part of the curriculum), or maybe your wise parents urged it upon you during the Met broadcasts. Surprise! They were right.

When you listened with full concentration, instead of squirming in your seat, you found that this strange "classical" music enveloped you with its imaginative power. Suddenly you became aware of intriguing instrumental colors, the fascinating ways melodies intertwine, and all sorts of other subtleties you didn't realize were in the music at all. A new awareness led to a new understanding of what your teacher was trying to tell you in the first place.

Color Them Instruments

Every instrument has its own special sound, and being able to tell one from the other enormously adds to your listening pleasure. Here's where watching television concerts can help, since the director will usually provide close-ups of trumpets sounding the alarm, flutes imitating the forest birds, or the kettledrummer stealing the composer's thunder. Another good system: Take your kids to a family concert. While they're enjoying the story of Peter and the Wolf, you'll get friendly with the grandfather (bassoon), cat (clarinet), bird (flute), and that dopey duck (oboe). Soon, you'll be able to tell the violins from their slightly bigger brothers, the violas; the low trombones from the even lower tubas; and the English horn from the French. Wow! You now can not only hear distinctive timbres you never realized were there, but applaud your own musical prowess along with the orchestra's.

Bet You Didn't Know

A group of environmentalists once picketed a performance of "Peter and the Wolf" because the endangered wolf is portrayed as a mean, nasty animal. Barbara Dunkel has written a sequel to the story (using other Prokofiev music) where Peter has a change of heart and helps the wolf escape from the zoo back to the forest; and one of your present authors wrote a follow-up tale to music by Margarita Zelenaia, wherein the Wolf's baby cousin and her forest friends outwit Peter's attempt to snag a second victim.

Combination Plates

It's easy with the visual arts. Look at a painting and you can immediately pick out the lines, colors, and shapes that make up the overall design (unless you're at an avant-garde exhibition, in which case all bets are off). One reason is that, except with mobiles, the patterns don't keep changing; you can stare at one corner of a piece of artwork for as long as you like, examine one section at a time, and if you come back for a second look a few minutes later, nothing will have changed.

Music allows no such permanent display. The melody is constantly moving, the rhythms and harmonies forever shifting, ideas and sounds appearing, evolving, being transformed into new figurations. Music exists in time, and time, as we all know, refuses to stand still.

If you're listening to a Gregorian chant, you don't have to worry about combinations because you won't find any. The voices spin out a unison melody in a long, seamless flow. But move to music of a later period, and you'll have to follow several voices, often moving in different directions at the same time. Be aware of shifting harmonies, the blending of instrumental or vocal colors and textures, and all manner of other nuances of rhythm and style. Sometimes one voice (or instrument) predominates, while others serve to enrich its theme or comment upon it. In other words, fine-tune your listening, and soon you'll be able to tell which instrument is sounding without watching the video.

Themes, Tunes, and Melodies

One of the most popular musical forms over the past four hundred years has been the theme and variations. Mozart wrote variations on the melody we know as "Twinkle, Twinkle, Little Star"; Beethoven wrote variations on an aria by Mozart; Liszt concocted variations on a Beethoven March; and so on. We can follow that chain of borrowed tunes right down to the present day, where we will recognize familiar melodies.

Music Word

A **melody** is a succession of notes, varying in pitch and having a recognizable musical shape. A **theme** is a melody that forms a building block of a musical piece. Usually the composer will make sure listeners knows that it's a theme by repeating it, sometimes exactly, sometimes changed or developed. Themes can do a lot of wandering, but if you listen intently, your ear can follow them through any and all permutations. Better still, you'll be able to recognize and welcome each reappearance of a theme, just as you might greet a returning friend. **Variations** are what we call those changes to the basic melody, and believe us, themes can do a lot of wandering.

Got Rhythm?

You may think you're the one person who can't sing the Gershwins' "I Got Rhythm" without feeling dishonest, but chances are you've just never given yourself a proper chance. Rhythm is the most basic element of music, as it is of life itself. Yes, it can get complicated in a symphony, with all those instrumental textures and interweaving melodic lines (though probably not as complex as the cross-rhythms produced by African drummers who never took a music lesson in their lives), but that's just another reason for attentive listening. Rhythm, like the beating of your heart or the tap-dancing in a Broadway musical, 42nd is the pulse that propels a work forward. The elements of rhythm are meter (the basic pulse) and accentuation (the emphasis on one part of a phrase). Even if you can't recognize a quarter note on paper (it's the black one with the straight stem), you'll have no problem stepping out to three of them in a waltz. And unless you have two left feet, you'll do fine marching along to "The Stars and Stripes Forever" with the accent on the first beat of every measure.

Getting Emotional With the Composer

We were talking earlier about instruments each producing a different sound. They can also produce different emotions. The harp is often used to suggest angelic serenity, for instance, the trumpet to evoke martial calls to battle. The trumpet can also be gentle, of course, and the harp obsessive, if that's how the composer so chooses, which is another thing that makes classical music so fascinating and unpredictable.

Tempo (the speed of the music) is another way to convey a mood. When a piece evolves with slowly shifting harmonies, it's safe to say that the composer was not thinking of euphoric celebrations; when the music races along with an exciting clatter of sound, it's probably not portraying sadness or grief. Many other elements can similarly allow listeners to share the composer's dramatic intent: Is the music harmonious or dissonant (harsh sounding), loud or soft, quiet or boisterous? Do the themes proceed in an orderly fashion or bounce around a lot?

When people speak of being "moved" by music, you know they were engaged in active listening. Even if you don't understand the German words, it's hard to imagine hearing Beethoven's "Ode to Joy" without becoming involved in the musical message, feeling uplifted in mind and spirit. Ditto listing to Wagner's "Tristan and Isolde" without being aware of its high eroticism, or the B Minor Mass without sensing Bach's abiding religious faith.

Bet You Didn't Know

You can't fool the critics when it comes to eroticism. More than a century before self-appointed guardians of the public morals were trying to save us from rock lyrics, a London critic wrote that "the story (of Wagner's 'Siegfried') is a chaotic mass of filth. Any half-hour of it would make you blush if you had a face on you as hard as a bronze statue."

The ABCs of CD Booklets

Important Things to Know

Allowing yourself to become part of the composer's emotional world involves more than distinguishing sad from happy sounds. You have to let the music permeate your own being, let yourself be transported into a virtual environment of sound.

In the old days of 12-inch LPs, liner notes were easy to read; now, assuming you can pry the booklet out of its plastic prison without destroying the cover, the tiny size of the page and print can lead to eyestrain. However tempting, though, don't just skip the notes: usually they contain extremely helpful information about the work you're about to hear, and/or the artists who created it.

That's not always the case, naturally. Every so often, you'll find notes that are pretentious, obscure, or so technically oriented as to be useless for normal people like you and me. In that case, you have our permission to use the booklet for kindling, and turn instead to any one of many fine books on the composer in the case. But first give the writer the benefit of the doubt. Most often, he or she has conveyed a genuine understanding of the music and thus will enhance your listening pleasure.

What Kind of Sound System Must I Have?

A good stereo system needn't cost a year's salary and have speakers taller than you. On the other hand, you do want to hear all of the qualities we've been discussing thus far, so if your set can't reproduce sounds accurately, you won't be able fully to partake of the musical meal at hand. If you can't hear the bass notes, for instance, if loud passages are distorted, if there's a hum or other noise not intended by composer or performer, the listening experience is degraded.

If your Beethoven is coming from a boombox, in other words, it'll still be great music, but you'll be coping with inferior reproduction and thus lowered that musical satisfaction.

The easy way to acquire decent sound is to buy a prepackaged system. Rarely will it include topnotch equipment, but it's a good start. Don't be fooled by a pretty case, though: it's what's inside that counts.

Better, though still something of a compromise, is to buy a stereo receiver, combination AM/FM tuner, preamplified and amplifier in one unit, plus a separate CD player and speakers. If you're limited in space, there are some tightly packaged systems (often called Compact Stereo) from Bose, Panasonic, Sony, and other companies. These usually have the speakers integrated into a single unit. Since the explosion of Home Theater, there's a limited choice of Stereo-in-a-Box units that bring together separate components, but you can find some of them at appliance/electronic stores like Best Buy, PC Richards, or more general stores such as Sears and Walmart.

An audio purist will scoff at this sort of package, but the audio purist we consulted—Richard Zuckerman, founder of Enveloping Sound in Briarcliff Manor, New York—admits that "It will give you a pretty good bang—not to mention a rat-a-tat-tat—for your money. If you cannot listen first, though, make sure the store offers a full money-back guarantee (as opposed to store credit only). Also be aware, that if you see a highly discounted price for a name brand product on the Internet, it is likely to be refurbished or even fake."

The third, and audiophiles agree, the best method is to purchase individual components—matching them to each other in quality, and being guided by your own personal listening tastes.

$1,000 to $1,500 as a long-term investment is not a lot of money, but the truth of the matter is that you really do have to spend a lot of money to get a good system—mine cost $10,000 and leaves a lot to be desired.

Computer geeks like to talk about "garbage in, garbage out," and that's a good motto when you're buying hi-fi equipment too. Resist the temptation to chintz on the amplifier and splurge on the speakers, because the front-end quality is far more critical. Remember that it all starts with the musical information on the recording: If the CD player can't decode that audio signal completely, or the amplifier fails to reproduce it properly, the best speakers in the world can't recall those lost details. In fact, high-quality speakers connected to an inferior system will often magnify the defects and may actually sound worse than cheaper speakers. You're playing a matching game here, so if you buy expensive speakers, equip them with electronics worthy of their unique qualities.

The cost of audiophile systems knows no bounds—you can buy a Mercedes for what a pair of some speakers will set you back—but a carefully chosen, moderately priced system will usually outperform a more expensive set where the components are not well matched. In the early days of stereo, people flipped out over thunderclaps in their living rooms or locomotives racing through the den. Now, enjoying music should be your primary goal, and that can happen if you're listening to the clock radio by your bedside. Yes, you'll miss the subtleties, but you will hear most of what the composer wanted you to hear.

Bet You Didn't Know

Last time we checked, at least seven companies offered speakers betweetn $30,000 and $50,000 for the pair. Unfortunately, the ones made out of solid gold (bargain-priced at under $7 million) are no longer available.

Assuming you want—and your budget allows—something better, visit a shop that specializes in high-fidelity components and is a factory-authorized outlet for a number of known brands. Most reputable dealers will have listening rooms where you can sample a great number of components and hear various equipment combinations. When you visit, bring along a favorite CD, since it will give you a better basis for comparison. Again, make sure the place has a reasonable return or exchange policy. The sound in a demonstration room may be quite different from that in your home, which has different dimensions, not to mention furniture, drapes, and carpets that could alter the listening experience. It might, in other words, take a bit of component-swapping before you get the setup just right.

Still, you should consider it as a long-term investment just as you do your furniture.

If you have only $100 to spend, don't despair—you can still hear most of the music on a good portable table radio—but it won't be hi-fi. You will miss the subleties, but you will hear most of what the composer wanted you to hear. An excellent hi-fi quality stereo table radio is made by Bose and sells for about $350 by mail order (800-444-2673). You can connect a CD player to it later on.

A Public Concert: The Ultimate in Active Listening

As thrilling as the sound may be on a high-priced system in a perfectly designed listening room (which rarely describes your home, anyway), it's still only an approximation of the acoustical qualities of an actual performance. Every time something comes between you and the original sound—whether it's the microphone in the studio, the encoding of the digital information on the CD, the feeding of that information through the audio equipment—something is lost. If you want to hear sound at its best, you have to hear it "live" in the hall.

Not all concert halls are created equal, and different auditoriums have varying acoustical properties. When musicians enter a new hall, they'll often clap their hands to test the reverberation rate, since that will affect the sonic quality of their performance, and perhaps even cause them to adjust the pace at which a piece will be played. If there's a great deal of echo, for instance, as in a cathedral, slower tempos can avoid a jumbling of the sound. Many new halls are designed with moveable panels so that the acoustics can be adjusted (up to a point) to reflect the size and type of the performing ensemble or the music being played.

Concert halls are also free from some of the distractions of home listening; you're not likely to be bothered by a package delivery or a phone call (you *did* turn off your cell and pager, right?). You can forget about the report that's half done on your laptop, the bills that need to be paid, and the filing that's six months overdue. All you need do is sit comfortably and enjoy the music. There, in the concert hall, is where you'll find the highest fi of all; plus you get to see as well as hear the performers and enjoy a communal experience with other concertgoers. Standing ovations are really no fun when you're alone in your living room.

CHAPTER 4

What Is Concert Hall Etiquette?

> **In This Chapter**
>
> ➤ What to wear at a performance
> ➤ Respect thy neighbor
> ➤ When to clap

Yes, it may be a bit more formal than going to hear a rock group, but don't let that spoil the high enjoyment of attending a classical concert. If you think concert hall decorum means observing a stiff, rigid code of behavior, you've been watching too many of those films from the 1930s where the whole audience at a concert was invariably in full dress. No one will be judging the way you act—unless, of course, you act in a way that keeps others from enjoying the performance. In short, most rules of concert hall manners are simple observances of common courtesy.

I Have Nothing to Wear

So long as that's a figure of speech, don't worry about it. Only in old films does everybody at a classical concert look as if they were being presented at Windsor Castle. Even before Casual Fridays, dressing to the teeth was not only unnecessary at a concert, but sometimes unwelcome, as though you were out to get more attention than the performers.

You don't want to look messy or dirty or make your neighbors feel uncomfortable by arriving in gym shorts and sneakers, but so long as you look presentable, nobody will give you dirty looks. Evening curtain times are usually at 7:30 or 8. For the men, business attire means the traditional suit and tie. For the ladies, it is a dress or suit, skirt or slacks, blouse and jacket, meaning you can leave the office and enjoy a leisurely dinner before heading for the performance. Some concerts are even scheduled at 5:30 or 6, so folks can go right from work to the music and be free for an even more leisurely dinner thereafter. Actually, that's a good rule of musical thumb: If the boss won't frown at your attire in the office, it'll be just dandy for that Mozart evening at the Y.

If the occasion is more imposing than usual—opening night at the Met, say, or a gala benefit—add common sense to your common courtesy. A suit or sport jacket is more likely to be appropriate for men; a dress, pants suit, or skirt, blouse, and jacket for women.

What about formal wear? Our policy is to get the designer gown out of the closet and press the tuxedo only when it specifically says "formal" on the invitation. Even then, if the thought of formal wear makes you squirm, stop wriggling and fall back on regular business attire. When you get there, you'll see that a good many rebels in the crowd have done the same thing, and guess what? Nobody gives a hoot. One exception: If you're going as a guest, it's a good idea to check with your hosts and follow their suggested dress code.

Casual Concerts

Some programs are deliberately, even proudly informal. These days, concerts take place in cafés, building lobbies, schools, and other locales where the situation is reversed: Come all dressed up and you'll look more like a waiter than your fellow music lovers. Even in the large halls, many programs are designed to be taken casually; the New York Philharmonic and many other orchestras and ensembles around the country often sponsor events designed to meet the needs of younger audiences. Here indeed you can come as you are. Just remember that neatness still counts: If your shoes are mud-covered and the rest of you looks like something the cat dragged in, better wait for an outdoor concert, where you can be slovenly to your heart's content.

Bet You Didn't Know

Some of the best composers were also the biggest slobs. When a certain Baron de Tremont visited Beethoven, he discovered "the most disorderly place imaginable—blotches of moisture covered the ceiling, the chairs were covered with plates bearing the remains of last night's supper, and an un-emptied chamber pot stood under the piano." Brahms wasn't much better. They say he grew his famous beard so he wouldn't have to wear a collar and tie, and R.H. Schauffler, in his biography of the composer, reported that "his hat would have been a windfall for a comedian playing the country cousin, there were patches and mends on the alpaca coat he always wore, and an accompanying pair of black trousers were adorned with an enormous brown patch on the seat and a black patch on the front."

Respect Thy Neighbor

If you're at a heavy metal concert, you probably won't mind your neighbors yakking all through the music (you probably won't be able to hear them anyway), but at a classical concert, where the music isn't designed to shake you out of your boots, it's important to avoid disturbing the person next to you. Even before the downbeat, be sure to arrive on time. It's great to turn up fashionably late to a party, but don't try it at a concert. Nothing is more irritating than to start enjoying a piece, only to have latecomers barge into your row, step on your toes, and slap your face with their coats while trundling to their appointed seats. Worse still, don't be the guilty party who does that unto others.

Many concert halls won't even seat you if the music has already started, and you'll have to listen through a closed door at the back of the auditorium. Some opera houses have closed circuit televisions to which they herd latecomers for the first act, but if you wanted to watch the thing on a small screen, you wouldn't have popped for a ticket in the first place.

Noises Off

Once the music begins, remember that your (and your neighbors') purpose in attending a concert is to enjoy a peak auditory experience. Any extraneous noise is a distraction, and making noise during a classical performance can be both annoying to others and—if you're the culprit—your neighbor and embarrassing to you. Loudly turning program pages, or digging around in pocket or purse for a tissue, can be visually as well as sonically disturbing. Not to worry if you're at a rock show: Rock music rarely has extreme modulations of volume; classical music has them all the time. Crashing cymbals and thundering timpani may disguise a comment to your seat-mate, but if the musical storm suddenly gives way to the sunshine of a solo flute, you could well be caught in mid-sentence for the entire hall to hear.

Important Things to Know

Your purposes in attending a concert is to enjoy a peak auditory experience. Any extraneous noise is a distraction, and making noise during a classical performance can be both annoying to your neighbor and embarrassing to you. Rock music rarely has extreme modulations of volume; classical music has them all the time. Crashing cymbals and thundering tympani may disguise a comment to your seat-mate, but if the musical storm suddenly gives way to the sunshine of a solo flute, you could well be caught in mid-sentence for all the hall to hear.

To Sleep or Not To Sleep

That's an easy one: by all means try to stay awake. Yes, it can be a problem sometimes to keep awake during a performance. You've enjoyed a nice dinner, perhaps with a glass of wine (or two), you've come in from the cold to a snuggly warm hall, and Wotan has been waving his spear around for 20 minutes already. Still, make every effort to avoid dozing off. Even if you don't snore, and your head doesn't slaw into the back of the seat in front of you, the bobbing and weaving can interrupt the concentration of those near you who might otherwise be excited by the music, and distracts the attention of those who might otherwise feel excited by the music. Besides, your ribs may get sore from the well-aimed blows of your companion. If you paid for your ticket, snoozing is a waste of money; if you came as a guest, don't expect ever to be invited again.

Are your eyelids getting heavy? Change your sitting position; focus more intently on the music; read the program notes (if there's enough light to do so); and, if all else fails, concentrate on some nonmusical matter that will require your later attention. Just remember that those around you have a right to appreciate the music, and make a mental note next time to choose a program that's more your cup of tonal tea.

Drop That Cough

High on the concert-going Pain-in-the-Neck list is the person who's forever sneezing, sniffling, coughing, and otherwise injecting unwanted medical sounds into the musical mix. Some theaters have bins of throat drops in the lobby, but just in case, bring your own lozenges or hard candy to suck on. There is, though, an obvious pitfall lying in wait: said lozenges have to be unwrapped. There are two ways to do this, both of them annoying beyond belief. One is to rip the thing open, with a snap, crackle and pop more suited to your breakfast cereal; the other, adopted by people whose heart, if not brain, is in the right place, involves a painfully slow unpeeling of the wrapper. The latter method is quieter, all right, but the process always seems to take longer than "Lohengrin."

Important Things to Know

So what's the best way to unwrap a lozenge if you have a cold or sore throat? For starters, use the dimming lights as a signal to put the first cough drop in your mouth. Then, either unwrap a whole bunch of lozenges and leave them accessible, or invest in a box of drops, keeping it unsealed in your lap, where you can quietly get them as needed. Ladies: Don't keep them in your pocketbook. By the time you've located them after rummaging through keys, combs, and other odds and ends, the concert will be half over, and you'll probably have created a greater disturbance than the coughing.

It's great to turn up fashionably late at a party, but never for a concert. Nothing is more irritating than to start enjoying a piece, only to have latecomers barge into your row, step on your toes, and slap your face with their coats while they trundle to their appointed seats.

Many concert halls won't even seat you if the music has already started, and you'll have to listen to the Overture from the back of the auditorium, usually through a closed door. Some opera houses have closed-circuit televisions.

When Do I Clap?

When should I applaud? When in doubt, listen. Not for the music this time, but for the clapping of others around you. Granted, it's a chicken's way out, but it works. Nobody will glare at you for coming in second, but jump out of your seat yelling, "Bravo!" before the piece has ended, and your face will be richly endowed with the proverbial egg—if not a whole omelet. Here are a few basic guidelines:

> ➤ In concerts, don't applaud between movements. It's very tempting to clap when you hear silence after a fine performance, but the end of a section within a longer work signifies a shift of mood or pacing, not a complete stop. Movements are part of a continuum, in other words, not complete starts and stops. Sometimes, especially after the first movement of a virtuoso concerto, the temptation is too great to resist,

Bet You Didn't Know

This no-applause-between-movements stuff is a fairly recent innovation. Berlioz cheerfully reported that, at the premiere of his "Symphonie Fantastique," the audience "simply let itself be carried along by the current of the music, and it applauded the 'March to the Scaffold' and the 'Witches' Sabbath' more warmly than the other three movements." About a century later, S. Frederick Starr, when he was president of Oberlin College, wrote a whole article titled "Why I Applaud Between Movements." "Would it really hurt to allow the violinist to take a bow after the movement in which he solos?" he asked; "what didn't offend Berlioz won't offend me. Quite the contrary. Our task, very simply, is to love the music, to enjoy the music, and to remove those impediments that prevent other Americans from doing so." This, of course, is standard operating procedure at jazz concerts; applause is expected after a rousing solo by any one of the players.

and the audience does applaud. If everybody around you is clapping, of course, feel free to add your own vote of approval.

➤ Do applaud at the end of complete pieces. That's the time to show your appreciation of the performance. If you didn't feel it was up to snuff, don't feel impelled to clap just because others around you are doing so; on the other hand, remember that most classical concerts are group efforts. Even if the brasses hit a few clinkers, or the clarinet cracked on the high note, a lot of other musicians were playing their hearts out, and some audible response from you is quite in order. Never boo or hiss. Booing or hissing is a way of expressing extreme dissatisfaction with a work, but it's also rude and often uncalled for, since it's the musicians, who did their best to present the piece, who have to bear the brunt of your displeasure.

Bet You Didn't Know

Vivaldi wrote a lot of his concertos for a convent school in Venice, and in those days, it wasn't considered dignified to applaud inside an institution of that supposed spirituality. So the audiences at the concerts didn't clap after a performance; they coughed, shuffled their feet and blew their noses loudly instead.

➤ Remember what we said about applauding at the end of complete pieces? It doesn't always apply with operas or at the ballet, when custom decrees that clapping and shouts of bravo are quite in order after exciting arias or pas de deux. Again, though, wait until others around you have clapped the first clap, since composers love false endings and insert other pauses into their scores that can entrap the novice into premature applause, not to mention the undying enmity of a savvy listener in the next seat. If you're really hopped up and want to add your vocal cries of approval to the general uproar, the proper shout for a male artist is "Bravo!" for a female "Brava!" and for two of more, of whatever sex, "Bravi!" If you're really ecstatic, you might try "Bravissimo!" "Bravissima!" or "Bravissimi!", but you risk sounding awfully pretentious. Better consult an Italian dictionary before proceeding with anything stronger.

Finally, two more excellent pieces of advice from the witty pens of music critics. Among Byron Belt's 10 Commandments of Concert Etiquette are "Thou Shalt Not Wear Loud-

Ticking Watches or Jangle Thy Jewelry. Owners are usually immune but the added percussion is disturbing to all." And from James Keller's Audience Oath: "I will not sprint up the aisle the instant the last piece ends. If I must exit without applauding the soloist, I will wait until he leaves the stage, sparing him the insult of seeing his efforts rewarded with a view of my backside."

PART TWO

The Sound of Music

CHAPTER 5

What Are the Basic Elements of Classical Music?

In This Chapter

> ➤ The elements of classical music
> ➤ The importance of rhythm, melody, harmony, and scales and keys
> ➤ Understanding tempo, form, and structure

Like water (which they told us in high school is made up of two parts hydrogen and one part water) and carbon dioxide (which you get by mixing two parts of oxygen to one part of carbon in a chemical reaction), music is made up of certain basic elements. Fortunately, you don't need a degree in chemistry to appreciate them—just an open mind and an attentive ear.

The Essence of Classical Music

From the simple folk tune to the most complex operatic ensemble, music is made up of certain basic ingredients, primarily melody, rhythm, harmony, and tone color. Some music evokes the power of a spiritual force, some displays wit and humor, and some is revered for its sheer beauty of sound.

Combination Platter

To the ingredients mentioned above, let's add texture, form, and structure. The composer has all of these tools of the trade at his or her disposal in the creation of sound. The composer can score a piece for strings, woodwinds, brass, percussion, or the marvelous combination of all of those instruments that we call the symphony orchestra. The composer can put ideas into a single instrument, like the guitar or piano, mix in electronic sounds, or merge words and music. The author can make us laugh or cry, depict bucolic scenes or fearsome battles, give musical life to conflicts between the Montagues and Capulets (or the Jets and the Sharks), or light up the stage with dueling divas (although sometimes that happens whether the libretto calls for it or not).

In effect, there's a lot that goes into a classical work. Just as a master chef intermixes ingredients so as to produce a gourmet meal that is pleasing both to the eye and palate, the composer swirls many musical components together in pursuit of a musical piece pleasing both to the ear and soul.

Too Many Cooks?

The analogy of chefs and composers isn't quite exact, since the performer is part of the process too, deciding to add a dash of presto to the polonaise, perhaps, or add a pinch more crescendo to the concerto. The composer, of course, wrote the original recipe, but it is the interpreter who follows that formula, shifting nuances of color or balance, but staying true to the intent of the composer, whose notes and harmonies must be followed in their prescribed order. In a way, it's the opposite of jazz, where improvisation is king; the wonder of classical music is that there remain so many different ways of playing or singing the same notes and rhythms.

In some works by John Cage, Alan Hovhaness, and many other composers, improvisation is either built into the score, or the notes of the piece are selected through some random or chance operation. (If you want to impress your literary or musicological friends, you can refer to this as aleatoric rather than chance music, but nobody else will know what you're talking about.) Music with random ingredients, needless to say, will change from performance to performance, but that was precisely the composer's intent. In other words, from the predictable formality of a baroque dance to the most unstructured modern work, the composer is still the master chef who cooks up the musical meal.

Bet You Didn't Know

Creating music by chance is nothing new. Mozart wrote a musical dice game, where each of the measures is numbered, and their order of performance is dictated by the results of consecutive throws of the dice.

I've Got Rhythm

Many famous poems are replete with rhythm: the texts often refer to familiar rhythmic patterns (tick-tock, ding-dong, etc.) while the imaginative use of rhymes, repetitions of phrases, alliteration, and sundry other tricks of the literary trade, all help us get caught up in the sound, as well as the specific meaning of the words. Not only do the words themselves refer to familiar rhythmic patterns, but try saying the lyrics to yourself: even if you're not sure of the intended meter, you'll find yourself caught in the spell of those sound repetitions, chanting the words rather than merely saying them. Rhythm is fundamental. If not for the steady beat of our hearts and the even flow of air entering and leaving our lungs, all life would cease. Babies learn early on to clap their hands in rhythmic patterns and respond to the catchy cadence of "Three Blind Mice." Granted, it's a bit more difficult to follow the rhythmic pulsings within a complex work like Scriabin's orgasmic "Poem of Ecstasy," but without some sense of pacing, we'd have no music at all.

Bet You Didn't Know

When the famous writer Henry Miller first heard Scriabin's "Poem of Ecstasy," he flipped out entirely. "I played it over and over," he said, "couldn't shut it off. It was like a bath of ice, cocaine and rainbows. For weeks I went about in a trance...."

There is the obvious left-right rhythm of a Sousa march (back in the Gay Nineties, his "Washington Post" sparked the dance craze known as the two-step). That makes perfect sense: after all, we have two feet, and if marchers had to wait while the composer added extra beats every so often, the parade would never pass by. The waltz, on the other hand, has to glide along in ONE-Two-Three fashion, even as the Danube (blue or otherwise) flows along rather than marching to an even beat. A mazurka also has three

Important Things to Know

To understand the concept of rhythm, think of it as the pulse of the music: It creates the beat of the tom-tom and the ticking of the clock. Meter is essentially the regular appearance of a beat.

beats, but the accent is on the second one, and that One-TWO-Three rhythm is part of the dance's special grace and charm.

Important Things to Know

Like so many musical terms, "tempo" comes from the Italian word for time, and it signifies the pace at which music flows. It's connected to rhythm in the sense that it dictates how quickly or slowly we get from one accent to the next, but it similarly controls the pace of harmonic changes and our perceptions of the emotions expressed within a piece. Composers often try to control the speed at which their music is played by putting precise metronome markings in the scores (a metronome is that clicky device you can adjust to tick off steady beats at specified speeds). Interpreters often take those instructions with a hefty grain of salt, slowing down here to make the work more spacious, speeding it up there to make it more exciting. Or so they think.

Tempo Time

Tempo markings are traditionally in Italian, just like those shouted "Bravos" and "Bravas" at the opera house. Here are a few of the most common:

➤ Largo: very slow, broad.

➤ Grave: how serious can you get?

➤ Lento: just plain slow.

➤ Adagio: see Lento. It's a little faster than Largo, if that helps any.

➤ Adagietto: a little Adagio, ergo, a touch faster.

➤ Andante: literally "going," moving along at a walking pace, at moderate speed.

➤ Andantino: you guessed it—a little andante, so a touch faster.

➤ Moderato: yep, at a moderate pace. This word is often used in conjunction with another tempo direction, such as andante moderato, meaning don't be overzealous about that slow stuff.

➤ Allegro: now we're getting someplace. It means lively, going at a reasonably fast pace.

➤ Allegretto: a little Allegro, hold your horses a bit.

➤ Allegro Molto: "molto" means much or very, so hop to.

➤ Vivace: very fast.

➤ Presto: as fast as possible.

➤ Prestissimo: a little faster than that. Well, try!

It's unlikely you'll encounter an interpreter who transforms a composer's adagio into a presto or vice versa, but even subtle changes in tempo can profoundly alter the mood and character of a work.

Steady, Hypnotic Beat

We're back to that tom-tom again. The regular, predictable throbbing of sound can indeed be hypnotic, whether it applies to the churning repetitive rhythms of a tarantella or the slow pulsing of drums at a Native American ritual. A steady beat is frequently used by composers who wish to evoke "primitive" elements.

Complex Patterns

Within the basic beat, we can find many patterns, sometimes complementing, sometimes clashing with each other. A lot of baroque music is characterized by energetic, steady and repetitive rhythms ("sewing machine music" is how some cynics describe it), but the textures are rich while the melodic counterpoint deftly sets one theme off against another. In short, Bach, Vivaldi, and Telemann stuffed their pieces full of intricate and complex decorations. And why not? The term "baroque" was borrowed from architecture, where it has connotations of elaborate, twisting, involved construction.

Bet You Didn't Know

Bach, Telemann and Vivaldi certainly didn't think of themselves as baroque composers. In the 18th century, the word meant uncouth, odd, rough, and antiquated in taste.

During the classical era, rhythms became more subtle and nuanced, compared with the more insistent patterns of the baroque. In the romantic period, the poetic spirit reigned supreme, and rhythmic freedom was encouraged. The 20th century, with its energy, vigor, and technological advancements led to a lot of rhythmic experimentation; Bartók, Stravinsky, and many other composers have used "polyrhythms," where several independent

Bet You Didn't Know

The American composer Henry Cowell, working together with the Soviet engineer Leon Theremin, invented a contraption called the Rhythmicon, which made possible the simultaneous production of 16 different rhythms on as many different pitch levels. Cowell also wrote a piece called "Rhythmicana," but it was so complicated that nobody could play it. The first performance, taking advantage of advanced electronic techniques, came at Stanford University in 1971, six years after his death.

patterns compete for the listener's attention at the same time.

Syncopation: It's Not the Same as What Olympic Performers Do

Syncopation is when the beat doesn't happen where you expect it, or more formally, the displacement of an accent to a beat that is usually unaccented. You can either get annoyed and sulk or enjoy the surprise. For most of us, this offbeat accent is a delightful ear-opener; it lies at the heart of jazz, blues, and ragtime, and adds a delectable spice to classical compositions as well. The word "syncopation" comes from the Greek word meaning "cutting short," so let's syncopate this discussion and proceed to...

It Propels the Music Forward

Rhythm—it becomes clear from the text. The rhythmic impulse that keeps a march marching or a waltz waltzing has its counterpart in vocal pieces, where sometimes the lyrics seem to drive the music ahead (think of a Gilbert and Sullivan patter song), while in other instances the melody leads the way, flowing up the lazy river while the words more or less float along with it. The rapidity or slowness with which the music progresses, the number of times rhythmic patterns are repeated, or the way they are altered each time all contribute to the musical current.

Merry Melodies

This is the part where the "beat beat beat of the tom-tom" goes into "Night and day, you are the one ...," where the rhythmic spurt of the verse gives way to a shapely tune, where the beauty of line replaces the urgency of the beat.

A Group of Single Notes

A melody or tune is a succession of musical notes that creates a recognizable musical entity. It can be as simple as "Happy Birthday to You" or as elaborate as an extended theme in a Mahler Symphony. The late musicologist and popular broadcaster Karl Haas said that

Music Word

The focal point of a melody, the center around which the tune flows, and usually the note on which it ends, is called the **tonic.** It's also the first degree, or keynote, of the scale in which it's written: A in the key of A Major or A minor, B in B Major or B minor, etc. The tune may wander far from that tonic note, but eventually it returns there, giving us a satisfying feeling of resolution, a comfortable "welcome home" after a long journey.

"melody has the musical flow of poetry. It subscribes to the same urges of symmetry and rhythmical division, and is governed by the same impulses of emotional stress and release."

Phrases—But Not the Grammatical Kind

A melody is usually constructed from smaller units, called motifs or phrases. These can be as short as the two-note cuckoo call, which has been often incorporated into major classical works, including (speaking of) Mahler's First Symphony. They can be constructed from two or three consecutive notes of a scale (try "Mary Had a Little Lamb" on your old kazoo: the opening notes are E-D-C-D-E-E-E), or they can span a whole octave (the opening of "The Star Spangled Banner").

Simple Or Complicated?

A melody can be easy to follow if it stands alone or predominates over a harmonic accompaniment, but play two or three melodies together and we tend to hear the resulting mix rather than each tune separately. Take a simple round, like "Frère Jacques." The first phrase is sung alone, and we have no trouble picking out the tune: "Frère Jacques, Frère Jacques." When singer #2 comes in with "Frère John, Frère John," we can still hear the tune because it's the same melody, only sung three notes higher. When Singer #3 chimes in with

---

Music Word

A **fugue** is an organization for several parts (often called "voices" whether they're sung or played), with each voice entering successively in imitation of each other. The opening motif is called the **subject,** the imitations the **answer,** and sections between complete entries of all voices are called **episodes.** A wit once described a fugue as "a piece where the instruments come in one after the other, and the audience goes out one after the other."

---

a different tune on "Sonnez les matines," though, and #4 adds yet another little melody with his "Ding Dong Ding," those four simple phrases add up to a fairly involved musical message.

Bet You Didn't Know

We often use words like "melodic" or "tuneful" to mean that a piece of music is pleasing to the ear, and historically, a lot of music was devised expressly for that purpose. A court composer to Elizabeth Tudor was not likely to take a chance on writing something that might displease the Queen, and even the great Haydn dutifully churned out pleasant pieces for everything from royal suppers to princely marionette shows.

Pleasing to the Senses

Great works of art, of course, can be disturbing as well as harmonious. They can serve as political protest, portray events of high tragedy, and in our own time, echo what W. H. Auden (and Leonard Bernstein in his symphony) called "The Age of Anxiety." All of which means that "pleasing to the senses" must be redefined to include a work of imagination, originality, and communicative power. We no longer need always to be soothed or placated; music has too much else to give us.

Live Together in Perfect Harmony

Harmony is the simultaneous sounding of two or more notes; it is the underpinning of a melody that gives it depth and perspective. "Harmony" may be synonymous with "consonance" in the dictionary, but that is not necessarily the case in music: Notes sounded together can be dulcet or dissonant. What harmony meant in the Middle Ages is that Brother Timothy and Brother John were no longer singing the same notes at the same time. Today, as the ever-wise Cole Porter pointed out, "Anything Goes."

Join Together With the Band

Important Things to Know

Harmony enriches a melody, accentuates rhythmic patterns, and moves the entire listening experience to a new realm. In its most common form, the melody predominates, with chords embellishing, supporting, and flavoring it. When all parts of the chord move along together, usually with the melody on top, as in a hymn at church, we have what musicologists call homophony. When the harmonies are produced by the interplay of different melodies, we have polyphony. In the Renaissance era and on into the baroque, polyphony was king. A decided shift toward melody came in the classical period, and reached its height with the romantics. Which is not to say that Bach didn't write some gorgeous melodies (listen to "Sheep May Safely Graze" or "Jesu, Joy of Man's Desiring") or that we don't have them in the 20th century (think of Barber's "Adagio for Strings").

Take a note, any note. Now take another one. The distance between them is called an interval, and intervals become harmony when you sound the two notes together. They also become a chord, although some purists insist that you have to have at least three notes sounding together to qualify as a chord. That's their problem.

The Birth of Harmony

We have pictures of ancient Egyptians and Greeks playing all sorts of instruments, so maybe the art of harmony is a lot older than we know, but until the 9th century, the Church in Europe frowned on harmony as the work of the devil. It was only in the 9th century that some rebellious monks decided to add a second voice to the chants, and eventually a third and a fourth. Around the year 1000, the heyday of Romanesque art and architecture, composers experimented with music for two voices that went their separate ways—a landmark step in the evolution of classical music since it became a determining factor in distinguishing Western music from its Asian and middle Eastern counterparts.

As the Renaissance began to spread through the European continent, freeing art from religious domination and reawakening scientific interest, composers of both religious and secular music began expanding the harmonic construction of their pieces, blending as many as six different vocal lines. By the time the Elizabethan madrigals came into favor, composers were exploring such highly secular topics as love, sex, and politics.

Enriching Your Soul—and the Melody

It may seem obvious to say that a chord produces a richer sound than a single note, but

Important Things to Know

Harmony is essential to the character of an instrumental piece. In vocal music, the lyrics in and of themselves can convey the emotional intent of the composer. In the absence of words, the music itself must establish the emotional mood. Consonant harmonies produce a lyrical, soothing, or romantic effect. Dissonant harmonies create tension, and evoke agitation or uncertainty. Of course, consonance and dissonance are very much in the ear of the listener: One man's music is another's mayhem.

adding supporting notes to a melody, or setting one tune against another, enriches the texture of a musical work. Harmony adds depth to music just as perspective adds depth to a painting, and indeed, for the past millennium, composers and artists have both been

Bet You Didn't Know

Most audiences today revel in the melodic invention of Debussy's "Prelude to the Afternoon of a Faun," but a Boston critic was less impressed in 1904. "The faun must have had a terrible afternoon," wrote Louis Elson, "for the poor beast avoided all trace of soothing melody until the audience began to share his sorrows." Another performance the following year took critic Elson back to his aisle seat, but he was still underwhelmed, writing, "There are moments when Debussy's suffering Faun seems to need a veterinary surgeon."

constantly experimenting with ways to enhance the three-dimensionality of their work.

Even when mood-setting is not the intent, harmony enriches the melodic substance of a work, it expands the sounds, points up the low and high points of themes, adds richness and a wide variety to the tonal spectrum.

Scaling New Heights With Musical Keys

A scale—from the Italian "scala," or stairway—is a progression of single notes, and like that staircase, the steps work equally well going up or down. A key is simply the name given to the notes of the scale, depending on where it starts and stops. If A is the base or "keynote," and the rest of the scale functions in relation to it, it's an A Major (or minor) scale, the notes progressing through B, C, D, E, F, G and back to A an octave (i.e., a span of eight notes) above.

Since the space relationships are the same whether the key is A, F, or anything else, the letters are sometimes replaced by syllables familiar to all crossword puzzle or "Sound of Music" fans. As Maria so aptly taught the kids, the keynote is "do" (as in a female deer), the one above that "re" (as in a drop of golden sun), and so on up through "mi," "fa," "sol," "la," "ti," and back to "do" again.

The best visual representation of this is the piano keyboard. The white keys are arranged in a seven-note sequence repeated throughout the keyboard. Within that octave are five black keys, in sequences of two and t------ ------- that we have 12 tones in all, each one

Music Word

A score is a written piece of music. In writing music, a measure is a rhythmic division of music marked on the score as the distance between two vertical lines. The vertical line is referred to as a bar. The key signature is indicated by noting the appropriate sharps and flats on the left side of the ruled lines on the score.

a half-step away from its neighbor. Since we don't have twelve letters between A and G, we use the term "sharp" or "flat" to indicate that the note is one half-step up or down from the base note. A sharp is denoted by a "#" and a flat by a "[fl]." Thus the first black note in the sequence of two would be a C-sharp if it's a halftone up from the basic key of C, but the same note would be a D-flat if it's a halftone down from the basic key of D.

A scale using all 12 tones (the seven white and five black notes within an octave) is called a chromatic scale; one using a specific selection of those notes, forming either a major or minor scale, is called diatonic. The major scales tend to have a bright, upbeat quality, most

Music Word

A **chromatic scale** is a scale based on an octave of 12 semitones, as opposed to a seven-note **diatonic** scale. Where a whole tone is represented by T and a semi-tone by S, a major scale is one that is built on the following sequence of intervals: T-T-SD-T-T-T-S, where T=tone and S=semitone. A minor scale is built on the following sequence of intervals: T-S-T-T-S-T-T.

easily illustrated by starting on a C and playing only the white keys, i.e., C-D-E-F-G-A-B-C. A major scale is made up of three whole tones followed by a half tone going up the scale. The minor scales reflect more melancholy moods. There are many types of minor scales, but for the sake of simplicity we will discuss only the "natural minor." Again, starting on C, it would be C-D-Eb-F-G-Ab-Bb-C."

Other selections of notes, often called modes, were in use during the Middle Ages and are still used today in other cultures. Nor is the division of an octave into twelve tones universally accepted: Arabic music has 17 tones, several Czech composers have used quarter-tone scorings, the Mexican composer Julian Carrillo constructed instruments capable of producing sixteenth-tones, and the American Harry Partch built a harpsichord-like keyboard contraption with 43 tones to the octave.

Keys to the Tonal Kingdom

Except for pieces in the 12-tone system, where every note is equal to every other note, most works—certainly those written before the 20th century—have a tonal center. When a work is listed in C Major or F# minor, it means that C (or F#) is the basic tone on which the rest of the music is constructed. The piece may shift into other keys as the piece goes along, but even so, each section of the work maintains that sense of unity, and gives us the

Important Things to Know

Composers choose different keys to evoke different moods. In very general terms, the major keys have a brighter, more optimistic sound, and the minor ones are more melancholy, even somber. Then, even within those two primary divisions, each scale has a slightly different center of pitch, and therefore a somewhat different emotional cast. Most composers look on C Major as a bright, carefree key, for instance, while G minor often signifies music of more serious or dramatic nature. The layman may not be able to distinguish between these keys, however, with experience you can tell the difference when a composer switches keys within a piece. The trained musician can tell the key upon hearing it.

feeling of starting from and returning to a home base. Usually, the sharps or flats that belong to each key are printed at the top of each score, at the left end of each line of music, and at any point within the score where the key changes; these listings are called key signatures. (In Mahler's Symphony No. 6, there are episodes in all 24 major and minor keys, each of them marked by an appropriate shift in key signature.)

One way to indicate how a composer views these subtleties of sound and mood is to consider the keys of the Beethoven Symphonies. The first two, shorter and lighter than most of the rest, are in the cheery majors of C and D Major, respectively. The groundbreaking, revolutionary "Eroica" bears the more heroic key of E-flat. The charming Fourth Symphony is in B-flat, while the far more powerful

Music Word

Modulation is the shifting from one key to another within a musical composition, the idea being to accomplish this in a continuous musical flow. It's no fair just stopping something in C Major and starting something else in G.

Fifth Symphony is in C minor. In the "Pastoral Symphony," the beauties of nature are displayed in the sunny key of F; the exhilarating Seventh dances along in A Major and the lighthearted (comparatively) Eighth returns to F Major. For the mighty Ninth Symphony, though, Beethoven chooses the darker key of D minor, until the "Ode to Joy" modulates to an jubilant D Major conclusion. Different composers, of course, will read widely diverse meanings into any given key, but that, as the saying goes, is what makes horse races.

Colorful Sounds

Color or timbre refers to the unique sound of each musical instrument or voice. A composer's judicious use of color, and clever combinations of different timbres, can help shape a melody, emphasize the rhythmic foundation of a piece, or widen its emotional range. Some composers, including Rimsky-Korsakov and Scriabin, saw music as reflections

Bet You Didn't Know

In his 1910 composition "Prometheus," Scriabin wrote in a part for a color organ, a keyboard contraption intended to project changing colors in step with the musical progressions. The coordination was too complex, and the technology too primitive. It was not until 1975, 50 years after the composer's death, that a reasonably successful fusion of music and color was accomplished (with a laser apparatus) at the University of Iowa.

of color and believed that each key had its own special visual counterpart. Both used G# minor to paint moonlight portraits, for instance, and E Major for rippling waters. Scriabin went much further in this color connection than his older colleague, though: He saw the key of C Major as red, F# Major as bright blue, and so forth.

Few composers have taken the parallel between sound and color so literally, but virtually all use instrumental and vocal timbres to evoke a mood, spirit, or emotion. And more generalized light shows, with large screen projections added to a performance, have helped illuminate the essence, if not the specifics, of musical works.

Form-Fitting the Structural Guidelines

Each era of music is identified with particular forms and structural guidelines. The baroque suite contains certain stylized dances and the first movements of Mozart sonatas have a recognizable shape (opening theme, second theme, development of both melodies, recapitulation of one or both of them); even Beethoven, ready to break with tradition at the drop of a baton, followed the prescribed four movement form in his symphonies. Adherence to such structures may seem inherently limiting, but the genius of the great composers ensured ongoing creativity, even as they poured exciting new wines into those familiar old bottles.

New forms came into being with the romantic era: The nocturne was pioneered by the Irish composer John Field, but elevated to never-eclipsed heights of beauty and inspiration when Chopin got hold of the form. Liszt developed the symphonic poem, fusing music and literature; Tchaikovsky broadened the musical scope of the ballet, with his full-length

Important Things to Know

Repetition and contrast are key words in describing musical structure. Repetition helps the listener keep track of the musical progress; it's like the windows in a house, the milestones on the road, it helps us keep our musical bearings. Sometimes the repetition can be exact; more often the theme or rhythmic motif is varied, shifted from key to key or major to minor, played by different instruments, or presented with different harmonies. Think of the familiar opening motif of Beethoven's Fifth Symphony: you'll hear it again and again in the course of the piece, each time in a newly compelling incarnation.

masterpieces "The Sleeping Beauty," "Swan Lake," and "The Nutcracker"; Wagner took the opera, with its set piece arias and ensemble numbers, and turned it into expansive music drama. In our own country, Charles Ives turned barn dances and hymn tunes into classical sonatas and symphonies; and John Cage blew form and structure out of the water altogether with his "4' 33'," a piece where the pianist is instructed to sit at the keyboard in silence for four minutes and 33 seconds. (The piece was later transcribed for other instruments, so five players came out and sat there for the required duration.)

CHAPTER 6

What Are the Instrumental Sounds of Music?

In This Chapter

➤ The four families of orchestral instruments

➤ Instrumental color

➤ Dynamic levels

➤ Non-orchestral instruments

Technology moves so quickly, and is so pervasive, that we quickly lose sight of what earlier generations took for granted. Most kids today would stare at you blankly if you asked them to prepare a paper on a Smith-Corona typewriter, with a carbon copy or two; most adults would have a similarly difficult time imagining life without a pocketful of credit cards. Evolution came about a bit more slowly in music, but we similarly have become so used to the sound of modern instruments, so accustomed to their more accurate pitch and greater virtuosic possibilities, that it can be unsettling to encounter performances on such ancestors of the oboe, trombone, and piano as the shawm, sackbut, and clavichord.

When the so-called "original instrument" or "early music" movement began a few decades ago, using those obscure contraptions was often a convenient excuse for playing out of tune, with all sorts of scrapings, squawkings, and screechings tolerated in the name of authenticity. Gradually, though, true virtuosos on the older instruments arrived on the scene, proving that historical accuracy and high musicianship could indeed walk hand in hand.

You Can't Make Music Without the Instruments

While the complex texture of Bach's orchestral pieces make it seem as if he had a large orchestra at his disposal, he was usually delighted if the court could round up a presentable 18-member ensemble. When Haydn was writing all those symphonies for Prince Esterhazy, he had an orchestra of merely 19 players. It was only when he first visited London, in 1790, that he found an orchestra of double that size.

Bet You Didn't Know

Large groups could be called in for special occasions, of course. When Handel conducted his Royal Fireworks Music in London in 1749, there were 3 sets of timpani, 6 trumpets, 9 horns, 12 bassoons, and no less than 24 oboes. They say there was such a crush of people trying to get to the first performance that London Bridge was tied up for three hours.

Today, of course, an orchestra of 40 players barely makes it into the symphonic ranks; most orchestras have 70 or 80 members, and the major ones have closer to 100. Unless, of course, they're playing Berlioz or Mahler, in which case they have to import additional musicians. Berlioz wanted an orchestra of 200 for his "Romeo and Juliet," which is probably why nobody plays it much any more.

Every Instrument Has Its Own Special Timbre

The timbre or tone of each instrument is different, and further variations in sound quality are possible in the hands (or mouth) of a skilled player. Some sounds seem to convey their own emotional or descriptive content: the agile flute is often used to portray twittering birds or cascading streams; skeletons rattle their bones on the xylophone; and romance often blossoms to the warm sounds of the cello.

Some Like to Play More Than One Note at a Time

The piano keyboard is arranged so that you can depress as many notes as you have fingers. (That wasn't enough for Henry Cowell, who invented "tone clusters" that you play with your entire forearm.) Sonorous chords can be played by one hand while the other races up and down in swirling melodic figurations. Violins and cellos have four strings, so they too can produce chords, and experts on keyboard-type percussion instruments, like the xylophone and marimba, often play four notes at a time (holding two mallets in each hand).

Most other percussion instruments concentrate on one note at a time. The cymbals crash; the triangle tinkles (so to speak); the bass drum pounds out the beat; and the gong can be used for anything exotic. Wind and brass instruments basically can only play one note at a time, but here again technology has rushed to the rescue with something called multiphonics, a special way of fingering the instrument that allows a skilled player to produce two tones at once.

Needless to say, synthesizers can produce as many simultaneous sounds as the programmer puts into them, but it seems unlikely that they'll replace the Los Angeles Philharmonic or Boston Symphony Orchestra any time soon.

Over the Rainbow

Just as each instrument has its own special sound, varying combinations of instruments produce distinctive colors that are called into being by the composer, then modified by the conductor. Adding a single trumpet to a body of strings produces a sonic texture totally different from the one you hear if that same trumpet is meshed within an ensemble of other brass and wind instruments. When a conductor signals the double basses to play with more vigor, he is trying to balance the orchestral sound, to ensure that the sonic essence of the piece is being presented in proper equilibrium.

Volume Control

The amount of sound any (unamplified) instrument can produce is a factor both of its construction—a guitar, obviously, cannot play as loudly as a trumpet—and the skill of the player in maximizing its inherent sonic spectrum. Generally speaking, the harder you pluck a string, hit a key, or blow into a tube, the louder the tone will be, but there are extra devices to cut down on the amount of sound being produced:

Important Things to Know

The four sections of the orchestra and the individual instruments within them create the dynamics of an orchestral performance. In one section of a piece, the composer may call for the brasses to play full-strength while the percussion provides a soft, steady underpinning. In another section, he may want the violas to carry a forceful theme, while the flutes gently comment on it from above; or vice versa. The composer's intent is then filtered through the conductor's judgment, and the players' ability to carry out his sonic vision.

mutes that fit into the bell of trumpets or tubas, or are placed across the strings of violins and violas. Even the pianist has a "soft pedal" to accomplish the same effect at the keyboard.

Pitching a Strike

Just as most of us can easily distinguish one color from the next, people with perfect pitch can recognize any note that is being played or sung. Pitch simply refers to the relative highness or lowness of a tone; acoustically, it is determined by the frequency of vibrations of that given note. In the orchestra, the highest string sounds are produced by the violins, the lowest by the double basses; the piccolos are the altitude champs of the woodwinds, the bassoons (or contrabassoons, which are even deeper) hit bottom. Amongst the brasses, it's the trumpet on top, the tuba down below. And handily outranging them all, with 88 notes and more than seven octaves, is the piano.

Four Category Combo

With the introduction of electronic instruments in the 20th century, it can be argued that there are more than four families of orchestral instruments, and we can sit here all night trying to figure out where to fit keyboards. For instance, is the piano a percussion instrument, since you strike the keys, or a string instrument, since that's what produces the sound? (Some experts call it a percussion instrument, while others take no chances and put the piano firmly into both categories.)

By the same token, we can well make the point that there are only three families, since there are only three non-vocal ways of making sounds: you can vibrate a string (violin or harp), vibrate the air within a hollow tube (flute or trumpet), or vibrate a solid object (xylophone or drum). So as not to complicate our life more than necessary, though, we'll stay with the usual designation of four basic orchestral classifications: strings, winds, brass, and percussion.

Stringing It Along

Strings have been prime players on the orchestral scene since the days when the concert hall was a palace ballroom and any audience member below the rank of earl or duchess was highly suspect. Basically, the strings are gentler-sounding instruments than their relatives in the other sections, which is why orchestras contain so many of them and why they sit right up front. Since composers love to write four simultaneous lines for strings (that's why there are so many string quartets), the violins are divided into firsts and seconds, the firsts usually playing the higher and more difficult parts, though there are no guarantees. The violas, slighter bigger and lower than the frisky fiddles, are in the middle, with the cellos and basses providing the deepest string sounds.

Though the term "string instrument" usually conjures up the image of bowed violins or cellos, there are many plucked instruments as well. The guitar, mandolin, and lute are occasional visitors to the symphony orchestra, and a more regular member of the family is the stringiest instrument of them all—the harp, with 47 (count 'em!) strings, not to mention seven foot pedals to move their pitches up or down.

The Answer Is Blowing in the Winds

Although the instruments in the winds section are now mostly (in some cases entirely) metal, they used to be made of wood and you blew through them, so the name woodwinds has stuck. Basically, there are three types: the kind where you blow across a hole, as we used to do with Coke bottles as a kid (flutes, piccolos); those where you blow into a mouthpiece containing a vibrating reed (clarinets); and those where you blow between two reeds fastened together (oboes, bassoons). The instruments in the last group, for obvious reasons, are called double-reeds. A reed is a vibrating strip of thin cane or metal, used to set the air column vibrating within an instrument. A reed can vibrate freely, as in a harmonica; up against a hard surface, as in a clarinet, where the reed is strapped to the mouthpiece; or against another reed, as in an oboe or bassoon. For obvious reasons, the last two are known as double-reed instruments. We'll tell you more about those blowhard types in Chapter 8. We promise.

Top Brass

The brass instruments have been more consistent in their construction. Back in medieval days, they were made of metal and still are today, although all sorts of other alloys are now added, both to improve and sound and cut the costs. Brasses have traditionally had a military flair, going back to the days when Joshua's trumpet made the Jericho walls come tumbling down. In ancient days, trumpets were great long things (the Tibetans still use a kind of trumpet that is sixteen feet long; it's called, if you'll pardon the expression, dung), but eventually somebody figured out that if you curved some of the tubing back into a sort of S-shape, you could carry it around without breaking your back. Eventually, valves were added, making nimble passage work far easier to accomplish.

Banging on Those Bongos

Percussion instruments include anything you bang, bong, rap, or slap. Some are hit; some are shaken (but not stirred); and some, called tuned percussion, can produce definite pitches. All are used to accentuate rhythms, create dramatic effects, or add an element of surprise to the orchestral proceedings.

It's not difficult to understand why percussion instruments are basic to virtually every society. Any child seeking attention has invented one or more of them. In fact, the traditional first baby toy—the rattle—is a form of untuned percussion. The gourd, used in so many Latin American ensembles, is really just a fancy rattle, and specimens of an ancient rattle-like instrument called the sistrum (with rings that jangle on a metal frame when the thing is shaken) have been unearthed from archaeological digs in Mesopotamia.

Orchestral Aliens

Since there are literally thousands of instruments in common use in our and other cultures around the world, we can't begin to list them all here, but let's name-drop a few that you may well encounter in the concert hall that are not generally considered orchestral instruments.

Guitars Don't Need To Be Electric

Not all guitars have long necks, flat bodies, and a cord leading to an amplifier. The classical six-string guitar is far more voluptuous in shape, mellow in sound, and striking in its ability to convey a remarkably wide range of tones. The national folk instrument of Spain, it was brought into the modern concert hall by the legendary Spanish virtuoso Andres Segovia. His mastery inspired dozens of composers to write solo pieces, chamber music, and concertos for the guitar. Today, thanks to such sterling performers as Christopher Parkening, Angel Romero, Sharon Isbin, David Starobin, Narciso Yepes, and a host of others, it is one of the more popular solo instruments on the American classical scene.

Loveable Lutes

One of the primary ancestors of the guitar, the lute was a favored instrument of the troubadours and until 1700 or so, was widely used for song accompaniments and ensembles. Bach wrote several suites for the lute, its subtle tones enriched because each of string is duplicated, the pairs (called courses) tuned either in unison or in octaves. Lutes come in many sizes, but they usually have five sets of double strings, plus a single string for the highest sound. (Some lutes have 11 courses, but they never became too popular since not too many players have 11 fingers).

Melodious Mandolins

The mandolin is a plucked string instrument, usually with eight strings tuned in pairs (to the same four notes as the violin); the player uses a plectrum to give the sound more substance. Mozart used a mandolin to accompany the Serenade in "Don Giovanni," and you'll even find one tucked away in the huge forces specified by Mahler for his Seventh Symphony.

Repertory for the mandolin goes back to the end of the 16th century. Parts for it appeared in concert music and opera in the late 17th century. Vivaldi wrote concertos for one and two mandolins. It is a popular "folk" instrument in the USA, Latin America and Japan.

Tinkling on the Ivories

"I love a piano," said Irving Berlin, and with the possible exception of kids who were forced to practice when they would rather have been out playing ball, so do we all. Its multi-octave keyboard permits a huge range of pitches; its solid construction gives it power enough to hold its own against a full symphony orchestra; and the pedals permit a further extension of its sound spectrum. The piano makes frequent cameo appearances in 20th century orchestral scores, but it's far more familiar in solo, chamber, and concerto circumstances. Piano is the normal abbreviation for pianoforte. The first pianoforte were made by Bartolomeo Cristofori, who began work on them in 1698. As it was able to play two or more notes at a time and both loud and soft, it was quickly appriciated by the likes of J.S. Bach, Beethoven and Mozart who wrote extensively for it.

Bet You Didn't Know

There's a sourpuss in every crowd. Ambrose Bierce wrote that the piano is operated by "depressing the keys of the machine and the spirits of the audience at the same time."

Heavenly Harpin' on the Harpsichords

Before there were pianos, there were sundry other keyboard instruments with softer tones (because the keys activated hammers that plucked the strings instead of striking them). The harpsichord evokes images of baroque drawing rooms and stately minuets (which is why it was used by The Rolling Stones to add an antique quality to their song "Lady Jane"), but it has had a renaissance in the 20th century, with more and more composers finding that infusing antique sounds with modern harmonies makes an intriguing musical mix.

Paging President Clinton: The Saxophone

The saxophone, named for its Belgian inventor Antoine Joseph Sax, is actually a kind of brass-woodwind hybrid since it has a metal body but is played with a mouthpiece and reed resembling a clarinet's. Like the strings, saxophones come in families, from the small, straight soprano to the curved alto and tenor, so familiar from jazz groups, and on down to the baritone, bass, and even contrabass saxophone. It was invented in 1840 and was soon taken up by French orchestral composers such as Bizet, Meyerbeer, and Massenet. Strauss, Ravel, Debussy, and Prokofiev have also used the saxophone for its unique color.

Humble Harmonicas

One of the most portable instruments in the world, the harmonica can easily be tucked into pocket or purse, so it's a favorite among folk and itinerant musicians. It's also known as a mouth organ, since the player blows air into, or sucks air out of it, the flow causing a series of metal reeds to vibrate. No clear-cut inventor has emerged for the harmonica, though one Friedrich Buschmann took out a whole batch of patents in Berlin in the early 1820s. The Hohner company started manufacturing the instruments in 1857, and to this day, remains the largest and best-known maker of harmonicas in the world.

It used to be considered a casual instrument—or worse, a children's toy—but the mouth organ has been rehabilitated in our own century. In the 1960s and beyond, Bob Dylan has created timeless folk and rock sounds with his harmonica. And the instrument has been elevated to concert status by such eminent virtuosos as Larry Adler, and such major composers as Morton Gould, Ralph Vaughan Williams, and many others who have written solo works for the instrument.

Bet You Didn't Know

Early in his career, while he was playing a vaudeville theater in Chicago, Larry Adler was introduced to an older man, "with a kindly face and gentle manner," who lectured the kid about writing home to his parents every day and attending a synagogue on weekends. "I don't care how many shows you go to do," he said sternly, "this Saturday you're gonna go to shule." Only later did Adler find out the source of this good advice was the infamous gangster Al Capone.

Opulent Organs

If you've ever been to church, you've heard the majestic sounds of the organ. A massive instrument with several keyboards and a whole series of foot pedals, it produces sound by forcing air into a large series of pipes. In the old days, some poor guy had to keep pumping air into the thing with bellows; now electricity does the job, the organ's hundreds of tubes and pipes creating a whole world of sound, not to mention a range of pitches wider than that of the full orchestra. No wonder the organ has long reigned as "the King of Instruments."

Switched-on Synthesizers

Theoretically, a synthesizer is capable of replacing the whole orchestra, since it can imitate almost any instrumental sound, and produce tones with mathematical accuracy. Big deal. We can also see the Mona Lisa on a picture postcard, but it would hardly be a substitute for the real thing. Synthesized Bach, Mozart, and Beethoven have all had their fifteen minutes of fame, but the future (one hopes) lies more in the route taken by a number of innovative composers, who use electronic effects selectively, fusing synthesized and natural sounds, juxtaposing technology and tradition in their never-ending search for intriguing new musical combinations.

CHAPTER 7

 How Can I Tell the Singers Apart Without a Program?

In This Chapter

➤ Who are the female singers?

➤ Who are the male singers?

➤ What do you get when you mix two or more singers?

➤ How to tell a chorus from just a group of singers

If the females are wearing helmets and battle dress, chances are they're Valkyries (maidens appearing in Norse mythology). Or else they're singing in an opera by Handel or one of those other early composers who wrote male parts so high that only women could sing them.

If the males are singing lustily and waving flagons around, chances are it's a drinking song, and if you see two guys with swords, they'll usually cross them in a couple of minutes. That's one of the nice things about opera: Even if you can't figure out exactly who's saying what to whom, the costumes and sets are there to give you a clue.

On the other hand, if you're in a concert hall and the singers are in formal attire and behaving in a dignified manner—even when hitting the high notes—you may want to consult the program to determine the performers' backgrounds, role specialties, and of course, who's who and what they might be singing about at any given moment.

Sing Out!

Singers refer to their voice as their "instrument," because even though the sound-producing mechanisms are tucked away inside their bodies, the voice is their sole means of making music. As Groucho Marx used to say, "It's something you always have with you." Babies make sounds the instant they're born, but not too many folks (beyond the doting parents, possibly) would consider that music. Producing beautiful sounds means cultivating the instrument, and developing the artistic wherewithall to use it to its best advantage.

As noted, not all singers head for the opera. We've all sung in the shower, and many of us in school glee clubs or church choirs. A lot of boomers and post-boomers even had a fling at singing with a rock group, although their focus may have been more on looking the part or tearing vocal cords than on hitting the right notes. Even professional artists frequently are quite content to work their vocal magic in non-operatic forms: as members of a chorus, possibly, or oratorio soloists, or singers of art songs, jazz, and musical comedy.

Bet You Didn't Know

Many of our most distinguished opera stars emerged from less exalted musical spheres. Rosa Ponselle, one of the first American-trained singers to take the Met by storm (she made her debut there in 1918), came out of Vaudeville, sharing the stage with animal acts, jugglers, and dialect comedians. The tenor Jan Peerce sang pop tunes at Radio City before reaching the Met, Birgit Nilsson and Sherrill Milnes sang till the cows came home (and needed milking) on the farms where they grew up, and Marilyn Horne paid her early rent by covering doo-wah pop hits in a West Coast recording studio.

There are some naturally gifted performers who seem to have sprung forth as fully developed artists from childhood on, but most singers—as indeed most instrumentalists— have to spend years developing their technical prowess and musical understanding, studying many stylistic periods and researching performing practices of past eras. Singers then have the added problem of words: they are expected to learn long texts in at least three or four foreign languages, in addition to not fainting when they have to add Russian or Spanish to the linguistic pot. Some singers are quite happy to sacrifice correct pronunciation and clear enunciation for better vocal projection, but more and more modern artists, especially amongst the younger generation, are ready, willing, and able to convey both clarity and expressive power without giving up one for the other.

The Ladies Take Center Stage

Just as many instruments come in several varieties, depending upon the range of pitches they produce, vocalists are grouped according to the basic nature of their voices. If you want to impress your musical friends, you can refer to a singer's tessitura, meaning the scope of notes within which he or she is most comfortable. In women's voices, as among men's, there are three basic categories (with considerable overlapping among them), fitting the broad designations of high, medium, and low.

Music Word

Tessitura is the range of notes in which a particular voice is at its best, most comfortable. The singer can go higher or lower if necessary, of course, but is happiest staying within those pitch confines. The term is also sometimes used to indicate the general range encompassed by a vocal part.

Shattering Glass with Sopranos

The highest voices belong to the sopranos, who—perhaps because of the strain inherent in pitching the sound so far above normal speaking range—tend to be among the more temperamental types. They also seem to get the most romantic roles and die the most colorful deaths.

There are several subdivisions of this voice type. The coloratura soprano is the daredevil of the crowd, with a light, limber quality and the ability to dazzle audiences with trills, runs, ornaments, and all sorts of other passages that theoretically should be physically impossible. The dramatic soprano produces a sound of high resonance and power, perfect for those Wagner and Strauss operas where the heroine has to be heard above the blaring of a huge orchestra. The lyric soprano is of a gentler, sweeter-toned nature, and therefore happier with the lighter, song-like arias found in many French and Italian operas.

Music Word

A **trill** is a musical ornament wherein the voice or instrument alternates rapidly between a written note and the note immediately above it. A **run** is the rapid traversal of many different notes. An **ornament** is any kind of embellishment of a melody by the addition of extra notes in and around it. As noted, a trill is just such an ornament.

The Middle Children: Mezzo-Sopranos

"Mezzo" is Italian for half, so these singers are halfway between sopranos and altos, whom we'll get to in a moment. Just don't confuse them with the "Messy Soprano" in Victor Borge's Mozart Opera routine, or the "Mezzanine Soprano" who has the leading role in P.D.Q. Bach's hilarious opera spoof, "The Stoned Guest," or they'll never speak to you again. Mezzos don't often get top billing, but when they do—in Bizet's "Carmen," for instance, or any of the many Rossini operas brought back to 20th century popularity by Marilyn Horne—you can expect dramatic and very exciting vocal fireworks. Some famous mezzos of the recent past include Conchita Supervia, Gladys Swarthout, Kirsten Thorberg, and Jennie Tourel.

Getting Down With the Altos

The word "alto" comes from the same root as altitude, meaning "high," making it a rather curious appellation for the lowest female voice. On the other hand, in the baroque era, many alto parts were sung by men, so the male alto really had to get up there. Meanwhile, female altos (or contraltos, which are like altos only more so) almost never land the romantic roles, but their rich, deep sound makes them perfect casting for what are referred to as the character parts in movies. The famous singer Betty Allen said that opera contraltos usually portray witches or bitches, but you'll also find them holding forth as nurses, mothers, confidantes, and other useful folks to have around the house. Some famous altos of the recent past are Marian Anderson, Louise Homer, Kathleen Ferrier, and Ernestine Schumann-Heink.

Bet You Didn't Know

When "Carmen" was in rehearsals before the first performance, the Toreador hated the aria Bizet had given him, and demanded a rewrite. Bizet, disgusted because his leading lady had already forced him to redo her entrance aria a dozen times, sat down and dashed off the immortal "Toreador Song," grumbling "If they want rubbish, they shall get it."

The Men Take Center Stage

Men get to play some of the most glamorous roles in opera: they're tsars and toreadors, saints and devils, leaders and lovers. In the early years of this century, Caruso and Chaliapin were among the most famous musicians in the world; not long ago we had the Three Tenors, whose round-the-world exploits will be documented in a later chapter, and one of whom—Placido Domingo—is still on the Metropolitan Opera roster, along with such other high-noters as Salvatore Licitra, Roberto Alagna, and Allan Glassman.

Some Men Can Reach Those High Notes, Too

We were talking before about male altos. These days, they're called countertenors (as opposed to P.D.Q. Bach's "Bargain-Counter Tenor"), and whether they muster a full high voice, or use falsetto, they can stay right up there with the ladies. Occasionally a countertenor will be heard in one of the "trouser" roles (male parts traditionally taken by women), but most often he settles for madrigals, oratorio solos, and other early music performances.

The regular tenors—the guys who get all the high C's and, in most operas, the girl—are the male counterparts of sopranos in range and, it is said, in egos. They tend to divide up their tonal territory into roles for the dramatic tenor, ready to do heroic battle with gods or earthly demons, and the lyric tenor, whose preference is for lighter, more flexible undertakings. Among the famous tenors of the recent past are Jussi Bjorling, Mario Lanza, Jan Peerce and Richard Tucker.

Bet You Didn't Know

Enrico Caruso was singing the part of the hero, Don Alvaro, in Verdi's "La Forza del Destino" when his gun failed to go off in the climactic scene of the first act. It's not clear whether the blanks didn't work or the stagehand who was supposed to supply the shot had dozed off, but there was silence. The singers on stage looked at each other in panic until Caruso saved the day: "Bang!" he shouted.

Those Funloving But Tricky Baritones

Baritones strike the happy medium within the male voice range, singing lower than the tenors (see above) but higher than the basses (see below). They make excellent drinking buddies (on stage) and often are cast as doting fathers, but they also portray some of the most mean and nasty villains, including the wormy Wurm (in Verdi's "Luisa Miller") and the dapper Dappertutto (in Offenbach's "Tales of Hoffmann"). Some famous baritones include Boris Christoff, Alexander Kipnis, Ezio Pinza, and Norman Treigle.

They're Very Deep: Basses

Bassos (or in less fancy form, basses) are the lowest members of the singing family, taking over where the baritones poop out. Baritones with very low notes, or basses with nifty high ones, are often called bass-baritones. Like altos, they get some of the best character roles, sometimes comic (like Bartolo and Basilio in Rossini's "The Barber of Seville"), sometimes menacing (Mefistofele in Boito's opera of that title, or if you refer to your devil as Mephistopheles, Gounod's "Faust"), and often very big (the giants Fafner and Fasolt in Wagner's "Das Rheingold"). Bassos also tend to do well in the royalty department, among many other lofty posts, portraying Kings of Cornwall, Spain, and Egypt (respectively in "Tristan," "Don Carlos," and "Aida"), not to mention Tsar Boris Godounov of Russia.

A Group Efforts

When the monks in their cloistered cells sang their unison chants, they were definitely singing in a group. As classical music evolved to encompass several voices singing independent themes, the group scene expanded and developed in a number of intriguing directions.

Two by Two: Let's Do a Duet

A vocal duet means that two voices are having at it. They can be focused in any way that the composer chooses. In a round, for instance, one voice begins, and when the second joins in, it echoes exactly the same tune. The voice parts in a duo can be of equal importance, or one can dominate, with the other adding harmonic color. They can be set in equal ranges (that is, for two sopranos or two tenors), or selected for contrast with one high voice and one low. In opera or musical theater, the libretto often dictates which voices are heard: If the hero and heroine are locked in a romantic embrace, we may assume an appropriate division of vocal activity. In other instances, the voices answer each other, as though in conversation; they may be heard a capella (that is, without accompaniment), or set against the tonal splash of a large orchestra.

Three's Company, But Four Or More's Not a Crowd

As composers grew more adventuresome, they began creating music for multiple voices, each part having its own importance, its own place in the musical scheme of things. In other pieces, the highest voice carries the melody, with the others serving more as an accompaniment. In opera, ensemble numbers (like the famous quartet from "Rigoletto" or the sextet in "Lucia") allow many characters to express simultaneous views or emotions, each singer having his or her own theme, pacing, and expression.

Chorus Lines of Angels

When does a chamber ensemble become an orchestra? If you can answer that one, you can tell us when a group of singers becomes a chorus. A good rule of thumb is whether there is more than one singer (or player) on a part. In other words, if you have two or three tenors singing the same notes, you might as well break down and call it a chorus (or choir, possibly, which usually signifies a small chorus). Normally, choirs are divided into groups by vocal range (soprano, alto, tenor, and bass being the most customary, although some composers specify six or even eight subdivisions).

Bet You Didn't Know

When Haydn went to London, he first heard Handel's "Messiah" in a performance at Westminster Abbey by a monster chorus of 1,000 voices, well over 950 more than Handel himself was able to muster at the premiere of the oratorio. According to contemporary reports, when the great "Hallelujah Chorus" reached its final measure, Haydn burst into tears, crying out, "He is the master of us all."

A mixed chorus—the ones we usually encounter at the opera or in oratorios—contains both male and female singers. When a chorus is made up entirely of women, it's called a women's chorus. We'll give you three guesses about what they call a chorus made up entirely of men.

PART THREE

Orchestra, My Kingdom for an Orchestra

CHAPTER 8

What is an Orchestra?

> **In This Chapter**
>
> ➤ The chamber orchestra
> ➤ The symphony orchestra
> ➤ The instruments of the orchestra
> ➤ The conductor

According to our Webster's, an orchestra is a large group of players of musical instruments. How large is large? Well, that's hard to say. If it's in the range of 12 to 30 players, it's usually called a chamber orchestra. The regular orchestra ranges up from there to the 100 or so musicians on the roster of the major symphonies around the country.

You'll generally see somebody in front of the orchestra, his or her back to the audience, waving a baton, and with a variety of gestures and other forms of body language, urging the players on to greater heights of musical glory. This is the Maestro, (or in the case of a woman, Maestra), well described by Laurence McKinney as "This backward man, this view obstructor, Who's known to us as The Conductor." There are some orchestras who get along just fine without a conductor, thank you, but they usually don't attempt really large-scale or complex modern works.

Music Word

A baton is a short stick used by conductors to make their hand motions easier for the players to see. It's usually made of light wood, painted white for greater visibility, and often with a cork base for more comfortable hand-holding.

Chamber-Made

Just because a chamber orchestra is smaller than the full symphony doesn't mean it can't have many of the same instruments. You'll find only one or two horns instead of four, ten violinists instead of sixty, and more than likely trombones and tubas will turn up on the missing list, but Bach's Brandenburg Concertos and most Mozart Symphonies were designed for ensembles of 20 to 30 players, so don't feel deprived. As a matter of fact, many large symphony orchestras, seeking some degree of historical authenticity, will ask half their membership to take a break during Bach and Mozart performances.

Music Word

The word **orchestra** comes from the Greek, meaning "dancing place," and in the Greek theater, orchestra meant the space in front of the stage where the chorus sang or danced. The French revived the term in the 17th century to indicate the stage where the instrumentalists sat, and by the early 18th century, the word was applied to the players themselves.

Sometimes a chamber orchestra can be made up exclusively of strings, in which case, oddly enough, it's called a string orchestra. But in many works, a composer modifies the all-string sound by adding one or more brass or wind (or keyboard) instruments. Often, this non-string interloper will be the featured instrument in a concerto. In any case, just keep in mind that "chamber" refers to the modest size of the performing ensemble, not to any lessening of musical values.

Sizable Symphonies

Orchestras in Bach's day were haphazard affairs, consisting pretty much of whatever players the composer could muster on any given day. Five years before Bach died, however, the Bohemian composer Johann Stamitz moved to the town of Mannheim, in southern Germany, where he developed and directed an orchestra so remarkable that it soon became famous all over Europe. For one thing, it pioneered gradations of sound that had been unknown before—swellings of volume (crescendo), and their opposite (diminuendo); a kind of drooping figure that became known as the "Mannheim Sigh"; and a leaping group of notes nicknamed the "Mannheim Rocket."

Local composers, members of the so-called Mannheim School, wrote pieces to take special advantage of these exciting orchestral possibilities, and by showing the world what creative imagination, effective leadership, and high performing discipline could accomplish, the Mannheimers gave the symphony orchestra a completely new significance in the musical world.

Bet You Didn't Know

Mozart first encountered clarinets at Mannheim and was so thrilled that he rushed home and included them in his next concerto. Schubert wrote to a friend that "no orchestra in the world has ever excelled the Mannheim."

Other composers, of course, continued that march of orchestral progress, gradually adding other instruments to the symphonic mix, devising ever more intriguing sonic combinations, and exploring all sorts of other new harmonic and rhythmic directions.

On to the 20th Century

By the middle of the 19th century, string instruments were being rebuilt to permit higher tension in the strings. The resulting increase in volume and brilliance of sound gave new presence and power to the orchestra, just as the many improvements to wind and brass instruments evened the balance and allowed the whole ensemble to reflect greater performing precision and virtuosity. Berlioz, Wagner, and other composers demanded, and often got, much larger orchestras to reproduce their expansive ideas. In the 20th century, the percussion section came more into its own as composers took advantage of more than just pounding out the rhythm on a big bass drum.

String 'em Up

The string instruments all have basically the same shape, with four strings that are either stroked with a bow or plucked with the fingers. The double bass is a little different, with more sloping shoulders and a flatter back, but you'll never mistake it for a tuba. Violins and violas are played tucked under the chin, while the cellos and double basses rest on an end pin extending from the bottom of the frame.

Bet You Didn't Know

Cellos didn't have those bottom pins until the middle of the 19th century, so the player had to hold the instrument off the floor with the pressure of his knees. That changed when a Belgian virtuoso named Adrien Francois Servais grew too tubby to clutch the cello easily, and decided to build a fixture at the base of the instrument into which he fit a peg that could be raised or lowered depending on how many second helpings he'd had that day. Pretty soon other cellists, even the thin ones, found it easier and more comfortable to use an end pin, and the custom became universal.

The string instruments we know today evolved from the Renaissance viols, which also came in four sizes. They were not as robust as their descendants, and by the end of the 17th century, when the violin, viola, and cello had been honed to perfection by such brilliant Italian instrument makers as Amati, Guarneri, and Stradivari, the viols pretty well went out of business. The amazing thing is that these master craftsmen, including Bergonzi, del Gesu, and others, all lived and worked in two tiny neighboring Italian towns, Brescia and Cremona.

The double bass remained sort of a stepchild in those days of courtly manners and minuets, but it was rehabilitated when Beethoven gave it a prominent place in his Fifth Symphony, and rose to stardom as a full-fledged member of the chamber music team in Schubert's "Trout" Quintet.

Music Word

A **trill** is the rapid alternation of a written note with the note immediately above it; a **run** indicates rapid traversal of many different notes.

More Winds in the Woods

The highest of the winds is the flute, although its baby brother, the piccolo, sounds an octave higher. Vivaldi wrote a few concertos for the piccolo, but for the most part, its shrill tone is used to add color or high-pitched sound to the orchestral blend. The flute itself has been called the coloratura soprano of the orchestra since its fluidity suits it well to trills, runs, and other bits of musical athleticism. The clarinet is another fluid instrument, whose ability to create flowing melodies as well as virtuosic racings up and down the scale has made it equally welcome in jazz and symphonic circles.

The bass clarinet is just what it sounds like: a larger version of the clarinet with a lower range.

The remaining four orchestral winds make up a four-member clan, just like the violins, violas, cellos, and basses do within the string section. The fiddle's equivalent is the oboe, with a rather nasal tone (sort of like a clarinet with a cold), and the distinction of being the instrument to which all the other instruments tune to. The windy version of the viola is the English horn, which as a wit once observed, is neither English nor a horn. It's actually an alto oboe, the misnomer probably arising from its French name "cor anglais," meaning angled (not English) since the instrument has a little bend near the mouthpiece, as opposed to the oboe, which is straight.

The cello and bass equivalents in the woodwind family are the bassoons and contrabassoons, and if you think they look like bundles of sticks tied together, welcome to the club: The Italians called the bassoon "fagotto," and the Germans "fagott," both words meaning a bundle of sticks.

Oompah-Oomps

The French horn looks like a whole lot of tubing curled up into a circle, which is not too surprising since the French horn is a whole lot of tubing curled up into a circle. It's not especially French, but you can't have everything. It has a wonderfully mellow sound, and in the orchestra, it often travels around in groups of four, like city buses, because a lot of composers wrote parts for four horns in their symphonies and other large-scale works. The instruments evolved from animal horns, which were among the first primitive instruments; the French part comes because the modern horn was developed primarily in France. Fingering the valves on a trumpet or horn (or tuba, which we'll get to in a moment) serves a similar purpose to pressing the strings on a violin or cello: It changes the length of the vibrating material, causing the pitch tone to rise or fall. The longer the tube (or string), the lower the tone; the shorter the tube, the higher the tone.

Music Word

The position of the player's mouth around the reed or mouthpiece of wind and brass instruments is called **embouchure**, which comes from the French word "boucher," to kiss. Watch a horn player next time, and you'll see why.

Trombones are funny-looking gadgets shaped like overgrown paper clips. They usually don't have valves to change the length of the vibrating tube, but a long, U-shaped slide that the player moves back and forth, preferably not poking the player sitting in front of him. Its renaissance ancestor was the sackbut, from the Moorish word for pump!

Tubas are those tubby things in the back row that give the orchestra its deepest brass notes, the symphonic harmony its most solid foundation. The tuba often hangs out with three trombones, forming a deep-voice instrumental choir that just can't be beat in moments of solemn pomp and circumstance.

Clanging and Banging

Again, we can generally divide percussion instruments into three units, although some noisemakers defy any such cubbyhole attempts. Perhaps the most familiar is the drum, where a parchment is stretched across a (usually round) frame. Then we have the cymbals and other discs or plates of metal that are either crashed together or struck with a stick. And there are the instruments with metal or wood bars laid out in the manner of a piano keyboard, such as the vibraphone, xylophone, and marimba, producing specific tones when struck by a mallet.

Other familiar orchestral percussion instruments are the triangle, the castanets, the gong, and the tambourine, although composers are forever coming up with other things that will make even more unusual noises. When Tchaikovsky wanted to emphasize the victory celebrations after Napoleon's defeat, he stuck bells into the score of his "1812 Overture." You can hear real anvils in Verdi's "Anvil Chorus," and Wagner asked for 18 anvils when the ring of the Nibelung is forged in "Das Rheingold."

Bet You Didn't Know

Edgar Varese's "Ionization" calls for 42 different percussion instruments plus two sirens, but even that pales alongside the performance of Verdi's "Anvil Chorus" during the 1872 Peace Jubilee in Boston, when the orchestra was augmented by 100 city firemen, each hammering away at an anvil.

Cast List

In the following paragraphs you'll learn about the lineup of the regular players in the symphony orchestra.

Fiddle-Faddle

The smallest of the stringed instruments, the violin is the soprano of the string family. Its strings are stretched over a hollow wooden structure and are designed to produce a clear and concise sound. The violin is the true melody maker of the orchestra; it is the most important player of all the instruments. The strings can be made of several materials, from sheep gut to nylon or steel. The violin's remarkable sounds are produced when the bow (horsehair stretched along a wooden bow) is drawn over the strings. The strings are of different thicknesses, with the thinner strings producing higher notes. The pitch is also changed as the violinist presses the string with a finger. The shorter the string, the higher the note. The violin has an amazing range of sounds and has been used to evoke just about every human emotion, as well as several members of the animal kingdom.

Second violinists were once selected by virtue of their not quite qualifying for first violin (sort of the runners-up). This distinction, however, no longer prevails in most major symphony orchestras, where first and second violinists are musicians of equal stature. The first violins are usually grouped to the conductor's left, with the second violins to the left of the first violins. First violins traditionally carry more of the melody, with the seconds providing more of the harmonic underpinnings.

Violin concertos and sonatas proliferate among classical works. Vivaldi's "The Four Seasons," one of the most popular works in the entire repertoire, is actually a set of four Violin Concertos. Mozart and Beethoven are celebrated for their violin concertos (is there any surprise?) as are Haydn, Prokofiev, Saint-Saens, Schumann, and a host of others, including Stravinsky.

Mozart composed 42 violin sonatas (only slightly surpassing the number of his symphonies). Beethoven, Bach, Mendelssohn, Prokofiev, and Bartók are among those who have created sonatas for violin.

Don't Call Them Second Fiddles, Going Down

The larger viola is the alto of the strings. It produces a richer, fuller, and deeper sound than the violin, although without quite so much brilliance and audacity. It does not step out in a solo role nearly so often as the violin, but it is indispensable to complete the string harmonies within the orchestra.

Bet You Didn't Know

The supposed lesser status of the violist, compared to his violin colleague, has spawned so many jokes that there's a whole page on the Internet devoted to them. Even violists like to tell them, wherefore this gem from the distinguished violist and Juilliard professor, Toby Appel. It seems an opera conductor got sick just before a performance of "La Bohème", and one of the violists had to take the podium in his stead. Everything went off without a hitch, but the next night, when the player returned to his regular seat, the violist in the next chair glared at him and snapped, "So, where the hell were you last night?"

Mozart's "Sinfonia Concertante" (K. 364) for violin, viola, and orchestra draws the viola out from its supporting status, as does Berlioz's "Harold in Italy" for viola and orchestra. Debussy featured the viola in "Sonata No. 2 for Flute, Viola, and Harp," and Bartók composed a "Concerto for Viola and Orchestra." The real fan of violas was Hindemith, who just happened to be a viola virtuoso. He composed several viola sonatas, along with "Der Schwanendreher" for viola and orchestra. To show his love for the instrument, Hindemith also composed both a concerto and a sonata for the viola d'amore of the Baroque period.

Hello Cello

Once known as the violoncello, the regal, resonant cello excels at evoking melancholy. Devotees of the cello marvel at its expressive quality, and played by a first-rate cellist, it is indeed evocative. The longer and thicker strings of the cello produce notes an octave deeper than the viola's, making it the tenor or baritone of the string family.

Beethoven, Chopin, Saint-Saens, and Rachmaninoff wrote beautiful cello sonatas, and composers as diverse as Bach, Debussy, Brahms, Hindemith, and Dvořák are among the composers who have created superb concertos for cello.

Bargain Bass-ment

The double bass can simply be called bass. Or you can choose from string bass (the choice of jazz musicians), bass viol, and contrabass. The instrument has also been dubbed the bull fiddle, but most double bass players would rather forget that one. With its thick strings, the double bass covers the lower registers of the musical spectrum. Like the other strings, it can be plucked as well as bowed. When used as a jazz instrument, it is usually plucked. Many orchestral instruments have an outrigging device attached over the scrollwork, called a "low-C extension." This enables the bassist to produce sounds two tones lower than the instrument's normal range.

Beethoven was a big fan of the double bass, and made it an important player in the Fifth Symphony. He also gave it some prominence in the Fourth and Ninth symphonies. And it may be argued that what was good enough for Beethoven is good for the symphony orchestra.

Music Word

Glissando. A quick sliding up or down the scale.

None But the Lonely Harp

The imposing triangular harp stands 68 inches tall, which makes it taller than some of the people who play it. With its roots in the Old Testament, the modern harp made its first appearance in Europe during the 12th century. Pedals were added a few centuries later. Its signature sound is the glissando, an effect produced by swiftly sliding the fingers over the strings. The unfortunate use of this device in movies—where all the good guys turn into angels—has made it seem a bit hackneyed to some critics. However, at the hands of a virtuoso harpist, and with music composed by the likes of Debussy, Berlioz, Liszt, Ravel, Mozart, or Wagner, the harp is a beautiful and lyrical instrument.

Piccolo Peepings

This is the one woodwind that is still frequently made of wood. The piccolo is a half-sized flute, with a range a full octave higher. It's the highest pitched of all orchestral instruments, and is used to evoke wild revelry and abandon.

Tutti Flutti

The flute is the soprano of the woodwinds. Its sound covers three octaves up from C. The flute has a crisp, clear sound that ranges from bright and festive to plaintive, depending on which end of the range is used. Whenever the composer wants us to hear twittering birds, that's usually the flute.

The modern flute, a descendant of the recorder, was once blown straight-on like its ancestor. Today, it's held sideways; the sound is produced when the player blows across the sharp edge of a hole near one side. The standard soprano flute is 27 inches long. There is also an alto flute, larger than its soprano sister, that produces a sensual, somewhat melancholy tone.

The flute has been a favored instrument for concertos and sonatas since the days it was featured by Bach and Telemann. Mozart immortalized it in his opera "The Magic Flute."

Little Oboe Peep

The oboe is the soprano of the double-reed woodwinds (or the mezzo of the whole wind family). Its range covers two octaves from just below middle C. The standard oboe is similar to the clarinet in appearance; it's distinguished by being three inches shorter (23 inches for the oboe; 26 inches for the clarinet) and because the flaring bell shape is not as pronounced. Less commonly seen is an alto oboe, the oboe d'amore. With its relatively high register, the oboe is capable of making lively music; however, most composers prefer its less cheerful moods. They like their instrument mysterious, mournful, and melancholy.

Part of the job of playing the oboe is mastering the art of honing reeds to the desired degree of slenderness—a tricky piece of work. Oboes have had a role in the vast majority of orchestral works composed over the past 300 years.

The Patient English Relative

The English horn is a one-and-one-half-sized oboe with an alto voice. It ranges from just below middle C up two octaves. It has a smokier, more exotic quality than the oboe.

A Case for Clarinets

The clarinet was the last woodwind to join the orchestral family and is a favorite of classical and jazz artists alike. The instrument has 18 holes, six of which are covered by fingers and the remainder by keys. The pitch of the tone is determined by which holes are stopped. The clarinet is an amazingly versatile instrument, capable of expressing a gamut of moods, and quickly going from loud to soft and back. As an example of its flexibility, in military band music where there are no strings, the clarinet takes the violin role.

There are several types of clarinets available. The most common instruments in symphony orchestras are the A (for keys with sharps) and the B-flat (for keys with flats). Clarinetists usually have both on hand. There is also a higher clarinet, the E-flat, and a lower-pitched clarinet or bass clarinet. In all, there are 13 types of clarinets. The lower register clarinets (alto, bass, and contrabass) have upturned metal bells, which makes them resemble saxophones. If the score calls for a saxophone and there is none in the orchestra, the part is played by a clarinet. Mozart was the earliest proponent of the clarinet and helped to raise the new instrument to its illustrious stature.

The bass clarinet was perfected by one Adolphe Sax, inventor of the saxophone, in 1840. Which helps to explain the uncanny resemblance between the two instruments. The bass clarinet is the woodwind equivalent to the cello in pitch. It ranges a full octave lower than the alto clarinet.

See You Bassoon

The bassoon is the lowest and largest of the standard wind instruments. It ranges from two octaves below middle C to almost an octave above it. If not doubled up, it would extend nine feet in length, which would make it inconvenient to play as well as unpleasant for neighboring musicians. Like its cousin, the oboe, the bassoon has a crook (called a bocal) on one end leading to a double reed. At the other end is an upward-turned bell. The bassoon is a heavy instrument requiring extra support to remain upright and in place. Its tonal range is comparable to the cello, although its nasal quality makes it more of a fun figure than a bearer of solemn tidings. Among other distinctions, the bassoon plays the opening notes in Stravinsky's "The Rite of Spring."

The contrabassoon is an octave lower and as long, and was probably a descendent of the Renaissance instrument known as the serpent. Beethoven was the first to use a contrabassoon in his Fifth and Ninth symphonies, and to invoke the darkness of a dungeon in "Fidelio." Not surprisingly, the melancholy Mahler favored the contrabassoon as well. Late 19th and 20th century composers seem to like its deep resonance, but the massive contrabassoon is used comparatively rarely in most orchestras today.

Trumpetuous, Sound the Trumpets

The forerunners of the modern trumpet were straight hollow tubes with no finger holes, valves, or slides. They appeared in most ancient societies, often to rouse soldiers to battle. During the Middle Ages, trumpets grew to unprecedented lengths, until finally the unwieldy size caused trumpet makers to bend it. The valves that are part of every trumpet today did not appear until the early 19th century.

The modern trumpet is four to four-and-one-half feet long before bending; the baroque trumpet was seven or eight feet long. Baroque works are often written for a trio of trumpets; two of these are played on a smaller instrument, called a piccolo trumpet. Trumpet players, like clarinet players, typically carry more than one instrument, tuned to different pitches. The standard pitches are B-flat, C, and D. Trumpets cover a range of about three octaves. Using the valves increases the length of available tube, therefore deepening the pitch. Trumpets—and all other brasses—can be muted to change the effect.

The cornet, a favorite instrument of military bands, is a cousin of the trumpet. It is the same length as the B-flat trumpet, but its configuration is conical instead of cylindrical. Composers of the last century often preferred its more refined tone. Another trumpet relative is the flugelhorn, which has a more mellow sound than either the trumpet or cornet.

Sound Your Horn

The horn is more commonly called the French horn, although why it is known by a longer and not entirely accurate appellation is a mystery. Possibly because the trumpet was once called a battle horn, and the two had to be distinguished.

The horn is one of the oldest instruments. Just hollow out an animal tusk, and voilà! Blowing into a conch shell can also be called playing a type of horn. By the 17th century, the horn had developed into 16 feet of coiled brass, with a wide, flaring bell. It was known as the "hunting horn" and designed to be slung on the user's shoulder. The invention of piston and rotary valves allowed the tube to be shortened and enabled the player to generate a much greater range of notes.

The French horn today is 11 feet of coiled brass, with the recognizable flare and a funnel-shaped mouthpiece. The player supports the instrument by placing a hand in the bell. There is also a popular larger version—a double instrument—which is coiled twice, four feet longer, and has an added fourth valve. The tube circles around the player, and the bell sits between the right shoulder and hip.

Like the oboe, the French horn is not a piece of cake to play. It can be temperamental, particularly in heat and humidity (but then, so are a lot of us). When played by an expert musician and not acting up, the instrument has a full, rich, mellow character that blends well with the other orchestral instruments. Horns are a staple of baroque music (lots of fanfares) and were favored by Schumann and Mahler.

Sliding Home

The word trombone comes from the Italian word for "big trumpet." Before it gained its Italian name, it was called the sackbut, from French words meaning "push-pull." The instrument sans slide dates back as early as the third century; the distinctive slide mechanism emerged during the Renaissance. Originally there were alto, tenor, and bass trombones, but the greater range of the modern instrument enables it to combine alto and tenor in one. The bass trombone still stands as a separate instrument (see below). The tenor trombone consists of nine feet of brass molded into three separate sections. The most identifiable feature is the U-shaped slide. The slide serves the same purpose as the valves or keys on the other brass instruments: Shifting the slide into one of seven basic positions changes the tones. Musicians also modulate tones by movement of the breath and lips. Like the harp, the trombone is capable of producing glissando, although of a totally different color and style. This comes from the musician blowing into the instrument and moving the slide simultaneously.

Monteverdi employed five trombones in his opera "L'Orfeo." Shortly thereafter, trombones fell from favor, only to be revived in another "Orfeo," this one by Gluck. Since then, trombones have been regular members of the orchestra.

When composers want to have the timbre of a particular instrument but at a lower pitch than it can encompass, they turn to larger and deeper-sounding members of the same family. We've already mentioned the alto flute, bass clarinet, and contrabassoon. For trombone, the designated low-hitter is the bass trombone, able to go several notes beyond the bottom range of the regular, so-called "tenor" trombone.

Tubby Tubas

The tuba is the youngest and biggest member of the brass family. It was invented during the 1820s, but was initially regarded as a bit rambunctious for genteel concert audiences. It took a decade or so for the massive brasswork to gain acceptance. The tuba is the lowest-pitched of the brasses, but like other instruments, it comes in several varieties. Listeners may be surprised to find out that there are soprano, alto, tenor, baritone, bass, and contrabass tubas—and that's just for starters. A featured tuba player may have 13 tubas and upwards of 40 mouthpieces. The mouthpieces are often changed to suit the tone color of a particular orchestral work. Like other brasses, the sound comes from the vibration of the musician's lips on the mouthpiece.

The primary orchestral tuba is tuned to B-flat, and covers a range of about two octaves (always below middle C). The bass tuba, originally called the bombardon) has a range of two-and-one-half octaves corresponding to the lowest notes on a piano. There's also a tenor tuba, with a sound quality similar to the tenor trombone. It's more commonly known as the euphonium. The baritone tuba also goes by the name baritone horn. Another variant is the sousaphone, named for John Philip Sousa, who cleverly realized that a removable bell would make the instrument more convenient for marching band members; like the hunting horn, it's constructed to fit comfortably over a shoulder.

Tuba players are unique: There is only one of them in each orchestra. Often, they play in conjunction with the bass trombone. The tuba was a favorite of Wagner and is featured in the powerful "Die Meistersinger" overture. The Wagner tuba is a synthesis of the tuba and French horn.

Drumbeats

The bass drum is always impressive to look at. It's the biggest member of the drum family. It migrated to the orchestra from military marching bands. A single-headed model (or gong drum) is popular in England, although the doubled-headed bass drum is the one generally found in American orchestras.

Strike Up the Band

The snare drum is the one we associate with soldiers in the American Revolution. It was about that time that the snare drum came to the orchestra from the military. In such marching bands, the small drum is slung at the drummer's side; in the orchestra, it rests on a stand. The snare drum has two heads; across the lower one are stretched long, slender metal strings (snares). The drummer strikes the top head; air hits the lower head, which in turn hits the snares. The result is a distinctive, reverberating sound. In its civilian form, the snare drum is a soloist in Rossini's overture to "The Thieving Magpie," and is featured in Ravel's "Bolero" and Berlioz's "Symphonie Fantastique."

T-Kettles

Timpani are more commonly known as kettledrums. They look like they'd be great fun to play—and probably are; but as the most important of the percussion group, it takes more than wild enthusiasm to play them well. Any mistake reverberates throughout the symphony hall. The kettledrum consists of a large copper or fiberglass bowl with skin stretched across one end; frets to be tightened for fine-tuning and a foot pedal for changing pitch complete the picture. The drumsticks are 14 inches long and come with both hard and soft heads. The original timpani were flatter, designed to be slung over a horse. They sounded throughout the Crusades—on the side of the Turks. In the orchestra, timpani come in five sizes and rest on wooden or metal frames.

Haydn composed one of the first timpani solos in his next to last symphony, No. 103, known as the "Drum Roll" Symphony. Beethoven and Mahler were big fans, and several composers have gone so far as to write concertos for timpani and orchestra.

Quadraladeral Triangles

The triangle is the instrument author George Plimpton played in his short sojourn as an orchestral musician. Aside from this radical departure from convention, orchestras do not commonly employ a musician to play triangle alone. A seven-inch equilateral triangle constructed by bending a metal rod, the triangle is struck with a thin steel rod. It can be held by the percussionist or as part of a large untuned percussion group suspended from a stand. Haydn, Mozart, and Beethoven all used the triangle in their symphonic scores, Liszt gave it a solo role in his First Piano Concerto (which is sometimes called the "Triangle Concerto" for that reason), and Wagner used it distinctively in "Die Meistersinger."

Bang a Gong, Get On

The gong or tam-tam does not only appear in *The King and I*. A gong sonata might be difficult for audiences to take (even John Cage never attempted it), but the gong fills out the untuned percussion section as well as filling the hall with vibrations. Ravel uses the gong for effect in "Daphnis and Chloe."

Xylophone Call

The xylophone is an example of tuned percussion. Each one of its progression of hard wood strips is tuned to a specific note. The instrument somewhat resembles a keyboard with spaces between the keys. The player strikes the keys with xylophone tappers made of wood or rubber. Probably the most well-known xylophone piece is the "skeleton" section of Saint-Saens' "Danse Macabre."

Carmean Marimba

The marimba is a Latin cousin of the xylophone. It produces deeper tones than the xylophone and is very popular in Mexico and Central America, where you can hear orchestras consisting of marimbas and nothing else.

Bells are Ringing

Chimes are a set of tuned, stationary bells suspended from a frame, including clock chimes and the orchestral tubular bells.

Clashing Cymbals

What would orchestral music be without the sound of cymbals crashing? Cymbals are two brass plates that can be loudly clashed or gently brushed, depending upon the composer's intent. A single cymbal can be held in the musician's hand and struck with a stick or mounted on a stand to be hit with two sticks. Stravinsky even used a cymbal struck by a triangle.

Who's with the Big Stick?

Comedian Victor Borge says that the conductor is a curious person. "He turns his back on his friends in the audience, shakes a stick at the players in his orchestra, and then wonders why nobody loves him. He makes the most noise at rehearsals, but there's not a peep out of him during the concerts, and he only shakes hands with the musicians when everybody's ready to go home."

Beating time to keep the rhythm is as old as classical music itself. In ancient Greece, somebody was assigned to stomp on a stool with a special kind of boot. In the 13th century, one of the singers in a choir would try to keep everybody together by rapping his hand on a book, and in the 16th, the director would bang on the floor with a large stick. In the 18th century, most performances were directed by the harpsichord player or the first violinist.

Among the more famous 19th century conductors were Mendelssohn, who kept time with a favorite white stick; Berlioz, who modestly declared that nobody could ever conduct his music better than he himself and liked to use a heavy oak staff; Schumann, who preferred a smaller baton, but kept dropping it until he devised a way of attaching it to his wrist with a string; and Wagner, who wrote a whole treatise on the art of keeping orchestral musicians in line.

Bet You Didn't Know

The premiere of the Berlioz Requiem in 1837 was almost turned into a shambles when the conductor, Francois-Antoine Habaneck, serenely laid down his baton and took a pinch of snuff at the very moment he was supposed to cue the brasses to come in with a tremendous fanfare. Berlioz, who habitually mistrusted all conductors—and therefore was hiding on stage, just in case—sprang in front of the astonished Habaneck and gave the proper signal. "Everything went off in order," the composer wrote in his memoirs, "and I conducted the piece to the end."

Bet You Didn't Know

Forget those exercise videos. Conducting might just be the secret to keeping fit: Bruno Walter was active until his death at age 85; Pierre Monteux becam   e music director of the London Symphony at the age of 86; Arturo Toscanini reluctantly slid into retirement at 87; and Leopold Stokowski made recordings into his 95th year. Stoki's philosophy was simple: "I would like to go on living for ever and ever," he said, "making music all the time."

Podium history in the first half of the 20th century is a legacy of such legendary artists as Toscanini, Furtwangler, Klemperer, Beecham, and Stokowski, to name only a handful. Within the recent memory of most of us were musical giants like Leonard Bernstein and Herbert von Karajan. Today, our cultural lives are enormously enriched by the work of such outstanding international personalities as Kurt Masur, Claudio Abbado, Zubin Mehta, Simon Rattle, Gutvao Dudamel and, not to overlook our superlative native American talents, Leonard Slatkin, Michael Tilson Thomas, David Zinman, Andrew Litton, Alan Gilbert, and so many others.

Part of the conductor's job is to select appropriate tempos, to control the dynamics and phrasing within a piece, to bring out and balance the many colors of the orchestral palette, and certainly not least, to persuade the players (through a combination of technique, psychology, and personal charisma) to follow his lead and thereby reveal the full artistic and expressive potential of the work at hand.

Some composers are also conductors (at least of their own works), and many conductors also compose, but few indeed are the artists (such as Leonard Bernstein) who are equally successful as creators and interpreters. Aaron Copland freely admitted that others could produce better performances of his compositions than he, but that didn't stop him from taking on many a guest-conducting assignment. "Conducting is a late passion of mine," he said. "If you've spent years, as I have, listening to others conduct your music, you gradually get the feeling that, oh gee, just once I'd like to get up there and do it the way I dreamt it…"

All conductors are working from the same scores, the same black notes on a white page, as Stokowski used to say, but those notes are filtered through each maestro's musical sensibilities and personal style. You'll find different recordings of the same piece that vary in time by five minutes or more, and have other major contrasts of color, phrasing or dynamics. It is this interpretive leeway that keeps classical music performances fresh, distinctive, and exhilarating.

One Conductor, Two Conductors

In days gone by, conductors were absolute dictators. They could hire and fire players at will, swear or throw things at their musicians, and in consequence, the players often responded as much out of fear as cooperative spirit. On the other hand, inspiration was very much part of the conducting package. Stokowski would say, "Play better!" to his orchestral musicians and without exactly knowing why or how, they did.

Bet You Didn't Know

The Polish conductor Artur Rodzinski, who was at various times music director of the Los Angeles Philharmonic, Cleveland Orchestra, and Chicago Symphony, began his tenure at the New York Philharmonic by dismissing more than forty players. He was forever embroiled in arguments with musicians and management, and he often conducted concerts with a revolver in his pocket. The pianist Oscar Levant once said it was "just Rodzinski's way of avoiding backtalk from the orchestra."

Nowadays, conductors can't get away with that stuff. Credit it to more savvy musicians, stronger unions, or just changing times, but most maestros are on much friendlier terms with their players and never indulge in personal attacks. (As Gilbert and Sullivan put it, "What, never? Well, hardly ever.")

The conductor also shares some of his duties with designated members of the orchestra. In England, the first violinist is called the leader; here we use the word concertmaster, which can refer to either a man or woman. (The politically correct sometimes substitute concertmistress in the latter situation.) In addition to taking any featured violin solos that the composer may have put into the music, the concertmaster serves as a sort of liaison between conductor and orchestra, putting the desired bowings or fingerings in all the violin parts, and generally supervising the other fiddlers in his domain. The first chair musician in each instrumental section functions in a similar manner, following through on the conductor's wishes regarding phrasing, the assignment of solos, etc. To signify his importance, the concertmaster usually walks on stage after the rest of the orchestra has taken its place on stage, and signals the oboe to sound the all-important A to which all the instruments then tune up.

Bet You Didn't Know

Richard Strauss was conducting a rehearsal of his Alpine Symphony and had just reached the exciting passage imitating a rainstorm when the concertmaster, in his excitement, let his bow slip from his hand. Strauss stopped the orchestra immediately, saying, "Just a moment, gentlemen, our leader has lost his umbrella!"

Big Sounds, Little Sounds

The overall sound of an orchestra is a combination of many factors: the strengths and weaknesses of the individual players; the acoustics of the hall; and the kind of tone and resonance demanded by the conductor. They say that Stokowski could stand before an ensemble of teenagers, and within a few minutes this non-professional orchestra would have the "Stokowski sound"—rich, flowing, and resonant. Some orchestras are especially noted for the lush quality of their strings, in others the winds are unusually precise, or the brasses give the performances an exciting thrust. There's nothing right or wrong about these different sonic weightings, which is why each conductor has his ardent devotees and equally strident critics. It's also why you should allow your own ears to be the judge. Forget about whether critic X loves conductor Y and hates orchestra Z—what do *you* like? What makes you sit up and take notice? What gives you the greatest listening satisfaction?

Buy two different recordings of the same piece, and compare their merits. Maybe listen to a third version on the radio. Soon enough you'll recognize nuances that passed right by you before, and you'll better appreciate the extraordinary diversity—not to mention the great commonality of enjoyment—that is the special province of classical music.

CHAPTER 9

How Does the Instrumental Garden Grow?

In This Chapter

➤ When two play together
➤ Trios
➤ String quartets and others
➤ And more

Corn is tasty and lima beans are lovely, but mix them together and you have succotash, a whole new vegetable with its own distinctive flavor. It's exactly the same way with musical instruments, so composers have long explored ways to create fascinating novel sounds, textures, and structural possibilities through the imaginative blending of the distinctive timbres of two or more instruments.

Double Header

The animals came into the Ark two by two, and some of the most thrilling music in the world arrives via the four hands of two players. Sometimes, the twosome plays the same instrument. Bartók, for instance, wrote 44 duos for two violinists, while Mozart and Schubert contributed sonatas, marches, and all sorts of other pieces for two pianists, sometimes at a single keyboard. You'll also come upon paired soloists in orchestral concerts: Bach wrote a Concerto for Two Harpsichords, Vivaldi has one for Two Trumpets, and Cimarosa came through with the Concerto for Two Flutes.

Put together two different instruments, of course, and the sonic possibilities expand greatly. Even when the match seems doomed from the start, a clever composer can preside over such unlikely musical marriages as cello and bassoon (Mozart), violin and guitar (Paganini), viola and clarinet (Rebecca Clarke), or guitar and organ (Chris DeBlasio). Even Beethoven wrote duos for clarinet and bassoon, viola and cello, and sundry other combinations.

Bet You Didn't Know

"I am not handsome," Paganini admitted, "but when women hear me play, they come crawling to my feet." Not that he minded. His "Duetto Amoroso" is in nine movements, with subtitles like "Entreaties", "Consent," and "Satisfaction," and he also wrote a "Scena Amorosa" as a conversation between lovers, the man speaking on the G string, the woman answering on the E.

Bet You Didn't Know

The German violinist Ludwig Spohr wrote dozens of pieces for his own use, but when he married another violinist, he made her switch to the harp because he didn't think it was dignified for a lady to hold anything under her chin in public. Spohr then proceeded to write a whole bunch of pieces for flute and harp, but since he also didn't think it was dignified for a lady to tune an instrument on stage, he used to do it for her—with everybody looking.

The most common partner for any string, woodwind, or brass instrument is the piano, which is logical enough, given its huge range of the keyboard and its ability to produce chords as well as melodic materials. In the baroque and early classical eras, the piano (or harpsichord) was often cast in the role of accompanist to the featured instrument. Mozart then turned the tables, using the fiddle as mere accompaniment in many of his early Violin and Piano Sonatas (some of which he had earlier published as solo keyboard works). In his later works for the two instruments (Mozart wound up writing more than three dozen of them), he brought violin and piano into more even balance. It took Beethoven to level out the playing field completely, and thereafter, most composers were content to create their music duos for equal partners.

Every period of music has its wealth of works that fuse contrasting tones and timbres, so pick your favorite composer, and chances are you'll find enough duets to fill a year of listening Sundays. Beethoven? There are ten violin sonatas, another five for cello and piano, and one for horn. Schubert? He wrote duets with flute, violin, and even a long-obsolete instrument called the arpeggione, for which the modern cello is the usual substitute. Hindemith wrote sonatas for violin, viola, and cello, but he also combined the piano with almost every wind and brass instrument in the book: flute, oboe, bassoon, clarinet, horn, English horn, trumpet, and trombone.

Three's a Happy Crowd

Trios, as you undoubtedly figured out long before this, involve three musical partners. Just to be difficult, though, the baroque trio sonatas sometimes required four players, the accompaniment split between a low instrument like the cello or bassoon, which would line out the bass notes, while the harmonies were filled in by a harpsichord or other keyboard instrument. Again, the combinations are almost endless. There are string trios (sometimes for two violins and viola, more often for violin, viola, and cello); wind or brass instrument threesomes; and pieces that combine members of two or even three musical families, such as Martinu's "Promenades" for flute, violin, and harpsichord.

Piano Plus

As in duos, the piano is the most often called-upon trio partner. In fact, the phrase "Piano Trio" almost always refers not to three Steinways jostling each other on stage, but to the most frequently encountered instrumental threesome of violin, cello, and piano. Once more, you'll find sterling examples of the form in the output of most major composers, from Mozart and Beethoven on through the romantic masterworks of Schubert, Brahms, Mendelssohn, and Tchaikovsky, and then forward into the 20th century with Copland, Shostakovich, and a host of younger generation composers.

Bet You Didn't Know

Little of Schubert's music was published during his lifetime (1797-1828), and there were few public concerts of his works. It remained for later generations to discover his genius, and significantly, several of his composing colleagues led the way: Schumann, who wrote eloquently about Schubert's Ninth Symphony; Mendelssohn who conducted its premiere; Arthur Sullivan, who found the lost score to "Rosamunde"; and Liszt, who prepared an edition of Schubert's piano music. "Like a bird in the air," wrote Liszt to the publisher, "he lived in music and sang in angelic fashion." And Schumann, after hearing Schubert's B-flat Piano Trio, said that "the troubles of our human existence disappear and all the world is fresh and bright again."

Two and Two Make ...

We don't have to say that a quartet is a piece for four players, do we? Didn't think so. Again in this category, the ensemble can be a mixed instrumental bag (Villa Lobos has one for flute, celesta, harp, and saxophone), but more often than not, the foursome involves instruments of the same family. Prokofiev wrote a "Humorous Scherzo" for four bassoons, and if you look hard enough, you'll find saxophone quartets, flute quartets, horn quartets, and even tuba quartets. Piano quartets, on the other hand, almost always refer to one keyboard and three of something else.

Perhaps the most familiar foursome, and certainly the one with the richest repertoire, is the string quartet. The family resemblance of the two violins, viola, and cello give the form a unity of sound and expression, yet each instrument retains its own dynamic personality and the ensemble overall has an astonishingly wide gamut of dramatic expression.

Although earlier examples exist of works that happen to be scored for four strings, the string quartet really came into general use around the middle of the 18th century. Haydn is often called the "father of the string quartet," but a Viennese composer of an earlier generation, one Georg Mathias Monn, published six string quartets. Haydn, in other words, didn't actually make the mold. He just filled it in with far higher inspiration than any of his predecessors—and in far greater numbers: his quartet output totals a bewildering 83.

Bet You Didn't Know

Monn is almost totally forgotten today, but he found a 20th century champion in Arnold Schoenberg, of all people. This master of atonality, many of whose works still scare away many listeners because of their austerity and dissonance, (see Chapter 17), not only edited one of Monn's symphonies and two of his harpsichord concertos, but converted another Monn harpsichord piece into a mild-mannered cello concerto.

Mozart wrote about 30 string quartets (six of them dedicated to Haydn, who responded with his famous remark to Mozart's father about Wolfgang being the greatest composer of whom he had any knowledge), and Beethoven followed with the 16 masterpieces that remain to this day the milestone works in the form.

The numbers dwindle somewhat as we move deeper into the 19th century—perhaps composers then were too busy pushing the boundaries of orchestral and keyboard music to spend much time on quartets—but what they may have lacked in quantity, they more than made up for in quality. Brahms, Schumann, and Tchaikovsky each wrote three magnificent string quartets. Mendelssohn completed half a dozen, and Dvořák actually equaled Beethoven's output at 16.

Quintuplets

All together now, class: a quintet is a piece for five players. You'll find some for strings only, usually with a second viola or cello added to the usual foursome. Beethoven and Mozart scored quintets for piano and four winds, while Schumann, Brahms, Franck, and Dvořák preferred to pit the keyboard against a string quartet. Interestingly, it was Schubert, aged 22, who first substituted a double bass for the second violin and produced what is arguably the most popular of all piano quintets, "The Trout."

Bet You Didn't Know

"The Trout" ("Die Forelle," in German) actually began as a song, although Schubert almost tore up the manuscript when a friend pointed out that the leaping figurations in the piano accompaniment (representing the water in which the fish is swimming), resembled a passage in Beethoven's Coriolan Overture. Fortunately, Schubert left the song intact, and when another friend urged him to convert it into a chamber piece, he used the tune, complete with that glistening accompaniment, as the "Theme and Variations" movement in his A Major Quintet.

Blowing in the Wind Quintet

There are many works where a single wind or brass instrument is juxtaposed with four strings—the gorgeous clarinet quintets of Mozart, Weber, and Brahms spring most readily to mind—but just as the string quartet ranked high in most composers' favor, a huge repertoire of works has arisen for five wind instruments. The usual complement of such wind quintets is flute, oboe, clarinet, horn, and bassoon, although other variations are occasionally encountered.

You Bet Your Brass

The blare of brasses is very different from the more sonorous strings or the leaner sounds of the winds, so the brass quintet (normally two trumpets, horn, trombone, and bass trombone or tuba) strides out with forceful power. Works for five brasses are in considerably shorter supply than those for winds or strings, so brass groups frequently use transcriptions of works for other instruments. On the other hand, virtuosity on brass instruments can be especially thrilling, which explains the worldwide popularity of ensembles like Canadian Brass, whose players, to quote the *Washington Post*, "have an agility that comes close to the phenomenal, achieving a wide dynamic range that fills their music with lights and shadows." The ensemble's incredible performing precision and delectable on-stage humor doesn't hurt either.

Bet You Didn't Know

When the Canadian Brass toured China in 1977, their hosts tried to be as helpful and accommodating as possible. Whenever the players would leave discarded trash in a hotel room, it was dutifully collected, packed up, and forwarded to them at the next touring stop.

Etcetera, Etcetera, Etcetera

You can continue on up the numerical ladder and enjoy sextets (Brahms has two great ones for two each of violins, violas, and cellos, while Poulenc has a sparkler for piano and winds), septets (Beethoven combined winds and strings in his and the Saint-Saens Septet adds a trumpet to the ensemble); and octets (the two most famous are by Schubert and Mendelssohn). Nonets pop up very occasionally, and Enesco actually wrote a piece for ten wind instruments that he called "Dixtuor."

Beyond that, of course, you're in the realm of the previously discussed chamber orchestra and the full-size symphony. The smaller combinations, by the way, can also be called into play as soloists with the orchestra. Poulenc, Mendelssohn, and Vaughan Williams are among the many composers who have written two-piano concertos; Vivaldi has one for two mandolins; Bach and Mozart each triple keyboard concertos; and there's a wonderful Schumann concert piece for four horns and orchestra.

Bet You Didn't Know

Some composers get all wrapped up in a particular instrument, particularly if they played it themselves. Vivaldi wrote violin concertos by the dozen, for instance, and the Brazilian master Heitor Villa-Lobos, who earned his living as a young man by playing the cello in cafés and restaurants, thereafter not only wrote cello sonatas and cello concertos, but scored his Bachianas Brasileiras #1 for an ensemble of eight cellos, and the even more famous Bachianas Brasileiras #5 for eight cellos plus solo singer.

Pieces for contrasting instruments with orchestra are also high on the masterworks list: Think of Mozart's Sinfonie Concertante for Violin and Viola or Haydn's for oboe, bassoon, violin, and cello. The Double Concerto (for violin and cello) is among Brahms' most popular works, and the Beethoven Triple Concerto (for violin, cello, and piano) is another frequent concert hall visitor. We even find pieces like Bartók's Concerto for Orchestra, where all sorts of instruments within the ensemble take turns stepping out into the solo spotlight.

The instrumental garden, in short, continues to grow and flourish as the composers of each new generation plant tonal seeds unimagined by their predecessors. It's yet another example of the vitality, energy, and endless fascination of classical music.

CHAPTER 10

What About All the Other Instruments?

In This Chapter

➤ The development of the piano

➤ Folk instruments

➤ The role of electronics in classical music

Before we get to some of the fascinating other instruments, let's return to the piano, since a) it's probably the most immediately recognizable instrument, b) a lot of us have played it, if only to bang out "Chopsticks," and c) with its seven-plus octave range and enormous sonic potential, it's practically an orchestra in itself.

Keyboards: In the Beginning

When li'l David played on his harp (in his pre Goliath-slaying days) and the Biblical psalmists sang praises unto God with psaltery of 10 strings, they were just pianists a few millennia ahead of themselves. They were making music by setting strings to vibrating, and it was just a matter of time (i.e., centuries) before somebody figured out a way to have a machine pluck the strings for them.

Actually, there is record of a 3rd century BC Greek water organ that used crude levers, but the keyboard didn't come into any real significance until the Middle Ages. Not that you'd recognize one if you saw it: The early keys were heavy levers, the player having to strike them with a clenched fist, usually protected by a leather glove. The idea of the keyboard was to have a continuous arrangement of available notes, making possible more rapid traversals of the scale and a better ability to play chords. Its earliest usage, though, wasn't to vibrate strings, but to vibrate the air flowing through organ pipes.

Bet You Didn't Know

"Chopsticks" was first published in England as "The Celebrated Chop Waltz," and all sorts of great composers—including Liszt, Borodin, and Rimsky-Korsakov— wrote variations on it. The European version of the tune is a little different from ours, but we won't tell if you don't.

Gradually, the keys became easier to press, more user friendly, and could be adapted to small instruments like the portative (translation: portable) organ. Those early medieval keyboards had only "natural" keys—the white ones on our modern piano—but gradually the five black notes were added and the chromatic scale of 12 notes to the octave was finally at hand.

The actual ancestors of the piano can be pinpointed as soft-toned keyboard instruments such as the clavichord, spinet, and virginals. Romantics like to think that the virginals were so named because they were considered most suitable for young maidens, but more likely the derivation is the Latin word "virga," meaning rod or jack and referring to the mechanism that connects the key to the quill plucking the strings. Reality is sometimes disappointing, but what can you do? Other early musicologists claimed that the virginals were named for Queen Elizabeth ("the Virgin Queen") since she liked to play them, but since the instrument was in use before she was born, that theory seems slightly flawed.

The most advanced, and best known, pre-piano instrument of this sort was the harpsichord, which evolved from the virginals and ruled the keyboard roost from about 1500 until nearly the end of 18th century. Bach conceived many of his keyboard pieces for the harpsichord, and while the instrument went into severe eclipse once the piano pushed it out of favor, the harpsichord story has a happy ending: The instrument has had a nifty 20th century revival thanks to such dynamic performing personalities as the Polish virtuoso Wanda Landowska. More and more 20th century composers, among them Francis Poulenc in France, Manuel de Falla in Spain, and America's own Elliott Carter, also discovered that the harpsichord's spiky tones could add a fascinating dash of antique color to their modern scores.

The main problem with the harpsichord is that no matter whether you put your finger gently on a key or bang it with all your might, the strings are plucked with exactly the same force.

Bet You Didn't Know

Even though the harpsichord was clearly the king of keyboard instruments in the 17th and 18th centuries (at the time of the French Revolution, the King's Library at Versailles included no less than 23 of them), all sorts of improvements were attempted. The clavicytherium tried to save space by standing a harpsichord on its end, and the Cembalo Angelico (Italian for angelic harpsichord) attempted to create a more mellow sound by replacing the standard quill plectra with velvet-covered leather ones. Other harpsichords were built with knee levers to change the tone quality, and a Polish instrument maker seems to have been the first to fit out his harpsichords with foot pedals to accomplish the same thing.

That fatal flaw led to the invention of the instrument that would sweep the harpsichord from its throne forever.

Pianistics

Although an Italian instrument-maker named Paliarino tinkered with a contraption he called the "Piano e Forte" (i.e., soft and loud) before 1600, the invention of the piano had to wait another century, with credit going to another Italian, Bartolommeo Cristofori. (Note that his name is not likely to come up in conversation, but for the record, it's pronounced Cris-TO-fori). He was a harpsichord maker, responsible for the care and feeding of the 40 or so instruments belonging to Prince Ferdinand de Medici, but in his spare time he too was fooling about with a way to make a keyboard instrument that could produce gradations of sound. The one he produced in 1709 was dubbed the "gravicembalo col piano e forte," which is a kind of Florentine dialect for "harpsichord with soft and loud." He achieved the desired result by changing the mechanism so that leather hammers struck the strings instead of plucking them, and two or three strings reproduced each note instead of just one.

By 1726, Cristofori had built about 20 of the new instruments, incorporating sundry other improvements, including a "soft" pedal that moved the whole keyboard sideways so that the hammers struck one string fewer than usual. There were still many technical problems left to solve—piano makers would struggle with them for the next 200 years—but such technical details need not detain us here. Suffice it to say that the pianos Bach heard and Mozart wrote for were altogether different in sound and appearance from our modern grands. If you're really burning with curiosity about the specifics of piano construction over the last two hundred years, head for the library and pull out any one of a number of illustrated books on the subject (two good volumes to start with are David S. Grover's "The Piano," for a complete chronology of the development of keyboard instruments, and Ronald Ratcliffe's "Steinway," a colorfully anecdotal history of the most famous piano—and piano family—in the world). Two recent, and fascinating volumes are James Barron's "Piano," which details the making of a Steinway concert grand, and Stuart Isacoff's "A Natural History of the World's Most Celebrated Instrument."

In 1732, the first music for piano was published in Florence—a set of 12 sonatas for "soft and loud harpsichord" by Ludovico Giustini—and in 1768, a chip off the old Bach, Johann

Bet You Didn't Know

Among the attempted innovations that didn't work was a contraption that its French maker called a "fortepiano a cordes de verre," since it had glass strings, and a "fortepiano clavier" that attempted to combine features of the piano and harpsichord. Later on, two Viennese instrument makers almost came to blows over which of them could claim the honor of having invented a weird sort of upright that, because of its odd shape, was called a Giraffe Piano. If you think that's funny, wait till you hear the German name for it: "Giraffenflugel."

Bet You Didn't Know

Haydn and Mozart were the first composers to put the newfangled piano to extensive use, although even they found it hard to keep up with the ongoing improvements to the instrument's range, power, and dexterity. In 1777, Mozart gave a ringing endorsement to the fortepianos built by Johann Andreas Stein, writing to his father that same year in delight that "whatever way I touch the keys, the tone is always even. It never jars, it is never strong or weaker or entirely absent." Needless to say, from that point on, all of Mozart's keyboard works were intended for the fortepiano.

Sebastian's son Johann Christian, sounded the early death knell for the harpsichord when he gave what seems to be the first-ever piano recital in London.

Not that the harpsichord gave up the ghost without a struggle. Twenty years later, there were still 19 harpsichord makers working in Paris alone, and it was not before the turn of the 19th century that the piano would displace the harpsichord once and for all as the keyboard instrument of choice. Meanwhile, Cristofori's piano-forte designation got switched around to fortepiano in common usage, so it was the fortepiano for which Haydn and Mozart wrote many of their keyboard sonatas.

The pianos of this period usually contained only five octaves, and Beethoven had to settle for that somewhat limited compass in the first 20 of his 32 sonatas and the first two of his five concertos. No doubt he did not accept those restrictions with good grace, and when various Viennese manufacturers added more notes to the keyboard and made other improvements that allowed a greater range of dynamics, Beethoven plunged in quickly to take advantage of them. The sonatas from the Waldstein onwards require a range of at least six octaves, and when he got to the great Hammerklavier Sonata (don't get nervous: old Ludwig didn't bang anything—he just used the German word for fortepiano), it demanded an even newer instrument that had six-and-a-half octaves.

Additional improvements, further extending the range and enlarging the sound were made

Bet You Didn't Know

Many of the early pianos had a square shape rather than the elongated, curved model we see today. In fact, the word "grand" came into being to distinguish the larger models from the square pianos that had a lighter touch and could more easily fit into people's homes. They also became popular in Oriental and Middle Eastern harems, usually with the legs cut down so that the player could sit on cushions placed on the floor. The pianist Leopold de Meyer was once invited to a palace in Turkey, and when he refused to sit on the floor, cushion or no cushion, the Sultan made three slaves come in and hold the piano on their backs while de Meyer played the whole concert seated on a regular chair.

in the 19th century, bringing with them a veritable parade of piano virtuosos. There was Jan Ladislav Dussek, who was the first person to place the piano sideways on stage so the ladies could swoon over his beautiful profile. There was Chopin, who explored all sorts of keyboard sonorities and shadings that no one before (or since) could achieve; and Liszt, whose keyboard prowess caused women to faint and moved strong men to tears. Russia gave the world Anton Rubinstein, who was dubbed "Ruby" when he came to America for a tour in 1872, his contract specifying that "he would not be obliged to play in beer gardens or tobacco establishments." And we had our very own Louis Moreau Gottschalk, who converted the cakewalk and other folk rhythms into some of the first truly American piano music.

Important Things to Know

What makes one pianist's style better or different from another? Assuming the notes are played with reasonable accuracy, there is no right or wrong to these infinite stylistic and sonic fluctuations; each artist projects the music in a manner that is his or hers alone. You should listen to as many of these musicians as possible and come to our own pianistic preferences. Radio and recordings can help here, especially since the unique conceptions of immortal pianists from the early part of the 20th century—Paderewski, Hofmann, de Pachmann, Godowsky, and dozens of others—have been reissued on CD.

Five-Finger Exercises

What makes one pianist different from another (note, we didn't say better) is the highly personal approach he or she takes both to the instrument itself and to the compositions at hand. Within the memory of many of us are incredible artists like Arthur Rubinstein, who aimed for a warm sound that would envelop an audience, and Vladimir Horowitz, who produced a glassier tone but whose finger dexterity allowed him to achieve virtuosic effects that seem beyond the reach of mere mortals. Each pianist projects different shadings of technical mastery, varying sensitivity to the dynamic and tempo markings in the score, and distinctive repertoire leanings.

Bet You Didn't Know

With greatness sometimes goes eccentricity. Vladimir de Pachmann milked cows because he said it kept his fingers well exercised; Paderewski insured his hands for $100,000, and in between tours served a term (in 1919) as Premier of Poland; and Glenn Gould (1932-1982) once made the studio technicians turn off the air conditioning at a recording session because he couldn't hear himself hum.

Steinway Spinoffs

The piano and the harpsichord (plus the organ, which we discussed back in Chapter 6) have pretty well cornered the market, but other keyboard instruments occasionally do pop up. There's the tinkly celesta, invented in 1866, which resembles a miniature piano with black and white keys causing tiny hammers to strike metal plates. Tchaikovsky was the first important composer to use a celesta: He heard it in Paris, and promptly had one shipped back to Russia in the greatest secrecy, lest Glazunov or Rimsky-Korsakov use it before he did. Tchaikovsky won the race, we're happy to say, and from that day to this, the sugarplum fairy dances with celestial sweetness in his Nutcracker ballet. In 1936, Bartók's Music for Strings, Percussion and Celesta gave the instrument one of its very rare chances to hold the spotlight through a whole piece.

Bet You Didn't Know

George Kleinsinger and Paul Tripp, who enchanted several generations of kids with the adventures of Tubby the Tuba, also tell "The Story of Celeste" in another delightful piece about an orphan instrument who finds her own place in the musical sun. You might, by the way, be able to find a wonderful old CD with "Tubby", "Celeste," and three other children's tales, narrated by Paul Tripp himself, on an Angel CD, #54330). Last time we checked, it was available through Amazon.com.

Dvořák scored several works for the harmonium, a small, organ-like instrument that was very popular in the 19th century; it had pedals generating an airstream that passed through a set of flexible metal strips. And keyboards entered the electronic age in the late 1920s, when Maurice Martenot developed what he first called "Ondes Musicales" (Musical Waves), but an instrument that later became known as the Ondes Martenot (Martenot's Waves). A number of important composers have written for the martenot, including Andre Jolivet, who made it the focus of a full-fledged Concerto in 1947.

Hands Off the Electronic Age

The first electronic instrument was the theremin, named for Leon Theremin, the Russian engineer who invented it around 1920. No less a Soviet luminary than Lenin himself tried it out (playing it very well, if he said so himself, as did everybody else who knew what was good for him). The instrument is unique in that the performer doesn't touch it except to turn the power on and off; it's constructed on the principal of the electric eye, the player's hands moving toward and away from two antennas (one controlling volume, the other pitch), each move breaking the magnetic field to create a haunting tone that can be mistaken for a cello or a wordless female song depending upon the range of pitches.

Bet You Didn't Know

Leon Theremin also invented a Dance Platform, where the player (Clara Rockmore at the first demonstration in Carnegie Hall) creates the music by movements of her entire body, and with the American composer Henry Cowell, developed a contraption called the Rhythmicon, which could create the most complicated rhythmic patterns, displaying them separately or simultaneously.

Hollywood composers used the theremin to create suspense in such classic films as "Spellbound" and "The Red House"; the Beach Boys added it to the musical mix in their big hit "Good Vibrations," and Clara Rockmore, whom Theremin himself dubbed "the greatest thereminist of them all," appeared in classical works with the Philadelphia Orchestra and other major symphonies, playing the theremin. The story of the inventor and the far-ranging effects of his musical creation were superbly retold in Steve M. Martin's prize-winning documentary film (which is now available as a video), "Theremin: An Electronic Odyssey." Clara Rockmore herself is represented in a wide range of solo and chamber performances in CDs issued by Delos, Bridge, and Romeo Records.

Bet You Didn't Know

New instruments are still being devised all the time. At a concert in January of 1997, Hal Rammel unveiled several of his latest inventions, including the snath and the triolin. He also played his "electro-acoustic sound palette" creating, in the composer's own words, "an assortment of staccato squeaks, gong-like tones, animalistic vocal gurgles, and deep bass groans."

The Techno-Musicians Take Over: Synthesizers

The synthesizer creates sounds according to precise instructions fed into it by the operator. By analyzing the distinctive sound pattern of any instrument, the machine can reproduce its tone quality more or less accurately, and through a range of octaves far beyond the capabilities of the instrument being copied. The race of technology has enormously expanded the capabilities of synthesizers and given rise to all sorts of specialized instruments that fuse electronic elements with more conventional performing methods. The future? It's anybody's guess, although ours is that nothing can ever replace the magic of music written and produced in its natural form, and heard live in its natural environment.

Before you decide to stay home with a good book, reflect on this comment on modern music by the composer Samuel Scheidt: "I am astonished at the foolish music written in these times. It is false and wrong, and no longer does anyone pay attention to what our beloved old masters wrote. I hope this worthless modern coinage will fall into disuse, and the new coins will be forged according the fine old stamp and standard." What makes this quote remarkable is its date: January 16, 1651.

Folk Instruments

Got a few weeks? Every country has literally dozens (if not hundreds) of instruments unique to its own culture, and there's no way we can even begin to cover them here. They range from A (a Korean percussion tube) to Zeze (an African drum). There's a bumbo and a bombo, a pang and a pong-pong, a going-going, and a gong. No kidding, you could look them up, only you don't have to because we already did.

Among the other world instruments you're more likely to encounter are the Japanese koto, with 13 silk strings; the Indian sitar, popularized by such classical virtuosos as Ravi Shankar, and appropriated for effective pop use by George Harrison of The Beatles in songs such as "Norwegian Wood (This Bird Has Flown)" and "Within You Without You"; the Chinese pipa (more properly spelled p'i p'a), a short-necked lute; and another lute-like instrument from the Middle East called the oud.

Here in the USA, of course, the banjo is a familiar staple, with strings running up a long neck from a kind of tambourine body. African in origin, the banjo (or "banjar," as Thomas Jefferson called it in his "Notes on Virginia"), soon became part and parcel of the American folk scene, both in its four-string version, beloved of minstrel show and vaudeville entertainers, and the five-string, preferred by Pete Seeger and most other urban folk song specialists.

The folk guitar (nowadays called acoustic to distinguished it from its electronic cousin) has six strings, although some performers prefer the richer, deeper sounds of the 12-string version. The ukulele (anybody remember Arthur Godfrey?) is a small guitar from Hawaii, and Latin American groups will often feature a large Spanish guitar called the guitarron.

Bet You Didn't Know

Leon Theremin also invented a Dance Platform, where the player (Clara Rockmore at the first demonstration in Carnegie Hall) creates the music by movements of her entire body, and with the American composer Henry Cowell, developed a contraption called the Rhythmicon, which could create the most complicated rhythmic patterns, displaying them separately or simultaneously.

Classical composers loved the guitar too, and wrote extensively for it. Boccherini combined the guitar with strings in a quintet, Schubert wrote a cantata for male voices and guitar (friends who visited him in the morning would often find him still in bed, "singing newly composed songs to his guitar"), and Weber put guitar accompaniments to thirty of his songs. "I love the guitar for its harmony," wrote the famous violinist-composer Niccolo Paganini. "It is my constant companion on all my travels."

In the 20th century, the much loved Spanish master Andres Segovia sparked a worldwide renaissance of interest in the guitar through his superb transcriptions, his own compelling performing personality, and by inspiring literally dozens of composers to write new solo pieces, chamber works, and concertos for his instrument. With the amazing flamenco players of Madrid, the country-pickers of Nashville, and the superb classical performers whose tastes and techniques have circled the globe, the guitar has indeed reclaimed its place of high honor in the instrumental scheme of things.

CHAPTER 11

 # Musicians are People Too: The Makers of Music

In This Chapter

➤ Music before the piano

➤ Pianist/composers

➤ Virtuosos on the rise

➤ 20th century legends

Those of us who grew up on "Fantasia" or those wonderful old Warner Brothers cartoons where Bugs Bunny wreaked his havoc in step to Liszt's "Hungarian Rhapsody No. 2" and other classical favorites may sometimes think that musicians' formal "tails" are the kind that come with four legs, floppy ears, and sundry other accessories of the animal kingdom.

Not too surprisingly, though, someone in human form has been putting those sound waves forward—writing the music, playing it, and enshrining it on the CDs we pop into our players without a second thought of the sweat and strain that went into their creation. Before the invention of the gramophone, of course, the only way to encounter music was to hear it live. Or better still, make it yourself, playing the flute, fiddle, or the keyboard that was a staple of so many pre-20th century households.

In any case, despite the halos that have been posthumously awarded to composers, singers, and players of earlier times, these artists were regular people as well as musical masters, beset by the same foibles and fantasies, problems and predicaments, laments and love stories that afflict the rest of us lowly non-genius types. In this chapter and the next, we'll look beyond the biographical facts and figures to consider the humanity of some of the composers whose music we love, and some of the artists whose performances gave them life.

Keys to the Keyboard Before Piano, There Was...

Although the young Mozart spent many childhood years going around to the courts of Europe, astonishing all and sundry with his prodigious skills, and Beethoven's dramatic temperament first surfaced at his keyboard concerts, the phenomenon of the touring piano virtuoso was largely an invention of the 19th century. There were fabulous keyboard masters before then, of course, but primarily the players were the composers, performing their own pieces since there was no use sitting around waiting for somebody else to do it. As noted in Chapter 11, the early players used clavichord, harpsichord, virginals, or other soft-toned keyboards whose sounds did not project far enough to permit performances in rooms even approaching modern concert hall size. No, these were instruments of palace or parlor, on which Bach could improvise complex works at the harpsichord, or the six-year-old Mozart could wow everybody with his prodigal feats at the fortepiano without feeling that they had to reach the back row of a 2,000-seat auditorium.

The clavichord was smaller and less expensive than its embellished peer, the harpsichord. It was (and still is, if you can find one) a rectangular box with a keyboard that works in a similar fashion to the piano: When you press the keys, a mechanism is activated that strikes the strings with a small blade called a tangent. There are no pedals, but the skilled player could achieve gradations of sound and texture.

Music Word

Tangent. In musical (as opposed to mathematical) usage, a tangent is a small, flat-ended metal pin attached to the inner end of a key. When the outer end of the key is pressed, the tangent strikes the string, which produces the sound.

Clavichords were in widespread use by the early 16th century, so had some mechanical mastermind come along to convert the clavichord into the piano, we might have taken a 200-year short cut. As it was, the harpsichord—where the mechanism plucks the strings instead of striking them—was soon top dog in the keyboard department. Bach, superb clavichordist though he was, wrote many of his most famous keyboard works, including the Goldberg Variations, the French and English Suites, and probably the Well-Tempered Clavier for the harpsichord, while Domenico Scarlatti, who was born in Naples just seven months after Bach, wrote more than 550 harpsichord sonatas.

Bet You Didn't Know

They say that one of Scarlatti's students brought his dog to a lesson one day, whereupon the composer's kitten, unused to such alien intrusions, leaped onto the harpsichord as the nearest means of escape. As the kitten hopped around angrily on the keyboard, Scarlatti came rushing delightedly into the room, grabbed some music paper, and copied down the notes the frustrated feline had pushed down. The student had no lesson that day: Scarlatti had to develop the theme into what is now known as "The Cat's Fugue." Fact or myth? Who knows. The same story is told about Chopin's cat, who allegedly gave him an idea for his F Major Waltz, Opus 34 no. 3.

It's Not Over Till the Thin Lady Plays

It was an amazing woman who almost single-handedly bought the harpsichord back to 20th century life. Born in Poland in 1879, Wanda Landowska began her keyboard training, like everybody else, at the piano, studying first at the Warsaw Conservatory and later in Berlin. In Paris, though, she heard and fell in love with the harpsichord, developing a lifelong passion for the instrument that would change the face of music. Her first public harpsichord recital was in Paris in 1903, and for the next 55 years, her superb performances and evangelical fervor would revive public fascination with the harpsichord. In fact, her accomplishments generated renewed excitement about baroque and early classical music altogether.

Important Things to Know

Although the harpsichord was an important instrument, however, it gradually came into disfavor because of its inherent limitation. Its tones could not be sustained, as they could be with the clavichord or piano, nor could its volume be changed by the players' heavier or lighter pressing of the keys. The bright clarity of the harpsichord made it perfectly suited to baroque polyphony, but once high drama entered the classical picture ("Sturm und drong," meaning Storm and Stress, is what musicologists like to call this stylistic development) it virtually disappeared from the musical horizon. Beethoven could not create his thunder at the harpsichord nor could Berlioz put one next to his dozen kettledrums.reeze over during an outing. Metal skimmers significantly outperform plastic ones.

Music Word

A **Cadenza** is a solo vocal or instrumental section interpolated into a longer piece of music, usually to allow the soloist a display of virtuosity. Most concertos have a *cadenza* just before the end of the first movement, sometimes the second movement as well.

Bet You Didn't Know

Musicians are forever arguing over details of ornamentation or other stylistic performing practices. One day Wanda Landowska was having an increasingly heated discussion with another early music specialist. The conversation came to an end when Landowska calmly said "Very well, my dear. You continue to play Bach your way, and I'll continue to play him his way."

Double Duty – They Played Piano and Wrote Music Too

Many music lovers try, whenever possible, to hear a work interpreted by its creator. Even if other artists have better voices or greater powers at the keyboard, it's always fascinating to learn how the composer really wanted the piece to go. Thanks to early recordings, we can actually listen to Grieg playing one of his piano pieces, or Gershwin sauntering through the "Rhapsody in Blue." What wouldn't we give to hear Bach playing his Italian Concerto, or Liszt tossing off one of his Hungarian Rhapsodies. Ah, dream on…

Mozart: The Whiz Kid

There's a delightfully comic little piece called the "Toy Symphony," because it uses a cuckoo whistle, ratchets, and other toy instruments. There's also a whimsical portrait of a Musical Sleigh Ride, complete with jingling bells (in German it's called, you should pardon the expression, "Schlittenfahrt"). Both pieces were composed by Leopold Mozart, who obviously imparted his sense of musical humor to his son Wolfgang Amadeus, not to mention bringing him up with careful training and strict discipline.

Alternately domineering and nurturing, this 18th century stage father not only encouraged the musical talents of his amazingly gifted son, but schlepped the tiny Wolfgang all over Europe starting in 1762, when the six-year-old prodigy astonished the Elector in Munich and captivated the Empress Maria Theresa in Vienna. Later they continued on to equal acclaim at the courts of Paris, London, and Rome.

Bet You Didn't Know

In London, Johann Christian Bach (Johann Sebastian's son) said that Wolfgang's playing "surpasses all understanding and all imagination"; but the stuffy Royal Society didn't believe him and dispatched one of its members to determine the truth. He accordingly ordered Wolfgang to play and sing music he was given for the first time, to compose in various styles, and even to play with the piano keys covered. In due course, the Honorable Daines Barrington submitted a paper to the Society expressing his own astonishment at the eight-year-old Wolfgang's prodigious abilities. He also added a personal note: "Whilst he was playing to me, a favourite cat came in, upon which he immediately left his harpsichord, nor could we bring him back for a considerable time. He would also sometimes run about the room with a stick between his legs by way of a horse...."

At this point, Mozart could sight-read virtually anything that was put before him. He improvised brilliantly, turning opera tunes into piano "fantasies" (a practice Beethoven would emulate, and Liszt turned into a whole cottage industry). He wrote dozens of sonatas, variations, and fugues for piano (plus 17 organ sonatas), and 24 piano concertos, which he would frequently embellish upon for on the spot during performances.

Was Wolfgang really the churlish, giggling mischief-maker that we met on stage (1979) and screen (1984) in "Amadeus"? The music historians and mavens are still arguing about that one, but even the much-honored Antonio Salieri, Mozart's chief rival (and possibly worst enemy) at the Viennese court, had to admit to the court composer that Mozart was an unexcelled virtuoso, an improviser without peer, and a guy who wrote a lot of pretty good music into the bargain.

Beethoven: The Heaven-Stormer

A great old New Yorker cartoon showed Ludwig van Beethoven (1770-1827) scowling over the piano keys in an elegant drawing room, while one fashionably-dressed listener whispered to another, "His music is good, but can't he comb his hair and smile a little?" Even without the film "Amadeus," it's easy to picture Mozart laughing and having fun. So much of his music has a lighthearted sparkle and the kind of graceful charm that puts a smile on the listener's face. But Beethoven? Liszt compared Beethoven's work to "the pillar of cloud and fire which guided the Israelites through the desert," while Bizet referred to Beethoven as "This Titan, this Prometheus of Music." (Prometheus was the Titan who defied the gods by giving mortals the gift of fire, and was punished for it when Zeus chained him to a mountain. He was finally freed by Hercules, but that's another legend.)

Important Things to Know

Beethoven was a memorable character. He angered many of those around him with his manner even as he guided music into the 19th century with his fiery gifts of composition and performance. He saw himself as alone against the world, he railed against the niceties of manners, and with equal disdain, broke the musical rules laid down by pedants of far lesser gifts. He is famous for his refusal to submit to his deafness, continuing to compose long after he could not hear the results. His inner torments colored both his life and his music.

Pushed by his father, Johann van Beethoven, who hoped to get rich quick by exhibiting his son as another Mozart, young Ludwig was forced to learn the harpsichord, organ, viola, and piano, and performed in concert at the age of eight (although his father pretended the lad was only six so his achievements would seem more impressive). Ludwig soon realized that while his most important creative outlet would be composition, he had to make a living, and even as a teenager, he was earning money as an instrumentalist. He became much in demand as one of the first virtuoso pianists, both at court and in the homes of the Viennese aristocracy. Even though he didn't smile a lot.

Bet You Didn't Know

Count Ferdinand Ernst Gabriel Waldstein, one of Beethoven's first patrons, also helped the young composer to his first great success. At an elegant soirée, the Count announced that he had in hand the manuscript of a new trio by an anonymous composer. Beethoven played the piano, while two other guests volunteered for the violin and cello parts. A five-minute ovation followed the performance, and the guests became wildly curious about the identity of its creator: the piece seemed too ardent for Haydn, too weighty for Mozart. Eventually, Count Waldstein gave credit where it was due, to pianist Beethoven, who had just premiered what would later be published as his no. Trio in E-flat, Opus 1, #1.

Beethoven continued to write extensively for the keyboard, his works increasing in complexity and dramatic sonority as improvements to the instrument itself gave the piano sufficient power and flexibility to accommodate his ever-expanding ideas. His 32 piano sonatas (not to mention the 10 for violin and piano and the five for cello and piano), plus the five immortal piano concertos, rank among the milestone works of classical music.

Rise of the Virtuoso

Think of the aura that surrounded the Beatles or the late Michael Jackson: today, that's how many listeners looked upon piano virtuosos in the romantic era. This, remember, was the age of individualism, of poetic extravagance, of breaking away from conventional manners and mores. For many a listener, hearing a high-powered virtuoso in action was as much an emotional experience as much as it was a musical one.

Liszt: Lion of the Piano

There were, of course, virtuosos before Franz Liszt (1811-1886). There was Clementi (1752-1832) whom many thought was the equal of Mozart (Mozart conceded Clementi's left-hand facility, but said "he has not a farthing's worth of feeling"); Jan Ladislav Dussek (1760-1812), so proud of his good looks ("le beau Dussek" they called him in Paris) that he turned the piano sideways on stage so the audience could admire the music and his handsome profile at the same time; and Carl Czerny (1791-1857), who studied with Beethoven, taught Liszt, and wrote well over 1,000 pieces, including the hundreds of exercises that have been the bane of piano students ever since.

Bet You Didn't Know

To give you an idea of Liszt's incredible output, his 1,000-plus exercises were published in three volumes and seven different opus numbers (299, 300, 335, 355, 399, 400, and 500, if you really want to know). The umbrella title was Complete Theoretical and Practical Pianoforte School, which is enough to scare anybody. Czerny, by the way published an arrangement of Rossini's William Tell Overture for 32 hands at eight pianos.

Music Word

Opus, from the Latin, just means work. When it's attached to a number, it usually signifies the chronological order in which a composer's piece was published. The first would be Opus 1, the second opus 2 and so forth. When several works are grouped together as a unit (as are the 12 Etudes in Chopin's Opus 10, for instance), a second number is used to indicate their place in the sequence: Opus 10, #4, or Opus 10, #12.

Liszt's father was a good amateur musician who taught young Franz to play the piano in their comfortable home. Giving a recital in a small Hungarian town, the 9-year-old Franz impressed a group of noblemen so much that they organized a fund enabling the lad to study with Czerny in Vienna. Liszt proved to be a remarkably adept student, making his concerto debut two years later, and while never a child prodigy in the Mozartian mold, he already was a composer at the age of 12, a touring pianist at 14, and a neurotic at 16 (who alternated between bouts of deep depression and periods of religious fervor, during which he considered both suicide and becoming a monk).

Bet You Didn't Know

Sometimes Liszt got so excited that he would swoon himself, right in the middle of a performance. According to one eyewitness, "he fainted in the arms of a friend who was turning pages for him, and we bore him out in a strong fit of hysterics."

In 1831, though, the 19-year-old Liszt heard Paganini give one of his stupendously exciting recitals (and saw women throwing themselves at the violinist's feet thereafter). Suddenly, his whole world changed. Liszt went into seclusion with his piano, determined to emerge as the greatest piano virtuoso known to mankind humankind, and if possible, the greatest lover known to womankind. He succeeded handsomely in both quests. His deep-set eyes and confident manner set women ablaze, while his playing induced them to shrieks of ecstasy and not infrequent swoonings. His fans would rush madly to the stage after a performance, desperate to collect bits of his clothing, or perhaps broken piano strings as prized mementos.

Liszt, ever the consummate showman, reveled in all the attention, and did what he could to contribute to it. He would sometimes appear wearing elegant doeskin gloves, which he would remove with sensual grace and casually toss to the floor; other times, he would have wreaths and garlands strewn around the piano, or else he'd walk out on stage with various medals and decorations dangling from his lapel. When he returned in triumph to his native Hungary, he appeared in full Hungarian Magyar costume, complete with a jewel-studded sword. Take that, Liberace!

Lizst Faces Some Competition: Thalberg and Alkan

Liszt was not without his rivals, chief among them Sigismond Thalberg (1812-1871), who had developed a method of outlining a melody with both thumbs, while his fingers traced all sorts of gymnastic figurations on either side. Contemporary reports indicate that his playing sounded as if three hands were traversing the keyboard, and during his concerts, otherwise refined ladies and gentlemen would stand on their velvet chairs to see how he did it. Like Liszt, Thalberg made a specialty of opera fantasies, taking one or more themes from popular stage works and swirling them through a whole series of virtuosic variations, usually including a quiet, melancholy episode for a soulful change of pace, but then bringing out the big virtuoso guns for a socko finish.

Bet You Didn't Know

An elegant Parisian apartment belonging to Princess Cristina Belgiojoso-Trivulzio was jammed to the rafters in 1837, when the entrepreneurial lady charged a hefty admission fee for a piano duel she had arranged between Liszt and Thalberg. (This was before the Princess was arrested for hiding the embalmed body of her ex-lover in her closet.) Thalberg played his splashy fantasy on themes from Rossini's Moses; Liszt followed with his own Grand Fantasy on Pacini's La Niobe. "At the close of the duel," reported the critic Jules Janin, "a profound silence fell over the noble arena. The two men were adjudged equals, Thus two victors, and none vanquished."

Alkan (1813-1888)—the stage name of Charles Henri Valentin Morhange—was another amazing pianist who might have become a much greater threat to Liszt's keyboard supremacy had he not become more and more eccentric as he went along. He had a morbid fear of the outdoors, often refusing to leave his apartment for months at a time; he would perform for a few years, then pull back and refuse to appear in public. (During one such lull, he didn't perform on stage for 28 years.) Eventually, Alkan retreated into a kind of monastic existence, leaving his mark on the world only through a series of incredibly difficult pieces, among them "Chemin de Fer" (1844), which seems to be the first ever description of a railroad train, and a set of 24 etudes in all the major and minor keys.

Gottschalk:One of Our Boys Made It Too

Bet You Didn't Know

Alkan's death was as odd as his life. Apparently, he was reaching for a religious volume on the top shelf when the bookcase toppled over and crushed him.

Europe was the center of the classical music universe in the 19th century, but Louis Moreau Gottschalk (1829-1869), born into a Creole family, staked out his keyboard claim in New Orleans, where he began to play the piano at the age of three. By the time he was seven, Louis had advanced sufficiently to replace his indisposed teacher at the organ of the St. Louis Cathedral, and at 12, his talents had become so prodigious that he was sent to study in Paris. (Seven-year-old Camille Saint-Saens was one of his classmates.) Chopin predicted that Gottschalk would become "the king of pianists," and Berlioz said that he was "one of the very small number who possess all the different elements of a consummate pianist."

All the while composing delightful little piano pieces based on Creole rhythms and folk tunes, Gottschalk went on concert tours in France, Switzerland, and Spain (where the Queen awarded him the Order of Isabella Cross), and he returned to America as a celebrity. Like Liszt, Gottschalk's good looks and dramatic stage manner (according to a one report, "his large and dark eyes had peculiarly drooping lids, which always appeared half-closed when he played") made him a favorite among the ladies, whose favors he gratefully accepted at any opportunity. There was a downside however; Gottschalk used to grumble that he kept hitting wrong notes because he was distracted by the pretty young girls who flocked to his concerts.

Gottschalk spent about five years in Central and South America, but returned to North America in 1862 to begin a three-year tour that took him from New York to California, where a newspaper figured out that in the process, he had travelled 15,000 miles by rail to give more than 1,100 concerts. He probably would have racked up even more mileage, except that one of his romantic exploits involved a young lady from a seminary in San Francisco, and the bad press—"Vagabond Musician Should Suffer Death" was one of the more complimentary headlines—made it seem wise to head back to South America. This he did, sneaking out of town in the dead of the night only a few steps ahead of a posse. He continued to compose, and to perform in many South American cities until he was felled by a mysterious disease, variously described as yellow fever, cholera, and peritonitis, collapsing on stage in Rio de Janeiro (as the probably apocryphal story goes, during a performance of his own piece "Morte—A Lamentation"). He died a month later, aged 40, and was buried in Greenwood Cemetery, Brooklyn, New York.

Bet You Didn't Know

Even though Gottschalk was a born and bred Southerner, his sympathies lay with the North in the Civil War. In 1862 he wrote a rabble-rousing piano piece called "The Union," its massive chords suggesting the sounds of war, while quotations from such patriotic tunes as "Yankee Doodle," "Hail Columbia," and "The Star Spangled Banner" made it clear which side was going to win.

Monkeying Around With Chopinzee and Other Peculiar Personalities

Not too many people alive today were lucky enough to hear the great turn-of the century pianists in person. If they did, they heard them at the end of their careers when their talents had started to erode.

There was Vladimir de Pachmann, a Chopin specialist whose grimaces, audience chats, and other stage antics were so outrageous that critic James Huneker dubbed him the "Chopinzee" (George Bernard Shaw once wrote that de Pachmann "gave his well-known pantomimic performance, with accompaniments by Chopin); and Leopold Godowsky, who decided that the Chopin études weren't difficult enough, so he devised a way of playing two of them at the same time (in an incredibly difficult piece called "Badinage"). There was Moriz Rosenthal, whose diminutive stature and great keyboard power earned him the nickname "The Little Giant of the Piano"; and Josef Hofmann, who made his American debut playing Beethoven's Piano Concerto #1 at the Metropolitan Opera House at age 11 to such wild acclaim that he was immediately booked on a 52-concert tour. He actually gave more than 40 recitals before the Society for Prevention of Cruelty to Children stepped in stop the exploitation. Godowsky and de Pachmann lived into the 1930s and Rosenthal and Hofmann into the 1940s, as did the two even more legendary pianists we'll discuss next in somewhat greater detail.

Piano Politics—Politics and Piano: Premier Paderewski

Presidents Truman and Nixon played the piano a bit, and Bill Clinton has been known to trot out his saxophone, but none of those eminent gentlemen could lay claim to being a highly skilled musician. Not so with Ignacy Jan Paderewski (1860-1941), the fabled pianist who served in Washington as the first representative of the new Polish republic after World War I. In 1919, he became the Premier of Poland, and later that country's delegate to the League of Nations.

Bet You Didn't Know

In his official post as Premier, Paderewski attended the Versailles Treaty Conference, where he was introduced to Prime Minister Clemenceau of France. "You are M. Paderewski, the famous pianist?" the Frenchman asked. "And now the Premier of Poland?" Receiving a bowed assent from the pianist-politician, Clemenceau is supposed to have heaved a great sigh, adding sadly, "What a comedown."

At the same time, Paderewski was one of the most celebrated and popular musicians on this side of the Atlantic. Americans rechristened him "Paderooski" or more simply "Paddy," endlessly played his Minuet in G at home, then flocked in record numbers to hear his concerts. Crowds would wait at railroad crossings hoping to get a glimpse of the pianist as his private car went by; sometimes his entire route from hotel to concert hall was lined with adoring fans.

Bet You Didn't Know

Paderewski designed his private railroad car by himself for utmost comfort, complete with easy chairs, separate heating and lighting systems (in case the ones on the rest of the train malfunctioned) and, naturally, his own grand piano.

One way and another, Americans couldn't get enough of Paderewski (on a single day in 1902, his opera "Manru" was performed at the Metropolitan Opera, while the pianist himself was giving two Carnegie Hall recitals), and in due course he became the highest paid musician of his day. He was also one of the most generous, allotting the profits from all his wartime concerts to Polish relief, donating the money needed for the construction of Chopin Memorial Hall in Warsaw, and eventually giving away millions of dollars to other worthy causes.

Rachmaninoff, the Super Romantic

Less than ten years separate the births of those mighty Russians, Sergei Rachmaninoff (1873-1943) and Igor Stravinsky (1882-1971), yet what a world of difference is to be found in their musical legacies. Whereas Stravinsky probed ever new and more challenging boundaries (we'll talk about him later, in our composers' chapter), Rachmaninoff remained true to his romantic calling, touring the world as a virtuoso pianist in the manner of Liszt, all the while composing works of the most extravagant beauty, even if they often seemed more in tune with 19th than 20th century sensibilities. His emotional, some would say sentimental, style often left him out of favor with critics, but not with audiences, who to this day are enchanted by the deep melodic warmth of his Piano Concerto #2, the brilliance of "Rhapsody on a Theme of Paganini," the thundering power of the Piano Concerto #3, and the dazzling virtuosity of the dozens of shorter pieces with which he enriched the solo piano repertory. Ironically, the most famous of them all, the Prelude in C# Minor, was so insistently requested at his concerts that Rachmaninoff himself grew to hate the thing with a passion.

Bet You Didn't Know

"The artist tries, and tries again to achieve the impossible," said Rachmaninoff in response to a comment about his brooding manner on stage. "Sometimes he is lucky and gets a little nearer to his goal. But all of the time he is forced way out someplace, way out where no one can comfort him, nothing can help him." No wonder his friend Abram Chasins described Rachmaninoff as having "a gaunt face, with the stern sorrows of the ages engraved upon it," while Stravinsky simply said he was "a six-and-a-half-foot-tall scowl."

Fortunately, Rachmaninoff's own ardent and bravura technique lives on through his many recordings, and his music—through its frequent appearance in the concert hall, films, and such classic pop-song ripoffs as "Full Moon and Empty Arms" written by Buddy Kave and Ted Mossman in 1946 (its luscious theme swiped from the Piano Concerto #2).

Super Man of the World: Rubinstein

"I was born to play the piano," said Arthur Rubinstein (1887-1982) on a radio broadcast, and that pretty well sums it up. His father tried to interest him in the violin, and young Arthur promptly smashed it to pieces. On the other hand, they couldn't keep the child away from his piano. He could play difficult pieces long before he learned to read music, and early on had a strong sense of his own destiny: he was barely five years old when he carefully designed little cards to give to his friends. On them was printed Arturic (his boyhood nickname), the Great Piano Virtuoso.

Rubinstein made his European debut in Berlin at the age of 13, conquered Paris while still in his teens, and made his Ameri   20th birthday. Thereafter, he came

Bet You Didn't Know

As much as he loved to play the piano, Rubinstein didn't much like practicing, so he came up with a clever little system: "I used to go into the practice room and lock the door behind me. I'd put a beautiful novel in with my sheet music, a box of cherries on the right side of the piano, and a box of chocolates on the left. I'd play runs with my left hand and eat cherries with my right, or the other way around, and all the time be reading my book."

back to the USA off and on, but not with anything approaching the universal acclaim that he would reap in his later years. The pianist freely admitted that much of this lukewarm response was his own fault. "I was lazy," he said. "I had talent, but there were many things in life more important than practicing. Good food, good cigars, great wines, women... I dropped many notes in those days…"

All that changed after a period of soul-searching and disciplined work, and when Rubinstein returned to the USA in 1935, it was as the supreme master so many of us remember with deep affection. Yes, he still dropped notes from time to time, but the obvious love he took in public performance, the exuberance of his personality, and the natural warmth of his piano sound combined to make him one of the most beloved artists of our time.

Although Rubinstein was especially known for his radiant Chopin performances, he was a master of music from almost every earlier and later era. He didn't often approach Bach and the other baroque composers, but he recorded a number of the Mozart concertos, all of the Beethoven (several times,   the premieres of works written for

Bet You Didn't Know

Once at the conclusion of a Carnegie Hall concert—as usual, with stage seats accommodating part of the overflow crowd—Rubinstein was backstage after having bowed several times to the still cheering audience. Just as he returned yet again, a lady in one of the stage seats got up to leave, whereupon the pianist stopped in his tracks, bowed, and graciously helped her on with her coat. That gentlemanly task accomplished, he proceeded to take another bow.

him by such notable 20th century composers as Villa-Lobos and Granados (whose "Nights in the Gardens of Spain" remains one of the most evocative concertos in the entire Spanish repertory).

His enormous popularity was further enhanced by Hollywood, which used his soundtrack performances in three films from the mid-1940s ("I've Always Loved You," "Song of Love," and "Night Song"), and featured him in two others, "Carnegie Hall" and "Of Men and Music." A 1975 film documentary called "Love of Life" chronicled his fascinating life and times, and a 90-minute television special, "Rubinstein at 90" followed by only one year his farewell recital in London.

A few days before Christmas, 1982, as Nicolas Slonimsky put it so poetically, Rubinstein "slid gently into death in his Geneva apartment, as in a pianissimo ending of a Chopin nocturne."

The Virtuoso's Virtuoso: Horowitz

The story goes that after a concert in Ann Arbor, Michigan, a young fan approached the great Vladimir Horowitz (1904-1989) with the words, "Maestro, how do you do it? You must have at least 20 degrees of subtlety between piano and pianissimo." "Ah," replied the pianist, "thank you my friend for noticing."

Horowitz had such incredible finger control that his technical prowess got a lot more press and audience attention than his musical gifts. As Harold Schonberg points out in his invaluable book *The Great Pianists*, "Horowitz never liked to be known as a stunt man. Aside from some extraordinary tours de force that he himself wrote as recital-closers—a transcription of Sousa's 'Stars and Stripes Forever,' arrangements of several Liszt rhapsodies, and so on—he considered himself an artist who used his technique for musical ends. Unfortunately, he was too rich technically for such a modest disclaimer, and his audiences generally came to see him turn the piano upside down."

Despite international stardom and the idolization of his audiences, Horowitz several times left the concert stage, once for a two-year hiatus in 1936 after his marriage to Wanda Toscanini (daughter of the famous conductor), then for a far lengthier retirement, from 1953 to 1965. His return to the stage—at Carnegie Hall, May 9, 1965—made international headlines, with all tickets sold out within a matter of a few hours. Fortunately, that entire recital was recorded by Columbia, is still available on a Sony CD, and thus will live forever as a golden moment in musical history. The CD is called "The Historic Return to Carnegie Hall"; it comes packaged with another Horowitz recital program, and includes works by Bach, Debussy, Schumann, Scriabin, Chopin, and more. The label is Sony Classical S3K 53461

Actually, Horowitz was making studio recordings all through those dozen years away from the concert platform, and indeed his discography spans the full musical gamut, from Scarlatti to Scriabin and on to such later 20th century masters as Prokofiev, Kabalevsky, Samuel Barber (whose celebrated piano sonata he premiered in 1949), and of course his friend Rachmaninoff.

Bet You Didn't Know

When tickets went on sale for that return concert, 57th Street was jammed with people waiting in the rain, desperate to be able to purchase one of the priceless tickets. Horowitz was so touched by this evidence of his fans' devotion that he ordered hundreds of cups of coffee to be delivered to them in line.

During a news conference, the nearly 80-year-old Horowitz told a *New York Times* reporter that he would keep playing as long "the devil and the angel" remained within him. "In the end I do everything," he said, and so he did. In 1982, he gave his first overseas concerts in more than 30 years. In 1986, he returned to Russia after a lifetime away (61 years, to be exact), including a never-to-be-forgotten concert at Tchaikovsky Hall in Moscow, which formed the basis of a worldwide television special.

Horowitz also continued to record: Scarlatti, Liszt, and Rachmaninoff at the Metropolitan Opera House (in 1981); Schumann, Scriabin, and Chopin (plus "God Save the Queen") at the Royal Festival Hall in London (1982); Bach and Schubert at home in New York (1985); Mozart and Moszkowski in Vienna's Musikverein (1987). In the fall of 1989, Horowitz decided to record various works of Haydn, Chopin, and Liszt that he had never played for

Bet You Didn't Know

It may have been a sentimental journey, but Horowitz didn't travel light: his own grand piano was cleaned and placed on a special plane to Moscow, and fresh sole and other food favorites were airmailed to him every day. He even brought along his cook to make sure that everything was prepared to his liking, and his own tuner, to attend to any potential ailments of his Steinway piano.

the American public. The last of six sessions was completed on November 1st; four days later, the pianist died suddenly in his Manhattan apartment. An era had ended. Music lovers around the world mourned his loss; Vladimir Horowitz, as the title of a film documentary put it, had been "the Last Romantic."

CHAPTER 12

More Makers of Music: Bows and Batons Department

> ## In This Chapter
>
> ➤ The Italian violin makers
> ➤ The early composers
> ➤ On the podium
> ➤ American conductors

A number of folk instruments are credited with being the ancestors of the violin, among them the Arabic rabab, which turned into the rebec when it arrived in Western Europe, and was often called the fiddle in England (without any of the slightly snide connotations the term later acquired). A more sophisticated branch of the bowed string family included many sizes of viols, and were in use until the 1700s, at which point the more pliant and expressive violins, violas, and cellos ran them out of town.

The Italian Touch

During the Renaissance, Italian artists and craftsmen revolutionized the way the world looked at painting, sculpture, and architecture, and thanks to an incredible group of instrument builders—who created the Davids and the Mona Lisas of the tonal world—music took a giant step forward as well.

Fiddle Faddle

Before 1600 or so, musicians were satisfied with viols, string instruments played with a bow that came in all the usual sizes, from the tiny viol de pochette (pocket viol) favored by dancing masters who had to carry their music around with them, to the large bass members of the family. For all their antique beauty, though, viols lacked the carrying power, the resonance, and the flexible tone colors we associate with the violin and cello. For those qualities, we had to await the arrival of the masters who built instruments so remarkable that they are prized to this day for their gorgeous sound and workmanship.

Master Maker: Andrea Amati

Andrea Amati (1520-1580) was one of the first of these remarkable violin makers. He set up shop in the small town of Cremona, where his work was later carried on by his two sons, Antonio and Geronimo, and his grandson Nicolo. Gaspara de Salo (1540-1609) lived not far away in Brescia, where his workshop was later maintained by his apprentice, Giovanni Maggini. Back in Cremona, Andrea Guarneri (1626-1698), having studied with Amati, proceeded to found his own dynasty of violin makers, the most famous being del Gesu.

Bet You Didn't Know

The Guarneris were incredible fiddle makers, but they ran out of steam when it came to naming their kids. Andrea's sons were Giuseppi and Pietro; meanwhile, there was a cousin, also named Pietro, and Giuseppe's son was another Giuseppe. He turned out to be the most distinguished Guarneri of them all, calling himself Giuseppe del Gesu (after the Jesuit movement), so folks could tell him apart from his father.

Top of the Line

If you go to Cremona and visit the house in the Piazza Roma where Antonio Stradivari (1644?–1737) spent most of his life, you'll find an inscription installed by the city fathers stating that he "brought the violin to perfection and left to Cremona an imperishable name as master of his craft." Having served an apprenticeship to Nicolo Amati for seven or eight years, the 22-year-old Stradivari went into business for himself, signing some of his instruments with the Latin form of his name, Antonius Stradivarius, usually adding a Maltese cross and enclosing his initials, A.S., within a double circle.

Important Things to Know

Stradivari's violins tended to be longer than Amati's, and he worked tirelessly on other improvements: larger sound holes, stronger arches, better forms of varnish, each time improving the instrument's visual symmetry as well as its sonic beauty. He is credited with having built at least 540 violins. Craftsmen of every succeeding generation—starting with Stradivari's own sons, Francesco and Omobono— have attempted without success to duplicate his mastery, to discover Stradivari's "secret," to build instruments of equivalent eloquence. The "Strads" remain in a class by themselves, however, never to be equaled, let alone surpassed.

The emergence of the violin as the instrumental king of the strings was due in no small measure to the amazing work of Amati, Guarneri, Stradivari, and other master craftsmen who built instruments more than 300 years ago that remain unsurpassed to this day (and don't think people haven't tried to surpass them!). During this era, the viola and cello, almost also vastly improved, became the essential middle and lower voices of the string family.

Bet You Didn't Know

Violinists maintain that fine instruments have distinct and very different personalities. In his book "The Glory of the Violin," Joseph Wechsberg maintains that old violins are like young women: "They want to be wooed and may lovingly respond to your efforts, but if you make a mistake, they scream." He also traded in his Amati because it "disliked bright lights" for a Strad that should have come with a Surgeon General's warning. "It is allergic to smoke, especially cigar smoke," Wechsberg said, "and doesn't like protracted fog, either."

The Italian Touch – Those Amazing Violinists

With all those fabulous fiddles being produced left and right, it inevitably followed that composers started putting them to good use, and violinists emerged who could play all that difficult new music.

Corelli and Torelli

Arcangelo Corelli (1653-1713) was born into a distinguished family of scholars, poets, and jurists, but he decided to become a musician and started to study violin at the age of 13, developing into a master player and composer even as he maintained his place in high society. Corelli's fans included Queen Christina of Sweden, who installed him as chamber musician in her palace (it's too complicated to explain why her palace was in Rome) and Cardinal Pietro Ottoboni, who invited Corelli to take up residence in his palace. The King of Naples tried repeatedly to get Corelli to move there, but how many palaces can a fellow use? Meanwhile, he dedicated his first 12 violin sonatas to Queen Christina, eventually publishing another five sets, each containing a dozen pieces. Taking into account his own technical mastery, his compositions for the instrument, and his development of new performing methods (playing chords, for instance), Corelli is generally considered to be the founder of modern violin technique.

Like Corelli, Giuseppe Torelli (1658-1709) began his training in Bologna and made his reputation as a court violinist (both there and in Vienna), churning out concertos and sonatas by the dozen. He expanded on Corelli's experiments with the concerto grosso (where several instruments within the large ensemble take on a kind of collective solo role), and was one of the first major composers to produce solo violin concertos.

Music Word

Concerto Grosso. Just as a regular concerto implies a solo instrument with orchestra, a Concerto Grosso (literally "grand concerto") indicates a piece where several instruments within the larger ensemble collectively make up the spotlighted instrumental force.

... and Tartini

We can pretty well forget about Francesco Manfredini (1684-1762) and Pietro Nardini (1722-1793), since their music sounds just as similar as their names. Besides, it hardly even appears on concert programs, with the occasional exception of a rather pretty Nardini concerto that Pinchas Zukerman recorded many years ago, and Manfredini's Christmas Concerto, which is sometimes played when they're tired of the Corelli Christmas Concerto.

Giuseppe Tartini (1692-1770) though, is a somebody to remember. For starters, he was the teacher of both Nardini and Manfredini (plus Pugnani, whose name, unfortunately doesn't rhyme), so he got there first. He was also another influential virtuoso, whose acoustical discoveries led to new performance possibilities (among other things, he made the violin strings thicker and the bow lighter), and whose dramatic style of playing became a model for later generations of fiddlers.

Bet You Didn't Know

Nardini was definitely the emotional type. They say he used to weep at the beauty of his own playing.

Tartini's most famous piece is called the Devil's Trill Sonata, because Satan himself came to his room one night and played "a sonata of such exquisite beauty that I felt enraptured." The next morning, Tartini scribbled down as much of the music as he could remember and voilà!—his devilishly difficult piece was born. At least that's what he told everybody.

Bet You Didn't Know

Many years earlier, the Cardinal of Padua had asked Tartini to give lessons to his niece, and Tartini obliged—unfortunately, he was teaching her just a little more than the fiddle and she ended up pregnant. When the baby was born, the Cardinal ordered Tartini's arrest, and poor Giuseppe had to grab his fiddle and sneak out of town disguised as a monk. He hid in the Monastery of Saint Francis of Assisi, practicing every day and waiting for the Cardinal to calm down. It took two years, so by then Tartini got to be a great virtuoso.

His Satanic Majesty: Paganini

A century and a half before The Rolling Stones came on the scene, Niccolo Paganini (1782-1840), perpetually clad in black with a gaunt, cadaverous look and seemingly supernatural skills, accentuated his persona as a Satanic Majesty. Actually, he was pretty strange as a kid, too: He would go into fits of ecstasy at the sound of cathedral bells, tremble all over when the organ sounded in church, and the first time he tried out his older brother's violin, he fainted dead away and lay in a trance for two days.

Important Things to Know

Paganini rewrote the book on violin playing, innovating the left-hand pizzicato. He made the violin imitate animal cries and human speech, achieving unexpected effects through unorthodox tunings. A favorite Paganini concert stunt was cutting through three of his strings with scissors so that he could play the most wildly brilliant passages on the remaining one. Which proves that he was just a 150 years or so early in the modern trend toward hard rock guitar-smashing and other on-stage demolitions.

Just as Beethoven's father had high hopes of turning his son into a money-making prodigy à la Mozart, Paganini's dad tried the same stunt with Niccolo, locking him up the practice room for hours at a time and thrashing him or taking away his supper if he hadn't worked hard enough. In one way, Papa's plan worked; in another it didn't. Paganini indeed became the greatest violinist of his time (possibly of all time), but not at the hoped-for age of seven or eight. He was an old-timer of 12 by the time he gave his first recital, and almost out of his teens when he took the first of several orchestral positions. His fame as a vagabond virtuoso would not be attained for another ten years or so, but once he began touring, his fabled prowess became the talk of Europe, his playing exciting audiences beyond belief.

Music Word

Pizzicato, like so many musical terms, comes from the Italian, meaning "pinched." It's an indication that notes on bowed string instruments are to be plucked by the player's fingers, not stroked with a separate bow.

Staccato, from the Italian, meaning "detached", indicates that a note is very short, and not connected to the note before or after it. On the violin, a staccato can be produced by a very quick bow stroke (with the right hand) or a fast plucking of a string with the left.

Bet You Didn't Know

As it was, rumors followed Paganini wherever he went: people whispered that the souls of his mistresses were locked inside his violin; that he could move the bow so fast because he had filled it small leaden bullets; that his tone was so exquisite because the fiddle strings had been spun from the intestines of his murdered rivals; that he had sold his soul to the devil in exchange for his incredible technique. Paganini once had to publish a letter from his mother, just to prove he really had human parents.

His popularity reached unprecedented heights. People flocked to buy Paganini fans and Paganini perfumes and Paganini walking sticks; you could eat marzipan Paganinis and Paganini rolls, baked in the form of little violins. Unfortunately, the violinist was stricken with a number of illnesses that forced him into semi-retirement for the last years of his life. In 1838 he developed cancer of the throat, and he died the following spring. Paganini's legacy, though, will live forever, both through modern performances of his Five Concertos and dozens of other shorter works for the violin, and in the virtuosic showmanship that quite possibly will never again be replicated.

The List Doesn't Stop There

They weren't all Italian, needless to say. Belgium's greatest violinist was Henri Vieuxtemps, and Poland gave us Henryk (or Henri) Wieniawski, who succeeded Vieuxtemps as professor at the Brussels Conservatory. Both men toured the United States in the mid-19th century and both composed concertos and shorter works that remain to this day in the repertoire of virtually all violinists.

Brahms' friend Joseph Joachim (for whom he wrote the Violin Concerto in D) was another highly regarded touring performer; and Norway boasted Ole Bull, who once gave 274 concerts in a single season (1836-37).

Music Word

Season. Unlike most of us, whose calendars run from January through December, and corporations, whose "fiscal years" can start and end at whatever month the treasurer deems best, concert "seasons" are usually reckoned from the fall through the spring. Most orchestras and opera houses begin their subscription programs in September or October, and wind them down in April or May. (There are also summer seasons, of course, but they will normally be specified as such.)

Bet You Didn't Know

Ole Bull had nine younger brothers and sisters. In any language, that's a lot of Bulls.

Spain had Pablo de Sarasate, who put Pamplona on the map long before Hemingway came along. He wrote dozens of showpieces in the Spanish style, and premiered concertos written for him by Saint-Saens, Lalo, and Bruch, among others.

Kreisler: The "Fooled You" Fiddler

The Austrian-born Fritz Kreisler (1875-1962), who reigned as one of the most popular musicians of the first half of the 20th century, was not so much a virtuoso as a deep-feeling musician for whom technical problems did not seem to exist. He could read music at the tender age of three, and at seven entered the Vienna Conservatory, winning prizes there and later in Paris, then making his American debut in 1889 (with the Boston Symphony, no less). Kreisler's interests extended far beyond the violin, however: He was a superb pianist, an accomplished painter, a linguist, an author, a composer, and a book collector. He gave up music for a time to enter medical school, then became an officer in the Austrian Army. "In my youthful days," he said, "I had some very weird thoughts about my future career. I envisaged myself operating on a patient in the morning, playing chess in the afternoon, giving a concert in the evening, and winning a battle at midnight."

Bet You Didn't Know

During World War I, Kreisler rejoined his regiment and was wounded in action. He chronicled some of those military impressions in a slim volume called Four Weeks in the Trenches: the War Story of a Violinist.

Kreisler's burnished tone, exemplary technique, and elegant phrasing made him one of the most admired violinists of his time, but perhaps the most enduring part of his legacy rests on a modest bit of deception. At a concert in 1905, he introduced three warm-hearted encore-type pieces, "Liebesfreud" (The Joy of Love), "Liebesleid" (The Pain of Love), and "Schön Rosmarin" (The Beautiful Rosemary), explaining that they were by one Joseph

Lanner, a Viennese composer who had died half a century earlier. Gradually, he introduced other works as transcriptions of music by Pugnani, Dittersdorf, Porpora, and sundry other earlier, if minor, masters.

Actually, it was Pugnani who blew his cover. In 1935, the *New York Times* critic Olin Downes, unable to track down the original source of the "Preludium and Allegro," called the violinist for the information. Thus cornered, Kreisler confessed that it—along with all those other wonderful miniatures—were in fact his own compositions. Why had he done it? "I wanted to enlarge my programs," said the always modest Kreisler, "but I found it tactless to repeat my name endlessly."

Aside from a few critics, who were highly put out at being taken in by the violinist-composer's little white lies, audiences were even more enchanted with his new-old miniatures than they had been in the first place, clamoring all the louder for them at every Kreisler concert. You can enjoy Kreisler's compositions in recordings by Itzhak Perlman and many other contemporary admirers. But try to hear Fritz Kreisler himself on one of the vintage CD reissues: Perhaps you'll sense the old-world elegance that was so much a part of his magic as a performer. When the violinist was given a testimonial dinner by the Musicians' Emergency Fund in 1950, Bruno Walter summed up Kreisler's musical sorcery with his own touch of eloquence: "He did not only play the violin," said the famed conductor, "he became the violin. Or better, the violin became him. To make music is for Fritz Kreisler what flying is for the birds, what swimming is for the fish."

Music, Maestro

Somebody has to lead the musicians, so enter the conductor, a virtuoso of a different stripe who has to know what every instrument in the orchestra is doing at every moment, yet lead the performance in silence (except at rehearsals, of course). In the early days, the conductor was almost always the composer or a member of the orchestra (usually the harpsichordist or first violinist).

A dictatorship is more efficient than a democracy, primarily because nobody dares talk back to the boss. For the first half of our 20th century, conductors pretty much made their own rules. They could hire and fire musicians at will, throw tantrums (or more tangible items like watches and batons) at the players, and generally proceed on their tonal ways without fear of contradiction. Those days, of course, are gone forever, but so, perhaps, are the conditions that made possible enhanced the storied legacies of some of the conducting giants of the recent past.

Beethoven: The Excitable Type

We've already discussed Beethoven's heaven-storming qualities as a composer and pianist. As you might have guessed, he wasn't any calmer as a conductor. In fact, with his high drama and drive, wildly flying hair, and explosive temper, Beethoven must have been something to see up on the podium. Since we can't produce a videotape, let's substitute an eyewitness account by the German conductor and composer Ludwig Spohr: "Beethoven became accustomed to indicating the marks of expression by all kinds of peculiar movements," he wrote. "Whenever a sforzando [a suddenly emphasized note or chord] occurred, he would vehemently open both arms, which had before been crossed on his chest. For a quiet passage, he would bend down, and the softer it was to be, the lower he would stoop, until he practically disappeared under the music stand. For a crescendo (increase in volume), he would draw himself up more and more, till at the arrival of the forte, he gave a leap into the air, screaming out to increase the volume…." They just don't make conductors like that any more!

Bet You Didn't Know

At the premiere of the Ninth Symphony in Vienna, Beethoven—now completely deaf—beat time in front of the orchestra while another musician stood behind him and did the actual conducting. At the end, the listeners broke into a wild, cheering ovation of which Beethoven, with his back to them, was completely unaware. At last, one of the singers approached the master and gently turned him around, so that he might see—if not hear—the jubilant reaction of the audience.

Mr. Elegant: Mendelssohn

Mendelssohn, in a way, was Beethoven's opposite. His music, like his personality, was refined, elegant, and well-mannered. Some critics have faulted this restraint (a characteristic we may be assured Beethoven was never accused of), but the melodic warmth that flows through Mendelssohn's music is ever a source of wonder. Although he was a superb pianist and organist, and remains best known as a composer, he was also an exemplary conductor. And why not? His doting (and wealthy) family gave him a little orchestra to play with, and from age 12 to 14, Felix led the players in a regular series of house concerts.

Bet You Didn't Know

When Beethoven was in love, he wrote "My thoughts go out to you, my Immortal Beloved, I send my soul enwrapped in you into the land of spirits…" When Mendelssohn was about to be married, he wrote his mother, "I wish to be calm and collected and go through this affair with the coolness I have always managed to preserve hitherto…" You might say these guys were type "A" and "B" personalities.

In 1829, Mendelssohn added yet another string to his illustrious musical bow, reviving the then all-but-forgotten "St. Mathew Passion" of Bach. His concern for music of the past led him to other important premieres as well, most notably Schubert's Ninth Symphony, and two symphonies of Schumann, not to mention his own compositions. With very rare exceptions, Mendelssohn never lost his conducting cool. When things were going well with an orchestra, he would often be content to set down his baton and, as one contemporary critic reported, "listen with seraphic transport, occasionally beckoning with eye or hand."

Appointed director of the celebrated Leipzig Gewandhaus Orchestra, Mendelssohn weeded out the inferior players, established rehearsal discipline and built what had been a fair-to-middling regional ensemble into a superb orchestra of international reputation. He was a much loved visitor in England, conducting his Scotch Symphony and the premiere of his oratorio Elijah to wildly enthusiastic response. He even hobnobbed with Queen Victoria and Prince Albert, pronouncing Buckingham Palace "the one pleasant English home where I can really feel at ease."

Toscanini: A Man Who Knew the Score

We were talking about Mendelssohn's historic resurrection of Bach's St. Mathew Passion. In the early 19th century, it was considered discourteous to the composer to conduct without music, so even though he had memorized the whole piece, Mendelssohn bowed to convention and had a score in front of him during the concert.

Toscanini also knew his scores without looking at the page, but his notoriously poor eyesight (probably caused by his teenage job of copying music at night) more than likely was a contributing factor in his decision to conduct everything by heart.

Born to a working class family in Parma, Italy, Arturo had a talent that was clear from the start. And so was his imperious manner—among his school nicknames were "Napoleon" and "Little Genius." Before the age of 18, he had graduated with the highest possible scores in both cello and composition.

Toscanini's emergence as a conductor the following year is one of those stories that any self-respecting Hollywood director would dismiss as totally unbelievable. Toscanini was playing second cello for an Italian opera company on tour in Brazil when the local conductor—furious because the audience had hissed the Prelude (to Verdi's *Aida*)—stalked out of the pit. With disaster—financial as well as artistic—staring him in the face, the company manager turned in desperation to Toscanini, who, it was rumored, knew the opera too. Calmly walking to the podium, Toscanini turned and gave the downbeat. In a moment, the booing had stopped, and before the end of Act I, the hostility and restlessness of the audience had turned to admiration. When the final curtain fell, there was pandemonium in the hall as the audience hailed a new genius. The untouched score still lay on the podium, opened to page 1: The 19-year-old lad had conducted the entire opera from memory. Within a few months, word had spread, and Toscanini's cello-playing days were over for good.

Bet You Didn't Know

The Toscanini temper could flare outside the studio as well. In his autobiography, "Unfinished Journey", Yehudi Menuhin describes a scene at New York's Hotel Astor, where he, as a teenaged violinist, had come to discuss the Beethoven Violin Concerto with the Maestro. In the middle of their discussions, the phone rang. The musicians ignored it. It rang again, at which point, Menuhin writes, "the pressure in the room was boiling up. At the third ring, Toscanini stopped, and with determined steps, walked not to the telephone, but to the installation in the wall and jerked the whole thing bodily out, wooden fitting, plaster, dust, severed dangling wires; then without a word, he came back to take up where we had stopped, in total serenity."

In short order, he became one of the most famous conductors in the world, serving as music director at the famous La Scala Opera House in Milan from 1898 to 1908, and again from 1921 to 1929. In the United States, he conducted opera at the Met from 1908 to 1915, returned to take over the New York Philharmonic from 1930 to 1936. He then began the association that would most indelibly stamp his artistry upon the American public: in 1937, he led the first concert of the newly formed NBC Symphony, sending the finest music around the country on wings of radio sound. His broadcasts included concert versions of operas, a full range of symphonic music, and performances with pianist Vladimir Horowitz, Jascha Heifetz, and many more of the most renowned soloists in the country. Through these programs, and the recordings that often followed, he made music accessible to audiences in a way that had not been possible before, converting casual listeners across the land into opera enthusiasts and avid classical music fans.

Toscanini remained at the helm of the NBC Symphony until 1954, when he grudgingly went into retirement at the age of 87. He died three years later at his home in Riverdale, New York.

Toscanini had a temper and his rehearsal rages became legendary—he would scream, yell, and throw things to get what he wanted from his performers. His podium manner at concerts was modest, however, lest audiences be distracted from the beauty of the music at hand.

Reiner: He Never Missed a Beat

Born in Hungary, Fritz Reiner (1888-1963) began his career in Budapest, where he conducted the Volksoper from 1911 to 1914. His next stop was Dresden, where he was principal conductor of the Court (later State) Opera until 1921. An appointment as music director of the Cincinnati Symphony in 1922 brought Reiner to what would thenceforth become his adopted homeland (he became an American citizen six years later). He taught at the Curtis Institute of Music in Philadelphia (where his more talented students included the soon-to-be famous composer Lukas Foss and the even sooner to be even more famous Leonard Bernstein), spent ten years as music director of the Pittsburgh Symphony, several more as a resident conductor at the Metropolitan Opera, and finally—in 1953—arrived at his last and most significant post: music director of the Chicago Symphony.

Like Toscanini, Reiner could be a hard taskmaster, and temper tantrums were not unknown to his players; on the other hand, his sturdy discipline and musical perfectionism raised the Chicago Symphony to a level of excellence equal to the best orchestras in the country—arguably the world.

Stokowski: Mr. Showmanship

Leopold Stokowski (1882-1977) was classical music's P.T. Barnum. He delighted in feeding the public (and even writers of major encyclopedias) false information about his age and background and affected a Polish accent, though he was born and raised in London. After some years using a baton, he dispensed with it so that audiences could more readily watch his graceful hand movements, and he would sometimes turn around on the podium and talk to his audience, urging the listeners to pay special attention to a

Bet You Didn't Know

One night, during one of Reiner's five seasons at the Met, a famous singer happened to notice Reiner enjoying a late dinner and stopped by to chat. "What opera was on?" she asked. "I don't know what they did," was Reiner's twinkling comeback, "I conducted *Meistersinger*."

new piece, or scolding the Philadelphia ladies who dared to bring their knitting to his performances.

Unlike most other conductors, who were concerned first and foremost with matters of musical interpretation, Stokowski was also a master of sound. He often changed the usual seating of orchestral players on stage to enhance certain acoustical qualities, or tamper with the orchestration of masterpiece scores—doubling the brass parts in certain sections, for instance, even adding percussion parts if he felt they could add rhythmic detail. He emphasized color in his interpretations, and during his 26-year tenure as music director in Philadelphia, created the glowing string sound that not only made the orchestra famous around the world, but remained in place through the even longer (43-year) reign of his successor, Eugene Ormandy.

Stokowski was always brimming with energy and innovation. He organized the All-American Youth Orchestra in 1940, and 22 years later, at the age of 80, founded the American Symphony Orchestra, making a point of welcoming many women musicians into both ensembles. His Bach and other transcriptions rescued dozens of pieces from their neglect on dusty archive shelves, but his enthusiasm for new music never dimmed either: he conducted the American premieres of Berg's "Wozzeck", Stravinsky's "The Rite of Spring," Ives' Symphony no. 4, Schoenberg's "Gurrelieder," Varese's "Ameriques," and a host of other important works. An early champion of hi-fidelity recordings, he experimented with stereophonic sound many years before stereo records reached the market, and he even made it to the movies, starring (as himself) in "A Thousand Men and Girl," a Deanna Durbin flick that still pops up on cable every so often. "Stoki," as he was widely known, was also the only conductor in history to have an on-screen chat with Mickey Mouse (in "Fantasia").

His detractors often dismissed Stokowski as an opportunistic showman, but his magnetic presence, deep personal charm, and undeniable musical gifts gave music a new lift in

Music Word

Stereophonic. Just as looking at a landscape with both eyes gives us a sense of depth, listening to music with both ears allows us spacial awareness of the sound sources. We can tell, for instance, that the bass drum is booming on the left, while the trumpet is calling from the right side of the orchestra. The old 78 rpm recordings and many early LPs were monophonic: that is, all the sounds came from a single source. Stereophonic recordings (stereo for short), allows the distribution of sounds among left, right and center, and thus provides a far more realistic reproduction of the music at hand.

America, and indeed around the world. Francis Robinson (author, broadcaster, and long-time assistant manager of the Metropolitan Opera) may have summed it up best, when he called Stokowski "the greatest propagandist for music of his time, perhaps of all time."

Made in America

Not so long ago, American ballet dancers would Russianize their names in order to be taken seriously, and American conductors had far better luck landing major jobs in Europe than here in their own country. Through the first half of our 20th century and beyond, every one of our top American orchestras was led by European born-and-trained maestros (Stokowski and Ormandy in Philadelphia; Reiner and later Solti in Chicago; Koussevitzky, Munch, and now Ozawa in Boston; Mahler, Toscanini, Barbirolli, and Mitropoulos in New York, and so on).

All that changed with the arrival on the scene of a young man from Lawrence, Massachusetts.

The Joy of Bernstein: The Joy of Music

If you leave Avery Fisher Hall in Lincoln Center, you'll see a street sign identifying 65th Street and Broadway as Leonard Bernstein Place, a fitting tribute to the prodigiously gifted artist who gave new impetus to classical music at home and abroad. He was a superb pianist, a galvanizing television personality, a published author and poet, and an incomparable lecturer and teacher. His compositions include symphonies, opera, ballet, film scores, songs, chamber music, and many choral works, including the ecumenical Mass, and one of most frequently performed of all 20th century pieces for chorus and orchestra, the Chichester Psalms. Oh yes, in his spare time, Bernstein also wrote such Broadway classics as "On the Town," "Wonderful Town," "Candide," and "West Side Story."

It was, though, as a conductor that Leonard Bernstein first sprang to national attention. On a Sunday afternoon in 1943, a few hours before he was scheduled to lead a live broadcast

Bet You Didn't Know

Bernstein's original name was Louis, but at age 16, he officially changed it to Leonard to avoid mixups with another member of the Bernstein family. He later worked for a publisher, earning the munificent sum of $25 per week for arranging pop and novelty tunes under the name of Lenny Amber. (Bernstein being the German word for amber.)

concert with the New York Philharmonic, Bruno Walter suddenly took ill. The emergency call went out to the orchestra's recently appointed assistant conductor. There was no time for rehearsal, not even to rustle up the customary white tie and tails. So wearing a gray business suit, the 27-year-old Bernstein stepped out onto the Carnegie Hall stage to conduct the same difficult program Walter had originally scheduled. Another of those understudy-makes-good stories, the event made front-page news, and launched what Nicolas Slonimsky (author, composer, conductor, and editor of the most recent edition (1994) of *Baker's Biographical Dictionary of Musicians*) quite aptly described as "one of the most extraordinary careers in the annals of American music."

Fifteen years later, the youngest man ever to conduct the New York Philharmonic had became the orchestra's first native-born music director. Describing Bernstein's later activities would take a book (and several of them are on the market): they included heading up the conducting department at the Berkshire Music Center at Tanglewood; hosting the celebrated Young People's Concerts on television; several times presenting the complete cycle of Mahler Symphonies; and making a bit of political history as well, conducting Beethoven's Ninth Symphony on both sides of the Berlin Wall (in 1989).

With good reason, Leonard Bernstein titled one of his books *The Joy of Music*. His inexhaustible energy, enthusiasm, and passion for life bubbled through everything he did, but it was as a peerless musical communicator that he will probably be best and longest remembered.

And Then Came...

Bernstein having proved conclusively that a born-and-bred American could indeed join the ranks of the most distinguished, famous, and popular conductors in the world, our native orchestras became less wary of giving opportunities to "local" talent. Today, needless to say, Americans on the podium are familiar and welcome visitors in every part of the country.

We can go coast-to-coast, with Alan Gilbert at the helm of the New York Philharmonic, while Michael Tilson Thomas rules the symphonic roost in San Francisco. Marin Alsop is music director in Baltimore, Leonard Slatkin in Detroit, and Robert Spano balances directorships at both the Atlanta Symphony and the Aspen Music Festival. James Levine, still struggling with health issues, for long years was a beloved figure at the Metropolitan Opera, and such other podium luminaries as Lorin Maazel, Andre Previn, and John Williams are still in demand as guest conductors here and abroad. It took long enough, but American conductors have—at long last—taken their rightful places on the American scene.

PART FOUR

So Tell Me About Me About Classical Music

CHAPTER 13

Understanding Those Scary Music Terms

MUSIC WORDS

In This Chapter

➤ What is a sonata?

➤ What is a symphony?

➤ What is a concerto?

➤ What are movements?

By now, you know that a symphony means a lot of instruments. And you heard about concertos ("concerti," if you want to get fancy about it), and sonatas. But what exactly makes each one what it is? With our jiffy guide, you can get your musical form straight without having to read the tiny print on liner notes, and you can even earn brownie points by explaining everything to your friends.

Sonatamania

Moonlight, Appassionata—what evocative names those Beethoven sonatas have (even though they were bestowed by publishers, not the composer himself). Beethoven's sonatas, just like the sonatas of contemporaries, predecessors, and descendants, have a few elements in common that make them sonatas. To pinpoint those specifics precisely, though, is not always easy.

The term "sonata" came into being in the late 16th century as a way of distinguishing instrumental from vocal music: if it was played, it was a sonata; if it was sung, it was a cantata. In the days when a handful of instruments was considered a "large" ensemble, a catchall term was probably good enough, but as ensembles grew into orchestras and then symphony orchestras, things got a bit more complicated. Today, the term sonata signifies an instrumental piece, usually in several movements, for one or two (sometimes three) players. Less frequently, the term is applied to a somewhat larger group, such as the string sonatas of Rossini and Mendelssohn. In the baroque era, a very popular type of sonata had a featured string or wind instrument with keyboard accompaniment; in later periods, the two instruments assumed equal importance.

Important Things to Know

The typical baroque sonata might feature a violin or flute, with accompaniment (continuo) on harpsichord and cello. It was usually in four movements, in the scheme of slow-fast-slow-fast. The classical sonata was more a showcase for the symmetry and proportion that symbolized the era of Mozart and Haydn, and usually emerged in three movements. Early Romantics wrote sonatas in the classical style, but as composers, in true romantic fashion, became more individualistic, the form became less structured. One radical departure arrived from the progressive Liszt, who cast his B Minor Piano Sonata in one 30-minute long movement.

Find that Form

The rules of sonata form are not quite as immutable as the laws of physics, but they do regulate the musical construction normally used in the first movement of a sonata (or, indeed, a symphony, which is essentially a sonata for orchestra). In simplest terms, the sonata is divided into three parts: exposition, development, and recapitulation.

Important Things to Know

The Exposition states a primary theme in the home key of the piece, and having established its texture and harmonic setting, moves on to a second theme in a different key. The Development, as its name suggests, expands on those materials (the German word for this section translates as "working-out"), while the Recapitulation restates the original material, but brings the second as well as the first theme back into the main key, so everybody can go home happy. The Exposition, incidentally, may be preceded by a mood-setting introduction, while the Recapitulation is often followed by a coda, allowing the composer to top off the piece with a grand musical gesture.

Music Word

The **Exposition** states a primary theme in the home key of the piece, and having established its texture and harmonic setting, moves on to a second theme in a different key. The **Development**, as its name suggests, expands on those themes in new and interesting ways (the German word for this section translates as "working-out"), while the **Recapitulation** restates the original material, but brings the second as well as the first theme back into the main key,

Haydn and Mozart believed that the two themes of the exposition should be contrasted in style, instrumentation, and, as noted, key. Rather than just stopping the presentation of the first theme and starting up the second in a different key, they made the music flow naturally from one tonality to the next, or to use another fancy phrase, it modulated. The first and second themes, in other words, are linked by a transition or bridge, the second theme often followed by a musical rounding-off and reaffirmation of the new key. These features are the activating forces of the sonata.

The development section allows the basic musical ideas to be presented in many different ways. Elements of the two main themes may be juxtaposed, for instance, or transformed by rhythmic shifts or unexpected modulations. This is where composers really get to show their stuff, entertaining their audiences with originality, wit, and sometimes, sheer surprise. After all those acrobatics, it's on to the recapitulation, where the original themes, having wandered far afield, get welcomed home. If the work has a coda, anything goes: it might be a refined farewell or a rip-roaring blastoff; it can be short and sweet or turn into an elaborate, extended finish.

Bet You Didn't Know

As a young man, Johannes Brahms paid a call on Franz Liszt, who read through some of his manuscripts and was so impressed that he sat Brahms down in an easy chair and gave him a private performance of his own B Minor Sonata. When the piece ended, Liszt wondered why there was no reaction from his audience. Then he looked over at the easy chair and saw why: Brahms was fast asleep.

I Hear a Symphony

This is the big one, the one where all those strings soar, the winds blow, the brasses shine, and the timpanist bangs away at every one of those five kettledrums. In the baroque era, folks didn't mind much what they called things, so the term "symphony" was used for overtures, ensemble pieces, short instrumental movements within oratorios, etc. Starting in the classical era, though, the word meant an orchestral work of substantial size and import, and that's still how we think of symphonies today. Interestingly, the first major composers to use this modern symphonic style—namely Haydn, Mozart, Schubert, and Beethoven—still account for a huge percentage of modern symphonic performances.

In the mid-18th century, at about the time that the Mannheim Orchestra grew to its then astounding size of 40 players, the four-movement symphony became the accepted norm. Mozart and Haydn knocked out symphonies by the dozen; Beethoven limited himself to nine, but raised the form to Olympian heights. Mendelssohn, Brahms, Dvořák, Schumann, and most other romantic composers adhered to the classical four-movement form, but there's a joker in every crowd, so the expansive Berlioz added a fifth section to his Symphonie Fantastique.

Early in the 20th century, Mahler outdid Berlioz with his passionate, super-romantic symphonies, and most later composers—while realistic enough to realize that demanding huge performing forces would inevitably limit their concert opportunities—filled the old forms with fresh and invigorating new musical wines. Shostakovich, Copland, Hovhaness, and Stravinsky all have left us great symphonic legacies, and composers today are continuing where they left off.

Bigger and Better

Mozart and Haydn did very nicely with their 40-piece orchestras, and so did Beethoven at first, though always on the lookout for coloristic opportunities, he soon added trombones, piccolo, and contrabassoon, and gave the timpanist a lot more work to do. As envisioned by romantic composers like Berlioz, though, the ideal symphony would be on a large enough scale to employ more workers than an automobile factory. Mahler's Eighth Symphony is called the "Symphony of a Thousand" because it demands a huge orchestra, with chimes, celesta, glockenspiel, harmonium, organ, and a host of fanfare trumpets, not to mention vocal soloists, and large choruses of both children's and adult voices. As we were saying, a symphony is a work for full orchestra. It's just that some orchestras are fuller than others.

Bet You Didn't Know

As is so often the case, Mahler did not himself give his work its "Symphony of a Thousand" nickname, but he didn't exactly object to it either. "In this Symphony," he said modestly, "the whole universe begins to sound in musical tones; it is no longer human voices, but planets and suns that are in motion here."

Important Things to Know

As the Classical symphony took on its characteristic structure, the opening movement was normally in sonata form, as described above. Then came a slow movement; next a lighter and livelier third movement (often a minuet, or its offspring, the scherzo, about which more in a moment); and finally, what else: a finale, normally the most robust and peppiest movement of the bunch. Sometimes composers inverted the order of the slow movement and the minuet or scherzo. Who knows? Maybe they just wanted to see if anybody was paying attention.

The slower pace of the second movement provided a good contrast with the first, and often contained some of the composer's most beautiful, lyric expressions. It could be in a modification of sonata form (perhaps without the development section), or just conceived as a lovely song, or possibly cast in the form of theme and variations, where a tune is embellished, transformed and otherwise taken to new heights of melodic or rhythmic glory.

Momentous Movements

The minuet was pretty well stuck in 3/4 time, given the dance origins of the movement, but in between the main section and its repetition came a new segment in a contrasting mood (called a Trio, because in the earliest days it was traditionally written for only three instruments). Beethoven, hardly the dainty minuet type, preferred the more vigorous scherzo (the Italian word means "joke"), which nonetheless stays pretty close to the form of Minuet and Trio, and normally stays in 3/4 time as well. Later composers refused to be bound by even those loose rules, and would substitute other forms as their third movements, a waltz, for example, or a march.

The last movement occasionally returns to sonata form, but far more often takes the more buoyant form of the rondo (which we will explain eventually. We promise).

The romantics embellished symphonic form, the better to evoke specific moods, pictures or passions. Even the basically conservative Brahms, who pretty much followed the Classical style, added innovative links between and within movements; other composers let themes (or parts of themes) from the first movement swirl through the later portions of the symphony as well. As noted earlier, most of the great 20th century composers, the list including Sibelius, Ives, Prokofiev, and Vaughan Williams, continued to pour their symphonic thoughts into some form of this traditional mold.

Concertomania

As late as the 17th century, the word concerto was sometimes applied to ensemble music for voices and instruments, but for all practical purposes, you can assume it means a composition for one or more soloists and orchestra. A favorite baroque form was the concerto grosso (literally "grand concerto"), where a group of instruments within the larger ensemble made up the solo contingent, but solo concertos for a single featured instrument were in use as well. Then, as in every succeeding musical period, the violin and keyboard were most frequently the solo instruments of choice, with the cello, trumpet, flute, and others rather distant runners-up.

Music Word

Concerto. A concerto is an extended work for one or more solo instruments and orchestra, usually in three movements. Sometimes composers use that designation for purely orchestral pieces when various individual instruments have opportunities to stand apart from the larger symphonic ensemble.

As always, there are rule-breaking concertos that range from a single movement up to four or five, but the great majority settle happily for three: the first usually being the longest and most dramatic, the centerpiece the slowest and most expressive, the finale the shortest and jolliest. Soloist and orchestra normally share the important themes, though the soloist is expected to demonstrate his or her virtuosity with strenuous passagework and other demanding flights of instrumental fancy. When the orchestra puts down its instruments and the soloist goes it alone (most often just before the end of the first movement, but sometimes before the conclusion of the second also), we're in a cadenza, the showoff vehicle par excellence, where the featured player can demonstrate his or her brilliant technique without interference from the conductor or anybody else.

Liszt, Brahms, and other icons of the romantic age, by giving greater emphasis to the symphonic elements in their scores, began converting the concerto from its original concept of solo with orchestra into something more aptly described as solo vs. orchestra. Instruments other than the featured one would be given extended solo passages, sometimes entire sections of the orchestra rose up as if to challenge the supremacy of the soloist. Pieces like Franck's Symphonic Variations and Prokofiev's Sinfonia Concertante—both of which are actually concertos in disguise, respectively for piano and cello—indicate another way in which concertos have gravitated towards a more equal division of musical labors.

Doubling Up

Bet You Didn't Know

Brahms' D Minor Piano Concerto so startled audiences that it was a total flop at its first couple of performances. "At its conclusion," the composer wrote to his friend Joachim, "three pairs of hands were brought together very slowly in applause, whereupon a perfect storm of hissing from all sides forbade any such further demonstration." Nearly 40 years later, a London critic still found the piece hard to take, conceding only that it was "distinctly less abominable than Brahms' other one" (the B-flat Piano Concerto).

Once past the baroque concerto grosso, the concerto normally pits a single soloist against the orchestral horde. Many composers, though, possibly wanting to even the odds a bit, have put two or three virtuosos into the solo spotlight. Bach composed a concerto for two violins, Mozart one for flute and harp; Mendelssohn wrote one (in fact two) concertos for two pianos, as the 20th century did Poulenc, Milhaud, and Walter Piston. In our own century, Brahms' radiant Double Concerto pairs violin and cello; the Beethoven triple brings together violin, cello and piano; and Schumann wrote a piece for four horns and orchestra. Other intriguing combinations worth searching out are the Shostakovich Piano Concerto no. 1, with its featured role for solo trumpet, and Samuel Barber's Capricorn Concerto for flute, oboe, trumpet, and strings.

Meet the Movements

Here are some of the forms you'll likely to run into in sonatas or symphonies.

Just a Minuet

Minuetto is how you say minuet in Italian, but since the dance is of French origin, we might as well stick with the word as we know in the good old USA. It's a dance in modern triple meter that gained favor at the court of Louis XIV, and until the late 18th century was popular with most of the European aristocracy. Lully was famous for introducing minuets into his operas and ballets, and the dance soon became a staple of baroque suites. The Italian minuet (sorry, minuetto), was often faster than its French counterpart. Interestingly, even as so many others of the old dance forms faded, the minuet not only survived but was transformed by Haydn and Mozart into an integral part of the classical symphony.

Music Word

Minuet is a dance in triple time that graduated from its rustic French beginnings to become a fashionable and highly popular dance at most 18th century European courts. Its form is A-A-B-A: a first section, which is repeated; a contrasting section (the Trio), and a return to the original.

Bet You Didn't Know

Louis XIV not only liked ballets, he used to dance in them, wearing pink tights, silk stockings, high heels, and big hats with ostrich plumes. That's our kind of king.

Scampering Scherzos

As we mentioned earlier, scherzo means "joke" in Italian, and the term came into use in the early 17th century to describe light madrigals. Later it was applied to movements that were faster or more robust than the delicate minuet, and Beethoven firmly established the scherzo as the preferred alternate in symphonies, sonatas, and chamber music. Eventually composers began writing scherzos as independent pieces, famous examples including Chopin's four piano works of that title, and Paul Dukas' "Sorcerer's Apprentice" (remember Mickey Mouse's battle with the water buckets in "Fantasia"?), which is officially listed as a symphonic scherzo.

Music Word

A **Divertimento** (from the Italian for "amusement") refers to a not overly serious work, usually cast in a number of short movements, and intended for performance by a smallish instrumental ensemble.

The term **Serenade** derives from "Sera", the Italian word for evening, and Serenata, which therefore is an evening song. Think of a lovelorn swain proclaiming his eternal devotion beneath his fair maiden's window. Later the word came to signify any sort of light entertainment music, like the Divertimento, usually scored for a small instrumental ensemble, but often specifically intended for open-air performance.

Various Variations

Variety is the spice of life, they say, and Nicolas Slonimsky dubbed variations "the sweet adornments of melody." In its simplest form, a theme is stated, then embellished with added figurations or otherwise altered in shape, rhythm, or texture. Mozart was a master of the form, employing it in concertos, divertimentos, serenades, and sometimes in his string quartets and piano sonatas. Beethoven was also an inveterate variation man (his output in the form including several sets based on Mozart themes), and composers of each succeeding generation have swiped everything from folk tunes to opera arias as grist for their own musical mills.

Bet You Didn't Know

In most cases, variations get more and more complicated as the work goes along, but the French composer Vincent d'Indy worked backwards in his "Istar Variations." The music describes a Babylonian goddess who passes through seven gates, depositing one of her garments at each stop. Thus the texture becomes lighter as the work progresses, and the actual theme on which the variations are built emerges only at the very end, as Istar stands nude at the seventh gate. Unfortunately, Walt Disney didn't include that one in "Fantasia."

A Round of Rondos

Thought we were going to forget rondo, didn't you? Never. The last movement of a composition is often cast as a rondo (from the French "rondeau" or round), an apt designation since the primary theme keeps coming round again and again. The form can be outlined as A-B-A-C-A, with the B and C sections (and those of as many subsequent letters as the composer chooses) providing materials other than those contained in the first tune, and usually cast in different keys for further variety. What gives the rondo its special delight is that each time the A section rolls around again and the now-familiar melody returns, the listener gets a feeling of comfortable recognition—sort of like coming back to your own neighborhood after a walk in the woods, or greeting an old friend after new introductions at a party.

How do you round off a rondo? Read on…

Coda: This Is the End

Coda is Italian for tail, and that's exactly what it is in music: a kind of appendage that's not a necessary part of the structure, but rounds it off, brings it to a more satisfying conclusion. Like this little section of the chapter. Or a Warner Brothers cartoon. After all, Elmer Fudd has chased Bugs Bunny all over the landscape, only to find that the pesky wabbit has outfoxed him again, so officially, that's it. The story is over, the picture is finished, but what really puts the exclamation point on the comedy? Porky Pig's "th…th…that's all folks!"

And with Porky's short tail bringing this long tale to its full finish, you may now stride off into the sunset in full confidence that you're up to speed with concert lingo, and ready to meet the composers whose genius made you want to explore classical music in the first place. Happy listening (and reading)!

CHAPTER 14

Go for Baroque

In This Chapter

➤ The most famous baroque composers

➤ The music of Bach

➤ Handel, Vivaldi, and Purcell

➤ Scarlatti and Telemann

The baroque period in music, usually reckoned as 1600 (a number probably chosen because it's easy to recall and round) to 1750 (the death of Bach) covers a very impressive historical era. It marked the Age of Reason in philosophy and science. It was the time of Rembrandt and El Greco in painting; Milton, Swift, and Molière in literature. In England, the Tudors gave way to the Restoration, and across the Atlantic, the American colonies were growing and thriving.

Important Things to Know

The Baroque period was an age of expansion, and no way could music remain unaffected. New instruments emerged and instrumental music took on an importance equal to vocal. Lovers of singing had to do something to keep up, and they did—they created opera. The texture of music grew more ornate and embellished; its structure became more formal. The world had entered a new age.

New Forms

With the rise of instrumental music, came new frameworks in which it could flourish; instrumental counterparts to motets and madrigals emerged, and the stirrings of what would eventually become the symphony.

Concerto Grosso

Most of those performing groups were comparatively small, sometimes with only one instrument per part; when you hear a concerto grosso today, it is often played on modern instruments in a large orchestra. This increases the musical drama while decreasing authenticity of presentation in approximately equal measure. Which is preferable? The debate rages on; this is Sinfonia.

Music, Music

Like a suite of rooms, a musical suite refers to an ordered set of pieces that come together to form a new entity, the word probably coming from the French, meaning "following." The character and purpose of the suite changed dramatically in the 19th century, but we'll worry about that in a later chapter.

Important Things to Know

As we discussed in Chapter 12, the emergence of the violin as the instrumental king of the strings was due in no small measure to the amazing work of Amity, Garner, Stradivarius.

Improved Violin and Other Strings

A number of folk instruments are credited with being the ancestors of the violin, among them the Arabic rabab, which turned into the rebec when it arrived in Western Europe, and was often called the fiddle in England (without any of the slightly snide connotations the term later acquired). A more sophisticated branch of the bowed string family included many sizes of viols, and were in use until the 1700s, at which point the more pliant and expressive violins and violas.

Bach: Just Your Average Genius

Robert Schumann once said that "music owes as much to Bach as religion to its founder," going on to add that "We are all bunglers next to him." Beethoven played several pieces from Bach's Well-Tempered Clavier; Chopin knew all 48 preludes and fugues by heart. Mozart made string transcriptions of Bach pieces and wrote to his father that he had finally found music with something to teach him. Perhaps Berlioz summed it up best when he wrote to a friend that "Bach is Bach, just as God is God."

Back on earth, though, Bach (1685-1750) was just like everybody else. He had to kiss up to his bosses to hold a job, got in constant trouble with the authorities, and when he wasn't turning out cantatas (more than 400 of them), he was producing children—at least 20 of them (although 13 of them died in infancy). Four of his offspring became renowned composers themselves—William Friedemann, Carl Philipp Emanuel, Johann Christoph Friedrich, and Johann Christian—and the list of Bach progeny was extended once again in our own day, when the ingenious musical mind of Peter Schickele cooked up the hilariously fictional P.D.Q. Bach, the last and least of the famous Bach clan.

For five generations, the Bachs had been musicians, so it's no wonder that Johann Sebastian followed suit.

Although his father taught him the violin as soon as the lad was big enough to hold one, Johann Sebastian also learned to sing and to play the organ, harpsichord, and every other keyboard instrument he could get his hands on. One of his first jobs was as a church organist and choirmaster in Arnstadt, but he was forever in trouble with the town fathers who kept complaining about everything from

Bach's playing "unseemly" variations on the organ while the congregation was singing its chorales to allowing "a stranger maiden" up in the organ loft with him. That was no lady, that was his cousin, Bach said, and to prove the point, he quit his job and married her.

He got his next post as organist in the town of Mulhausen by agreeing to avoid "all unseemly society and suspicious company," but that got pretty dull, so he moved on to Weimar, where he stayed for nine years, writing his organ toccatas, chorales, and fugues. When another musician was promoted over him, Bach raised such a fuss that he was tossed out on his ear. You can't fire me, said Bach, I quit, whereupon he was hauled up on charges of "too obstinately forcing the issue of his dismissal" and tossed into the local jail for a month.

Music Word

Toccata, from the Italian meaning to strike or touch, usually refers to a piece that takes advantage of the clarity inherent in keyboard instruments, while also serving as a showcase for the performer's virtuosity. In the 16th century, the term was often used to indicate an improvisational prelude before the central section of a piece, but by the 17th, it applied to any sort of short keyboard composition in rapid tempo and brilliant sound.

Chorale, from the Latin "choralis", or belonging to the chorus, refers to a type of hymn-tune for congregational use in the Lutheran Church, many of them written or adapted by Martin Luther himself for singing in Protestant services. Eventually these vocal works were used as the basis of instrumental compositions, reaching their highest form in the hands of Bach, who harmonized hundreds of these melodies, and composed many more.

Fortunately, Bach's reputation was already well-established, so he was soon out of the hoosegow and into the position of Kapellmeister to Prince Leopold of Anhalt-Cothen, where the salary was higher, the food better, and the court lacked only one rather important ingredient for the best organ virtuoso in Germany: a decent organ. Oh well, waste not, want not: the Prince did have some good harpsichords around the palace, and he also maintained a presentable orchestra, so Bach switched instrumental courses and started writing harpsichord pieces and all sorts of larger ensemble works, among them the Orchestral Suites, the two violin concertos, and the famous Brandenburg Concertos.

On the other hand, the Calvinism of the court at Anhalt-Cothen rendered unnecessary all but the simplest hymn tunes, and eventually the greatest composer in the history of sacred music couldn't stand it any more. Besides, when the Prince married a lady who didn't like music at all, Bach could see the handwriting on the castle wall. Since the music director at St. Thomas Church in Leipzig had just died, Bach applied for the post (auditioning for it, so the legend goes, by writing the St. John Passion). The elders really wanted Telemann (see below) for the job, but when he turned it down, they grudgingly gave the nod to the 38-year-old Bach, who soon moved to the city where he would remain, and the position he would hold, for the rest of his life.

Not that Bach had it easy there. In addition to turning out cantatas at the drop of a church holiday, he had to act as a kind of dormitory master for the 70 boys at the church school, teach them Latin, and train them for emergency musical service in his choirs and orchestras. The regular orchestra contained a motley crew of town bandsmen, with only a couple of fiddlers amongst the trumpets and oboes, so drastic measures were necessary. "Discretion deters me," Bach told the town council, "from revealing anything near the truth as to their quality and musical knowledge."

Bet You Didn't Know

Poor Bach had problems with good climate in Leipzig, since it kept people from getting sick, and a lot of his free-lance income came in from playing funerals. "Last year," he wrote to a friend, "a healthy wind blew and I lost fees that would ordinarily come in from funerals to an amount of more than 100 thaler" (about one-seventh of his annual income). Bach also had to deal with the high cost of living in Leipzig. So what else is new?

Nonetheless, Bach stuck it out, continuing to compose some of the most glorious music ever to come from quill to paper. In an ironic twist, the works of this towering musical genius all but disappeared from public view following his death in 1750. Other composers continued to admire and study Bach, but not until the young Felix Mendelssohn revived the "Passion According to St. Matthew" did music lovers at large begin to realize the storehouse of greatness that is Bach's unique legacy to us all.

Bach's Works You Need to Know

Almost everything Bach wrote is worthy of high attention, so where do we begin? Perhaps with the Brandenburg Concertos, those six magical works that were never performed during

Music Word

Counterpoint, from the Latin "punctum contra punctum" (meaning point against point) is the simultaneous combination of two or more melodies in such a way as to make a satisfying musical unity.

Bach's lifetime, but which are now an indelible part of our concert life. Each has its own special instrumental timbre: no. 2, for instance, has solo parts for flute, violin, oboe, and high trumpets; no. 3 is for strings alone; no. 5 features the harpsichord, and so forth.

Then try the two violin concertos and the Concerto for Two Violins; take an international sampling of keyboard pieces with the French and English Suites and the Italian Concerto. Listen to the six great sonatas and partitas for violin alone (the D Minor Partita contains the famous "Chaconne," one of the supreme achievements of the string repertoire).

On the vocal scene, take a few hours off and be inspired by the B Minor Mass; or for lighter listening, sip a bit of the Coffee Cantata. Bach was justly renowned for his mastery of counterpoint, but if you seek gorgeous melody, pure and simple, try "Sheep May Safely Graze" or "Jesu, Joy of Man's Desiring," the latter providing a spiritual uplift into the bargain. As Mendelssohn put it so feelingly, "when anything of Bach's has been once heard, it will be easy to discover that it is beautiful and to hear it again; the only difficulty is the beginning."

Handel: Royal Flush

Beethoven, not generally known for considering other mortals his equal, let alone his superior, called George Frederic Handel (1685-1759) "the greatest of us all." Not bad for the son of a valet and sometime barber at court. The first time Handel packed up and left his native Germany, he headed for the sunnier climes of Italy, where he stayed for more than three years, composing secular cantatas in Florence, displaying his abilities as a virtuoso organist in Rome, and learning to write Italian-style operas in Venice.

Returning to Germany, he became Kapellmeister to the Elector of Hannover, but his heart (and quite often his body) was in London, which he visited on several occasions, and where his music was received with great enthusiasm. An amazing event settled Handel's dilemma: For reasons too complicated to explain here, the Elector became King George I of England, and Handel followed him, bag, baggage, and music paper, to live happily ever after in London. The new king, delighted to have somebody he could still speak German to, lavished a good salary and many other favors on the delighted composer; Handel, in turn, wrote the famous Water Music Suite so King George could barge up the Thames in high style.

After that, composer George and King George got along swimmingly, and when George II came along, Handel protected his investment by writing four coronation anthems. All the while, he was producing enormously popular (and financially rewarding) operas to Italian texts, and when public interest in them began to wane, he turned to writing the oratorios that elevated him into the pantheon of musical giants.

Much of Handel's music was intended for the stage, so it has an outgoing quality, perhaps a little more accessible, less demanding, than that of Bach. Some experts characterize Bach as the introvert, Handel the extrovert; Bach may have had a sense of humor, but we know Handel did, even when he was the target. Once when a friend was complaining about the terrible piece he had heard at Vauxhall Gardens, Handel answered, "You are right, sir, it is very poor stuff. I thought so myself when I wrote it."

Perhaps the crowning achievement of Handel's life—certainly the work by which he is most often represented today—is Messiah," an oratorio he wrote in the incredible short span of 24 days. We've all heard the great "Hallelujah Chorus"; Handel said that when he wrote it, "I saw all heaven before me, and the great God Himself."

Handel conducted many more performances of the oratorio in the remaining 17 years of his life, and his last public appearance—just a week a day before he died—was at yet another Messiah in London. As befitting an English hero, Handel was buried in Westminster Abbey.

Bet You Didn't Know

When "Messiah" was premiered in Dublin, there was such a crush for tickets that the ladies were asked to wear skirts without hoops and the gentlemen to leave their swords behind so that more people could fit into the hall. At the London premiere a year later, King George rose to his feet during the performance of the "Hallelujah Chorus," prompting the rest of the listeners to follow suit and establishing the tradition of standing during this most thrilling of

Handel's Works You Need to Know

"Messiah," of course, is an annual treat at Christmas and Easter, but a joy at any time of year. Then get further Bible lessons from a few other inspiring oratorios, such as "Saul," "Judas Maccabaeus," and "Israel in Egypt." For shorter samplings of Handel's choral writing, there are the chandos and the coronation anthems.

History has not dealt too kindly with Handel's Italian operas, so even though quite a few of them have been recorded, you might get a more comfortable sense of his Italianate leanings from the two great sets of Concerti Grossi (opus 3 and 6). He followed the lead of Corelli and Vivaldi here, yet gave the music his own special stamp of energy and good cheer.

Right behind Messiah in popularity are his two kingly commissions, the Water Music and Royal Fireworks Music, both of them bright, energetic and—at this point in time—encouragingly familiar.

Other instrumental pieces you'll enjoy are the regal "Arrival of the Queen of Sheba" and the attractive keyboard suites, especially the one dubbed (not by Handel, though) "The Harmonious Blacksmith."

Want more? There's the charming harp concerto, the frisky D Major Harpsichord Concerto (though you may prefer it in one of the many piano recordings), and if you like the king of instruments, try a few of Handel's 16 concertos for organ and orchestra.

Vivaldi: The Red Priest

Antonio Vivaldi (1678-1741) was a fully ordained clergyman whose red hair earned him the nickname of "The Red Priest," but he soon gave up the ministry for music (rumor had it that he'd stop right in the middle of a service if he thought of a good tune and wanted to write it down fast). Vivaldi's music is noted for its clarity, color, and energetic rhythms, and boy is there a lot of it. Off and on for more than 35 years, Vivaldi was music master at a school for orphan girls in Venice, and the opportunity to compose pieces for all manner of unorthodox instrumental combinations obviously appealed to his experimental nature.

Soon Vivaldi became the undisputed concerto champion of the world. You name it, he wrote a concerto for it. He wrote flute concertos and oboe concertos and cello concertos; he tossed off concertos for mandolin, clavier, piccolo, and guitar. He left nearly 40 bassoon concertos (he also wrote 40 operas, but that was in his spare time), and for his own instrument—the

Bet You Didn't Know

Concerts at the orphanage where Vivaldi worked became quite a fashionable event for the eligible bachelors (even a few ineligible ones) of Venice. "I vow to you," wrote one smitten listener, "that there is nothing so diverting as a sight of a young and pretty nun in a white habit, with a bunch of pomegranate blossoms over her ear, conducting the orchestra with all the grace and precision imaginable."

violin—the concerto total is up in the hundreds. When he got tired of the regular garden variety, Vivaldi came up with double, triple, and even quadruple concertos, usually issuing them in groups of 6 or 12 to help with the bookkeeping.

This is also true of his most popular work, "The Four Seasons," which if you look closely, turns out to be separate violin concertos, the first four of the dozen in Vivaldi's opus 8. It's hard to escape "The Four Seasons" nowadays: you'll find in playing in coffee bars, in elevators, it even served as the background score and gave the title to the popular film

Important Things to Know

It was his series of twelve Concerti Grossi, published in 1712 as his Opus 3, that first established Vivaldi's fame. Bach was so impressed by the set that he proceeded to arrange half of them for other instruments. Vivaldi also had a passion for affixing picturesque subtitles to his works, but even when something went by the name of "The Hunt," "Storm at Sea," or "The Bullfinch," like as not it was a concerto anyway.

starring Alan Alda. Listen carefully, though, and you'll find it a marvelous example of descriptive music, with clever images of twittering birds, burbling brooks, snoozing shepherds, chattering teeth, horses at the hunt and pelting hailstorms (not necessarily in that order).

Vivaldi's Works You Need to Know

It's hardly surprising—given his incredibly prolific output—that many Vivaldi pieces sound like many other Vivaldi pieces, so for the same money, start with "The Four Seasons." Thereafter, make your concerto choices by your instrumental preferences, or take the easy way out and get one of the many recordings devoted to "Concertos for Diverse Instruments."

Vivaldi's most popular choral work is the brilliant Gloria in D, and if that whets your vocal appetite, go on to his many other sacred works, including a pair of magnificats and several lovely settings of Biblical psalms.

Music Word

The , named for the first word of the canticle of the Blessed Virgin Mary ("Magnificat anima mea Dominum", Luke 1:46-55), is the most important hymn of the Vespers service in Roman Catholic liturgy. In Anglican churches, the Magnificat is part of the evening prayer, using the English words "My soul doth magnify the Lord." Through the centuries, many composers have written Magnificats as separate choral pieces.

Purcell: Get Him to the Church on Time

Although Henry Purcell (1659-1695) is today recognized as one of the greatest native-born English composers, his star has been overshadowed by Handel, who lived twice as long and had infinitely more commercial success in London. Purcell wrote six operas to Handel's nearly 40, spending much of his compositional time on shorter pieces: incidental music for plays, sacred songs and anthems, and a group of fantasias for strings.

Bet You Didn't Know

Some of the stage plays that benefitted from Purcell's songs and other incidental music sound like pips: the list includes The Wives' Excuse or Cuckolds Make Themselves, The Married Beau, Innocent Adultery, and The Virtuous Wife or Good Luck at Last.

Holder of a number of positions at court and church—among them, Keeper of the King's Instruments and organist at Westminster Abbey—Purcell paid his courtly debt by writing coronation anthems, royal birthday odes, and welcome songs, even a funeral anthem for Queen Mary that, ironically, was sung at Purcell's own funeral later that same year. The story goes, by the way, that Purcell's early death (at age 36) was indirectly the result of a domestic battle. Mrs. P, annoyed at her husband's penchant for staying out late at the local tavern, locked the door at midnight and ordered the servants not to admit the wayward composer. Forced to stay outside in the pouring rain all through the night, Purcell caught the cold from which he never recovered.

If his wife failed to appreciate Purcell's independent spirit, his countrymen held his achievements in the highest regard. He was buried in Westminster Abbey, where a plaque over his grave in the north aisle reads "Here lyes Henry Purcell, Esq., who left this Lyfe and is gone to that Blessed Place where only his Harmony can be exceeded."

Purcell's Works You Need to Know

Purcell's "Dido and Aenaes" is usually listed as the first great English opera, but you can find many shorter examples of his vocal artistry in collections of songs, the two Odes to St. Cecilia's Day, and the two works the composer dubbed "semi-operas," "King Arthur" and "The Fairy Queen."

Instrumental suites have been derived from many of these works, plus those he wrote for theatrical dramas, and from there by all means proceed to the lively Trumpet Sonata in D, several harpsichord suites and lots of other chamber music.

Scarlatti: The Keyboard King

Domenico Scarlatti (1685-1757) came by his musical instincts naturally. His father, Alessandro Scarlatti (1660-1725), was even more famous in his era and did for vocal music what his son would do for the keyboard sonata, namely turn them out by the hundreds. Papa's list includes 20 oratorios, 50 motets, 100 operas, 200 masses, 600 cantatas…well, you get the idea.

Domenico started out meekly following in his father's musical footsteps, playing organ at the Royal Chapel in Naples where Alessandro was music director, and composing operas. His passion for the keyboard soon overwhelmed everything else, though, and it was not long before he was being hailed as a supreme virtuoso. When Domenico met Handel in Rome, the two men engaged in a friendly performance duel, Scarlatti apparently carrying off the harpsichord honors while Handel reigned supreme at the organ.

Bet You Didn't Know

Another version of the story puts the first Scarlatti-Handel meeting in Venice, and the circumstance a masquerade party at which a man in a black mask was improvising at the harpsichord. Among the listeners was the 21-year-old Scarlatti, who marveling at the unknown player's astonishing virtuosity and musical insights, said out loud, "This must either be the Devil himself, or that famous Saxon." It was the latter, of course, and from that day forward, the flattered Handel and the admiring Scarlatti became friends for life.

Meanwhile, Scarlatti became music director to the Portuguese ambassador to the Holy See in Rome, and by 1724, he had moved to the Lisbon court, where his duties included teaching the king's daughter, the Infanta Maria Barbara. When Maria married the Spanish Crown Prince Fernando five years later, she brought Scarlatti with her to Seville, where the composer spent the rest of his life in contented service to the royal family.

Bet You Didn't Know

Scarlatti became so associated with the musical life of his adopted country that some publishers decided to make his name more Spanish as well: they printed his pieces under the name of Domingo Escarlatti.

Speaking of contentment, on a visit to Italy, Scarlatti met and married Maria Caterina Gentili, with whom he had five children; later he wed Anastasia Zimenes of Cadiz, bringing his offspring total up to nine. None of them, however, pursued a career in music.

Scarlatti's fame rests securely on his brilliant keyboard sonatas, many of which were originally entitled "Essercizi." Needless to say, these are "exercises" only in the sense that Chopin's Études are study pieces: They do indeed pose formidable technical difficulties, but it is their depth of musical content and expression that have given them eternal life. Scarlatti wrote more than 500 of these dazzling sonatas, obtaining novel and often striking effects by such innovative techniques as frequent crossing of hands, repeated-note figures, and other types of embellishments. Add to this mix daring modulations and dissonant (for that era) harmonies, and you have some of the most creative, original, and compelling works in the keyboard repertoire.

Scarlatti's Works You Need to Know

If you insist, there are several recordings of Scarlatti's "Stabat Mater" and a clutch of Cantatas, but for all practical purposes, your Scarlatti sessions can begin and end with the sonatas. Purists prefer to hear them on the harpsichord, but Queen Maria Barbara is known to have pianos at her Spanish court, so quite possibly Scarlatti conceived some of them for the more modern keyboard. In any event, there are dozens of recordings on both instruments and if you crave further sonic variety, you'll find that quite a few of the Sonatas have been transcribed for (and sound exceedingly well on) the guitar.

Telemann: Fastest Pen in the West

Georg Philipp Telemann (1681-1767) started composing at the age of 10, and thereafter wrote music as if there were no tomorrow. Since he wound up having an unusually large numbers of tomorrows after all (he died at the ripe old age of 86), he quite possibly produced a greater bulk of pieces than any composer before or since.

Handel said that Telemann could produce an eight-part motet as easily as anybody else could write a letter, and Georg Philipp himself was quoted as saying that "a proper composer should be able to set a placard to music." He churned out operas and oratorios by the dozen, chamber pieces by the hundreds, cantatas and songs by the thousands. He wrote installation music for clergymen, captain's music for the seafaring community, and table music for the Hamburg aristocracy. Telemann was the first composer to produce cantatas for every Sunday in the year, and in his spare time he wrote poetry, engraved scores, published a method book for harpsichordists, and completed his autobiography.

Bet You Didn't Know

When he wasn't producing music, Telemann was creating children. His wife gave birth to eight sons and two daughters before thinking better of the whole deal and running off with a Swedish army officer.

Telemann acquired huge favor during his lifetime, and while some contemporaries regarded him as a radical, it is precisely his fresh and imaginative ideas that make his works so highly attractive to modern ears. As Nicolas Slonimsky puts it, "While Telemann never approached the genius of Bach and Handel, he nevertheless became an exemplar of the German Baroque at its grandest development."

Telemann's Works You Need to Know

How many hours do you have? Some of Telemann's vocal music has made its way to CD (you'll find a bunch of cantatas, a magnificat, and even a Messiah on the list), but perhaps start instrumentally with the popular "Suite in A Minor for Flute and Strings," many other artists. Another great piece is the "Don Quichotte Suite," with its humorously pictorial account of the Man of la Mancha and his faithful Sancho Panza. It can't match the descriptive power of Richard Strauss' "Don Quixote" (after all, Strauss got to use a wind machine, while Telemann had to make do with a rush of 16th notes), but it's a lively and likable portrait nonetheless.

On the concerto front, take your pick amongst those for oboe, horn, trumpet, recorder, viola, and violin; if you want to double up, browse through the two-violas and two-horn concertos; for a triple play, there's the "Concerto for Three Violins"—and upping the numerical ante yet again—the "Concerto for Three Trumpets, Two Oboes and Orchestra."

There's an endless fount of chamber music too, so don't get us started.

Postscripts

If you find that you've developed a real taste for the baroque, look for music by some of the other composers of the era, ranging from Albinoni to Zelenka. We've already talked about Tartini and Corelli in an earlier chapter; you'll also find much to enjoy in Sammartini's vigorous Harpsichord Concerto, the charming Sonatas for Guitar, Cello and Harpsichord by Geminiani, Torelli's exciting Concertos for One and Two Trumpets. Look for music by the Marcello boys, including Alessandro's lilting Oboe Concerto and the elegant Flute and Cello Sonatas by brother Benedetto, and if you need a lift at holiday time, ease into Manfredini's warm-hearted Christmas Concerto.

 # Roll Over, Beethoven: The Classical Composers

In This Chapter

➤ Most famous classical composers

➤ The music of Haydn

➤ Mozart and Beethoven

➤ Weber and Schubert

The classical era is usually reckoned from 1760 to 1820, though don't take those numbers too seriously. There were composers well beyond the first date who refused to give up the baroque ghost, and some well before the latter year who were already pounding at the romantic gates. Basically, the major stylistic difference between the baroque and classical era was the latter's focus on purity, simplicity, and formal elegance. In the baroque, ornamentation and embellishment were an integral part of both composition and performance, singers and players not only allowed, but expected to improvise upon and embroider the written parts. Beethoven, on the other hand, would not have been amused had a singer added an extra roulade or two in the Ninth Symphony.

Even though if you may still look on classical music as an impenetrable forest, you may have climbed more of the trees than you realize. You know about Beethoven, if only because Beatles experts tell us you can hear the "Moonlight Sonata" backwards in the song "Because" off their "Abbey Road" album, and you like that big shaggy dog in the "Beethoven" movies. You know Mozart if you saw the play "Amadeus", saw the movie "Elvira Madigan" or watched the final episode of "Mash". Well, in this chapter you'll find out about these and other mighty men of music, along with some of the foibles and frailties that made them human, just like us.

The dual phenomena of an expanding orchestra and a growing bourgeoisie created a demand for new listening arenas. Not everyone could wangle an invitation to court, so public concert rooms sprang up, and then larger halls, since the rapid improvement in instrument technology had made it possible to generate the carrying power needed to let the sounds of music fill these new larger spaces.

New Instruments

The classical orchestra more than tripled in size from the 18-piece ensembles Bach worked with. With 60-member orchestras came larger performance spaces, and with the larger halls came the need for more powerful instruments.

Recorder to Flute

During the Renaissance, the recorder, with its sweet but tiny tone, was rarely used in any sort of soloistic fashion, but that changed in the baroque, where Vivaldi wrote concertos for the recorder (of course he wrote concertos for everything he could find), Telemann used them in a number of chamber pieces, and Bach gave them prominence in two of the six Brandenburg Concertos.

During the Classical era, Parisian craftsmen developed the recorder into the transverse flute, so-called because the player held the instrument sideways instead of vertically. By the end of 18th century, the flute's technical superiority and greater carrying power made it the high woodwind instrument of choice.

Natural to Valved Instruments

Most of the other orchestral wind and brass instruments underwent comparable reconstructions around this time. By the middle of the 17th century, for instance, the so-called natural horn was an impressive 16 feet of coiled brass, great for signalling the hunt, but not of much use in more expressive music. The addition of rotary and piston valves refined the sound and simplified the process of playing in different keys, making the horn a welcome addition to the symphonic assemblage.

Creating wind instruments by poking holes in tubes of wood was an ancient invention, but the addition of valves and keys similarly marked giant steps forward in the technical proficiency of the oboe, trumpet, flute, and bassoon. Their added power also permitted more virtuosic displays when they took center stage in solo concertos.

Harpsichord to Piano

The harpsichord was another instrument whose limited power and dynamically inflexible range needed serious renovation if it was to be heard in large concert halls instead of courtly drawing rooms. Enter the pianoforte, whose very name (from the Italian for soft-loud) indicated one of its primary advantages over the harpsichord. The strings of the pianoforte were struck by hammers instead of being plucked by quills, so the player could control the quality as well as the volume of sound. This greater capacity for expression was seized upon by many composers, notably Haydn, Mozart, and Beethoven, whose explosive nature could in no way be fit within the narrow sonic confines of the harpsichord.

Symphony Rules the Roost

As orchestras grew larger, even the Hall of Mirrors at Versailles may have seemed a bit cramped. Besides, don't forget that during the Classical era, royalty was not-so-politely asked to leave Versailles by angry citizens demanding their rights. In France and all over Europe, the old order was changing rapidly, and music followed suit, moving well beyond the exclusive domain of court and church. Most composers still had to find royal patrons to underwrite their creative work (Mozart was the first freelancer, and look what happened to him), but middle-class listeners were beginning to discover the joys of concert-going, and larger audiences clamored for larger performing forces. Like rock and roll two centuries later, the Classical symphony burst on the scene and became the ultimate success story of the era.

Composers Wrote a Lot of Them

Before Beethoven, composers were happy to toss off symphonies at the drop of a royal command. A Symphony just didn't seem like such a big deal. Haydn wrote 104 of them, Mozart, even in his short life span, 41. After Beethoven came forward with his mighty nine, though, the whole form seemed to take on a new seriousness of purpose, and later composers were less ready to use it for anything less than their most weighty musical statements. Brahms and Schumann called it symphonic quits at four, Tchaikovsky at six. Even when totals grew larger, many composers felt intimidated by the very thought of seeming to out-produce Beethoven: Schubert and Dvořák stopped at 9, and Mahler learned a lesson when he started on #10: he died, leaving the work unfinished.

Bet You Didn't Know

The 20th century's champion symphony writers were Nikolai Miaskovsky, a professor at the Moscow Conservatory who managed to dodge Soviet interference and wound up with 24 of them, and Massachusetts-born Alan Hovhaness, who had composed well over 60 last time we checked. That was a few weeks ago, however, so the total is probably much higher by now.

Haydn—Father of the Symphony

"Since God has given me a cheerful heart," Haydn once said, "He will forgive me for serving Him cheerfully." This Haydn did, pepping his music with little jokes and upbeat surprises. If you have any concerns about classical symphonies being ponderous or dull, listen to the barnyard squawkings in his Hen Symphony; the loud chords in the slow movement of the Surprise Symphony, designed to startle the royal audience out of its collective snooze. Try the Farewell, during which the orchestral players literally pack up their instruments one by one and trundle off the stage, until the conductor has only the concertmaster left to fiddle with.

Franz Joseph Haydn (1732-1809), born in the little Austrian town of Rohrau, near the Hungarian border, grew up surrounded by music and siblings. One of 12 children, he had a clear and beautiful voice, so by the age seven he was singing in the local church choir, and learning to play the violin, keyboards, tambourine, and any other instrument he happened to find around the place.... etc.

Bet You Didn't Know

There didn't seem to be any Kevins or Laurens or Averys around in those days, so people were kind of stuck for names in large families, often using the same ones—in various combinations—for different kids. It probably didn't hurt to have several Josephs and Marias, since that way if one got lost or ran away from home, there would still be some left. Maria was an especially good bet, since it was used for both girls and boys. Mozart's mother, for instance, was Anna Maria, his sister was Maria Anna, and his godson was Karl Maria von Weber, whom we'll be talking about in a few pages.

One day, a talent-scouting choirmaster from Vienna heard the child sing and chose him for service in that city's famous St. Stephen's Cathedral. Haydn stayed there for nine years. He stayed, but one day he cut off another singer's pigtails as a joke. Unfortunately, neither the singer nor the headmaster laughed, and the next day Haydn was out of a job.

Undaunted (well, slightly daunted, but not too badly), Haydn stayed in Vienna for another seven or eight years, studying music on his own, reading books, and indulging in the occasional counterpoint lesson. In other words, he was an itinerant musician, available for dances, outdoor parties, and other paying gigs, while he patiently waited for his ship to come in.

When it did, the captain was Prince Paul Anton Esterhazy, whose family owned several palaces, including Eisenstadt, which had 200 guest rooms and paintings that later became the founding collection of the Budapest Museum of Fine Arts. On May 1, 1761, the Prince made Haydn conductor of his court orchestra. He moved into Eisenstadt and agreed to conduct the orchestra and compose weekly operas and operettas, ceremonial music, chamber pieces, and anything else the Prince wanted. Haydn also was responsible for fixing broken violins, making sure the players' uniforms were wrinkle-free, coaching singers, and turning in attendance reports on his musicians.

Bet You Didn't Know

As befitting a high-class servant, Haydn agreed to wear "white stockings, white linen, and either a powdered queue or a tie-wig," and to refrain from "undue familiarity" with the other musicians.

Despite the oppressive list of rules, regulations, and assignments, Haydn realized his good fortune in having an unprecedented degree of musical freedom. He had at hand every composer's dream: vocal and instrumental ensembles ready to try out every tonal experiment, every new combination of sounds. True, he was cut off from the mainstream of musical life in Vienna, but even that worked to his advantage. As he put it many years later, "I was forced to become original."

A year after Haydn arrived, Prince Paul died and was succeeded by his brother, Nicholas, who modestly called himself "The Magnificent" possibly because he owned 21 castles and liked to wear jackets covered with diamonds. Eventually Nicholas decided that he needed a little getaway house in the country. So he had a swamp cleared and another palace built, complete with flower gardens, game parks, hothouses, guest cottages, and a hall of clocks with golden cuckoos. It was called Esterhaz.

The bottom line, though, was that Nicholas loved music as much as his brother, so Haydn's job was safe, and for nearly 30 years more he continued pouring out a glorious series of sonatas and symphonies and quartets. When Prince Nicholas died, leaving his musically indifferent son Antal in charge, musical life at Esterhaz began to fizzle and Haydn knew it was time to move on.

London Calling

Fortunately, a British bigwig in the concert world, the violinist and impresario Johann Peter Salomon, offered Haydn a package deal that included commissions for a dozen new symphonies, various conducting gigs, and publication contracts.

Bet You Didn't Know

The story goes that Mozart cautioned his friend Haydn about going to a foreign country so late in life, pointing out that he didn't know a word of English. "My language is understood everywhere," said Haydn, and started packing.

In London, his new symphonies were wildly successful, the audiences cheering so long and loudly that whole movements often had to be repeated. Haydn was wined and dined, and given an honorary doctorate from Oxford University. He didn't know enough English to give a speech of thanks, so he just took off his scholar's gown and waved it at everyone. Haydn also gave command performances at more than two dozen parties thrown by the Prince of Wales and even sang for the King and Queen.

Bet You Didn't Know

Haydn had a rather unhappy encounter with a London surgeon, one Dr. Hunter, who noticed that the composer had a nasal polyp, and suggested an office visit. Haydn, not understanding English too well, was under the impression he was being invited to high tea. "After the first greetings," Haydn reported, "several big strong fellows entered the room, seized me and tried to seat me in a chair. I shouted, and kicked them black and blue until I freed myself and made it clear to Mr. Hunter, who was standing all ready with his instruments, that I would not be operated on." With that, Haydn, his precious polyp intact, made good his escape.

When Haydn was in his mid-sixties he became homesick and retired to Vienna, where he swore off composing symphonies, and contented himself with writing masses, oratorios, string quartets, hundreds of songs, and the Austrian National Anthem. In 1805, a London newspaper printed his obituary, starting a period of international mourning that continued until Haydn himself gently pointed out that he was "still of this base world." "How can I die now?" he asked, "I have only just begun to understand the wind instruments."

Four years later, Franz Joseph Haydn caught up with the press and left the world. He was wealthy, famous, and revered (then and evermore) for his hundreds of masterful compositions. Haydn may not have been the creator of the symphony or the string quartet, but he defined their forms and produced an incredible body of exemplary works that gave music a majestic push down its evolutionary path. Said Mozart, "It was from Haydn that I first learned the true way to compose quartets."

Haydn's Works You Need to Know

So much music, so little time. Start with the nicknamed symphonies, since they're easier to remember, and you're more likely to encounter them on the air or in concerts. On the list: the aforementioned Farewell (no. 45), "Hen" (no. 83), Surprise (no. 94), plus Horn Signal (no. 31), no. Oxford (no. 92), and the magnificent final four: the Military (no. 100), Clock (no. 101), Drum Roll (no. 103), and "London" (no. 104).

The Trumpet Concerto is a special treat, so is the D Major Harpsichord (or Piano) Concerto, and you'll find other concerto delights for oboe, horn, cello, and organ. The trios for Piano, Violin, and Cello make wonderfully lighthearted listening, while any of the string quartets are perfect for more intimate listening. Here, too, you might do well to start with some of the titled quartets, such as the Lark (op. 64, no. 5), Emperor (op. 76, no. 3), and Sunrise (op. 76, no. 4).

They say it's not over till the fat lady sings, so open your ears to Haydn's mighty oratorios, The Creation and The Seasons and same of the other sacred scores, including the bright-hued Coronation Mass or the heartfelt Mass in Time of War.

Mozart: The Wunderkind

He may not have been the giggling cutup portrayed in the Oscar-winning film "Amadeus," but Mozart (1756-1791) was certainly not the model of temperance that Haydn was required to be. On the other hand, Haydn was in awe of his younger colleague. "Friends often flatter me that I have some genius," he said, "but Mozart stood far above me." And in a letter to Mozart's father, Leopold, Haydn referred to Wolfgang Amadeus as "the greatest composer known to me, either in person or by name."

Bet You Didn't Know

Never mind Amadeus: Mozart's real name was Johannes Chrysostomus Wolfgangus Theophilus. Try saying that one three times fast. The Wolfgang, of course is short for Wolfgangus, but his father preferred Gottlieb to Theophilus, and in Latin that translates into Amadeus (love of God).

Mozart was born in Salzburg, Austria, and it didn't take long for his father, Leopold, to figure out that the kid was pretty unusual. At the age of three, Wolfgang began to repeat his older sister's keyboard exercises by ear, and he started correcting Papa Mozart whenever his fiddle wandered off key. Next thing you know, Wolfgang was handing the old man a page full of ink-blots marked Symphony no. 1. With visions of fame and fortune dancing in his head, Leopold took his wunderkind out on the road, zipping him all over Europe and showing him off for all he was worth

Music Word

Wunderkind is a word we swiped from the German. It simply means wonder-child, and is used to refer to a prodigy: any, meaning any youngster with talent or achievements far beyond the expectation of his years.

Actually, he was worth plenty. Little Wolfgang wowed audiences everywhere he went, improvising sonatas on tunes people sang to him, making up new accompaniments for old songs, or performing with a napkin covering the keyboard. In Rome, the Pope decorated him like a Christmas tree (even though the boy had broken the papal rule by putting down on paper the allegedly top-secret score to a nine-voiced "Miserere" after hearing it just twice). In London, Wolfgang played for King George III and accompanied Queen Charlotte while she sang some arias; and in France, Wolfgang proposed to Marie Antoinette, though nothing came of it, since they were both seven years old at the time. Everywhere they went, in fact, royalty showered the prodigy with useful gifts, like golden toothpick holders and silver snuffboxes.

Bet You Didn't Know

As an adult, Mozart was no longer happy when royal patrons gave him silly presents instead of far more urgently needed cash. "I now have five watches," he grumbled, "and am seriously thinking of having an additional watch pocket sewn on each leg of my trousers, so when I visit some great lord, it will not occur to him to present me with another."

I Was a Teenage Kapellmeister

After a number of very busy years, the novelty of little Wolfgang wore off even as his littleness itself had disappeared. By the time he reached his pre- and early teen years, his prodigy appeal had vanished and his touring blitzes petered out.

At 15, Mozart followed his father into the service of the Archbishop of Salzburg, who promptly died, leaving the boy in the clutches of a musically unappreciative replacement Archbishop, who paid peanuts for all sorts of masterworks to which he was utterly indifferent. Financially struggling (as he would be the rest of his life), largely unappreciated, and no doubt emotionally miserable, Mozart nonetheless spent the next half a dozen years in Salzburg, really settling down to the business of composition. Brilliantly endowed with vast imagination as well as amazing technical facility, Wolfgang worked much harder and with more discipline than, again, the entertaining "Amadeus" film would have us believe. He wrote opera after symphony after oratorio after sonata; he tried his hand (in fact both hands) at conducting, and was available for piano or violin performances on demand. During this Salzburg period, he finished his first 13 piano sonatas; a Flute Quartet, ; his Mass in C Minor, the five violin concertos; and the opera "Idomeneo."

During those years, Mozart also began synthesizing German and Italian music to create a style uniquely his own. The Italians tended to view music as light and entertaining, the Germans leaned toward more serious expressions; Germans preferred instrumental pieces, Italians melted at the sound of a beautiful voice; Italian composers sought to charm audiences with soaring melody, the Germans were more concerned with form and texture. When you listen to Mozart, all of those ingredients are combined; we bask in the best of both musical worlds.

Wedding Belles

By age 21, Mozart was desperately anxious to have a woman in his life. "The voice of nature speaks as loud in me as in others," he told his father, and when he met the beautiful 16-year-old Aloysia Weber, who had a lovely voice (and even played the harpsichord a bit), he figured he was all set. Papa Mozart, however, was not too keen on having anyone take Wolfgang's mind off his music, so he whisked his son away on a concert tour to Paris. By the time Wolfgang came back, Aloysia was unavailable. (She had become the mistress of the Elector of Salzburg, if you must know.) Not to worry, there were plenty more Webers where she came from, namely her three fresh, young sisters. Mozart moved in with the family, where he could explore his options more easily, and eventually settled on Constanza. "She understands housekeeping," he explained to Papa.

So Wolfgang and Constanza moved to Vienna, and there Mozart spent his last years, plagued by poor health and dreary finances. Here was a case of life and art taking separate paths. Even as Mozart's genius reached the pinnacle of expression with his four greatest operas, the Clarinet Quintet and Concerto, his most acclaimed symphonies, and a magical body of chamber music, his life deteriorated beyond repair. His last work was the Requiem, which remained unfinished when his final illness—likely typhoid fever—led Mozart to a pauper's grave on a wet winter day in December 1791. He was 35 years old.

Important Things to Know

If you see a Mozart piece on a concert program, it usually will be followed by the letter "K" and a number. What on earth, you wonder, does that mean? His Symphony no. 25, for instance, is K. 183, while the ever-popular Eine Kleine Nachtmusik adds up to K. 525. No, the K. doesn't stand for Konzert, nor even Potassium. It refers to Köchel, as in Ludwig Alois Ferdinand Ritter van Köchel, an Austrian botanist, mineralogist, and part-time musicologist. Most composers and publishers settled for identifying pieces by opus numbers ("opus" simply meaning "work"), but Mozart wrote music so quickly, and in such profusion, that even he sometimes lost count (his Symphony no. 24 is really no. 31, he seems to have forgotten #37 altogether, going right from Symphony #36 to 38, etc.). To bring order out of this creative chaos, Köchel systematically catalogued every one of Mozart's compositions, assigning each one a number from 1 (a keyboard minuet written at the age of four) to 626 (the Requiem). Theoretically, the listing was in chronological order, but Köchel goofed up fairly often, so you can't always be sure. Oh well, nobody's perfect.

Mozart's Works You Need to Know

As with Haydn, many of Mozart's most popular symphonies come with titles attached, like the Haffner (no. 35), named for a wealthy Salzburg family (if you're in a hurry, try the shorter and sweeter "Haffner Serenade"), and two symphonies named for the cities where they were premiered: Linz (no. 36) and Prague (no. 38). Under no circumstances, however, should you fail to hear the superb final three symphonies, written within the incredibly short span of six weeks in 1788: no. 39 in E-flat, no. 40 in G Minor, and no. 41 in C, the last of those also equipped with a nifty nickname, the Jupiter.

The sparkling Eine Kleine Nachtmusik is great at any time of day, and for a round of pure slapstick, try "A Musical Joke." You won't go wrong with any of the Mozart Concertos, including those for Bassoon, Clarinet, Flute, and Flute and Harp together. There are four Horn Concertos, five for Violin, and twenty-five for Piano (plus one for Two Pianos and another for Three).

Bet You Didn't Know

You won't find a trumpet concerto on Mozart's list, because from earliest childhood until the age of nine and beyond, Mozart couldn't abide the sound of the solo trumpet. "Merely holding a trumpet towards him was like aiming a loaded pistol at his heart," reported a family friend. "Papa wanted to cure him of this fear and once asked me to blow my trumpet at him, but my God! Wolfgang had scarcely heard the sound when he turned pale and began to collapse."

In chamber music, the list of delights is endless, with all sorts of solo and duo sonatas, trios, quartets, and some quintets, too. Want background music for your next dinner party? Several of the divertimenti and serenades have lost none of their charm since they first served that very purpose in 18th-century drawing rooms.

On the vocal aisle, Requiem is a must, though by all means counterbalance its poignancy with the bright and virtuosic joy of the motet "Exultate Jubilate." The great Coronation Mass is bursting with energy, while the "Ave Verum Corpus," like the Requiem written in the last year of Mozart's short life, is serenity personified.

For the opera aficionado, Don Giovanni, The Magic Flute, and The Marriage of Figaro are the best starting points, though you may well want to proceed to Cosi fan Tutte and Idomineo as well.™

In fact, there is hardly a Mozart work that will fail to please. As Aaron Copland put it, "Mozart tapped the source from which all music flows, expressing himself with a spontaneity and refinement and breathtaking rightness that has never since been duplicated."

Beethoven: Larger Than Life

You can't really escape Beethoven. We've all heard the "Da-Da-Da-Dummm" opening of the Fifth Symphony (during World War II, it became the American equivalent of Churchill's "V for Victory" sign); we've met Beethoven in the movies, either as that big cuddly dog, complete with symphonic snippets on the soundtrack, or in person in the recent biographical film "Immortal Beloved." He's even made it to the top of the pop charts with "Roll Over Beethoven" and a disco version of the Fifth Symphony. What was Beethoven like as a person, and how did he come to write all that incredible music? Read on... Ludwig van Beethoven (1770-1827) was a hard man to get along with. He was sloppy, rude, and egotistical (although, to be fair, he had plenty to be egostical about). "With whom need I be afraid of measuring my strength?" he asked, presumably not expecting an answer. He disdained the rules of polite society, just as he broke the compositional chains that bound so many of his composing colleagues. Even his concerts tended to be monumental. On one evening in 1803, the program listed his oratorio Christ on the Mount of Olives, the First and Second Symphonies, and the Third Piano Concerto, with a few arias thrown in, lest the audience worry about not getting its money's worth.

Bet You Didn't Know

Given some of the traits mentioned above, it's little wonder Beethoven had trouble keeping household help. His calendar for 1820 include the following entries:

April 17: The kitchen-maid entered upon her duties.

May 16: Gave notice to the kitchen-maid.

July 1: [Another] kitchen-maid entered upon her duties.

July 28: The kitchen-maid ran away in the evening.

September 9: A girl entered service.

October 22: The girl left.

December 12: The new kitchen-maid entered service.

December 18: The kitchen-maid gave notice.

Beethoven lived and died a rebel. His defiance was rooted in his genius and in a passion for independence. Why not? He grew up in the wake of the French and American Revolutions. But he also possessed the defiance that comes with abuse and exploitation. Sorry to say, he was born into an unhappy family of alcoholics, and his father's approach to developing his son's talent was tyrannical, often violent. When Ludwig showed early signs of musical promise, his father, remembering all those stories about the way Mozart had been welcomed by royalty, figured that his kid could be a similarly rich source of beer money. He forced the child to practice long hours, beating him if he made too many mistakes, and when Ludwig was eight, he plastered the town with posters announcing the debut of his six-year-old son. Whether six or eight, it didn't really matter. The audience was underwhelmed. Beethoven was a late bloomer (at least by musical prodigy standards).

By age 13, he was working as a harpsichordist in the court orchestra, and before long he was promoted to assistant organist and was starting to pile up a good-sized stash of pocket change. Not yet 17, he got up the nerve to try Vienna out for size, playing for Mozart, who predicted great success for him, and studying under Haydn, who never felt entirely comfortable dealing with this headstrong youngster.

Bet You Didn't Know

Johann Albrechtsberger, a respected teacher but hidebound conservative, was outraged at the younger Beethoven's blossoming originality. "Beethoven has never learned anything, and never will learn anything," he said. "As a composer he is hopeless." This pretty well describes Albrechtsberger's gifts as a fortune-teller.

Gradually, Beethoven found himself accepted by the Viennese aristocracy. Not, to be sure, for his looks or personality. He was short (5'4"), had a massive, bullet-shaped head, a prize-fighter's nose, protruding teeth, and pockmarked skin. (Prince Anton Esterhazy called him "the Moor" because of his leathery complexion.) His temper was erratic and volatile, but he could improvise up a storm at fancy dinner parties, and the improved pianos had power enough to match his volcanic temperament. He was one of the first pianists to extract nearly orchestral sound from the instrument, and he impressed enough members of high society to start earning a living with incoming commissions.

Bet You Didn't Know

Once, having entertained guests with his keyboard prowess at an elegant soirée, Beethoven was asked to eat with the servants, as Haydn and Mozart had done before him. Ludwig would have none of that, of course, so he created a big scene and stalked out angrily. The story, for once, had a happy ending though: One of the guests was Prince Ferdinand of Prussia, who promptly threw another party, inviting Beethoven to sit on his left side, while the now-contrite hostess of the previous evening was placed at his right.

Beethoven's irascible nature was well in place by his mid-20s, but his sense of isolation was enormously heightened with the onset of the ultimate tragedy for a musician: deafness. He withdrew from society more and more, partly in shame of his affliction, partly because his commitment to music was becoming evermore passionate and all-consuming.

However, this withdrawal was not all-consuming enough to prevent his passions from seeking human connections. Beethoven was forever falling in love, though usually the targets of his affection were unattainable women who were either married or royalty or both. He did teach a few of his pretty piano students more than what was on the music page, and he was known to dally with some of his landladies. He also wrote long, burning letters to his "Immortal Beloved," but refused to tell anybody who she was, because it might have upset her husband and sundry children.

Meanwhile, music was pouring from Beethoven's pen. Usually, his creative life is divided into three segments. The so-called "early period," roughly from 1792-1803, contains works that stayed more or less within the bounds of the classical conventions established by Haydn and Mozart, though with highly individual bursts of energy and originality. Included here are the first two symphonies, three piano concertos, six string quartets, and nine piano sonatas.

With the "Eroica" Symphony, #3—longer, harmonically more daring, and emotionally more powerful than any symphony had been before—Beethoven embarked on a revolutionary path. From here on, he would experiment with new forms even as he was expanding the old ones, invent his own musical parameters, produce works on a vast and heroic scale, and ultimately shatter existing preconceptions about the expressive potential of music altogether. This "middle period" encompasses the Symphonies #3 through 8, the next three String Quartets and fourteen Piano Sonatas, the last two Piano Concertos and the Violin Concerto, and Beethoven's only opera, "Fidelio."

Bet You Didn't Know

Not surprisingly, Beethoven's powerful new ideas ruffled all sorts of critical feathers. "All impartial connoisseurs are fully agreed," wrote one critic about Fidelio, "that never has anything been written so shrill, chaotic, and ear-splitting. The most piercing dissonances clash in atrocious harmony, and the few puny ideas only increase the deafening effect."

With deafness almost complete, Beethoven entered the "late period" with deep introspection and artistry honed to its highest level. No longer was there the least concern for performers' limitations, or audience preferences. Beethoven was writing for the ages. From these final years came the lofty Missa Solemnis, the powerful Ninth Symphony, the radiant final string quartets and piano sonatas, including the nearly hour-long Hammerklavier Sonata, which has been described as "herculean" and "gargantuan." Would one expect less from a titan?

Despite all the controversy that had swirled about him, all the rumors of his disreputable behavior, and his self-imposed retirement from society, the public well knew that a giant had been walking among them. Thirty thousand people attended his funeral, with a little-known composer named Franz Schubert among the torchbearers. His tombstone bears his dates of birth and death and a single word: Beethoven.

Beethoven's Works You Need to Know

All nine of Beethoven's symphonies are pretty indispensable to a basic library, and fortunately, you'll find many inexpensively-priced boxed sets. Cart home one of those and you'll get a lot of Beethoven for your buck. For some reason, the odd-numbered symphonies (once beyond the cheery Symphony no. 1) have the greater drama: think of the revolutionary "Eroica", #3, and the stormy Fifth sandwiching the lyric and graceful Fourth Symphony. Schumann called that Symphony #4 "a slender Greek maiden standing between two Norse giants." The warm-hearted country landscape of the Pastoral Symphony, #6, leads into the expansive Seventh, with its jubilant dance finale. #8 is again on a smaller scale, witty and lighthearted, and standing in startling contrast to its successor, the stupendous Ninth Symphony, with its great choral finale.

Try the jaunty Piano Concerto no. 1 (which was actually written after Concerto no. 2, but don't let that bother you) and the spaciously dramatic Emperor Piano Concerto no. 5. The Violin Concerto is another popular masterpiece, and to get your soloistic money's worth, there's always the Triple Concerto for Piano, Violin, Cello, and Orchestra.

Those same three instruments without any symphonic help are available in a set of terrific trios, or try any of the 16 string quartets. For pianophiles, the list of 32 sonatas includes such favorites as the Pathetique, Moonlight, Waldstein (dedicated to Beethoven's friend and patron from his Bonn years, Count Ferdinand von Waldstein), and the aptly subtitled Appassionata. The ten violin sonatas and five more for cello and piano are also well worth exploring.Beethoven only wrote one opera, Fidelio, but it took him four overtures before he got to one he liked (the others being the Leonore Overtures nos. 1, 2, and 3). Come to think of it, the Overtures are a good way to enjoy Beethoven's dramatic style without spending three hours at it: listen to the Egmont, King Stephen, and the Ruins of Athens Overtures (all heading up suites of incidental music—my little operas, Beethoven used to call them) and Consecration of the House, written to celebrate the opening of a new theater in Vienna.

Weber: Romantic Rumblings

Wagner called Karl Maria von Weber (1786-1826) the most German of German composers, by which he probably meant that he (Wagner) had cribbed more ideas from Weber than almost anybody else, including the use of leitmotifs, freer forms, and subjects derived from medieval German legends.

Music Word

German for "leading motive", the **leitmotif** is a musical phrase that symbolizes a person, place, idea, or emotion. We encounter it all the time on TV and at the movies (think of the pulsing music from "Jaws" that gets us on the edge of our seat even before the shark is anywhere in view), but it was a revolutionary concept in Weber's day.

Weber was born in the little town of Eutin, near Lubeck in Germany. His father was a traveling-theater violinist, his mother a singing actress, and perhaps because they were on the road so much, they forgot to browbeat the kid into endless hours of practicing. As a result, Karl Maria was a late bloomer. He studied painting with more diligence than the violin, taking piano lessons but not beginning really serious study until the age of 11 when the family moved to Salzburg and signed him up for lessons with Haydn's greatly gifted, but far less famous brother, Michael.

Although Weber later maintained that he had learned little from Michael Haydn (and, he grumbled, "that little with great effort"), he had assimilated enough knowledge by the age of 14 to write his first opera. It was a flop, but the experience filled the young composer with a sense of operatic mission, and he was soon hard at work on another one called "Peter Schmoll and His Neighbors." Michael Haydn called it "full of fire, great delicacy, and appropriate feeling," but the thing flopped anyway. While Weber was sulking and wondering how to find the secret of success, he started conducting other people's operas, first in Breslau and then in Prague, where he reorganized the whole operation and revived the sagging fortunes of the opera company there.

Even while he was becoming a superb conductor, Weber kept trying to establish himself in the composing business. He had another disaster with the opera Silvana, but at least it wasn't a total loss because he eventually married the leading soprano. Next came Abu Hassan, a reasonably successful one-acter based on a tale from The Arabian Nights, and then his first big hit, a dramatic cantata, "The First Note," dealing with no less momentous an event than the creation of the world. That cantata, by the way, was more important historically than musically because it included the first important use of the leitmotif technique that Wagner would later elevate to such glorious heights.

While Weber was rather frantically searching for a good libretto he met the brilliant clarinetist Heinrich Barmann, and wrote a whole series of pieces for him—among them two concertos, a concertino, and the gorgeous quintet—that are still mainstays of the clarinet repertoire.

Still, opera was Weber's grand passion, and gradually he evolved the idea of creating a kind of German folk opera, based on ancient legends, and occasionally using actual (or imitation) folk melodies. By now his reputation had spread sufficiently for the King of Saxony to choose Weber as music director of the opera in Dresden. This was a bit of a sticky wicket, since the Dresdenites were huge fans of Italian opera at the time, and here was Weber pushing German themes. On the other hand, nobody was about to argue with the King of Saxony, so that was that.

Weber immediately put his stamp on the company by forbidding the singers from taking liberties with scores and interpolating fancy cadenzas along the way, as was their custom in Italian operas. He also rearranged the seating plan of the opera orchestra, started conducting with a baton so the players would know who was boss, and then unveiled one of the three operas on which his reputation still stands, Der Freischütz. (The title doesn't translate neatly in English, but it's something like "The Free-Shooter.")

Here was a wildly romantic tale indeed, complete with magic bullets, forest demons, sorcery in a wolf's glen, and a hunter's pact with the devil. To project these scenes of supernatural mystery, Weber innovated all sorts of orchestral effects, using instruments at the extremes of their ranges, subdividing the strings, combining massed voices with the instruments, and in general creating a hitherto unknown synthesis of orchestral music and stage drama. The premiere was a wild success; with the overture and several arias cheered so loudly that they had to be encored. Fifty performances followed, bringing the composer a higher degree of fame and fortune than he had ever experienced, with only some diehard critics remaining unconvinced.

After the enormous acclaim of Der Freischütz, and its productions in most of the opera houses of Europe, Weber wrote Euryanthe. This time, though, the libretto—based on another medieval tale—was so wildly implausible, even incomprehensible, that a great deal of his beautiful music came to naught, and only the overture remains in the active files today.

Weber's favorite amongst his own operas proved to be his final achievement. Commissioned by the celebrated Covent Garden Opera House in London, Oberon had an almost as hopelessly confused plot as Euryanthe, but maybe the English were used to that. In any case, it was another stupendous success. At its premiere, the composer was treated to a 15-minute ovation even before the curtain rose, and when it fell again, Weber pronounced the whole experience "simply unbelievable: The emotion produced by such a triumph is more than I can describe." Despite poor health, Weber conducted the opera 11 more times and played at a number of other London concerts. Two months later, still in England, Weber felt ill, bid his host goodnight and went to sleep, never to wake again. He was buried in London, where he lay peacefully for 18 years, until his body was reclaimed by his homeland. On December 14, 1844, Weber was re-interred at the Catholic cemetery in Dresden, while themes from Der Freischutz were played as funeral music.

Bet You Didn't Know

Weber's Dresden funeral ceremony was presided over by Wagner, who gave the eulogy and conducted "At Weber's Grave," a choral piece he had written for the occasion, little imagining that it would be sung again at his own funeral many years later.

Weber's Works You Need to Know

The remarkable orchestrations for which Weber was so justly renowned are on display in his Overtures to Der Freischutz, Euryanthe, and Oberon, but to appreciate fully the dramatic tension and explosion of supernatural terror he was able to achieve on the operatic stage, listen to the "Wolf's Glen" Scene" from Der Freischutz.

To slake your virtuosic thirst, there are the Clarinet Concertos, another pair for piano, plus the shorter "Konzertstuck" (Concert Piece) in F Minor. Clarinet fans should also partake of the Quintet, the Concertino, and some delightful themes and variations; and if you happen to have a thing for the lower winds, try the Bassoon Concerto or the quirky Hungarian Rondo, available in versions for both bassoon and viola.

Schubert: Man of Song

"A divine spark lives in Schubert," said Beethoven; "he will yet attract much attention in the world." He was right, of course, but Beethoven died a few months later, and a year after that, Schubert was gone too, at the tragically early age of 31. Schubert had written upwards of 600 songs, not to mention all sorts of piano works, chamber pieces and nine symphonies, yet almost none of it was published, and indeed history records only one public concert of his music during his lifetime (on the first anniversary of Beethoven's death).

Franz Peter Schubert (1797-1828) was the twelfth child to be born into the Schubert family in Vienna, Austria, so there were plenty of older siblings to teach him the piano, organ, violin, and viola. At the age of 11, he became a choir boy at the Imperial Chapel Choir, and served time at the State Konvict, which is what they called the school next door. Actually it was pretty jail-like at that, with cold rooms, poor food, and annoying work assignments (like oiling the oboes and lighting the tallow candles), but Schubert stuck it out until his voice changed and he became an ex-Konvict.

He next took a job as a school teacher. At least that's what he told everybody he was doing. Actually, he was scribbling down songs a-mile-a-minute, trying to finish them before the "little devils" (as he called his students) would bother him with their foolish math problems. The amazing speed with which he composed may have been honed here. Still a teenager himself, he tossed off what are now some of the most famous songs in the world, including "Gretchen at the Spinning Wheel" and "The Erl King," the latter while two friends stood by his writing desk watching him "hurl notes at the page." He composed "Hark, Hark the Lark" on the back of a beer-garden menu, and by the time he quit posing as teacher, his output included more than 350 songs, 4 symphonies, several operas, 2 masses, some sonatas, and a string quartet.

With hardly any source of income, Schubert was supported by the generosity of his friends. Only they recognized that this short, near-sighted, plump fellow was indeed a composer of genius; only they heard his new songs and chamber music at their private musical evenings, which became known as Schubertiads.

Bet You Didn't Know

When Schubert sent off "The Erl King" to a publisher, the song was not only rejected, but returned to the wrong Franz Schubert, who described himself as a "Royal Court Composer," but seems rather to have been an itinerant double-bass player. In any case, he thanked the publisher, but said he was holding on to the manuscript "in hopes of discovering the scoundrel who so impertinently traded on my name by sending you such rubbish."

Melody was Schubert's forte. He painted pictures in song; gave chamber music a new burst of lyricism; and his expressive gifts brought the German art song, or lieder, to its greatest heights, his exquisite music exalting even the minor poets whose works he set. Schubert also pioneered the song cycle, groups of integrated pieces usually taken from the lyrics of a single poet, such as "Die Schöne Mullerin" (The Miller's Beautiful Daughter) or "Die Winterreise" (Winter's Journey).

Music Word

Lieder is German for songs (one song would be a Lied), but the word is normally used to indicate art songs—as opposed to folk or popular ballads—deriving from poetic sources. Customary usage also limits the usage of the word "lieder" to songs in German.

Cycles are groups of songs (in any language) that are connected by subject matter, author of the poems, or some other unifying factor.

Later critics faulted Schubert's orchestral pieces for structural weaknesses, but none could help marveling at his incredible melodic gifts. It was only after he died, of some pre-penicillin plague variously described as syphilis or typhoid fever, that his place in the pantheon of musical greats was gradually, but unshakably, established. Eleven years after Schubert's death, his majestic Ninth Symphony found a champion in Schumann, who persuaded his friend Mendelssohn to conduct its premiere. Another quarter of a century would pass before a Viennese conductor found the manuscript of the "Unfinished Symphony" and introduced it to the public; and it wasn't until 1867 that Arthur Sullivan (still three years away from becoming the other half of the famous Gilbert And…) located Schubert's incidental music to "Rosamunde" stuffed away in a Vienna cupboard.

Schubert's Works You Need to Know

In several instances, you can enjoy the same melody in vocal and instrumental form: "Die Forelle" is both a short song, and the theme of the Variations movement in the delectably long "Trout Quintet"; you can encounter "Death and the Maiden" in one of Schubert's most touching lieder or the radiant String Quartet bearing that title; you can hike along with the singing "Wanderer" or follow his path into the piano fantasy (later arranged by Liszt for piano and orchestra).

There are many wonderful piano sonatas, but for shorter keyboard sittings, try the delectable "Moments Musicaux" (Musical Moments). On the symphonic list, your best introduction is the familiar Unfinished (no. 8), though the charming Fifth Symphony makes absolutely delightful listening, and the Ninth finds Schubert at his most orchestrally expansive. "All the instruments are human voices," wrote Schumann after hearing the Ninth, which perhaps explains its unique allure.

We've mentioned some of the more famous Schubert songs, but almost any of the hundreds more are equally worth hearing. Then, while you're browsing in the vocal section, explore some of the masses and other church music, and the exquisite "Shepherd on the Rock" for voice, clarinet, and piano.

Rossini

A quick quiz: Rossini was:

a) an over-priced Italian wine, as in Rossini Spumanti

b) a songbird in the rossignol family

c) a prolific Italian opera composer

If you guessed "c"—Si!—then you're our kind of music lover. Gioacchino Rossini (1792-1868) was indeed one of the great early 19th-century contributors to the art of Italian opera.

Bet You Didn't Know

Over the next 40 years, Rossini turned into a great gourmet, grew very fat, and wrote pieces called "Anchovies," "Radishes," and "Hors d'Oeuvres." He also composed "Profound Sleep with Startled Awakenings" and a "Hygienic Prelude for Morning Use," but no more operas.

"Give me a laundry list," Rossini said, "and I will set it to music." By the time he was 38, he had turned 38 laundry lists—sorry, librettos—into operas, then figuring "enough is enough," he quit.

Meanwhile, back in 1792, Rossini was born on February 29th, leap-yearing into the world slightly ahead of schedule, since his parents had been married only five months earlier. His mother was a singer and his father alternated between being the town trumpeter and the town butcher, so young Gioacchino grew up with a love for opera and all the bologna to that goes with it. He was, however, a troublemaker as a kid, pulling off practical jokes in church and throwing stones at his playmates. He was also extremely lazy, ducking the odd jobs he was supposed to do around the house, refusing to practice, goofing off whenever he could, and generally giving everybody a hard time. A perfectly normal teenager, in other words.

When Rossini figured out that composing is a physically passive activity, in fact one that can be quite happily accomplished in bed, he began to take a greater interest in music. He sang in an opera at age 11, then made his first attempt at writing one a year later. His exceptional talents really began to take shape after his family moved to—here we go again—Bologna. Rossini never really went in for had much formal training, but he did take a few courses at the Conservatory, even winning a medal for counterpoint, and writing a cantata that was played at his school's annual ceremonies.

His early operas didn't really go anyplace, but Rossini worked fast when he wanted to, and churned them out at astonishing pace: four in 1812, another four in 1813. He went steady with The Italian Girl in Algiers, made a hit with The Turk in Italy, even fooled around with The Barber of Seville, but you can put those eyebrows back down: those are all opera titles. So are "The Thieving Magpie," and "Tancredi," and "La Cenerentola" ("Cinderella"), and the dozens of other works that made Rossini one of the most famous men in Europe. Heads of state from Sweden to Turkey sent him presents, gave him honorary titles, invited him to court, and generally treated him like the (musical) royalty he was.

Rossini's music is often described as bel canto, which simply means "beautiful singing." Unlike Weber, Rossini had no interest in portraying supernatural events, bringing ancient legends to life, or infusing his stageworks with nationalistic fervor. His gifts lay in making opera a delicious entertainment. "His melodies have chuckles and sparkles in every bar," wrote David Ewen, "his effervescent music bubbles like champagne." So let's have a toast to old Gioacchino, a bit of an eccentric perhaps, but an opera composer for the ages.

Bet You Didn't Know

Rossini could also be quite acerbic. When Meyerbeer died, one of his nephews visited Rossini, proudly showing him a Funeral March he had written in honor of his uncle. "Very nice," Rossini said after scanning the score, "but don't you think it would have been better if you had died and Meyerbeer had written the March?"

On February 29, 1868, Rossini gathered friends and family around to celebrate his 19th birthday. He had a been a leap-year baby, remember, and indeed there been only nineteen February 29ths since his first one in 1792. On the other hand, he was increasingly troubled by a superstitious fear that something terrible would happen on Friday the 13th. Oddly enough, he was right: Rossini died on November the 13th of that same year. Believe it or not, it was a Friday.

Rossini's Works You Need to Know

If you're up to a whole opera, start with "The Barber of Seville." It's funny, it has the tongue-twisting "Largo al Factotum" and other great tunes (a few of which were appropriated by Bugs Bunny), some marvelous ensemble numbers, and there are many superb recordings to choose among.

Otherwise, get the flavor of his witty and animated music from the marvelous Overtures, including, besides those already mentioned, "The Silken Ladder," "Semiramide," "The Thieving Magpie," and "William Tell," from which emerged the galloping theme that old-time radio fans will forever associate with the Lone Ranger. (Old Joke: "Where does the Lone Ranger take his garbage? Ta-da-dump, ta-da-dump, ta-da-dump, dump, dump!" Even Older Joke: What's the definition of an intellectual? Someone who can listen to the "William Tell Overture" and not think of the Lone Ranger.)

Just for fun, sample some of the witty miniatures that Rossini tossed off during his retirement years under the umbrella title "Sins of My Old Age." And for moments of inspirational guidance, listen to one of his final works that well atones for any sins Rossini may have committed earlier on: the beautiful "Petite Messe Solonelle," which is neither little, nor solemn, just very beautiful. Rossini attached to the score an open letter to God. "Here is my poor little Mass," it says, "done with a little skill, a bit of heart and that's about all. Be Thou blessed, and admit me to Paradise."

Now you know where to find Rossini if you're looking for him.

CHAPTER 16

So You Want a Revolution: The Romantic Era

In This Chapter

➤ The age of individualism

➤ Art forms

➤ Poetic influences

➤ Songs

➤ The symphonic poem

➤ The most famous romantic composers

Musicians and other artists in the 18th century more or less played by the rules. In the 19th, they tried to break free of the old conventions, to make their own individual statements. Imaginations soared, passions roared, and legends loomed larger than life. Emotions held sway, replacing the reason and intellect so integral to the classical era. Moods became the stuff of art: joy and sorrow, hope and despair, love of humanity or homeland, all found their way into musical expression. There was a fascination with the exotic, the supernatural, the sensual. The Romantic approach also encouraged a fusion of art forms, with poetry inspiring music and music enhancing the drama. Goethe went so far as to call architecture "petrified music."

Poetry in Musical Motion

Speaking of Goethe (1749-1832), here was both an early romantic and a renaissance man, who distinguished himself as much in science and politics as in letters. Already in the mid-1770s, his "Prometheus" set forth the ideal that man must believe in himself rather than submit to the will of the gods; Goethe's poems "The Erl King" and "Gretchen at the Spinning Wheel" were turned into glorious songs by Franz Schubert, and his play "The Tragedy of Faust," based on a medieval German legend, served as the basis of Gounod's most famous opera. Faust, in fact, was the prototype of dozens of later literary characters who sell their souls to the devil in exchange for beauty, riches, fame or (in Faust's case) youth, then live to regret the bargain. As they soon enough discover, it's pretty hard to pry a refund out of Satan.

Follow the Lieder

The word "lieder," used in English as well as German, is plural for the German word "lied" (pronounced "leed"), meaning song. Beethoven is sometimes heralded as the creator of romantic lieder (and he did write one of the first song cycles), but it was really Schubert who set the pace with his settings of Goethe verses and those by dozens of other poets. Mendelssohn, Schumann, Brahms, Liszt, and Wagner were among the masters who followed in those songful footsteps. Hugo Wolf made the piano a more integral partner in the musical equation and brought in more modern harmonies, for which he was dubbed "the Wagner of the Lied." Lieder with piano began to wane in popularity towards the end of the 19th century, but Mahler, Richard Strauss, and others solved the problem by giving many of their songs orchestral accompaniments.

Music Word

The terms **symphonic poem** and tone poem are interchangeable: they both refer to an orchestral work with a literary antecedent. It can be a general mood piece, inspired by landscape descriptions, it can portray characters within a novel, play or poem; or it can actually try to convert events from printed word into musical sound descriptions.

Of Poems and Tones

The tone poem (or symphonic poem if you want to be a little more elegant about it), is just a fancy-pants title for an orchestral piece inspired by a literary work or an attempt to tell a story in music. Although composers of earlier eras did depict dramatic events in their music, it was Franz Liszt who pioneered the form, writing a Faust Symphony and a dozen shorter works attempting to translate images, scenes, and emotions from the printed page to a musical score. Liszt's list includes Les Preludes after Lamartine, Hamlet via Shakespeare, and Tasso, based on verses about the Italian Renaissance poet by Goethe and Byron.

Other composers were similarly intrigued by the challenge of turning literary works into the sounds of music, with Shakespeare, not surprisingly, a frequent source of inspiration, as witness Berlioz's "King Lear," Dvořák's "Othello," and Tchaikovsky's "Romeo and Juliet."

Toward the end of the 18th century, the American and French Revolutions sparked a whole series of social convolutions, and in the 19th, there arose a new wave of nationalistic fervor. You'll have to glean the historical, geographical, and political particulars from other sources than this modest volume, but musically there was a similar turn toward works that evoked pride in the creator's homeland. Composers in the romantic era took special note of traditions in their native countries, giving symphonic life to country folk tunes and rustic dance rhythms, painting tonal landscapes of rivers, mountains and castles, bringing national poetry and other literary works to bear on their musical intincts. Thus we find classical pieces deriving from on local legends Franck's "The Accursed Huntsman" and Moussorgsky's "Night on Bald Mountain"), nature sketches (Smetana's "The Moldau" and Borodin's "In the Steppes of Central Asia"), or historic personages (Glazunov's "Stenka Razin" and Schumann's "Manfred"). Another major champion of the symphonic poem was Richard Strauss, whose pictorial subjects covered most of the above bases, from Shakespeare (Macbeth) to folklore heros (Till Eulenspiegel) from a legendary lover (Don Juan) to himself (A Hero's Life).

Bet You Didn't Know

Somebody **once** was remarked to Strauss that it wasn't very seemly for a composer to make himself the subject of a musical work, as he did both in A Hero's Life (where he quoted themes from **a variety** of his earlier compositions to make sure everybody knew for sure who the Hero was) and in the Domestic Symphony, which includes a love scene between husband and wife. "And why not?" Strauss allegedly snapped back. "I consider myself at least as interesting as Napoleon or Alexander the Great." He had a point there.

Women on the Move

As recently as 1890, an allegedly intelligent critic wrote that "women were not, in general, intellectually capable of grasping the intricacies of music composition." Putting aside such hogwash, it is a sad fact that for many centuries it was deemed a mark of proper upbringing for a young lady to learn the harpsichord, flute, or other instrument of non-threatening nature, but rather scandalous for her to take her expertise beyond the confines of home and family. Playing such "masculine" instruments are trumpet, tuba, or tympani, of course, was considered totally beyond the pale.

There were, of course, women through the ages who defied this double standard. One of the earliest was the German-born Hildegard of Bingen (1098-1197), who managed to combine religious and diplomatic careers, while writing mystical poetry and songs, even "harmonic symphonies of celestial revelation." In Italy, Francesca Caccini (1587-1640), a solo singer in church and opera, entered the history books as the first woman opera composer, and possibly the first to cause a national scandal when, during the Florence Carnival of 1619, she dared unveil a work that included the scandalous sight of a pregnant woman on stage.

Two of the most gifted women of the 19th century carry names that are far more indelibly associated with their male kinfolk. Indeed, it is only in our own time that their unique composing talents have been fully appreciated and their scores become available to the public.

All in the Family: Fanny Mendelssohn and Clara Schumann

Born in Hamburg, four years earlier than her more famous brother, Felix Mendelssohn (you'll hear more about him later in this chapter), Fanny Mendelssohn (1805-1847) grew up in the same cultural environment, became an equally fine pianist, and turned to composition at the age of 14, when she created a song in honor of her father's birthday. Thereafter, she wrote more than 500 songs and piano pieces, plus a piano trio, string quartet, and other chamber music. Due to the prevailing prejudice against women composers, few if any of these works were published in her lifetime.

During the 1830s, some of Fanny Mendelssohn's passion for music was gratified when she became something of a musical magnet, presiding over salon evenings that were the talk of

Bet You Didn't Know

In frustration, Fanny allowed six of her "songs without words" to be printed under her brother's name; they are of such high quality that only recently have musicologists been able to determine which pieces were hers and which were Felix's.

the town. The major personalities in the arts swarmed to those cultural evenings at which Fanny played—and sometimes conducted—her own latest compositions. Her letters and diaries provide a vivid chronicle of the musical world of her time.

If Fanny Mendélssohn was a wonderful sister, Clara Schumann was a great wife. Her father, Friedrich Wieck, was a martinet, a cruel taskmaster, and all around meanie, but realizing that his daughter had extraordinary talent, he made no attempt to keep her from a life on the musical stage. Clara Wieck (1819-1896) gave her first recital in Leipzig at age 9, played in Paris at 12, was a tremendous success with the Viennese at 18, and soon thereafter was appointed Chamber Virtuoso to the Austrian court.

Clara blossomed early, and by the time she was 15, another of her father's students, Robert Schumann, set his sights on her. Her father responded in typical ogre fashion, locking his daughter away and tearing up Schumann's letters. When that didn't seem to produce the desired results, Friedrich Wieck tried a different approach, introducing the passionate young man to another of his students, Ernestine von Fricken who, we're told, was "physically luxuriant, emotionally strongly developed, and intellectually insignificant." Two out of three isn't bad, so Schumann dallied with Ernestine for a while, before realizing that Clara was the only one for him. We won't bore you with the gory details, but it took a two-year legal battle before the marriage could go forward.

Once the couple was together, Clara's own career went on hold, because she had enough on her hands taking care of their eight children. Soon there was another person to care for: Robert himself, who was beginning his tragic descent into madness. After her husband's death, though, Clara resumed her profession, earning the nickname "Queen of the Piano" from her many tours throughout Europe and the British Isles (19 in England alone), and personally seeing to it that her husband's music—plus that of her close friend Brahms—were played to the widest possible audiences.

If women composers were looked on as something of an anomaly in the 19th century, the pattern of the composer-virtuoso had been firmly established by Liszt and Paganini, so Clara Schumann (after the wedding she always used her married name) cleverly straddled the musical fence by writing works for her own concert use, including a Piano Trio, two concertos, and a raft of songs and shorter keyboard pieces.

Mendelssohn: Nice Guys Don't Always Finish Last

Felix Mendelssohn (1809-1847), born four years after his sister into the same warmly nurturing, culturally aware household, grew up as a man of high education and attainments that went far beyond the world of music: he was a fine horseman and swimmer, an elegant dancer, a skilled painter, a chess master, and pretty hot stuff at the billiard table. His music reflects this aura of refinement; like his personality, it is literate, handsome, and harmonious.

Mendelssohn, never lacking for material comforts or popular acclaim, was no rebel; he was content to live as he composed: with grace and gentility.

Music surrounded Felix from birth, and by the time he was five, he had contributed his first song to the family archives. Every Sunday there would be a morning musicale at the Mendelssohn house, with Fanny displaying her expertise at the piano, while brother Paul played the cello, their sister Rebecca sang, while other family members and visiting friends filled out the performing forces. In the middle of it all was little Felix, sometimes accompanying at the piano, sometimes helping out at the fiddle, and not infrequently lugging out a stool so the other players could see him while he conducted one of his new pieces. And those new scores kept coming. By the time he was 14, Felix had signed his name to a dozen short symphonies, not to mention three concertos, several operettas, and a few cantatas.

Unlike many prodigies, whose surface talents cannot survive the harsher glare of adult scrutiny, Mendelssohn continued to grow in stature and international fame throughout his all-too-short life. As music director of the famous Gewandhaus Orchestra in Leipzig, and co-founder of the Leipzig Conservatory, he was a major force in the cultural life of his own country, and as biographer Herbert Kupferberg wrote, "possibly no other composer's music had ever spread through the world so quickly." Mendelssohn's Violin Concerto is arguably the most loved in the whole repertoire, and untold millions have been spurred to the altar by the "Wedding March" (from his music to Shakespeare's *A Midsummer Night's Dream*).

Though he traveled widely, both as tourist and performer, Britain rapidly became his destination of choice. Mendelssohn made ten separate trips to England, conducting the

Important Things to Know

If you are going to go down the bridal path, you will want some great appropriate music. Great as it is, Mendelssohn's Wedding March is a tad clichéd at this point, as is the "Here Comes the Bride" theme from Wagner's "Lohengrin", so consider a few tonal alternatives for your matrimonial matinée. The Wedding March from Mozart's "The Marriage of Figaro" is a nifty one, or try Grieg's "Wedding Day at Troldhaugen". Saint-Saens' lighthearted "Wedding Cake" might be better suited to skipping, rather than marching down the aisle, so consider an instrumental section from one of Bach's five Wedding Cantatas. Most importantly, have a happy life!

premieres of his oratorios St. Paul and Elijah to wild acclaim, becoming the darling of British society and—as the most distinguished semi-resident since Haydn—something of an English hero as well. Mendelssohn gave organ recitals at St. Paul's Cathedral, played his piano concertos, and was even welcomed at Buckingham Palace by Queen Victoria and Prince Albert

A conductor, teacher, festival organizer, composer, pianist, **and** composer, Mendelssohn made the most of the scant 38 years allotted to him. Musical snobs often denigrate his works as not being profound enough, but audiences continue to bask in his luxurious melodies and warm harmonic invention. "Let us honor and love Mendelssohn," said Robert Schumann. "He is the prophet of a glorious future, his road leads to happiness."

Bet You Didn't Know

The Nazis, contemptuous **of** Mendelssohn's Jewish heritage, tore down his statues, removed his name from musical textbooks, got a state-approved composer to write a substitute Wedding March, and tried desperately to ban his compositions altogether. "Mendelssohn was an ersatz (fake) for a true German master," stated one official document. "His music can perhaps still be used as material for practicing, but never as a full-valued work of art." Needless to say, the Nazis could no more erase musical history than they could rule the world.

Mendelssohn's Works You Need to Know

"A Midsummer Night's Dream" is a perfect introduction to the warmth and radiance of Mendelssohn's music: the complete set of Incidental Music contains vocal solos, choruses and—in some recordings—interpolations of Shakespeareian readings, but you'll get the flavor in the shorter "Suite," with its luminous Overture, scampering Scherzo, and the aforementioned Wedding March.

The composer's love for travel is well displayed in the Italian and Scotch Symphonies, plus the Hebrides Overture, and the Venetian Boat Songs (included among his many "Songs without Words" for solo piano). On a more expansive keyboard level, there are two solo piano concertos and the aptly titled Rondo Brilliant, plus another pair of concertos for Two Pianos and Orchestra. Unquestionably, though, the E Minor Violin Concerto is Mendelssohn's greatest achievement in the form. The themes are glowing and gorgeous, and the soloist has enough opportunities for virtuoso razzle-dazzle to make the Concerto as delectable to hear as it is challenging to play.

Enchantments abound in his chamber music, too, the bulging roster including two piano trios (the D Minor is especially scintillating), seven quartets (try the op. 44, no. 1), and the peerless Octet.

Schumann: It's a Hard-Knock Life

Robert Schumann (1810-1856) possessed the true romantic's affinity for poetry, drama, and dreams. He once wrote, "I do not know myself what I really am. If I am a poet—for no one can really become one—destiny will decide." Destiny, meanwhile, was preparing a double-edged sword. The burning romantic spirit that allowed Schumann's musical imagination to soar also turned his life into improbable melodrama and, ultimately, tragedy. Schumann's sister, Emilie, drowned herself at the age of 20; his three brothers died young, and signs of his own mental instability became apparent as early as his 23rd year.

Born in Zwichau, Germany, Robert Schumann's childhood gave no indication of the darkness to come in his life. There was no poverty, no harsh or abusive parents. His father owned a publishing house and lending library, and his propensity for dark and gloomy fantasies may have helped shape young Robert's own poetic personality; certainly it instilled in the boy an early love for literature. Although Robert wrote a few childish pieces at the age of six, and five years later was directing his school band, he devoted far more of his creative time during his teenage years to writing poems, essays, and even novels. Indeed, his fame as a music critic well preceded the acceptance of his own compositions.

After the death of his father, Schumann's more conventionally minded mother enrolled Robert in law school, but his first rummagings in legalistic textbooks convinced him that music was his intended path after all. He signed up for piano lessons with Friedrich Wieck, who promised his mother to turn Robert into a great virtuoso within three years. He might have done it, too, had not Schumann's impatient and impulsive nature caused him to invent a device that was supposed to strengthen his fourth finger. Instead, it crippled his fourth finger, ending his virtuoso dreams, and forcing him to channel his musical creativity into composition.

The time spent with Wieck was not entirely wasted. If you remember from a few pages back, Schumann fell for his daughter, and despite Papa's protests and ploys, the romance flourished. When Clara and Robert couldn't meet, they wrote; when Clara's father tore up Robert's letters, they spoke of their love through music. Schumann described his F Minor Sonata as his heart's cry for her, and Clara played it right under her father's nose because, as she later wrote, "I knew no other way of showing something of my inmost heart. I could not do it in secret, so I did it in public."

If the years of courtship inspired Schumann to some of his most impassioned piano music, including "Kreisleriana," the C Major Fantasy ("my profound lament about you," Robert

Bet You Didn't Know

On Clara's 18th birthday, she and Robert became engaged, and while they waited impatiently for her father's grudging approval, Robert wrote her several other musical love letters "with many a bridal thought, amid the most splendid exaltation that I can ever recall." Was he a "Romantic" or what?

wrote to Clara), and the "Fantasiestucke," Robert proclaimed his newfound happiness after their marriage in 1840, with a "year of song." Here he poured out his love in dozens of magical lieder, and such exquisite song cycles as "Frauenliebe und Leben" (Woman's Life and Love) and "Dichterliebe" (Poet's Love).

In 1841, Schumann expanded into the first of his four symphonies, appropriately dubbed *Spring*. Then chamber music came to the fore, and in 1842 alone Schumann completed three string quartets, plus the beautiful Piano Quartet and Piano Quintet.

Alas, Schumann's mental health, always a bit iffy, began to deteriorate much more seriously. He experienced bouts of extreme melancholy and, began to have lapses of memory. He heard voices in his head, the shrieks of demons alternating with angelic choirs. He claimed to have been visited by the spirits of Schubert and Mendelssohn. In February of 1854, he bade farewell to his Clara, close to delivering their eighth child, and threw himself into the Rhine. Passersby rescued him, but a week later, Robert was moved to a sanitorium. He lived another two years, with only occasional moments of lucidity; on July 29, 1856, Clara held him for the last time. "He smiled at me," she recalled, "and put his arms around me with great difficulty, for he had almost lost control of his limbs. Never shall I forget that moment. I would not give that embrace for all the treasures on earth."

Schumann's Works You Need to Know

As with Chopin, whom we'll get to in a little bit, the keyboard looms large in Schumann's output, whether in the great solo suites, among them "Carnaval," "Kinderscenen" (Scenes from Childhood), "Kreisleriana" and "Fantasiestucke", or the enormously popular Piano Concerto in A Minor.

The piano then appears as partner to the voice in a barrage of lieder and the great song cycles "Dichterliebe" and "Frauenliebe und Leben," and as a chamber music participant with strings in the three trios, the quartet, and quintet.

In the non-keyboard department, the First ("Spring") and Third ("Rhenish") Symphonies are probably the most appealing of the four; the Cello Concerto is a warmly lyric piece, and for a real sonic novelty get out the Konzertstuck (Concert Piece) for Four Horns and Orchestra.

Berlioz

Berlioz' "Symphonie Fantastique" was hailed as the most sensational first symphony ever written, which made it a hard act to follow. Berlioz was up to the task, though, brandishing the banner of revolutionary Romanticism by vastly expanding the era's choral and orchestral horizons.

Hector Berlioz (1803-1869) was born in a small French village near Grenoble. His father was a prosperous physician who appreciated the classics and the arts, so Hector grew up playing the guitar, flute, and piano, though none of them well enough to earn a living by. This was fine with Papa Berlioz, who wanted his son to follow him into the medical trade anyway, and when the time came, he shipped the lad off to medical school in Paris.

Berlioz stuck it out for a year, but it was no use. He would sing arias in the dissecting room and copy opera scores instead of doing his osteology homework. Eventually, he quit his medical studies altogether and enrolled at the Paris Conservatory. His father was so upset that he cut off Hector's allowance, but the lad got by as a singer in a vaudeville chorus and by writing articles for a local newspaper.

As it turned out, the bulk of Berlioz's income in later years came from music journalism,

Bet You Didn't Know

Berlioz was pretty nervous about his first literary assignments, but he got used to them later. "My brain seemed ready to burst, my blood was on fire," he wrote in his Memoirs; "I felt as if burning embers were scorching my veins. I tore my hair and wept, I beat with my fists against my skull." Another true "romantic!"

because it didn't cost a fortune to print reviews, articles, and letters, the way it did to mount such miniatures as Romeo and Juliet, which is scored for an orchestra of 200 players, plus three vocal soloists, and a huge chorus; and The Trojans, a five-act marathon so long that even Berlioz had to break down and divide it up into two full-evening operas.

Despite his illusions of grandeur, Berlioz was indeed a master painter of sound canvasses,

Bet You Didn't Know

Berlioz liked things on a grand scale, even when it didn't involve his own compositions. At an 1844 concert in Paris, he conducted Weber's "Die Freischutz" Overture using 24 French horns; Beethoven's Fifth Symphony with 36 double-basses; and the "Prayer" from Rossini's opera Moses with 25 harps added to the orchestra. Somebody else was paying the bills, naturally.

using music to convey vivid pictures and tell melodramatic stories. He also excelled as a conductor, his strength of personality (and his insistence on sectional rehearsals) raising performance levels to new heights of power and precision. He defied convention and opened bright new vistas in the orchestration.

Berlioz's Works You Need to Know

Start with the "Symphonie Fantastique," with its high passion and graphic descriptions of everything from the beauties of nature to a witches' sabbath, from a glittering ball to the composer's opium-clouded vision of his own execution.

"Harold in Italy" is a sumptuous travelogue in sound for viola and orchestra, and for those with shorter attention spans, consider the Roman Carnival, King Lear, Benvenuto Cellini, and his many other overtures, with or without operas attached.

The glorious Requiem, with its four brass bands sounding from all sides of the hall, will give your home stereo a good run for its money, or for a more intimate vocal experience, listen to the meltingly beautiful orchestral song cycle Les Nuits d'été (Nights of Summer).

Chopin: Star of the Pianistic Galaxy

What Handel was to oratorio, Beethoven to symphony, and Schubert to lieder, such was Frederic Chopin (1810-1849) to the piano. He left us a dozen songs, a cello sonata, and a few other chamber pieces, but otherwise Chopin poured all of his love and inspiration into the solo keyboard, bestowing upon it such a wide array of sonorities and expressive nuances, that a whole new age of piano artistry came into being.

Born in a little Polish town outside of Warsaw, Frederic Chopin was precocious in many ways, writing poetry at age 6, showing considerable gifts for drawing and acting, and already starting to compose little pieces at the piano. When he played a difficult concerto by the Bohemian composer Adalbert Gyrowetz two years later, the Polish public dubbed him "the new Mozart," and welcomed the child into the aristocratic salons of Warsaw. As a teenager, Chopin dutifully studied at the Conservatory, but his international fame began with his greatly acclaimed Vienna debut in August 1829, when he played his own Krakowiak (a Polish dance) for piano and orchestra.

A year later, Chopin gave his farewell concerts in Poland, and prepared to embark on a tour of Europe, with a possible visit across the Atlantic to the United States. The best laid plans of mice and musicians being what they are, the hoped-for grand tour fell through. Italy, for a change, was a hotbed of political unrest, while America seemed terribly remote and still a bit on the barbaric side. Chopin had to settle for scattered performances in Germany, during one of which, in 1831, he received news of the Russian occupation of Warsaw. Legend has it that the fiercely patriotic Pole responded by rushing to his desk to compose the "Revolutionary" Étude; in any case, in company with many other greatly talented exiles, Chopin soon arrived in Paris.

Very quickly, the young expatriate was inducted into French high society, his performances much in demand at elegant soirées, his reputation as a composer growing almost as quickly. "Hats off, gentlemen!" exulted Robert Schumann, further urging everyone to "bow before Chopin's lofty aims and masterful, spontaneous genius."

Chopin was no Berlioz or Wagner, propounding the theory that bigger is better; nor was he like Liszt, ready to subvert any music to virtuoso display, adorning everything he could get his fingers on. On the other hand, Chopin had attained full mastery of the keyboard; his works are at once passionate and delicate, intense and warmly melodic. He was not out to revolutionize music, but he did so nonetheless, at least insofar as the piano is concerned.

Chopin's health was indeed fragile and deteriorating, nor was it helped by his emotionally

Important Things to Know

In his mazurkas and polonaises, Chopin proudly recalled the music of his homeland; his waltzes exemplified the bright-hued elegance of the Parisian salons; in the Bballades, he was the romantic story-teller; in the nocturnes, he sighed with the soul of the poet. His talents as interpretive artist apparently mirrored his creative gifts. Critics at the time described his playing as precise, clean, and free from embellishment. Liszt, quick enough to recognize Chopin's art as miles apart from his own, nonetheless recognized his unique qualities. He is a poet—elegiac, profound, chaste, and dreaming," said Liszt after attending one of Chopin's Paris recitals. "He sought delicate sympathy rather than noisy acclaim." Chopin, in other words, may have put all of himself into his music, but as a performer, he never lost his cool.

Music Word

The **Mazurka** and **Polonaise** are both Polish dances, the former of rustic origin, the latter a more stately, elegant step that became popular at many European courts.

The **Ballade** is an instrumental piece that—as its deriviation from "ballad" suggests—either tells a story or is inspired by a literary poem or narrative tale.

The **Nocturne** is a night piece (in Italian: notturno), usually short, lyric, and serene. All of these forms were brought to exquisite concert life by Chopin, though he neither invented them, nor was the last to use them.

draining work methods. Perhaps the most intimate—and touching—account of Chopin's creative universe came from George Sand, the brilliant, tuxedo-clad, cigar-smoking novelist who became his live-in lover for more than ten years (don't worry, George was a woman!). "His creation was spontaneous and miraculous," she wrote. "He found it without seeking it, without foreseeing it. It came suddenly, complete, sublime, singing in his head during a walk. But then began the most heart-rending labor I ever saw, a series of efforts, of irresolutions and frettings to seize again certain details of the theme he had heard. He shut himself up in his room for whole days, weeping, walking, breaking his pens, repeating a bar a hundred times.

By the time of his last recital in Paris in February 1848, Chopin was already dying of

Bet You Didn't Know

Chopin's music was said **to** heat up the **work** production lines. In England, a statistical study made in 1940 by the Parliamentary Secretary to the Ministry of Information reported that "the playing of music by Chopin produces an increase of the munitions output from 6 to 12 percent."

tuberculosis. Within days, the 1848 Revolution broke out, and Chopin took refuge across the Channel in England, where his diminishing strength was taxed further by more concerts, the last of them a benefit for Polish emigrés. He returned to Paris in the fall of 1849, and died there on October 17. Thousands of mourners gathered to hear the Mozart Requiem sung in his memory, and Chopin's body was laid to rest between the tombs of Cherubini and Bellini. His heart, however, literally remains in Poland, where, at his own request, it was transported for reburial in his homeland.

Chopin's Works You Need to Know

If you don't like the piano, better cross Chopin off your listening list. Otherwise, hours of musical heaven await you, and it almost doesn't matter where you begin. For high virtuosity, make it the études; the nocturnes are better for moments of reflection and introspection; to sample of Chopin's Polish fervor, try the mazurkas and polonaises. Some of all those qualities swirl through the ballades and scherzos, and if you grew up on old-time pop songs, the "Fantasie Impromptu" ought to bring back fond memories: one of its main tunes was pilfered by Joseph McCarthy and Harry Carroll for "I'm Always Chasing Rainbows."

For Chopin on a larger scale, listen to the B-flat Minor Sonata, with the famous "Funeral March," and the two Piano Concertos. Less often encountered, but worth the hunt, are his Variations on Mozart's "La ci darem la Mano" and another sparkling work for piano and orchestra, the "Grand Fantasy on Polish Airs."

Bravo Brahms: Beethoven's Tenth

Given the zillions of composers whose names begin with B— from Buxtehude to Britten— it's a pretty high honor to make to the fabled "Three B's," as happened when Johannes Brahms joined the pantheon of Bach and Beethoven. The linkage is appropriate though, because unlike Berlioz, who epitomized the Romantic era and stretched its poetic boundaries ever farther, Brahms was a classicist at heart, who had an 18th century respect for structure, and followed classical form even while his musical language kept up with the romantic times.

Johannes Brahms (1833-1897) was born in Hamburg, Germany, where his father was a town musician, and Johannes began earning his own keep at the age of 15 giving piano lessons, arranging marches for brass bands, and playing dance music for ladies of the night and their seafaring customers at waterfront bars.

This provided young Brahms with a good education (in life, if not music), but he knew he was destined for better things, and they started happening when he met the famous Hungarian violinist, Joseph Joachim. Joachim was sufficiently impressed by Brahms to send him on with letters of introduction to Liszt in Weimar and Schumann in Dusseldorf.

The Liszt connection, alas, never amounted to anything because Brahms managed to doze off while the older pianist was demonstrating his keyboard prowess (Brahms didn't much care for Liszt's music, even when he was awake), but when the young man played for the Schumanns, the results were far different. Robert immediately pronounced his new friend a genius "who would not show us his mastery in gradual development, but like Minerva spring full-armed from the head of Zeus." Brahms, meanwhile, found in Clara an ardent admirer and lifelong friend.

With Schumann's help, Brahms' rise to fame was nearly immediate, although he was

Bet You Didn't Know

Clara was impressed by more than Brahms' compositions, writing in her diary about his "beautiful hands and interesting young face, which becomes transfigured when he plays." For his part, Brahms dashed off a set of Variations "on a Theme by Him, Dedicated to Her." Hmmm...

sometimes caught in the crossfire of the two warring camps in mid-19th century Vienna. There were the devotees of "music of the future," who fell to their knees at the mere mention of Liszt and Wagner; and there were the classicists who exalted Brahms and Mendelssohn, and not-so-secretly hoped that the new music enthusiasts would be attacked by roving bands of Valkyries.

Brahms, meanwhile, ignored both sides and proceeded to produce a stream of glorious music in a style that was his alone. He did, though, stall for quite some time on the composition of a symphony, because he fretted about coming up to the standards set up by his idol, Beethoven. Brahms planned out a symphony in a two-piano score, then thought better of the idea and turned the sketches into the D Minor Piano Concerto. He labelled two other symphonic-type pieces Serenades, while a third became the Variations on a Theme of Haydn. Finally, twenty years after he had begun the agonizing process, Brahms came forward with his First Symphony. The famous conductor Hans von Bulow immediately dubbed it "Beethoven's Tenth." The musical logjam broken, Brahms proceeded to add three more masterworks to the symphonic ranks, all the while continuing to compose reams of piano, vocal, and chamber music.

Bet You Didn't Know

Don't think appreciation of Brahms' music **was** universal, even amongst his fellow composers. Hugo Wolf said that the Second Piano Concerto had the "nutritional equivalent of window glass, cork stoppers, and stove pipes," while Tchaikovsky, too polite to say anything nasty in public, expressed himself quite clearly in his diary: "I played over the music of that scoundrel Brahms. What a giftless bastard."

Brahms' last public appearance was at a concert in Vienna, where his Fourth Symphony was played, and the audience endlessly cheered the cancer-stricken composer. Less than a month later, the world was mourning the loss of the last of the Three B's.

Brahms' Works You Need to Know

There are the four great symphonies, of course, the two mighty Piano Concertos, the great Violin Concerto, and the spacious Double Concerto for Violin, Cello, and Orchestra. But for Brahms at his most jovial, put on any of the sparkling Hungarian Dances, and then the boisterous "Academic Festival" Overture, with its symphonic treatment of the ancient student song "Gaudeamus Igitur."

Listen to the ravishingly lovely "German Requiem," and if you like that, dig deeper into Brahms' vocal artistry with the "Alto Rhapsody" and some of the exquisite songs.

For keyboard fans, start with the rhapsodies and proceed to the two-piano dazzlements of the "Variations on a Theme of Paganini." The chamber enticements are too many to enumerate here, but don't miss the Clarinet Sonatas, Cello Sonatas and Sextets (there are two of each), plus the three Sonatas for Violin and Piano and, for dessert, the Piano and Clarinet Quintets.

Tchaikovsky: The Russian Soul

The flag-waving propensity of the romantic era was nowhere stronger than in Russia. Michael Glinka started writing music "that would make my countrymen feel at home" and was rewarded with the title "Father of Russian Music." His figurative children included the proudly nationalistic composers who became known as "The Russian Five": Balakirev and Rimsky-Korsakov, both of whom arranged and published extensive collections of Russian folk songs, Borodin, Cui, and Moussorgsky. Standing apart from this circle was Tchaikovsky, who recognized the gifts of those five composers, but pronounced them (with the exception of Rimsky-Korsakov) "impregnated with the purely amateur conviction of their superiority to all other musicians in the universe."

While he too would more than occasionally write patriotic pieces and quote folk tunes in his symphonic works, Tchaikovsky was far more universal in his approach, his music incorporating elements of Italian opera, French ballet, German symphony and song. On the other hand, his soul was always rooted in his homeland, and more than most other composers, he poured his soul into his music. Without wanting to, Tchaikovsky became, as Igor Stravinsky put it, "the most Russian of us all."

Peter (or Piotr, to put the proper Russian spin on his first name) Ilyich (i.e., the son of Ilya) Tchaikovsky (1840-1893) was born in Votkinsk, a remote village at the foot of the Ural Mountains. Not quite the same as Leipzig or Vienna for nurturing an awareness of the arts, and even after the family moved to St. Petersburg, Tchaikovsky's musical gifts were slow to emerge. He went to a school of jurisprudence and worked for a while as a government clerk before, at the age of 21, entering a new musical institute that would later become the celebrated St. Petersburg Conservatory. Four years later, he won a silver medal for his cantata on Schiller's "Ode to Joy," and thereafter composition became his prime focus.

Bet You Didn't Know

Medal or no medal, Tchaikovsky was so afraid that people would be upset with him for having used the same text as Beethoven for the finale of the Ninth Symphony, that he refused to allow the piece to be published during his lifetime. Unfortunately, nobody bothered to publish it after his lifetime either, **so** the cantata did not actually appearing in print until 1960.

As Tchaikovsky's fame and fortune increased, so did his psychological torment. Rumors were spreading about his homosexuality, and in a tortured attempt to quell them, Tchaikovsky married a young conservatory student. Predictably, the union was a disaster, the composer fleeing after nine days, then trying to commit suicide by walking into the Moskva River. (The idea was to get pneumonia, but he only wound up with a lousy cold.)

The next woman who came into his life was Nadezhda von Meck, and talk about an ideal relationship (under the circumstances): she paid Tchaikovsky's debts, lent him money, then bestowed upon him a generous annual allowance, the only condition being that composer and benefactress never meet face to face. "My beloved friend," the grateful and highly relieved Tchaikovsky wrote to her, "every note which comes from my pen in future is dedicated to you. To you I owe this reawakening love of work, and I shall never forget for a moment that you have made it possible for me to carry on my career."

Bet You Didn't Know

Mme. von Meck tried to be nice to other musicians too, hiring the then 19-year-old Claude Debussy to give her children piano lessons. When the composer tried to give one of her daughters bedroom lessons as well, she kicked him out of the house.

For all his inner turmoil, Tchaikovsky's international career was quite on track. His music was being performed all over the world, he received an honorary degree from Cambridge, and was invited to conduct his own works in Poland, Germany, and America where, in 1891, he presided at the inaugural concert in Carnegie Hall. Ironically, two of his (now) most popular concertos were heartily denounced by critics and rejected by the soloists for whom they were written: "The First Piano Concerto, like the first pancake, is a flop," was one of the kinder comments; another critic called the Violin Concerto "music that stinks to the ear."

In October 1893, Tchaikovsky was back in St. Petersburg conducting the premiere of his "Pathetique Symphony," a deeply personal work over which, he admitted, "I often wept bitterly while composing it." Typhoid was prevalent in the city, and despite public warnings, the composer unthinkingly drank a glass of unboiled water. In less than two weeks, the dreaded epidemic had claimed its most famous victim.

Though beset by personal demons, Tchaikovsky knew well the worth of his music. "My faith in the judgement of the future is immovable," he wrote to Mme. von Meck; "I have had a foretaste during my lifetime of the fame that will be meted out to me when the history of Russian music comes to be written. I have no right to complain."

Tchaikovsky's Works You Need to KNow

To hear Tchaikovsky in full orchestral glory, start with the last three symphonies (no's. 4, 5, and 6), continue with suites from his three radiant ballets, Swan Lake, The Nutcracker, and Sleeping Beauty. For the literary-minded, take out Tchaikovsky's sumptuous symphonic translations of Romeo and Juliet, Francesca da Rimini, and Hamlet; the lush sonorities of his Serenade for Strings came long before Mantovani; and for blatantly patriotic, delectably noisy hi-jinks, you just can't top the 1812 Overture.

Despite what some of his contemporaries thought, the Violin and the First Piano Concertos are among the most accessible in the entire repertoire, and if you feel adventuresome, take a gamble on the far less familiar, but highly attractive Second Piano Concerto. For cellophiles, there's the elegant "Variations on a Rococo Theme," and by all means, enjoy some of the shorter pieces for violin and orchestra, including the exquisite "Serenade Melancolique."

Eugene Onegin and Pique Dame (Queen of Spades) should head up your operatic ticket, while for quieter moments, curl up with the String Quartet no. #1 (which contains the famous "Andante Cantabile," such a gorgeous piece that it often ventures into the concert hall on its own). A longer chamber work of single beauty is the A Minor Piano Trio.

Apologies Department

Once again we have tried to point up trends and tendencies within the Romantic era, and to spotlight some of the composers who made them happen. We couldn't include them all, though, so forgive us our sins of omission, and try to investigate other giants of 19th century music on your own. Start with Antonin Dvorak,perhaps: the Czech master saluted his homeland with the jaunty Slavonic Dances and the ebullient Carnival Overture, then came across the Atlantic to set an example for our composers with his "New World" Symphony and the "American" String Quartet. For more Slavonic flavorings, Czech out some of the delightful music of Bedrich Smetana, especially his tonal portrait of a ride down the river Moldau, or the rollicking Overture to "The Bartered Bride."

Want some music with the French touch? You can go to the opera with Jules Massenet and Charles Gounod, the chamber music room with Cesar Franck and Gabriel Fauré, the ballet theatre with Adolphe Adam and Leo Delibes. Edvard Grieg in Norway and Alexander Borodin in Russia wrote such gorgeous melodies that—fitted out with lyrics by Robert Wright and George Forrest—they lit up the Great White Way (respectively, in "Song of Norway" and "Kismet"). The list goes on and on, adding up to a never-ending source of delight for the curious music listener.

CHAPTER 17

 # Grooving to the Classics in the 20th Century

In This Chapter

➤ The romance is over

➤ A change of taste

➤ Mighty Mahler

➤ Richard Strauss

➤ Vaughan Williams, Debussy, and Ives

➤ Schoenberg, Cowell, and Stravinsky

Many of the composers whose lives crossed the millennium were still romantics at heart. They favored lush melodies, sensuous harmonies, and took sides in the perpetual battle between Good and Evil. Before long, though, musical chinks appeared in the romantic armor. Debussy, denouncing emotional excesses and preferring to have his music create a mood rather than tell a clear-cut story, led the way to Impressionism. Igor Stravinsky's plunge into savage rhythms and clashing harmonies caused riots, as did Henry Cowell in America when he attacked the piano with forearms and elbows. Arnold Schoenberg, refusing to be bound by the old rules of keys and scales, led hordes of followers down the 12-tone trail. Well before the middle of the 20th century, in other words, the face of classical music had completely changed.

Music Word

Impressionism is a term borrowed from the art world (where it was applied to such painters as Degas, Whistler, Monet, and others), and used to describe music that suggests moods, perceptions, or feelings rather than being specifically descriptive of events or scenes.

Diehard Romantics

Call them Neo-Romantics. Their music was rich and embellished, their instrumentations bold and expansive, their orchestrations massive. Herr Wagner was a hard act to follow, but they gave it their best shot.

The Mighty Mahler

During his own lifetime, Gustav Mahler (1860-1911) was better known as a conductor than a composer—and a fairly ruthless taskmaster at that. "I have encountered frightful habits in every orchestra," he said, mincing no further words in whipping the musicians into shape. Players rebelled at his grueling standards of perfection, while theatrical managements resented his iron-willed determination to produce concerts and operas his way: fully researched, thoroughly rehearsed, uncut. The results pleased audiences, but audiences don't hire conductors: Within ten years, Mahler bounced around in posts at Kassel, Prague, Leipzig, Budapest, Hamburg, and Vienna, where he lasted three whole seasons before calling it quits.

It was in 1880 that Mahler, fresh from the Vienna Conservatory, got a summer job as music director of Bad Hall, a light-opera theatre that quite lived up to its name: the repertoire was cheesy, the facilities inadequate, the players slovenly. Nonetheless, Mahler caught the conducting bug there, and it became a serious itch that he continued scratching the rest of his life. Indeed, in 1907 he crossed the Atlantic to shake a stick both at the Metropolitan Opera and the New York Philharmonic, until he fell seriously ill with a blood infection. He returned to Vienna, where he died in 1911.

Mahler's perfectionism led to considerable turmoil in his compositional work, too. He couldn't leave a piece alone. He would constantly rework details, sometimes engaging in massive rewritings and re-orchestrations, even of scores that had already been successfully performed and circulated. In sharp contrast to Puccini, who loved "small things" (be patient—we'll get to that later in this book), Mahler thought big. His expansive symphonies have mystical and philosophical subtexts, while many of his songs are passionate expressions of despair and longing.

As it happens, Mahler knew sadness all too well. Five of his siblings succumbed to diphtheria in childhood, another died of a brain tumor, and one more committed suicide. It was in music that he found both an escape from real-world tragedies, and a burning desire to communicate his deeply-felt ideas about life and death. The passion in Mahler's music often suggests a personality on the edge.

Mahler's orchestral songs require a large ensemble, and his symphonies call for rows and rows of winds and brass, a sea of strings, and all sorts of oddball percussion instruments. Mahler also achieved special sounds by unusual instructions: in certain scores, for instance, the oboes and clarinets have to play "bells up," (that is, with the players' heads tilted uncomfortably up so that their instruments were aimed toward the top balcony. Other works require off-stage brass, on-stage church bells, and such infrequent symphonic visitors as mandolin and organ.

Mahler's Works You Need to Know

Like most of his Ssymphonies, the Fifth takes well over an hour, but spare ten minutes for the Adagietto movement, a meltingly beautiful elegy for harp and strings that could make a Mahler fan out of anybody. Once you're hooked, move on to his First Symphony, especially the third movement, with its "Frère Jacques" tune. The Second, or "Resurrection" Symphony adds vocal soloists and chorus to the musical mix, and the surprisingly gentle Fourth Symphony brings in a soprano to give us a child's eye view of Heaven. Mahler completed nine symphonies, but don't panic if you see a tenth listed on a concert program: the unfinished work was completed by English musicologist Deryck Cooke.

Other vocal pieces with orchestra include the heartbreaking "Kindertotenlieder" (Songs on the Death of Children); the robust "Lieder eines fahrenden Gesellen" (Songs of a Wayfarer); the often rollicking settings of lyrics from the collection of folk poetry known as "Das Knaben Wunderhorn" (The Youth's Magic Horn), which are equally effective as lieder, with piano accompaniments; and "Das Lied von der Erde" (Song of the Earth), a richly varied work that Mahler himself admitted was less a song cycle than a symphony for voices and orchestra.

Richard Strauss: Wizard of the Orchestral Oz, or: Orchestral Fireworks

Not to be confused with Johann Strauss (1864-1949), the father of the "Blue Danube" (or Oscar, the double-s-less Straus, who wrote "The Chocolate Soldier"), Richard Strauss was the son of the principal horn player in the Munich Court Orchestra. Daddy Franz had suffered through so many Wagner operas that he was one of the most rabid of the anti-Wagner voices in Germany. Highly protective of the tender ears of his talented son, he allowed Richard to study only the "classics": Mozart, Beethoven, and Mendelssohn. The results were predictable. At the age of ten, when other boys were sneaking out to smoke their first cigarette, the rebellious Richard got hooked on the music of Wagner. He was smitten by its power and drama, and it only remained for him to learn how to create pieces as big, bold, and brassy as that of his idol.

Important Things to Know

Stressed by all the Strausses? Here's a quick reference guide. The old man of the family was Johann Sr. (1804-1849), known as the Father of the Waltz. Unfortunately, his son was also named Johann Strauss (1825-1899), so make sure you see the Jr. sign if you're looking for "The Blue Danube" or any of the hundreds of other great dance pieces that earned him the title of The Waltz King. Don't put away the phone book just yet, though. Johann Jr. had two composer-brothers, Josef (1827-1870) and Eduard (1835-1916), and Eduard had a composer-conductor son whom, in a fit of wild originality, he dubbed Johann Strauss III (1866-1939).

No relation to any of those guys was Franz Josef Strauss (1822-1905), a German composer and horn player whose most important creation was his son, the Richard Strauss under present discussion. Oh yes, one more composer of high repute, but one less "s" than usual, was Oscar Straus (1870-1954), who wrote the immensely popular operetta "The Chocolate Soldier".

Growing up in a professional music environment, Strauss had become a fairly capable pianist and a promising young conductor, but still in his teens, he was attracted most strongly to composition. He wrote a Wind Serenade, numerous songs and chamber pieces, a Horn Concerto (which he made as difficult as possible to get back at his father), and even a Symphony that won the esteem of Brahms.

Once into his twenties, however, Strauss' conservative streak faded quickly. In 1885, he struck up an important friendship with violinist Alexander Ritter, an ardent Wagnerian who just happened to be married to Wagner's niece. "His influence was in the nature of a stormwind," Strauss later recalled. "He urged me to the development of the poetic, the expressive in music, as exemplified in the works of Liszt, Berlioz, and Wagner."

With that, Strauss was off. He began with the symphonic fantasy "Aus Italien" (from Italy), modestly proclaiming it "the connecting link between the old and the new." Critics proclaimed it a few less complimentary things, such as incoherent, noisy, and vulgar, but undaunted, the young composer proceeded to a whole slew of tone poems. "Don Juan" was his first rousing success, after which he tackled Shakespeare ("Macbeth"), Nietzsche ("Thus Spake Zarathustra"), Cervantes ("Don Quixote") and—no shrinking viole—Richard Strauss himself ("A Hero's Life"). By adapting Wagner's leitmotifs to symphonic usage, he earned himself the nickname "Richard the Second." Unlike so many other composers, Puccini, who cloaked the agonies of real life in musical beauty, Strauss portrayed exotic fantasies with everyday sounds, his music graphically imitating horses' hoofbeats, the bleating of sheep, claps of thunder, even the feeding of a baby.

With the turn of the century, came a turning of Strauss' interests towards opera. His first one ("Guntram"), written in 1894, was a total disaster (except that Strauss married the leading soprano), but after a reasonable cooling-off period, the slightly bawdy "Feuersnot" did much better in 1901. "It is not seemly for men and women to talk to one another about the lewd plot," said one critic, so naturally everybody rushed to see it. Next came "Salome," after the Oscar Wilde play, with such a shocking plot and such sensual music, including the stripteasing "Dance of the Seven Veils," that the Viennese censors banned it altogether. Even the presumably less prudish and more enlightened Metropolitan Opera bowed to a storm of protests and removed it after only two performances.

Bet You Didn't Know

The critic in The New York Tribune referred to the "moral stench with which Salome fills the nostrils of humanity"; a letter to the New York Times called it "a detailed and explicit exposition of the most unmentionable features of degeneracy that I have ever heard, read of, or imagined"; and a minister preached a sermon to his Boston congregation railing against this "degrading, loathsome opera whose theme cannot be discussed in a mixed audience." Needless to say, Salome turned into a tremendous hit.

Still on a roll in terms of offending genteel sensibilities, Strauss next turned to the cheery subject of matricide with "Elektra" in 1909. The critics had had three years to recuperate from "Salome," but they were still shocked by the vivid musical portrayal of a sensational subject ("a prodigious orgy," was the verdict of the man at the *New York Times*, guaranteeing yet another sold-out house). Having made his stimulating points, though, Strauss mellowed in 1911 with the witty, light, gracefully satiric "Der Rosenkavalier" (The Knight of the Rose). For once, both audiences and critics loved it. They still do.

Important Things to Know

Unlike many of his colleagues, Strauss did not leave Germany when the Nazis came to power, and this politically aloof musician soon found himself on the wrong side of two different fences. The Nazis, having initially embraced him as a valuable propaganda figure, were upset when he commissioned a libretto from a Jewish writer (Stefan Zweig) and even more outraged when they discovered he had a Jewish daughter-in-law. Strauss did knuckle under and write a hymn for the 1936 Olympic games in Berlin, but his later refusals to obey Nazi propaganda orders put him even further under a government cloud, and he sat out most of the war under virtual house arrest at his villa in Garmisch.

Everybody outside of Germany, meanwhile, went on thinking he was a Nazi collaborator, and it was not until 1948 that Strauss was officially exonerated. By then, he was in poor health and near the end of his life.

In that same year of 1948, Strauss had a final burst of musical inspiration, writing his Four Last Songs for soprano and orchestra. On June 11th, 1949, after saying that the process of dying was just as he had depicted it, nearly 60 years earlier, in his tone poem "Death and Transfiguration," Strauss left this world at the age of 85.

Strauss' Works You Need to Know

The tone poems are an excellent way to make Strauss' musical acquaintance, because they tell stories with wit and high imagination. *Till Eulenspiegel's Merry Pranks* is filled with little orchestral jokes; passionate throbbings indicate the major preoccupation of "*Don Juan*"; in "*Don Quixote,*" the Man of La Mancha (solo cello) and his faithful Sancho Panza (solo viola) do battle with the windmills (wind machine); and while the philosophical meanderings of *Also Spake Zarathustra* can get tiresome after a while, the spectacular opening music will be familiar from its portrayal of the dawn of civilization in the Stanley Kubrick film *2001: A Space Odyssey*.

Opera-wise, *Salome* is short, though not sweet, and *Der Rosenkavalier* is sweet, but not short, so you might want to start orchestrally with the former's "Dance of the Seven Veils" and the lilting "Suite of Waltzes" from the latter. If you're vocally inspired, try a few of Strauss' other 11 operas, especially the fanciful *Die Frau Ohne Schatten* (The Woman Without a Shadow) or the melodramatic *Elektra*. Don't miss the aforementioned *Four Last Songs*, either, and gradually try to hear some of the more than 100 splendid non-last songs with piano accompaniment.

Though Strauss is known mostly for his operas, songs, and tone poems, there are **a** few chamber and solo works worth noting as well. Among them are his impassioned Violin and Piano Sonata, two Horn Concertos, completed 59 years apart (in 1883 and 1942), and two examples of Strauss' superb writing for woodwind instruments that similarly span virtually his entire creative life, the 1881 "Serenade for Thirteen Winds" and the 1948 Oboe Concerto.

Vaughan Williams: A True Englishman

"If the roots of your art are firmly planted in your own soil," said Ralph (or "Rafe," as he pronounced it) Vaughan Williams (1872–1958), "you may gain the whole world and not lose your own soul." **For** inspiration he turned to traditional folk tunes and choral music of the late Middle Ages, he created music for Shakespeare plays, and made settings of verses by Walt Whitman. He even wrote a "Sinfonia Antarctica," but in style, and often content, he was English to the core, whether turning "Greensleeves" into a warm-hearted instrumental Fantasia, portraying the sights and sounds of London, complete with chimes of Westminster, or sauntering through the countryside in his three Norfolk Rhapsodies.

The son of a clergyman who died when Ralph was still a child, the boy was introduced to music through piano and harmony lessons from an aunt. He played violin and viola in his school orchestra, later held down a post as a church organist, and dreamed of greater glory as a composer.

Bet You Didn't Know

Vaughan Williams' family was overly encouraging about his music. "He is hopelessly bad at it," said his Aunt Etty. "He's been working hard all his life, yet he still can't play the simplest thing decently." Aunt Etty, by the way, had similarly dire predictions for the famous writer E.M. Forster, a family friend at the time. "His novels are too unpleasant for the girls to read," she wrote to her niece. "I very much hope he will turn to something else, though I am sure I don't know what."

Gradually, Vaughan Williams' skills strengthened. He studied for a while in Germany with Max Bruch, the composer of the popular "Scottish Fantasy" and another work beloved of concert violinists, the G Minor Concerto; later he went to Paris to pick up a few orchestration hints from Maurice Ravel, whose "Bolero" is practically a textbook on how to write skillfully for instruments; and all the while he was collecting the English folksongs that would form so important a part of his musical output. Traditional tunes swirl through dozens of his compositions, and even when the music is entirely original, the spirit of Britain—her history, her poets, her traditions—is strongly felt.

Vaughan Williams' creative energies extended to the end of his long life (as did his other energies: he married the poet Ursula Wood at age 80). Two years later after his marriage to Wood, he wrote a Tuba Cconcerto; his Eighth Symphony, premiered in his 83rd year, is one of the few classical pieces to incorporate a vibraphone; and in his Ninth Symphony, premiered the following year, Vaughan Williams again defied custom by including three saxophones in the scoring (with the caution that they behave themselves and not play "like demented cats"). As did Richard Strauss, Vaughan Williams closed his life with "Four Last Songs," dying in London on August 28th, six weeks shy of his 86th birthday.

Vaughan Williams' Works You Need to Know

Start with some of the many pieces in which Vaughan Williams gave folksongs a chance to shine. The "Fantasia on Greensleeves" takes only four minutes or so, but it's four minutes of bliss. Want a longer spell of ecstasy? Listen to his haunting "Fantasia on a Theme of Thomas Tallis" (a 16th century English composer), or the equally gorgeous romance for violin and orchestra evocatively titled "A Lark Ascending."

Of the nine symphonies, the "London Symphony" (no. 2) and "Pastoral Symphony" (no. 3) are probably the most accessible, with their folk-inspired portrayals of town and country; also try the "English Folksong Suite," "Studies in English Folksong," "From the Fen Country," and the first of the "Norfolk Rhapsodies."

Lovers of song and poetry will find them magically merged in dozens of individual pieces, plus such cycles as "Songs of Travel" (Robert Louis Stevenson), "Three Poems" (Walt Whitman), and the "Five Mystical Songs" (George Herbert). For vocal ensemble enchantment, you'll do no better than Vaughan Williams' "Serenade to Music" fashioned after Shakespeare, and if you like that, plunge ahead into his more substantial choral pieces, including "Magnificat," "Te Deum," and the Christmas cantata "Hodie" (This Day), a glowing product of the composer's 82nd year.

Along with those early 20th century composers who carried romantic ideals to ever more expansive levels, came those musicians who sought to travel a different road. Some shifted gradually away from the old forms, others exploded them with a barrage of new concepts and methods.

Debussy: Making a Good Impression(ist)

"I am more and more convinced," said Claude Debussy (1862-1918), "that music by its very nature, is something that cannot be cast in a traditional and fixed form. It is made up of colors and rhythms. The rest is a lot of humbug invented by frigid imbeciles riding on the backs of the masters."

Although Debussy's own favorite painters were not Impressionists, and he disclaimed the label in referring to his own compositions, history had other ideas, and the name of this notable French composer will be indelibly and forever be associated with musical Impressionism. The word originated in the Parisian art world of the 1870s, so it was almost passe by the time Debussy began replacing strong musical pictures with shifting, misty images, and disturbing listeners' harmonic expectations with what the poet Verlaine called "harmoniously dissonant chords."

Indeed, Debussy often turned to poetry for inspiration, setting verses of Paul Verlaine, Heinrich Heine, Charles Baudelaire, and other literary icons, but it was his innovative use of exotic colors and startling nuances of phrase that made listeners experience what was happening in his music, rather than just hearing it.

Bet You Didn't Know

The French novelist Joris-Karl Huysmans took that experiential idea one step further when he decided that instrumental colors added up to an "organ of liqueurs." The tone of the clarinet was like curaçao, he announced, the flute was anisette, the lowly trombone brought forth images of whisky and gin, and if you want a glass of vodka, let the tuba blow!

Debussy's first orchestral masterpiece, also suggested by a poem (by Stephane Mallarme) was "L'Aprés-Midi d'un Faune" (The Afternoon of a Faun). Right from its opening flute solo, the work appeals to us today as one of serenity and lustrous warmth, seducing rather than shocking, but it certainly rattled the early critics. One of them called it "nothing, expressed in musical terms," while another suggested that "the suffering Faun seems to need a veterinary surgeon." That, mind you, was before the music was used for a highly erotic ballet, during which Vaslav Nijinsky, in a skintight costume, undulated his way to a realistic depiction of the Faun's sexual longing and release. Even Debussy was a little shocked by that one.

Other orchestral works followed, then his only opera, "Pelleas et Melisande" (after the Maeterlinck play), and a whole series of piano works, from the technically challenging etudes to the charming and fun-filled "Children's Corner Suite," dedicated to his daughter and titled in English since Claude-Emma (or Chochou for short) had a British nanny.

Debussy was always looking for something more than was being handed down to him. He didn't want to follow older recipes, to use anyone else's ingredients, and as a result his musical dishes were not to every taste. On the other hand, his distinct concepts of structure, color, and harmonic shadings paved an important road, one of several bridges that allowed music to flow from 19th century romanticism into the mainstream of modern thought in the 20th.

Debussy's Works You Need to Know

"L'Aprés Midi d' un Faun" is a good way to slide into Debussy's shimmering world, and if you want waves, sail on with "La Mer" (the Sea). Other great portraits in sound are the "Images and Nocturnes." For ensemble music on a more intimate plane, his early (and only) String Quartet is enormously appealing, as is his three-way Sonata for Flute, Viola and Harp.

Debussy's opera "Pelleas et Melisande" has long had a cult following, but it's definitely an acquired taste, so you might find a better vocal introduction via some of his exquisite songs, or the cycle "Chansons de Bilitis."

From the splendid body of piano music, start with the Suite Bergamasque, since it contains the ever-popular "Clair du Lune" (also available in numerous orchestral transcriptions), or the delectable "Children's Corner," with its snippets of early ragtime. The two books of preludes paint a wide array of vivid pictures in sound, as do "Estampes" (Engravings), while the Études are as easy to hear as they are difficult to play.

Ives: A Connecticut Yankee

"It may be possible," Charles Ives (1874-1954) wrote in one of his essays, "that a day in a Kansas wheat field will do more good for an American composer than three years in Rome." Ives was born pretty far from those wheat fields—in Danbury, Connecticut—but he maintained a lifelong separation from the conservatories of Vienna, Leipzig, Paris, and the other European centers where most composers (including Americans) sought their musical muses. He was the quintessential Yankee: original, experimental, eccentric, reclusive, and not one to allow outsiders to tell him what to do.

Ives' father, George, was an ex-bandsman and music teacher whose love of the unusual was obviously a spur to the young Charles. George introduced his kids (Charles and his brother) to military marches, patriotic songs, hymns, spirituals, and all manner of other musical Americana. He's also stretched their ears by getting them to play the piano with the right and left hands in different keys, or else he'd play an accompaniment while the boys sang the tune in a different key. "Why do I like these things?" Charles wondered. "Are my ears on wrong?"

For a while, the young Ives behaved himself. At 14, he became the youngest salaried church organist in Connecticut, and after doing fine in prep school, he was admitted to Yale University in 1894. There, his battles with conventionality began. He barely passed his non-music courses, and he was constantly torturing his famous, albeit ultra-conservative teacher, Horatio Parker, by dropping bits of folk tunes into his exercises, or submitting pieces with free rhythms, quarter-tones and multi-layered textures that give the impression of several things happening at once. Parker railed at his stubborn student until Ives decided to do his interesting stuff on the side, pacifying the professor and earning his degree with a well-behaved, unthreatening Symphony no.1.

His diploma in hand, Ives swore off well-behaved music once and for all, trying out his fascinating new ideas in feverish bursts of composing activity (his "resident disturbances" his roommates called them). Realizing that his oddball music would not bring in a living, Ives went into business, taking a job with the Mutual Insurance Company in New York, and later starting up a new agency with his friend Julian Myrick.

Bet You Didn't Know

"No genius ever stopped creating because he knew he never could make a million dollars," said Ives, but he made his million dollars anyway, since his passion for originality applied to his insurance savvy as well: One of his innovations was a strategy for preserving wealth that we now know as estate planning.

With his financial house in order and his private life in equally happy state (in 1908, he had married the sister of one of his Yale classmates, a lady with the glorious name of Harmony Twitchell), Ives could afford to be a part-time composer, writing anything that struck his far-out fancy, and worrying not a whit about what critics or anybody else might have to say. Virtually none of his music was published, and hardly any of it saw public performance, but Ives continued to turn out one fascinating, fresh, and inventive work after another. A heart attack and diabetes caused him gradually to lessen his activities, and he formally retired from business in 1930, four years after his musical star had set with a final song, ironically titled "Sunrise."

Over the nearly quarter of **a** century left to him, Ives revised some of his pieces, and tried to put some order into the chaos of the undated and often unnumbered manuscript pages that were strewn around the house. "Vagueness is at times an indication of nearness to perfect truth," he said, and musicologists are still trying to sort out the truth from some of the vague and conflicting instructions about his music that he left behind. Ives did, however, live long enough to see his pieces rise from obscurity to worldwide public acclaim, among them the Symphony no. 3, which won the Pulitzer Prize in 1947, a mere 36 years after its composition.

Ives' Works You Need to Know

Don't expect to fall in love with Ives' music right away, except possibly for his irreverent "Variations on 'America,'" originally for organ solo, but far more entertaining in William Schuman's brilliant orchestration. The Second Symphony, with its deliciously thumb-to-nose finale, and the Third Symphony, with its folk connections (the movements are titled "Old Folks Gatherin'," "Children's Day," and "Communion"), will reward careful listening. So will "Three Places in New England," one of which recreates a scene Ives remembered from childhood, where two marching bands approached, crossed each other's paths in a blare of sonic dissonance, then went their separate ways again. There's also an intriguing "Holidays Symphony," its four movements depicting events on Washington's Birthday, Decoration Day, Fourth of July, and Thanksgiving; it took Ives 10 years to complete the set, so we ought to be able to spend 40 minutes listening to it.

Folk tunes also swirl about in the Fourth Violin Sonata, many of his 150 songs, and while it's not easy listening, be brave and tackle the ground-breaking "Concord" Piano Sonata, honoring the famous New England authors Emerson, Hawthorne, the Alcotts, and Thoreau.

Schoenberg: Twelve-tone Taskmaster

Perhaps no name on a program terrifies the average concert-goer more than that of Arnold Schoenberg. Well over half a century after their composition, many of his works are still difficult to penetrate, and even those of a warmly romantic bent tend to be shunned because they came from the same dreaded pen.

Born in Vienna to a set of unmusical parents (his father was a shoemaker), Arnold Schoenberg (1874-1951) found his way to the art only gradually, starting violin lessons at age eight, and later becoming reasonably proficient on the cello. When his father died, the 16-year-old Schoenberg took a job as a bank clerk, earning extra cash by arranging popular songs and orchestrating operettas. Only at age 20 did he come forward with his first original composition, a set of three piano pieces, and then decide to pursue formal lessons with the composer Alexander Zemlinsky.

Bet You Didn't Know

It was a busy time **for Schoenberg**. In addition to his studies, he played cello in his teacher's instrumental ensemble, Polyhymnia, and went waltzing with Mathilde, Zemlinsky's sister, whom he married in 1901. Later, he took painting lessons, and Mathilde had an affair with his art teacher, but that's gossip for another day.

Schoenberg's first major works appeared around the corner of the 20th century: "Verklarte Nacht" (Transfigured Night) for String Sextet in 1899; "Pelleas und Melisande" a symphonic poem notable for its first-time use of a trombone glissando, in 1903; and his expansive "Gurrelieder" (Songs of Gurre, a medieval Danish castle), settings for chorus, orchestra, and narrator of verses by the Danish poet Jens Peter Jacobsen. The first two parts of this monumental cycle—conceived for such large forces that Schoenberg had to order special music paper long enough to include all the parts—were written in 1901, but the work was not finished for another ten years, and had to wait two years after that for its premiere.

Another expressive innovation appeared in his 1912 "Pierrot Lunaire" (Moonstruck Pierrot) with something called "sprechstimme," a gliding method of vocal performance midway between speech and song, the singer touching a note but not sustaining it. This produces an eerie effect, perfect for the work's graphic portrayal of creeping madness.

Perhaps Schoenberg realized he had pushed those romantic boundaries as far as they would go. Enter his famous (or infamous, depending on your point of view) 12 tones. Having come to the conclusion that key signatures were outdated, but realizing that some sort of system was necessary to avoid compositional confusion, if not chaos, he came up with the idea of giving each of the 12 notes in a scale (i.e., C, C#, D, D#, E, F, F#, G, G#, A, A#, B) equal importance. There is no tonic, no dominant, no home key, no modulation from one key to another; there are just those twelve notes and their relationships to each other. Since there is no key involved, the music came to be called atonal.

Music Word

Historically in Western music, the tones within an octave scale were organized into sequences called keys. Atonality simply means that there is no key or predictable relationship between the tones; or, to put it the other way around, atonality indicates a synthesis of all possible keys, and therefore the equal use of all twelve tones.

Instead of melodies, Schoenberg based his new method on what he called a tone row, in which the notes are placed in a specific sequence. There's a catch, though: each of the 12 tones must be sounded before any of them can be repeated. On the other hand, by sounding the notes in the row upside down (inversion), backwards (retrograde), or upside down and backwards (retrograde inversion), composers could create themes and build recognizable structures within the system.

Music Word

The tone row represents the composer's particular sequencing of the 12 tones within the octave. All sorts of permutations may follow, but the strict rule says that before any one of those 12 notes is heard again, the other 11 have to have been presented as well.

Here was a genuine musical revolution. Virtually every composer of note, from Stravinsky to Bernstein, experimented with atonality; some, like Berg and Webern, dedicated their lives to its development and implementation. Somewhat left out in the cold by all these mathematically precise formulas were audiences, who found the music more intellectually stimulating than emotionally satisfying. In Vienna, Schoenberg helped found the Society for Private Performances, thereby excluding the razor-tongued critics and insult-screaming listeners who had made a shamble of so many open concerts.

Bet You Didn't Know

One of his major creations, a Biblical opera, was called "Moses und Aaron" until a friend pointed out that the title had **13** letters. In something of a panic, Schoenberg considered changing the name altogether, but finally hit upon the compromise solution of crossing out the second "a" in Aaron. Moses und Aron thus passed muster at an acceptable 12-letter total.

Fleeing the Nazi takeover, Schoenberg came to the United States, where he held teaching posts at the University of Southern California, and later U.C.L.A. (which forced him into retirement at age 70 with the munificent pension of $38 per month). Like Rossini, Schoenberg was morbidly afraid of the number 13, and during his final illness, he verbalized his fear that, having been born on the 13th of one month (October), he would not live beyond the 13th of another. He was right: Arnold Schoenberg died on July 13th, 1951.

Schoenberg's Works You Need to Know

By and large, Schoenberg's earlier works are still the easiest to take, given their Straussian predilections, so start with the sumptuously scored "Transfigured Night," either in its original version for string sextet or the composer's own larger orchestration. Add the Chamber Symphony no. 1, and the "Gurrelieder" (the texts are obscure, but the music is incandescent). Advanced Schonbergians may proceed to his "Variations for Orchestra" and the Piano Concerto, but don't say we didn't warn you.

Cowell: Hit 'Em Again

Henry Cowell (1897-1965) was one of the first native-born Californians to hit it big in the world of composition. As a child he studied violin, but left to his own keyboard devices, he began finding his own way around the piano. Since nobody told him he wasn't supposed to do it, he experimented with plucking or stroking the piano strings, producing the harp-like sounds of "The Fairy Answer" and the otherwordly shriekings of "The Banshee." Sometimes he would hit the strings with a darning egg, or change their timbre by sticking pencils in between them. Then, not satisfied with the keyboard sounds that could be generated by a mere ten fingers, Cowell devised what he called "tone clusters," whole groups of notes sounded simultaneously by the application of fists and forearms.

Music Word

A **tone cluster** is a group of adjacent notes on the keyboard. You can play five such notes at the same time (or ten if you use the fingers on both hands), but Cowell extended the possibilities by instructing the player to press down all the notes within an octave with the flat of his hand, or to get achieve a cluster of two octaves or more, the entire forearm. A tone cluster is notated on the music page by an indication of its top and bottom notes, with a thick black line connecting them.

Now audiences could be shocked by sight as well as sound, and were they ever. Riots ensued, newspapers sent sports writers to cover his recitals (one headline read "Battling Cowell vs. Kid Knabe"), and Cowell became known as the "bad boy" of American music. He persevered, though, taking his startling music around the world, even to the Soviet Union, where a number of his pieces were published, and gradually the hysterics died down. Meanwhile, Cowell himself had veered off onto other paths of exploration, investigating world music, spicing his scores with unusual percussion instruments, and infiltrating folk themes that added a lilting quality quite at odds with his fearsome reputation of old. His "Hymns" and "Fuguing Tunes," based on early American forms, are almost as harmonious as Bach's chorales.

Today, Cowell's "bizarre" keyboard effects are part of the creative arsenal of almost every major composer, and worldwide celebrations of his centennial revived many of his pieces, and reconfirmed his acceptance amongst the front ranks of 20th century musicians.

Cowell's Works You Need to Know

Start, as Cowell himself did, with the piano pieces. A few of them may still seem pretty wild and wooly, but others exhibit delicious wit ("Advertisement"), gentle restraint ("Aeolian Harp") and marvelous rhythmic spirit ("Lilt of the Reel"). Only some of his 20 symphonies are currently available on CD, but latch on to as many of the 16 Hymn and Fuguing Tunes as you can find, and pounce if you see concert listings of his "Celtic Set," the warmhearted "Ballad for Strings," the exotic "Persian Set," or the folksy suite titled "American Melting Pot."

Bet You Didn't Know

"Why is he so coy about it?" wondered a German critic about Cowell; "with his rear end, he could cover many more notes."

Stravinsky – The Rite Touch

Who wrote this fiendish Rite of Spring?
What right had he to write this thing,
Against our helpless ears to fling
It's crash, clash, cling clang, bing, bang bing.
He who could write the 'Rite of Spring'
If I be right, by right should swing!

— from a letter to the *Boston Herald*, 1924.

Igor Stravinsky (1882-1971) towers above most of his 20th century colleagues as did Bach and Beethoven over theirs. His compositions changed the face of music in our time; his harmonic and rhythmic innovations have become part of contemporary musical language; and while each of his stylistic shifts prompted a horde of imitators, Stravinsky continued to dwarf them all.

The son of a leading bass player at the St. Petersburg Opera, Stravinsky grew up surrounded by music, although he considered it just a hobby at first, and was trundled off to the University as a budding lawyer. Since one of his school mates happened to be the son of Nicolai Rimsky-Korsakov, Igor was able to show a few of his fledgling attempts at writing music to the famous composer, and while Rimsky was not exactly overwhelmed ("Don't quit law school" was the upshot of his advice), he did suggest that the young man take counterpoint lessons from one of his assistants. By 1905, the young man had progressed to the point where Rimsky agreed to take him on as a private student, and for the next three years, Stravinsky worked closely with his idol, assimilating the older man's consummate mastery of orchestration, along with his abiding love for the folk tales and tunes of Mother Russia.

It was a short, jubilant piece called "Fireworks," written in celebration of the wedding of Rimsky's daughter, that gave Stravinsky his big chance. In the audience at its 1909 premiere was Serge Diaghilev, father figure of the new Ballet Russe, who felt that the music was "new and original, with a tonal quality that should surprise the public." First testing Stravinsky with a minor commission, the orchestration of a Chopin waltz and nocturne for use in the ballet "Les Sylphides," Diaghilev cabled him to start work on an original dancework based on several Russian legends about "The Firebird."

Bet You Didn't Know

Diaghilev had originally assigned the score to Anton Liadov, but when that notoriously procrastinating Russian composer diddled around too long for Diaghilev's volatile temperament, Stravinsky got the job.

The premiere **of** "The Firebird" ballet on June 25, 1910, a week and a day after Stravinsky's 28th birthday, catapulted the unknown composer to international fame; next came another highly acclaimed folklore-inspired ballet, "Petrouchka," and then the roof fell in with the third Diaghilev-Stravinsky collaboration, "Le Sacre du Printemps" (The Rite of Spring). "It will be jolting and emotional experience for the viewer," predicted the dancer Nijinsky, in what proved to be the understatement of the decade.

The Paris premiere literally caused a riot heard around the world. Legends have emerged about the duels that were fought between pro- and anti-Stravinsky proponents in the crowd, and how swooning women had to be carted out of the hall in droves, but distinguished literary personalities left us objective eyewitness accounts that are hardly less astonishing. According to the American novelist and critic Carl Van Vechten, "a certain part of the audience began, very soon after the rise of the curtain, to make cat-calls, and to offer audible suggestions as to how the performance should proceed. The young man seated behind me stood up, and the intense excitement under which he was laboring betrayed itself when he began to beat rhythmically on top of my head with his fists."

From another seat in the Theatre des Champs Elysees, 24-year old Jean Cocteau, then still a newspaper reporter, experienced much the same thing. "People laughed, booed, hissed, and imitated animal noises," he wrote. "Possibly they would have tired themselves out had not a handful of musicians insulted and roughly handled them. The uproar degenerated into a free fight. Standing up in her loge, her tiara awry, the Comtesse de Pourtales flourished her fan, and red in the face shouted 'I'm sixty years old, and this is the first time that anyone's dared to make a fool out of me!'"

Even the musicians in attendance were a house divided. Saint-Saens bellowed that Stravinsky was a faker, Ravel yelled back that he was a genius, and in between them stood Debussy, pathetically trying to shush everybody up so the music could be heard at all. Stravinsky, meanwhile, slammed out of the hall in a fury, and rushed backstage. "For the rest of the performance," he recalled much later, "I stood in the wings behind Nijinsky, holding the tails of his jacket while he stood on a chair shouting numbers to the dancers like a coxswain."

The scandal may have ruined the premiere, but its reportage, and several highly successful subsequent concert performances, cemented Stravinsky's reputation. The music itself, meanwhile, sent shock waves through the entire musical community. As Harold Schonberg wrote, "'Le Sacre', with its metrical shiftings and shattering force, its near-total dissonance and breakaway from established canons of harmony and melody, was a genuine explosion. For decades there were repercussions, as composers all over the world imitated the new Stravinsky rhythms and sonorities"

With the onset of World War I, Stravinsky moved to Switzerland, where his musical path took a neoclassic turn. War, even in a neutral country, means shortages, and that includes the pool of available performers. Having turned the musical world upside down with his large-scale ballets, Stravinsky pulled in his dissonant horns and produced such smaller-scale and far more accessible works as the witty "L'Histoire du Soldat" (The Soldier's Tale) for narrator and seven players, and the jaunty "Ragtime for Eleven Instruments."

Returning to Paris after the war, Stravinsky paid homage to earlier masters, wrapping music of Pergolesi and other Italian composers in the spiky harmonies of his "Pulcinella," and swiping Tchaikovsky themes for us in the ballet "Le Baiser de la Fée" (The Fairy's Kiss). He explored other aspects of his Russian heritage in "Les Noces" (the title translates as "Little Wedding"), a portrait of a peasant marriage ceremony, and "Mavra," a short opera based on a Pushkin story. He explored baroque forms in his "Capriccio for Piano and Orchestra" and the Brandenburg-like "Dumbarton Oaks Concerto" (named for the Washington, D.C., estate of the couple who had commissioned it); he daringly combined vocal and instrumental concepts in the "Symphony of Psalms."

After 29 years in France, the gathering war clouds again forced Stravinsky to move, and he found his way to America in 1939, his adopted homeland giving impetus to his "Ebony Concerto for Clarinet and Swing Band (written for jazz great Artie Shaw), the "Circus Polka" (which brightened performances at the Ringling Brothers Circus), and even some ballet music for the Broadway musical "The Seven Lively Arts" (a show that also boasted an Ooverture by William Schuman and an intermission display of Salvadore Dali paintings).

Stravinsky's longtime association with choreographer George Balanchine at the New York City Ballet yielded three masterpieces based on Greek legend: Orpheus, Apollo, and Agon; he contributed a score for a CBS-TV special "Noah and the Flood," and among his final works was an "Elegy for J.F.K."

All through his long life, Stravinsky allowed his music to evolve in unexpected stylistic directions. Sticking to any one pattern, he felt, was not only failing to progress, but actually going backwards. "I live neither in the past nor in the future," he said. "I am in the present. I cannot know what tomorrow will bring forth; I can only know what the truth is or me today." As a result, you never knew what Stravinsky would come up with next; all you did know is that it would be well worth waiting for.

Bet You Didn't Know

You never know where inspiration will strike. After a visit to the men's room at Harvard, Stravinsky wrote a piece for unaccompanied treble voice called "Do Not Throw Paper Towels in Toilet."

Stravinsky's place in the pantheon of immortal composers is secure, and for a change, the composer lived long enough to reap a full measure of critical and audience acclamation. "Le Sacre du Printemps," which once caused such hysteria, has long since been a staple of our concert repertory, and while some of his more prickly pieces have yet to find full public favor, Stravinsky evenings at the ballet are predictable sellouts. No riots, now, just bountiful applause.

Stravinsky's Works You Need to Know

Start with the mighty ballet trilogy: "Firebird," "Petrouchka," and "Rite of Spring." "Agon" is pretty tough going, so better move along to Stravinsky's more gracious musical depictions of "Apollo" and "Orpheus," and perhaps sit in on the zesty "Jeu de Cartes" (Card Game), which Stravinsky described as "a Ballet in Three Deals." The old Italian flavorings of "Pulcinella" and the Tchaikovskian spirit of "The Fairy's Kiss" are both thoroughgoing delights, as is "L'Histoire du Soldat," which you can enjoy as a chamber trio, ensemble suite, or full-fledged drama with spoken narration.

"The Ebony Concerto," "Ragtime for Eleven Instruments," and "Circus Polka" are hardly works of high import, but Stravinsky's use of popular idioms gives them a quirky wit. And for those with short attention spans, sample such other easy-to-take miniatures as the "Scherzo à la Russe," the two "Suites for Small Orchestra," and the early wedding piece that ignited Stravinsky's long ride to musical glory, "Fireworks."

Missing Links

In this chapter, we've moved from Mahler, whose heart and soul throbbed with all the fabled fervor of the romantics, to Stravinsky, who revolutionized the creative spirit in our own century. Along the way, we visited with composers in France, Germany, and the USA who, each in his own way, contributed to the ongoing evolution of classical music as we know it today. We only touched on a few highlights, of course, so we urge you to explore many more of the creative geniuses who are also part of this link from past to future. Start with Maurice Ravel, Debussy's partner in bringing Impressionism to world attention and enticement; then, to further pursue the French connection, consider such upholders of the Gallic spirit as Camille Saint-Saens, Erik Satie and Francis Poulenc. If you like Vaughan Williams, help yourself to some of the lovely musical landscapes of his fellow Englishmen, Frederick Delius and Benjamin Britten. For pianophiles, sample the expressive work of Russia's Alexander Scriabin, and America's own Edward MacDowell, who wrote some of the most beautiful piano music this side of Chopin. And if Schoenberg is your cup of atonal tea, follow the 12-tone trail to the music of his disciples, Alban Berg and Anton Webern.

The main thing is to enlarge the scope of your musical enjoyment as much as possible, without getting too hooked on any particular style or era. As the famous poet and playright Oliver Goldsmith so wisely observed more than 200 years ago: "Women and music should never be dated."

CHAPTER 18

The 20th Century Mainstream and Beyond

> ## In This Chapter
>
> ➤ Those Russian composers
> ➤ America the beautiful
> ➤ Synthesizers and electronic orchestras
> ➤ Music from the movies

History is rarely cooperative enough to have its dates work out in round numbers, but more or less, the 17th century was baroque, the 18th classical, the 19th romantic. That brings us to our own 20th century, which has been conservative, radical, absurdist, neo-classical, neo-romantic, neo-baroque, experimental, minimalist, and sundry other labels that will no doubt give pause (if not merriment) to future historians. Which of these many trends will be considered dominant in the 22nd century? Call us in a 100 years or so, and we'll let you know.

Music chroniclers sometimes date the dawn of the modern age to that historic, not to mention hysterical, 1913 premiere of "The Rite of Spring." The world would thereafter be in incredible flux, what with two horrific wars, the atomic age, the space age, and the information highway, so who would expect music to stay cool, calm, and collected?

The Russians are Coming

Hot on the heels of Stravinsky's musical time bomb came the political and social explosions of the Russian Revolution. Some composers, including Stravinsky, sought their fortunes outside the Soviet Union. Others tried, then rejected, the expatriate life; some never left. But home or abroad, they proved that the Russian soul could not be quenched by Communism.

Prokofiev

Born in Ukraine, Sergei Prokofiev (1892-1953) started his musical climb to fame as a daring firebrand, a brilliant pianist whose brash, percussive, highly dissonant (or so it seemed at the time) pieces caused great consternation among his conservative professors at the St. Petersburg Conservatory. Like Stravinsky, Prokofiev studied with Rimsky-Korsakov, soaking up the older master's flair for colorful orchestration; thereafter (like Stravinsky as well), he struck out in totally new musical directions. He wrote one piano piece where the right and left hands played in different keys, and withheld several more from Anatol Liadov, another of his teachers, because "he would probably expel me from the class." Finally, instead of dutifully playing a classical concerto as his graduation piece, Prokofiev stormed through his own First Piano Concerto, sending the head of the conservatory rushing from the hall in anguish.

Bet You Didn't Know

Such was Prokofiev's reputation as a modernist that Leonid Sabaneyev, a famous Moscow critic, decided not to attend the premiere of the "Scythian Suite", but wrote a review anyway, kvetching that the music "offered no pleasure or artistic satisfaction even though the composer conducted it with barbaric abandon." Was Sabaneyev's face red (and this before the Revolution, mind you) when he found out the next day that the performance had been cancelled!

When the Revolution came, Prokofiev set out for more peaceful climes, touring as pianist and conductor to such distant ports of musical call as Japan, and unveiling his satiric comic opera "The Love for Three Oranges," in Chicago. Not that things were any more peaceful on the critical front. The *New York Herald* called Prokofiev "a Bolshevist musical agitator," while the man at the *Times* grimly sat through the First Concerto, cheering up only when the composer-pianist refused to grant an encore. "The Russian heart may be a dark place," he wrote, "but its capacity for mercy is infinite."

In 1927 and again in 1929, Prokofiev gave concerts in Russia, and eventually made the fateful decision to return to his homeland. It had less to do with politics than homesickness. "I've got to see real winters again," he wrote, "and springs that burst into being from one moment to the next. I've got to hear the Russian language echoing in my ears, I've got to talk to people who are of my own flesh and blood, so that they can give me back something I lack—their songs, my songs."

The Soviets, never too happy about artists escaping their clutches (for years, Stravinsky was considered a turncoat and his music was tabu in the USSR), welcomed Prokofiev back as a musical hero. He fell in step with the ruling cliques, composing all sorts of governmentally approved works, like "Hail to Stalin" and "Hymn to the Soviet Union," and scored several patriotic film scores, most notably "Alexander Nevsky." He also produced such delectable apolitical works as the ballet "Romeo and Juliet" and the children's tale of "Peter and the Wolf." During World War II, Prokofiev's "Leningrad Sonata" and the Fifth Symphony expressed the nation's turmoil, a sense of tragedy, and suffering tied to faith and hope in a better future.

Prokofiev's own future, meanwhile, along with that of Shostakovich, Khatchaturian, and several other of the most significant Russian composers, became seriously clouded in 1948, when the Central Committee of the Soviet Union issued its infamous public denunciation of music that didn't toe the Communist line (i.e., wasn't simple-minded enough for the Commissars to figure out what it was all about). The decree, among other things, accused the composers of "decadence" and rejected "as useless and harmful garbage all the relics of bourgeois formalism in musical art." Nobody quite knew what bourgeois formalism was, but Stalin didn't like it, so composers had better stop writing it, if they wanted to stay healthy. Fortunately, Prokofiev was 57 years old at the time, and had already created enough harmful garbage to please the dissolute senses of the rest of the world; his place amongst the great composers of the 20th century was secure.

"In my view," wrote Prokofiev four years later, "the composer must beautify human life and defend it. He must be a citizen first and foremost, so that his art may consciously extol human life and lead man to a radiant future." Ironically, his death preceded Stalin's by only a few hours.

Prokofiev's Works You Need to Know

If you haven't actually grown up with "Peter and the Wolf," this delicious piece offers children (and anybody who ever was a child) a breezy introduction to the instruments of the orchestra and even the Wagnerian concept of the leitmotif (since each of the characters in the story has its own tune). You can also (mentally) follow the story line in Prokofiev's incomparable ballet scores to "Cinderella" and "Romeo and Juliet," and sample his satiric wit in the "Suites from Lt. Kije" and "Love for Three Oranges."

"The Classical Symphony" is a charming work in olden style (though early critics inexplicably still found it to be "an orgy of discordant sounds"), and pianophiles have much to explore, perhaps starting with the Third Concerto and the Seventh Sonata. Finally, don't miss "Alexander Nevsky," converted by Prokofiev himself from the background score for the classic film into a powerfully dramatic cantata.

Shostakovich

Dmitri Shostakovich (1906-1975) spent his teenage years during the most difficult days of the Russian Revolution. Political goals had far outshouted social needs, and famine had wreaked havoc among the population of St. Petersburg (the city renamed Petrograd, then Leningrad, before finally returning to its original designation). When Dmitri entered the Conservatory, the director actually had to apply to the Commissar of Education to get an increased food ration for the undernourished child.

Shostakovich's creative originality won him high praise at first, but as the commissars began getting their repressive act together, and Soviet society became more and more prudish, satiric works like his opera "The Nose," and sensational ones, such as "Lady MacBeth of Mtsensk" became the subject of ridicule in the government press, with organs like *Pravda* scorning the "bourgeois decadence" of the former and dismissing the latter as "a bedlam of noise."

Bet You Didn't Know

Even when Shostakovich tried to produce a politically acceptable piece, such as "The Limpid Brook," a pastoral ballet about life on a collective farm, Pravda panned it for not treating Soviet workers with sufficient dignity.

It was not until his Fifth Symphony that Shostakovich managed to reconcile his own artistic integrity with the demands of political necessity. He subtitled the work "A Soviet Artist's Reply to Fair Criticism," just to make sure the Commissars got the point, and the apology worked wonders with *Pravda*. "The powerful sounds stirred the audience," wrote their now-enthusiastic critic at the premiere. "Joy and happiness streamed from the orchestra like a spring breeze."

Joy and happiness, alas, were not to be Shostakovich's lot. Fearful of ruination (or worse) at government hands, he treaded very carefully, burying many of his creative instincts behind a façade of acceptance, squirreling away works likely to cause controversy—such as a cycle of songs on Jewish texts—against the day when a less repressive regime would make their publication less life-threatening. With domination of the arts getting comparatively low priority during World War II, Shostakovich could continue his work relatively undisturbed, winning Stalin Prizes for his 1940 Piano Quintet and his stunning "Leningrad" Symphony (no. #7), the latter dedicated by the composer "to our struggle against Fascism, to our future victory, and to my native city."

In 1948, though, as earlier mentioned, the cultural roof fell in, and Shostakovich was in the political doghouse again. In public, he proclaimed his contrite allegiance to Soviet ideals ("I shall try again to create symphony works close to the spirit of the people from the standpoint of ideological subject matter, musical language and form"); in private, he poured out his tormented soul in instrumental pieces—sonatas, string quartets, symphonies—the true meaning of which he revealed only to family and trusted friends. Under the guise of political correctness, Shostakovich continued to display deep personal heroism, writing poignant and heartfelt music that would long outlive the attempts of petty functionaries to control his creative spirit.

Shostakovich's Works You Need to Know

In order both to appease his critics and make a living, Shostakovich turned out barrels of charming, lighthearted music for films and the ballet. "The Age of Gold", "The Gadfly" and several other suites offer an easy entrée to at least one side of his musical personality. The Piano Concerto #1 with its bright an bouncy finale, complete with co-solos from the trumpet, the Festival Overture, and the playful little Ninth Symphony are in similarly easy-to-take style. Like Beethoven's, the Fifth is the best known of the Shostakovich Symphonies, but the Seventh Symphony and Eighth String Quartet, both inspired by the horrific war years, are unforgettable, as is the Symphony #13, subtitled "Baba Yar" after the place where Jews were massacred by the Nazis during the occupation of Kiev.

Khatchaturian

Aram Khatchaturian was born in Tbilisi (1903-1978), and proudly displayed his Armenian heritage in many works, most notably the ballet "Gayne," home of the wildly popular "Sabre Dance". He didn't often quote actual folk melodies, but dance rhythms were fair game, and his scores gain color and character from modes and scales used in traditional Armenian songs.

On the musical enemies list of the Central Committee in that fateful year of 1948, Khatchaturian made a formal apology like all the others who wanted to stay among the living ("How could I have come to formalism in my art?" he said, "What can be nobler than writing music understandable to our people?"). Then, just in case the commissars were even more stupid than he thought, he wrote an "Ode in Memory of Lenin" and music for the film "The Battle of Stalingrad."

Rehabilitated and returned to the OK list, Khatchaturian resumed his high status among Russian composers, and eventually was even allowed to travel outside of the Soviet Union, conducting his own works in England, Japan, and in 1968, the United States.

Khatchaturian's Works You Need to Know

With his flamboyant use of folk-derived rhythms, his frequent quotations of oriental-sounding tunes in the style of music from Armenia, Uzbekistan, and other republics of the former Soviet Union, his imitations of exotic folk instruments, and his essentially romantic spirit, Khatchaturian is an easy composer to get close to. His Piano and Violin Concertos are in the grand style; his incidental music to Masquerade is light and appealing; there's lots more to "Gayne" than the "Sabre Dance"; and for further balletics, lend an ear to "Spartacus."

America the Beautiful

Musicians from every part of the world have made America their adopted home, and just as immigrants have done in every line of work, these men and women of artistic bent added enormously to the vitality and diversity of our national heritage. Until well into the 20th century, however, American composers suffered from something of an inferiority complex. They rushed to study in Europe, they emulated old-world styles and musical mannerisms, they tried to out-Wagner Wagner and to go Liszt and Tchaikovsky one better. It took the Czech master Antonin Dvořák to lecture American composers on the need to establish their own national identity and to use native themes and rhythms in their classical writings (meanwhile giving them an orchestral case in point with his "New World Symphony"). The lessons must have sunk in, since gradually a new breed of composers arose to become proud exemplars of the American character.

Gershwin

Biographers of George Gershwin (1898-1937) and his lyricist-brother Ira (1896-1983) love to dwell on their humble beginnings in immigrant Brooklyn, and on the lads having to plug their music to cold-hearted, cynical Tin Pan Alley songbrokers. Gershwin himself said that he developed his improvisational skills to keep from going bonkers as he played the same song over and over in front of Remick's publishing house. By his late teens, though, George Gershwin's fortunes were already improving. Al Jolson got down on one knee to sing "Swanee", and Gershwin got up from his song-plugging chair to write such big-time musicals as "Lady Be Good," "Strike Up the Band," and "Of Thee I Sing," a political satire that won the 1931 Pulitzer Prize. Subsequently, he wrote hit songs for Hollywood films, the blazingly original folk opera "Porgy and Bess," (both with brother Ira) and concert pieces that remain among the most frequently performed of all American works.

Bet You Didn't Know

Having had minimal formal training, Gershwin approached "classical" music with a great deal of trepidation, obsessed with the notion that his work was full of technical flaws. He sounded out Stravinsky about taking some composition lessons (the Russian master, upon determining Gershwin's annual salary, suggested that he take lessons from Gershwin instead), and when the American approached Ravel on a similar mission, the composer of Bolero supposedly responded "Why do you want to be a second-hand Ravel when you're already a first-rate Gershwin?".

Gershwin sprang into the concert arena at the age of 25, when his "Rhapsody in Blue" sparked one of the first successful fusions of jazz and classical music. The next year, he undertook the far more ambitious Piano Concerto in F, and at the premiere, conductor Walter Damrosch made a little speech about it. "Until George Gershwin accomplished this miracle," he said, "Lady Jazz had encountered no knight who could lift her to a level that would enable her to be received as a respectable member in musical circles. He has done it boldly, by dressing this extremely independent and up-to-date young lady in the classic garb of a concerto, without detracting one whit from her fascinating personality."

A visit to France inspired "An American in Paris," complete with three types of saxophones and a genuine French taxi-horns. Several years later, Gershwin spent the summer of 1934 in a little cottage on Folly Island, not far from Charleston, South Carolina, listening to fishermen's songs and street vendors' cries and attending revival meetings. The ideas and atmosphere he soaked up there would soon arrive on stage in his operatic masterpiece "Porgy and Bess."

Who knows what other works of genius might have poured from his pen had not Gershwin succumbed to a brain tumor at the age of 38. The novelist John O'Hara spoke for all Americans when he wrote "George Gershwin died on July 11, 1937, but I don't have to believe it if I don't want to."

Gershwin's Works You Need to Know

We'll leave the endless delights of Gershwin's film and Broadway show tunes to other listings, but a number of overtures have attracted major symphonic attention, and you can enjoy a further fusion in the virtuoso "Variations on 'I Got Rhythm'" for piano and orchestra. Everybody loves the "Rhapsody in Blue," but you might sample the Second

Rhapsody as well (an urban portrait in sound, it was originally titled "Rhapsody in Rivets"); and after joining "An American in Paris," with or without Gene Kelly, continue your tonal travels with the "Cuban Overture." There are endless ways to experience "Porgy and Bess," the best, of course, being to attend a performance of the opera. Otherwise, take home the great songs on a variety of excerpt albums, or just sing along with the instrumental suites available in piano solo, two-piano, and several competing orchestral versions.

Copland

Aaron Copland (1900-1990), the first generation offspring of Russian emigré parents, grew up in Brooklyn where he attended Boys High School and his compositional stirrings began. His first published piece, a little piano scherzo called "Cat and Mouse," suggested a talent worth nurturing. At the age of 20, Copland went to France, enrolling as a student of Nadia Boulanger at the American Conservatory in Fontainebleau. What an incredible group of composers came to gather at the Boulanger shrine: naming only the Americans, the roster included Walter Piston, Elliott Carter, Virgil Thomson (see David Diamond, Elie Siegmeister, and Roy Harris. It is high tribute to Boulanger's wisdom and pedagogical skills that her protégés all emerged with strong compositional discipline, yet totally distinctive musical personalities.

Copland returned to the USA in 1924 (the same year Gershwin unveiled his "Rhapsody in Blue"), and began developing what he called "plain music," infiltrating elements of jazz, folk tunes, and dance rhythms into his classical scores. Happy to champion the music of other American composers as well as his own, Copland joined with Roger Sessions to produce a series of new music concerts in the late 1920s. In 1937, Copland was one of the founders of the American Composers Alliance, an organization designed to publish, promote, and encourage performances of music by our national composers. He wrote books, lectured, and traveled the world as an artistic ambassador of good will.

Not that the critics always returned that good will. One Boston paper called Copland's Piano Concerto "a harrowing horror from beginning to end," while fellow composer Lazare Saminsky, who presumably should have known better, dismissed the gorgeous "Appalachian Spring" as "a feeble score, anemic and insignificant."

It was Copland's brilliantly imaginative use of American folk themes that gave his career new impetus and brought him international acclaim. Using infectious cowboy tunes and hoedown rhythms, this Brooklyn boy was able to encapsulate the high spirits of the American West in "Billy the Kid" (1938) and "Rodeo" (1942). He used a traditional Shaker hymn ("Simple Gifts") as a primary theme in another milestone ballet, "Appalachian Spring," and brought a homey Americana flavor to his film scores for "Of Mice and Men" (1939), "Our Town" (1940), and "The Red Pony: (1949). He even won an Oscar for "The Heiress" in

1950.

Copland's "Fanfare for the Common Man" was so successful that he later incorporated it, almost note for note, into his Third Symphony; and "A Lincoln Portrait," like the Fanfare, dating from the war year of 1942, remains an brilliant fusion of patriotic text and music. Lincoln biographer Carl Sandburg was the first narrator, but through the years, the inspiring words of our 16th president have become the province of everyone from Katherine Hepburn to General Norman Schwarzkopf.

Not that Copland's music ever got into a stylistic rut. He experimented with 12-tone writing, and his warm-hearted, folksy scores butt up against other works of dissonant and astringent nature. But always, there is the mark of an original thinker, a man not afraid to try new paths in his never-ending search for musical truths. "Copland's work," said his friend and colleague William Schuman, "is recognized as part of our heritage. That special Copland sound has enriched us all. It is a sound that was not in music before, and so personal an expression that not one of his many imitators has been able to make it convincingly his own. We glory in his achievements and count our good fortune in his presence."

Copland's Works You Need to Know

Just as Stravinsky came into his own with the mighty ballet trilogy of "Firebird," "Petrouchka," and "The Rite of Spring," you'll find a splendid introduction to Copland's Americana in his three great danceworks, "Rodeo," "Billy the Kid," and "Appalachian Spring." Don't miss "A Lincoln Portrait," and continue around the country with his settings of "Old American Songs," "An Outdoor Overture," and "The Tender Land" (either in its operatic original or the composer's own orchestral suite). Next, go south of the border to "El Salon Mexico" and "Danzon Cubano," and come back home with the jazzy "Clarinet Concerto," originally written for Benny Goodman.

Thomson

Born in Kansas City and trained at Harvard, Virgil Thomson (1896-1989), like Copland, went to study in France with Nadia Boulanger. Unlike Copland, though, Thomson was so captivated by the artistic life of Paris that he returned there after completing his college studies, and made the French capital his headquarters until the war clouds brought him home again in 1940. In Paris, he was an integral member of Gertrude Stein's literary salon, and indeed his two most famous operas, "Four Saints in Three Acts" and "The Mother of Us All," the latter based on the life of the famed suffragette Susan B. Anthony, both have Stein

Important Things to Know

Gertrude Stein was quite a character. Like Thomson, she was an American who put down strong roots in Paris, putting aside her training in psychology and medicine (she specialized in brain anatomy), to become a poet, critic, and novelist. She lived openly with her secretary, Alice B. Toklas, and flouting literary conventions as easily as social, often used words for their sound associations rather than for their literal meaning. Among her more famous lines are "A rose is a rose is a rose is a rose", and "Pigeons on the grass, alas", the latter finding its way into Thomson's opera "Four Saints in Three Acts."

librettos.

For all his years in France, Thomson's roots remained firmly planted in America. "I wrote music in Paris that was always, in one way or another, about Kansas City," he said. "I wanted Paris to know Kansas City, to understand the way we think and feel on the banks of the Missouri." Hymn tunes remembered from childhood, folk songs learned as a teenager, music that echoed the independent, sometimes eccentric spirit of America, this was Thomson's tonal road. "His music," said Thomson's Parisian friend and fellow composer Erik Satie, "is as simple, as straightforward, as devastating, as the remarks of a child. To the uninitiated, they may sound trifling. To those who love them, they are fresh and beautiful and firmly right."

For 15 years, starting upon his return to the United States in 1940, Thomson took on a new role, that of music critic for the *New York Herald Tribune*. Far more than a reviewer, he became a keen observer of the American cultural scene and an ardent champion of new music and its composers. His comments could be highly personal (some would say biased), but his articles combined musical erudition, literary wit, and an abiding love for the art to which he devoted his life.

Thomson's Works You Need to Know

One of Thomson's unique contributions was the musical portrait. Many composers have translated landscapes or paintings into sound, but Thomson literally worked from life. The subject would be there in his studio, while Thomson sketched out a piece suggested by his or her features, personality or other distinguishing traits. He wrote almost 150 of these portraits from life; many are piano miniatures, others are more substantial works for orchestra—all are fascinating.

Even easier to assimilate are Thomson's folk-inspired pieces, including his scores to the documentary films "The River," "The Plow That Broke the Plains," and "Louisiana Story" (the last sometimes listed as "Acadian Songs and Dances"). The two Gertrude Stein operas are more of an acquired taste, but the "Symphony on Hymn Tunes" is immediately accessible, as is his "Autumn Concertino" for harp, strings, and percussion.

Schuman

William Schuman (1910-1992) reached greatness in several fields. Born and bred in New York City, he was drafted into playing the double bass (because the George Washington High Scuhool orchestra didn't ha   ɪ to form Billy Schuman and his

Bet You Didn't Know

One of Schuman's buddies was the great theatre lyricst andcomposer-to-be, Frank Loesser, and Loesser's first published song, "In Love with the Memory of You," had music by Bill Schuman. In his 20th year, attending a New York Philharmonic concert changed Schuman's life. "I was astounded at seeing the sea of stringed instruments, and everybody bowing together," he recalled years later. "The visual thing alone was astonishing. But the sound! I was overwhelmed. I had never heard anything like it. The very next day, I decided to become a composer."

Alamo Society Orchestra, a modified jazz band that played local weddings and bar mitzvahs.

His first taste of success came in the mid-1930s, with performances of his First Symphony and First String Quartet, but the super-critical Schuman later withdrew them from further performance. The earliest of his works in current circulation is thus his 1939 "American Festival Overture," after which the masterpieces flowed forth without cease. The *New Yorker* proclaimed Schuman "the composer of the hour by virtue of the popular and critical success of his Third Symphony," and when the first Pulitzer Prize for music was given out in 1943, it went to William Schuman.

In the quarter century following World War II, America stepped forward as an international catalyst of the arts. With no need to rebuild cities or recalculate borders, the economic strength of the U.S.A. allowed us to lead the world in reestablishing the arts as a cornerstone of civilized society. Through his energy, initiative, and good business sense, Schuman became one the leading figures in this modern musical renaissance. As President of the Juilliard School and then the fledgling Lincoln Center for the Performing Arts, Schuman

Important Things to Know

Students from every land vie for entrance to this most famous music conservatory in the world, but few of the singers, players, dancers, and actors who crowd its practice rooms and performance studios know who Mr. Juilliard actually was. Perhaps that's because Augustus D. Juilliard (1836-1919) was not a musician at all, but a music-loving industrialist who willed much of his large estate to a foundation designed to help worthy students gain a musical education. The Juilliard Graduate School opened its doors in 1924, then merged with the older Institute of Musical Arts (founded in 1905) to become the Juilliard School. In 1968, it became one of the consituent organizations of the Lincoln Center for the Performing Arts.

was instrumental in shaping how America perceived and supported music, dance, and drama in the second half of the 20th century.

It was Schuman who struck down the color barrier at Juilliard—an action directly responsible for Leontyne Price's debut at the Met—and it was he who raised the banner of Mostly Mozart, sparking a host of similar summer festivals all over the country. It was also on his Lincoln Center watch that the Juilliard String Quartet was born and the new Metropolitan Opera House opened its doors.

All the while, Schuman was producing pieces that reflected the highest standards of American achievement. "The composer's job is to be faithful to his gifts by composing the best music of which he is capable," Schuman said. "The continuing flow of the art of music through the centuries, and the possibility, however modest, that his music may enter the stream, is sufficient reward."

Schuman's Works You Need to Know

As with Copland, the best introduction to William Schuman's output is through the scores that make imaginative use of American themes and rhythms. "New England Triptych" is high on that list, its finale a stirring setting of "Chester," the anthem by William Billings that became a rallying cry of the American Revolution. The "American Festival Overture" is lively and fun, and since you can't get more American than baseball, take a swing with "The Mighty Casey," an operatic retelling of Casey at the Bat. Schuman's orchestration of Ives' "Variations on America" is also so fresh and cleverly appealing that it almost qualifies as an original piece. Of his 10 symphonies, the Third is probably the most striking, and his Piano and Violin Concertos will reward serious listening as well.

Bernstein

Where do we start? Here was a man of such gargantuan and multifaceted talents that he stood alone in the musical life of America, and indeed the world. As fellow composer Ned Rorem put it so eloquently, Leonard Bernstein (1918-1990) is "the epitome of glamour combined with quality, and thank heaven for him. His books and lectures have reshaped the way America listens. His mastery of keyboard and podium has defined the notion of American performance. While the scope of his programs spans centuries, it italicized his homeland, bringing into relief our sense of American craft."

Bernstein illumined whatever he touched. Young People's TV broadcasts introduced millions of listeners to the joys of classical music. His podium mastery gave us new understanding of symphonies from Beethoven to Mahler, and his charismatic energy gave wings to dozens of pieces by American composers. A major composer himself, Bernstein wrote music that reflects many faiths, covers many stylistic bases; it sparkles with equal luster at the ballet, in the concert hall, and on the Broadway stage.

The public loved the first two Bernstein shows. The familiar "New York, New York" theme from "On the Town" has been used countless times to introduce film scenes and radio or TV shows set in the Big Apple; "Wonderful Town" made a musical comedy star out of Rosalind Russell, its initial Broadway run racking up more than 500 performances. "Candide" didn't do too well the first time around (a mere 73 performances), but has led a charmed life in numerous revivals since then. Let's not talk about "1600 Pennsylvania Avenue," which flopped in less than a week (though leaving us a superb song that has become something of an American anthem: "Take Care of This House"); instead, let's hail "West Side Story" which had a nearly 1,000-performance stay on Broadway, ran even longer in London, then made it to the movies, best-selling recordings, and countless revivals.

It was to Broadway that Bernstein brought a unique combination of rhythmic drive, melodic warmth, and intellectual honesty. First came "Fancy Free," Jerome Robbins' ballet about three sailors on shore leave in New York City, and its musical comedy offspring, "On the Town," which wedded his music to the brilliant book and lyrics of Betty Comden and Adolph Green. The long-running show also became (four years later) a hit movie starring Frank Sinatra and Gene Kelly.

"Wonderful Town" was next, in 1952, followed by "Candide" four years later, during which interval Bernstein made his one and only foray into film scoring. His dramatic music helping Marlon Brando's Terry Malloy ("I coulda been a contenda instead of a bum") take on the corrupt union bosses "On the Waterfront." Then, in 1957, came "West Side Story," a shattering updating of the Romeo and Juliet story that has gone around the world on stage and screen. The libretto has been printed in German, Norwegian, and Bulgarian; the show has been sung in Swedish, Czech, Danish, Japanese, and Serbo-Croatian. Pop and rock versions have been issued, and a set of Symphonic Dances from "West Side Story" has become a concert hall staple.

Bernstein's keen theatrical sense pervades many of his classical pieces as well, including the following:

➤ "Jeremiah Symphony" (1943), with its Biblical texts;

➤ "Age of Anxiety" (1949), a musical translation of the long poem by W.H. Auden;

➤ The Third or "Kaddish" Symphony (1961-63), dedicated to the memory of John F. Kennedy;

➤ The poignant "Chichester Psalms" (1965), celebrating the rebuilt Chichester Cathedral in England;

➤ And "Mass," an ecumenical theatre piece that opened the John F. Kennedy Center for the Performing Arts in Washington, D.C., in 1971.

Bernstein was sometimes criticized for spreading himself too thin, but his enthusiasms and creative spirit were far too compelling to be curtailed, let alone cubby-holed. True, he could have composed more had he conducted less (or vice versa), but Bernstein chose his own paths. He was unique in his ability to bridge the artificial chasm that so often exists between classical and popular idioms, passionate in his desire to guide all of us along the path Candide sought, to "the best of all possible worlds."

"Any composer's writing is the sum of himself, of all his roots and influences," Bernstein said. "I have deep roots, each different from one another. They are American, Jewish, and cosmic in the sense they come from the great tradition of all music. I have been as influenced by Handel and Haydn as by jazz, folk songs, Hassidic melodies, or prayers I heard as a child. My music is not one or the other but a mixture of all. I can only hope it adds up to something you could call universal."

Bernstein's Works You Need to Know

As we were saying, where do we start? Maybe with "West Side Story," a magical show with a power and beauty that is indeed universal, and while you're in a Broadway mood, listen to "Candide" and "Wonderful Town." Then try the ballet music from "On the Town" ("New York, New York," it's a wonderful town…) and the Symphonic Suite from "On the Waterfront." For a more restful listening experience, try the exquisite "Chichester Psalms," and if you're ready to pull out all the dramatic stops, there's no topping "Mass," which Bernstein himself admitted was really "a theatre piece for singers, players, and dancers."

Music at the Movies

There was soundtrack music long before Al Jolson got down on one knee to serenade his Mammy in "The Jazz Singer"; indeed, all the way back to the end of the 19th century. In 1888, Thomas Edison was tinkering with a gadget (he called it a Kinetoscope) through which "we may see and hear a whole opera as perfectly as if actually present, although the performance may have taken place years before." Within half a dozen years, Edison's Kinetograph camera was filming snippets of Broadway musicals, and by 1895, he had developed the Kinetophone, so that when peepshow patrons plunked down their dimes, they could not only watch five consecutive scenes from "A Gaiety Girl" or some other stage hit of the day, but listen through ear tubes to an accompanying recording.

By 1900, no less the three companies validated Edison's predictions at the Paris Exhibition, with ballet and grand opera excerpts included in their competing versions of talking pictures. It would take another generation to develop the technology to make sound movies viable for general production and distribution, but just because most of the major pictures of the teens and 1920s were silents doesn't mean they lacked music. Engraved in American lore and legend, after all, is the image of the put-upon piano player at the ratty old upright, raiding the classics to improvise accompaniments for the train robbery, the kiss, or whatever else might materialize on screen.

Gradually, producers of important films began distributing cue sheets and "suggested music," so the tonal wherewithal might have a closer kinship to the on-screen action. The more ambitious studios even sent out scores, to be played by orchestras in the lavish, big-city film emporia.

Bet You Didn't Know

When the gigantic Strand opened on Broadway in 1914, it boasted high-pile plush carpets, crystal chandeliers, original artwork, and a pit where more than 30 musicians accompanied the film of the day (not to mention the inevitable vaudeville stage show). Ah, the good old days...

Other theatres astonished their patrons with the variety of sound effects possible on "the mighty Wurlitzer" organ. Smaller-town halls made do with a more modest band of five or six instrumentalists or, in a pinch, fell back upon the aforementioned piano player. With these live music capabilities in place, producers began commissioning and distributing full background scores (usually in a variety of orchestrations). This continued even after the advent of the sound era, primarily because the live orchestra was a lot more pleasing to the ear than the tinny music emanating from the primitive theater speakers. As technologies continued to advance, synchronized sound and sight became the norm that prevails to this day.

Bet You Didn't Know

Just as live music helped draw an audience into the silent screen action, it sometimes motivated the actors while the pictures were being shot. A number of early silent-film directors, among them Alfred Hitchcock, actually hired musicians to perform on the set, hoping thereby to inspire the players to higher levels of thespian glory.

Almost from the very beginning of the art form, in other words, music and motion pictures were natural partners. Sometimes music served as a subtle enhancement, "like a small lamp placed beneath the screen to warm it", as Aaron Copland put it. But it could be a powerful emotional tool as well, delineating characters, creating suspense, and counterpointing the dramatic highs and lows of the story action. The best film music not only did that, but went on to transcend its original screen function to thrive in the concert hall. And producing that music since the 1930s has been a brilliant cadre of classically trained composers.

We've already mentioned the film scores of Copland, Thomson, and Bernstein, but however excellent their work, Hollywood was clearly a diversion from their more usual concert or theatrical venues. The composers of whom we now speak, wrote sonatas and symphonies and operas too, but their abilities in the cinematic medium were so remarkable that their names are, for better or worse, indelibly associated with Hollywood and the blockbuster films they scored.

Tiomkin

The biography of Dimitri Tiomkin (1894-1979) begins almost the same as Prokofiev's. He was born in Ukraine, studied at the St. Petersburg Conservatory, and began his career as a virtuoso pianist. Tiomkin made his debut with the Berlin Philharmonic in 1924, playing the Liszt Concerto no. 1, and four years later brought Gershwin's Piano Concerto to Paris for the first time, where he also gave joint concerts with Gershwin at the Paris Opera. As a rising star, Tiomkin was booked onto the vaudeville circuit in the United States, but when the stock market crashed and the Great Depression stalked the land, the dates dried up. Only the movies—those blessed havens of escapism— were still booming, and Tiomkin managed to boom with them, especially when a producer decided that only a Russian composer could properly score a film version of Tolstoy's Resurrection complete, as Tiomkin recalled it, "with beards and Cossacks."

One thing led to another, and Tiomkin was off on a 40-year Hollwood binge that included such memorable films as "Mr. Smith Goes to Washington" (1939), "The Moon and Sixpence" (1943), "Dial M for Murder" (1954), "Giant" (1956), and "The Guns of Navarone" (1961). And those were the scores that didn't win Academy Awards; those that did were "High Noon" (1952), "The High and the Mighty" (1954), and "The Old Man and the Sea" (1958).

Bet You Didn't Know

Tiomkin was the hit of the 1954 Oscar ceremonies, when he accepted the trophy with a little speech expressing his appreciation of "the very important factor, which makes me successful and adds to the quality of this town. I like to thank Johannes Brahms, Johann Strauss, Richard Strauss, Richard Wagner..."

Tiomkin made his conducting debut with the Los Angeles Philharmonic in 1937, and he composed non-film music for the dance. But it is his richly romantic screen scores, reflecting his Russian heritage, yet flecked with jazz from his adopted homeland, that influenced successive generations of film composers, and keep his name high on the list of American originals.

Rozsa

Born in Hungary, Miklos Rozsa (1907-1995) was already on stage at age eight playing the violin, conducting a children's orchestra in Leopold Mozart's "Toy Symphony" and starting to jot down original music, much of it flavored by the gypsy and Hungarian folk tunes he heard around him. At the Budapest High School, he organized concerts of music by such then modern composers as Bartók and Kodaly, and at age 18, he won the Franz Liszt prize for a trio based on a folk tune called "The Sunset."

For more than 20 years, Rozsa had no thought of films: he was far too busy writing concertos, chamber music, ballets, and all sorts of other concert pieces. When Leonard

Bernstein made his historic debut at Carnegie Hall, one of the pieces he conducted was Rozsa's "Theme, Variations and Finale." According to the New York Times, "it brought down the house."

In 1937, Rozsa, then living in London, was asked to write the music for "Knight without Armour," an Alexander Korda film starring Robert Donat and Marlene Dietrich. Its success engendered another scoring assignment, this time for "Thunder in the City," and then Korda made Rozsa his official composer, a collaboration that led to seven more distinctive movies, among them "The Thief of Baghdad" (1940) and "The Jungle Book" (1942).

During World War II, much of Britain's film production work was transferred to Hollywood, and there Rozsa came in 1940, subsequently winning Oscars for his scores to "Spellbound" (1945), "A Double Life" (1948), and "Ben Hur: (1959), but also writing music for about 75 other films. On that voluminous list: "Quo Vadis" (1951), "El Cid" (1960), and "The Private Life of Sherlock Holmes" (1970).

For most of this time (1945-1965), Rozsa was on the music faculty at the University of Southern California, and even after he left off teaching, he continued to flourish as a concert organizer and conductor, and maintained a separate classical composing career.

Important Things to Know

Among the distinguished classical musicians who premiered Rozsa's concert works were Jascha Heifetz, Pinchas Zukerman, Janos Starker, and Leonard Pennario (the concertos respectively for violin, viola, cello, and piano. Rozsa also wrote a double concerto for Heifetz and the great Russian cellist Gregor Piatigorsky.

In addition to dozens of CDs devoted to Rozsa's film scores, some 30 of his classical pieces are available as well.

North

The son of a Russian blacksmith, Alex North (1910-1991) was born in Chester, Pennsylvania, studied at the Curtis Institute, the Juilliard School, and later—choosing an unusual alma mater for a native American—the Moscow Conservatory. Upon returning to the U.S., North studied with Aaron Copland and Ernst Toch and became music director of the Anna Sokolow Dance Troupe at a time when the spiritual daughters of Martha Graham were redefining modern dance in America.

During World War II, North became a Captain in the Army, and oddly enough, it was here that he started on the yellow brick road to Hollywood, scoring more than 25 documentary films for the Office of War Information. His interests were still centered on concert music, though, and after the war, he wrote "Revue," a clarinet concerto that was premiered by Benny Goodman, with Leonard Bernstein conducting. He also wrote several children's pieces on commission from the New York Philharmonic, two Cantatas, and his First Symphony.

Called upon by director Elia Kazan to write background music for his film edition of Tennessee Williams' "A Streetcar Named Desire"—over the objections of the Warner Brothers Music Department, which looked upon North as an inexperienced outsider— the composer established himself as a major creative artist on the Hollywood scene. He innovated the use of jazz, played by a stage band, within the context of a classically oriented score, and created instrumental leitmotifs that emphasized the dramatic impact of the action. Blanche du Bois' torment is identified with the plaintive and sensuous alto sax; the faraway tingling of a celesta suggests her lessening grip on reality.

North considered his forte to be intimate drama and character development. His skills were evidenced in his music for "Death of a Salesman" (1951) and another Williams play, "The Rose Tattoo" (1955), but he didn't shy away from such literate spectaculars as "Spartacus" (1960), "Cleopatra" (1963), and "The Agony and the Ecstasy" (1965). One of North's greatest frustrations was that his score for 2001 was discarded in favor of Strauss' "Blue Danube" and other classical snippets (North later resurrected the lost music for use in his Third Symphony); one of his final achievements, in 1988, was the remarkable score for "Good Morning, Vietnam."

All in all, Alex North wrote music for more than 60 pictures. In the inscrutable Hollywood manner, he was nominated for Academy Awards 15 times, but came home empty-handed until 1986, when he received a special Lifetime Achievement Oscar. "It is the genius of Alex North to convey an emotion to the audience," said the great director John Huston, who had collaborated with the composer on a number of pictures, among them "The Misfits" and "Prizzi's Honor." Sadly, North's many orchestral, choral, and chamber pieces still await significant performances and recordings; as long as there are movie channels, however, his music will continue to sound forth around the world.

The Other Bernstein

Following the now-familiar trail from classical conservatory to film studio, Elmer Bernstein (1922-2004) graduated from the Juilliard School, and dabbled in dance before deciding to cast his lot among the Hollywood composers. (His name, by the way, is pronounced "steen," as opposed to Leonard Bern"styne"). When you're the new kid on the block, you'll take any assignment that comes along, and what came along first for Bernstein was "Robot Monster" one of those sci-fi B-movies that used to be a great lure for teenagers on their first dates. Two years later, in 1955, came a biggie—"Man with the Golden Arm," starring Frank Sinatra as a heroin-adddicted jazz musician trying to kick the habit—and the year after that, Bernstein graduated from the seedy to the sublime, with his richly orchestrated music to one of Cecil B. DeMille's Biblical sagas, The Ten Commandments."

Soon, Bernstein's versatility was known throughout the industry and he was pegged for films as diverse as the pulse-pounding "The Magnificent Seven" (1960), the poignant and intimate "To Kill a Mockingbird" (1962), and the action-packed "The Great Escape" (1963). Elmer Bernstein won his only Oscar for "Thoroughly Modern Millie" in 1967, and when his elaborate orchestrations seem**ed** a bit out of place in the film directions of the 1970s, he responded with a parody of his own style in "Animal House" (1978), adding further to his comedic total with appropriately wacky scores for "Airplane!" (1980) and "Ghostbusters" (1984). His more recent cinematic achievements added terror to "Cape Fear" (**1**991) and romantic warmth to Rambling Rose (1992). His last contribution, to the 2002 film "Far From Heaven," earned an Oscar nomination for Best Original score.

Williams

Is there anybody over the age of six who hasn't flown with Superman, gasped at Jaws, or rooted for E.T. to call home? What desert island do you come from if you haven't gone with the Force in Star Wars, or wondered at Close Encounters of the Third Kind? What all these films have in common, aside from being box-office bonanzas, is that they boasted music by John Williams (1932-). The venerable Royal Academy of Music in London has a strict dress code, but when this proudly American composer was awarded honorary membership, one guest came dressed as Darth Vader; another arrived wearing a shark costume. Were they turned away? Of course not.

Important Things to Know

Along with the films mentioned above**earlier**, the Williams touch—sweeping themes, lush orchestrations (heavy on the brasses) and throbbing climaxes—enlivened such other film adventures as Raiders of the Lost Ark, The Empire Strikes Back, and Return of the Jedi.

Born in New York, where his father was a film studio musician, John Williams became a well-rounded musician himself. He learned to play trumpet, clarinet, and trombone, studied piano with the legendary Rosina Lhévinne at the Juilliard School, then took composition lessons from Mario Castelnuovo Tedesco when the family moved to Los Angeles. He put his feet into the cinematic waters gingerly at first, transcribing other people's music for films and TV; then, after winning an Oscar in 1971 for his arrangements and conducting in Fiddler on the Roof, he moved over into important composing assignments.

The man who won an Oscar for the jagged suspense of Jaws and the soaring, full-throated ecstasy of Superman would seem to have been an unlikely choice for Schindler's List, Steven Spielberg's harrowing, heartbreaking, and ultimately inspiring chronicle of death and life during the Holocaust. Genius cannot be cubby-holed, however, and Williams provided a score at once powerful, understated, and totally in keeping with the serious theme of this extraordinary film.

Speaking of non-cubby-holes, even while he was producing this long list of film scores, John Williams was also busy in the concert arena, writing two symphonies, concertos for flute and violin, a number of chamber pieces, and for more than a dozen years, starting in 1980, he succeeded Arthur Fiedler as music director of the Boston Pops.

Play It Again, Steve

Every action has a reaction, we learned in high school, and when the bubble of super romanticism burst in the first part of the 20th century, composers made their reactive moves in different directions. Stravinsky went one way, Schoenberg another, and— sad to say—many audience members went a third. Finding themselves out of the listening loop, as it were, their comfort level challenged by pieces that were dissonant or otherwise difficult to grasp, they simply said No to a lot **of** the music being written in their own time, contenting themselves with the cultural riches of earlier generations. Composers kept writing new works, but they were applauded largely by other composers and guardians of the academic trust. The lines of communication were badly damaged between the creators of music and their audiences, and some composers decided to do something about it.

Again, their remedies took divergent paths. Some returned to warmly lyric writing more often associated with the 19th than the 20th century ("neo-romantics," Jacob Druckman called them); others tried to provide a soothing alternate to the stresses and strains of modern life with a kind of wallpaper-like background music that came be known as "New Age." Threading a tonal course between those two approaches were the composers called "minimalists" because they pared music down to its simplest, most basic ingredients, attempting to get the greatest effect from the least amount of input.

If you hear a chord over and over again, until a very slight variation establishes a new harmony, which then itself gets repeated many times, you've probably stumbled onto a minimalist piece. If a tune or a rhythmic phrase keeps coming at you like a sonic mantra— and you get let yourself go with the flow instead of getting edgy at the monotony of it all—you may well find yourself drifting into a new dimension, entering, as Richard Jeffries so eloquently put it, "a timeless universe of contemplation and inner peace." See you in the morning.

Reich

Steve Reich all but coined the term minimalism, but the inner peace he was seeking to convey can be traced back to the mystics of ancient days; it can be found in the hypnotic power of the Gregorian chants, the exotic gamelan (percussion) music of Bali, and other non-Western cultures. "In composing music," Reich said, "it isn't what you do, it's how you do it. I find it basically impossible to separate the emotional and intellectual aspects of a piece of music."

Born in New York City, Steve Reich (1936-)grew up in a musical family where jazz, show tunes, and the classics were in equally full supply. His own musical directions were further influenced by the drum lessons he took as a teenager from Roland Kohloff (later principal timpanist of the New York Philharmonic). "The combination of tastes for Stravinsky, Bach, and jazz," he says, "coupled with my early training as a drummer, has persisted as a basic musical outlook in my compositions."

Following his graduation from Cornell University (as a philosophy major), Reich studied at the Juilliard School with Vincent Persichetti and William Bergsma, and at Mills College with Darius Milhaud and Luciano Berio. While those major composers instilled in him high knowledge and rigorous discipline, it was outside the mainstream that Reich's distinctive personality would blossom. Non-Western forms and concepts, including repetitive rhythms, are an integral feature of his music. In 1970, Reich went to Ghana to study West African rhythms with a master drummer of the Ewe tribe; several years later, he was in Jerusalem, learning about traditional forms of Hebraic cantillations. He also evolved what he called "pulse music," where sound patterns are created by the sounding of tones in and out of phrase with each other.

Finding that many artists had little or no knowledge of non-Western musical traditions, concepts and performing methods, Reich put together his own ensemble. Over the years, "Steve Reich and Musicians" have given us many many definitive recordings of his works; as for their concert performances, New Yorker critic Nicholas Kenyon summed them up as "an extraordinary experience: exhilarating, engrossing, hypnotizing, disorienting." Or, as the musicologist Nicolas Slonimsky puts it,"By rejecting the conventional way of music making, and thus infuriating the academics, Reich finds a direct avenue to the hearts, minds, and ears of the young."

Reich's Works You Need to Know

Don't try to use Reich's music as background, or have it on while you're doing the dishes. It demands total concentration, preferably with dimmed lights and a glass of wine. You needn't fear wild dissonances or jolting rhythms; this is music for contemplation, for the suspension of time; you have to immerse yourself into his very special sonic world, to share his karma, as it were. You can follow the creative unfolding of Reich's musical style with "Drummings" (1970-71), "Music for a Large Ensemble" (1978), "Tehillim" (Psalms for voices and chamber orchestra, 1981), and "Different Trains" (1988). You might also try his Double Sextet, which won the Pulitzer Prize for Music in 2008.

Glass

Philip Glass 1937-) is another of the "minimalist" composers who combines rhythmic cycles and other non-Western devices with repetition, stripping musical form down to its barest essentials, then letting those patterns play out in extended works, sometimes lasting as long as four hours.

Important Things to Know

Behavioral scientists have proved that if certain areas of the brain are not stimulated in early childhood, they may never develop to thier full potential. Kids who grow up with fine music around them—even if it's only a mother's lullaby or classical radio broadcasts providing playtime accompaniment—will often develop a lifelong love for music; conversely, youngsters whose only tonal encounters come from the screechings of a rock-and-roll boombox may forever be deprived of that enriching potential.

Glass' father serviced radios and sold records. When a disc was a poor seller, he'd take it home, play it for his three kids, and the gang would ponder the reasons why it didn't go. Since the things that didn't go included Schubert Sonatas and Beethoven Quartets, young Philip decided early on that he had better explore other paths. He, like Steve Reich, Glass majored in philosophy (at the University of Chicago), then studied music with Persichetti and Bergsma at the Juilliard School, and Darius Milhaud out west.

The young composer seemed well on his way, with some two dozen pieces published and many more performed, when he began rethinking his outlook. "I had reached a kind of dead end," he said. "I just didn't believe in my music any more." He applied for, and was awarded, a Fulbright Fellowship to study with Nadia Boulanger in Paris, and then in 1965, he found the breakthrough he had been looking for in the music of Ravi Shankar. The world-renowned Indian sitar virtuoso, in France to score a film, hired Glass to notate his improvised music so that the western-trained musicians could play it.

The experience galvanized the young American as nothing had before. Discovering a completely different tradition of music-making, Glass abandoned his earlier concepts of composition. He researched music in North Africa, India, and the Himalayas, then used some of those Eastern techniques to evolve a new system based on short rhythmic phrases and static harmonies. He also put together a seven-player ensemble, the Philip Glass Ensemble, specifically to develop and perform his new works.

Audience response was mixed: some listeners were mesmerized by the repetitive patterns; others just found them boring. But Glass was gradually developing a cult following. Virgin Records, a company specializing in rock, issued excerpts from his "Music in 12 Parts" in 1974, and two years later, "Einstein on the Beach" solidified Glass' international reputation. A sensation at its premiere in France, this four-and-a-half hour, multimedia opera, created with the architect, painter, and theatrical avant-gardist Robert Wilson, went on to major exposure in Austria, France, Germany, and Holland, before exploding onto the stage of the Metropolitan Opera House for two completely sold-out performances. His opera "Satyagraha" (the word is a Sansrit term meaning the force of truth), based on the life of Gandhi, has been another unlikely hit at the Met.

Glass has continued to produce works of great theatrical effect, among them three other expansive operas, Akhnaten, Satyagraha, and The Voyage (which had its world premiere at the Metropolitan Opera in 1992), several film scores, danceworks, and a striking "collaboration" with the late director Jean Cocteau, whereby new music and stage action are presented against a screening of Cocteau's classic film Les Enfants Terribles.

Glass' Works You Need to Know

We've just mentioned the operas (there's also another, called The Photographer). Add the scores for the films The Thin Blue Line and Koyaanisquatsi, the Low Symphony, based on the pop hit by Brian Eno and David Bowie, "Dance Pieces" for voices and instruments, and Hydrogen Jukebox, a theatre piece derived from poems of Allen Ginsberg, and you'll have a fair notion of Glass' far-ranging interests and explorations.

Adams

John Adams has been called the modernist among the minimalists, because in addition to trying to slow down the passage of time with repetitive phrases and rhythms, Adams incorporates shifting tempos, colors, textures, and dynamics. A New Englander by birth (Massachusetts, 1947), upbringing (Vermont and New Hampshire), and training (Harvard), Adams went west in 1971. He headed up the composition department at the San Francisco Conservatory for more than 10 years and served (for most of that time) as advisor to, and later composer in residence for, the San Francisco Symphony. Recently, he has added an active conducting career to his busy schedule, leading his own music and that of other 20th century composers with the Los Angeles, Cleveland, and other major orchestras.

Adams' Works You Need to Know

Two short pieces that pop up fairly regularly on orchestral programs are both derived from longer works: "Shaker Loops" from Adams' String Quartet, and "The Chairman Dances" from the opera "Nixon in China"; you'll also have fun with a a dazzling little curtain-raiser intriguingly titled "Short Ride on a Fast Machine." Like "Nixon in China," "The Death of Klinghoffer" brought a headline story on the operatic stage, and contemporary themes swirl through "Doctor Atomic," which was so successful on stage in 2005 that two years later Adams converted themes from the opera into his Doctor Atomic Symphony.

New Technologies

Electronic keyboards are so much a part of modern culture that we tend to forget that guitars weren't always plugged in, and that the organ used to have air pumped through its pipes by manual labor. The advent of sound recordings put electricity to useful cultural service, and radio made music accessible to people everywhere. The first electronic instrument dates from as recently as 1920, when a Russian scientist, Lev Termen (known in America as Leon Theremin) demonstrated what he then called an Aetherphone. **He** produced sounds by moving his hands in the air (breaking an electromagnetic field, the way opening a door can set off a car alarm). Later renamed "theremin-vox" for the inventor and subsequently shortened simply to theremin, it had quite a vogue in the 1920s and 30s. This led to semi-mass production of the instrument by RCA, concerts by theremin ensembles, and creation of such important works as Anis Fuliehan's Concerto for Theremin, which was premiered in 1945 by Clara Rockmore, with Leopold Stokowski conducting. Widely acknowledged as the supreme theremin virtuoso, Rockmore's art is documented on CDs on the Bridge, Delos, and Romeo labels.

Synthesizers

The synthesizer is a contraption capable of generating and processing a vast array of sounds. There are any number of models, differing in capabilities, manner of operation, size, and appearance, but once the operator has input the necessary musical information, it must pass through an external amplifier and loudspeakers to be heard as sound. Synthesizers, like other forms of electronics, are customarily divided into analog and digital types. In principle, an analog synthesizer uses continuously varying voltages to fashion its sound waves, whereas a digital synthesizer uses discrete units of information.

The first synthesizers appeared in the late 1950s. They were programmable composition machines which, like their office computer counterparts, took up an awful lot of space and had a limited range of capabilities. Before this, virtually all electronic music had to be created by laying down tracks, one at a time, on magnetic tape and then fusing the tracks into a completed product. The synthesizer greatly simplified some of these procedures, and made others unnecessary. The use of voltage control, for instance, made it possible to create an infinite variety of pitches, amplitudes, timbres, and reverberations; in short, machines could duplicate most of the components of what we call music.

The early synthesizers, such as those developed by the pioneering American engineer Robert Moog (that's pronounced Mow-g in case you want to order a theremin: his company now manufactures them), were controlled manually; later models added all sorts of devices to produce predetermined sounds or rhythms on demand. The Moog was the instrument of choice for "Switched-on Bach" and other electrified versions of revered classics. Some music lovers were horrified at the onslaught, but unquestionably the new electronics switched a lot of young listeners on to the ineffable joys of Father Bach and his classical descendants.

The next step was taking synthesizers out of the studio and onto the stage as actual performance instruments. They were smaller now, had fewer component parts, and as a result were a lot easier to set up and operate. Composers of note began using synthesizers alongside standard instruments, until at last electronic music had come full circle. Like the theremin, which its inventor showed off to Lenin way back in 1920, the synthesizer was being used to create and supplement other sounds of beauty, not just to produce startling effects or imitate other instruments.

Electronic Orchestras

Theoretically, a synthesizer that can reproduce any sound would make musicians obsolete, let alone the baton-waver up on the podium. Ironically, one of the earliest explorations of this formidable possibility came from Pierre Boulez, who for half a dozen years was the chief baton-waver at the New York Philharmonic. In his "Repons," Boulez used computers to analyze, synthesize, and replace symphonic sounds. Producers of Broadway shows have more than once threatened to use synthesizers in place of recalcitrant or striking musicians, and who knows what further manipulations await. One hopes, of course, that wise heads will prevail, and that electronics will expand the scope of our musical horizons, not foist upon us imitations of the real thing

The Vocal Chord

CHAPTER 19

Singing in the Main

What's more important, the words or the music? The question has fomented centuries of controversy and sparked a famous opera by Richard Strauss, but the answer is clear: neither. The singers are the true stars, the real audience draws, the actual makers of headlines. Sure Carmen has some good tunes, and Tristan some great half-hours, but it's the diva (or divo in the case of a man) who is the box-office magnet. Way back in 1757, Parisians flipped over a young soprano named Sophie Arnould, literally fighting with each other to get tickets to her performances. As one French observer put it, "I doubt they would take such pains to get into paradise."

Pre-Madonnas—100-Year-Old Prima Donnas

Let's stroll down the lanes of vocal history over the last hundred years or so, stopping to consider some of the first ladies of operatic song, and a few of the first gentlemen into the bargain. Most of them lived into the early years of sound recordings, long enough to have their voices enshrined on early recordings, so we can still partake of their artistry on CD reissues. Many reached their heights of vocal glory within the happy memory of us over-forty types; and before our chapter is through, we'll also have touched upon a few of the legendary personalities whose gifts of song and aria continue still to enrich our lives and broaden our musical horizons. We begin, though, with a couple of the prima donnas (literally, first ladies) who brightened the operatic scene a century ago.

Jenny Lind

They called her the "Swedish Nightingale," and indeed Johanna Maria Lind (1820-1887) was born in Stockholm (1820-1887). Though she studied in Paris, she became America's favorite singer and lived the last 30 years of her life in London. Among her many admirers were the composers Giacomo Meyerbeer, who helped jump-start her career by getting her the starring role in a Berlin production of Bellini's Norma, and Giuseppe Verdi, who wrote the role of Amalia in I Masnadieri expressly for her.

Bet You Didn't Know

Meyerbeer also had arranged an audition for Lind at the Paris Opera, but she was turned down. The soprano never forgot the insult, and when she became the most popular singer in the world, she took special delight in refusing every offer to perform in the French capital.

Unlike many other singing stars, Jenny Lind was modest in her personal life and unflashy in her professional dealings. In 1849, deciding that too many plots were immoral, she stepped down from the operatic stage, only to agree to an American concert tour organized by that noted arbiter of morality and taste, P.T. Barnum. She made her New York debut the following year, adding another 92 recitals (and marrying her accompanist) before returning to Europe. There she restricted her singing to oratorios and concerts, and later became a professor at London's Royal College of Music.

Adelina Patti

Adelina (actually Adele Juana Maria) Patti (1843-1919) seems to have been born to the operatic life. Her father was an impresario, her mother a noted soprano (Caterina Barilli), an iron-willed lady who continued performing strenuous roles throughout her pregnancy. According to one report, Adelina made her entrance into the world while her mother was singing Norma. That would have been an even greater story had it been true.

In any case, Adelina showed exceptional talent at an early age (her mother claimed that Adelina's first cry was a perfectly pitched F-sharp). At the age of four, she could sing popular ballads and even a few arias. When Barilli signed on to do another Norma, her prodigal daughter was given a role as one of the priestess' children. They say she unnerved the cast at rehearsals by singing along with her Mom in the duet "Miro, O Norma." Adelina gave her first recital at the age of eight, went on her first tour a year later, then made her operatic debut at sweet 16 in the title role of Donizetti's Lucia di Lammermoor. This was all in America, by the way, the family having moved from Madrid to New York when Papa Patti became manager of the Astor Place Opera House.

Thereafter, the world was Patti's musical oyster. She sang for 25 seasons at Covent Garden, made wildly successful tours of Europe and the USA, and continued to give farewell concerts for many years after her official operatic retirement. Her final performance, at a charity gala for the Red Cross, was in 1914: she was over 70, in the twilight of a magical career that had lasted for 63 years.

Bet You Didn't Know

When Adelina Patti came to San Francisco in 1884, she literally caused riots, with tickets scalped at wildly excessive prices and places in line at the opera house bought and sold like blue-chip stocks. The impresario, Colonel Mapleson, was arrested for overcrowding the theatre (the judge dismissed the charge in exchange for a pair of Mapleson's own house seats). The local newspaper reported, "It seemed that a large number of people had run completely mad over the desire to hear Patti sing. After the throng had melted away, the approaches to the box-office looked as if they had been visited by a first-class Kansas cyclone in one of its worst moods."

Patti was far more the stereotypical prima donna than Jenny Lind. She managed to squeeze three husbands and quite a few high-profile lovers into her schedule. In addition, she rarely showed up on time for rehearsals (in fact, her right to skip them was put into her contracts), and she sometimes didn't even bother to meet her fellow artists before going out to sing with them on stage. Long before Lorelei Lee figured out that diamonds are a girl's best friend, Adelina Patti never lost an opportunity to flaunt her fabulous jewelry, much of it gifts from royalty. During her last Traviata season, the London press estimated that she went on stage wearing nearly half-a-million dollars worth of diamonds.

By the age of the gramophone, Patti's voice had lost much of its sheen, but even those primitive early recordings reveal the subtle beauty, rhythmic sensitivity, and expressive power of her singing. According to another story, the great diva was very impressed when she heard her own voice on records, finally understanding why everyone adored her so. Now there's a great story that might just be true.

The Great Caruso

He was short and plumpish and hardly the glamorous figure that Mario Lanza portrayed in the movie, but Enrico Caruso was not only the most popular singer of his day, but probably the most famous singer in the history of opera. The 18th of 20 children in Naples, Italy, he had to help support his family by working in a machine shop, but his goal of becoming a singer never wavered. He joined his church choir and sang on street corners to earn money for lessons. Drafted into military service, he was a hopeless misfit, but he so impressed a high-ranking officer with his powerful voice that he was actually released to pursue his musical studies, his older brother Giuseppe reluctantly replacing him in the unit.

Unlike anything you may have gathered from the film, Caruso's career actually got off to a fairly bumpy start. As a young man, he sang by ear well enough to land a part in Mignon, but when he couldn't follow the orchestra at the first rehearsal, he was unceremoniously dumped from the cast. His first stage appearance in 1894 wasn't much better, because Caruso was stuck in a bomb called L'amico Francesco by an amateur composer, one Mario Morelli.

Four years later, though, he had increased his reputation to the point where he was chosen to create the role of Loris in Giordano's Fedora, and after the national acclaim for those performances, there was no looking back. The story goes that the 24-year-old Caruso turned up unannounced at Puccini's house, asking for an audition. The composer reluctantly allowed him in and asked him to sing "Che gelida manina" (from "La Bohema"). Caruso did so, ending his impromptu performance with a spectacular high C. In amazement, Puccini asked "Who has sent you to me? God?" (Another version of that tale has it that Puccini asked Caruso "Who are you?" and Caruso fell right into character, picking up the operatic text at that point "I am a poet…") Either way, Puccini soon convinced the powers to be at La Scala that Caruso should sing La Boheme there, and later the tenor gave stellar performances of Puccini's Tosca, Madame Butterfly, and Girl of the Golden West.

Bet You Didn't Know

It was during another Boheme performance that Caruso saved the show when Andres de Segurola became too ill to get through the famous "Coat Aria" in the last act. Years before Milli Vanilli came up with the idea, Caruso told the basso to mouth the words while the tenor turned his back to the audience and sang the whole aria for him.

In later years, Puccini became jealous of Caruso's fame and fortune (especially fortune), when the tenor amassed what was then a king's ransom for recording his arias. (Composers didn't get royalties in those days.) Even at his most upset, however, Puccini always gave Caruso his vocal due, once ending a letter with the phrase "I salute you, O singer of many notes," and admitting to anyone who asked that "his voice is magnificent."

Few people would disagree with that assessment. Caruso sang with Nellie Melba at Monte Carlo, swept through Europe and South America to universal acclaim, and in 1903 made his debut at the Metropolitan as the Duke of Mantua in Rigoletto. He sang in the first radio broadcast from the Met in 1910, continued to make dozens of recordings, and was still in his vocal prime at the time of his tragically early death (from pleurisy) at the age of 48.

Feuding and Fussing

"In a chorus girl, it's bad taste," goes a famous line from the musical "42nd Street", "in a star, it's temperament." When two stars collide in the heavens, there is a spectacular explosion. Why should it be any different down here?

In Handel's day, Francesca Cuzzoni and Faustina Bordoni actually came to blows on stage when they were cast in the same opera, their fans divided into two camps, wildly applauding one while hysterically booing her rival until the performance lay in total shambles. Their feud caused such a stir that it became the subject of a popular satire in London called Contretemps, or The Rival Queens.

A century later, Adelina Patti grew so convinced that another soprano, Etelka Gerster, was out to get her that she would extend the first and fourth fingers of her right hand whenever Gerster's name was mentioned, the classic horn sign designed to ward off the Evil Eye of her nemesis.

Sometimes, of course, a singer's temper flares up against the audience rather than a colleague. Caruso, booed (by jealous rivals) when he sang in his hometown, vowed never to perform there again. "I will come to Naples only to eat a plate of spaghetti," he said. The same thing happened in Barcelona, with the same results (minus the spaghetti); years later, Caruso turned down full-fee engagements in Madrid because it was only 350 miles away from Barcelona.

Bet You Didn't Know

Back in Naples, there was another tenor named Armandi who, even on his best days, was pretty terrible. Landing a contract to sing in six performances of Norma, he was roundly hissed at the premiere, whereupon, after the end of Act I, he stepped in front of the curtain and made a deal with the audience: if they would treat him with respect, he'd leave town after that night's show. If they kept booing, he vowed to stay and sing the remaining five performances too.

Maria Callas

As if to prove that the 19th century had no monopoly on operatic fireworks, the 20th gave us Maria Callas (1923-1977). She was of Greek heritage, but she was actually born in New York (1923-1977), and lived there until the age of 13, when her family moved back to Athens. Maria studied at the Conservatory there, made her stage debut in a school production of Cavalleria Rusticana at 15, and took on her first major professional role as Tosca four years after that. Her operatic debut in Italy came in 1947, when she starred as La Gioconda in Verona. The conductor Tullio Serafin, greatly admiring her work, helped promote her blossoming international career and led her towards the stardom that seemed to be her birthright.

Bet You Didn't Know

The soprano had long since changed her name. Maria Callas fits your average marquee a lot better than Anna Sofia Cecilia Kalogeropoulos.

Prodigious as her vocal gifts were, and as famous as she became for many bel canto (literally "beautiful singing") operas, Callas achieved her place in vocal history through the dramatic intensity of her performances. "Some of the texts we have to sing are not distinctive poetry," she said. "To convey the dramatic effect to the audience, and to myself, I must sometimes produce sounds that are not beautiful. I don't mind if they're ugly, so long as they are true."

Bet You Didn't Know

The Met manager at the time, Rudolf Bing, got his revenge: he arranged to have Callas' husband paid in a unmanageably large wad of $5 bills. Not that Callas herself was disinterested in money. When a reporter questioned her about her American birth, her Greek upbringing, and her Italian residence, wondering in which language she felt most comfortable, the soprano answered, "I count in English."

Callas' electrifying presence on stage (Nicolas Slonimsky called her "an incarnation of carnality") was matched by her tempestuous private life. Her liaison with Aristotle Onassis was a source of sensational gossip in the press (this, of course, before the Greek shipping magnate's romance with Jacqueline Kennedy ushered in an equivalent barrage of tabloid coverage), and her battles with opera impresarios and managers were legendary. She more than once stalked off the stage in a fury over some disagreement (in Rome, she walked out at the end of the first act of an opera even though the Italian President was in the audience) or failed to show up for a scheduled performance altogether. She canceled her first contract at the Met, delayed signing a second one because she didn't like the conductor assigned to her debut, and demanded (at least her manager-husband demanded) payment in cash before the curtain rose each night.

Sparks continued to fly between Bing and Callas. She held onto her next Met contract for 10 weeks before signing it and later cancelled a run of Traviatas because Renata Tebaldi had been offered them first. When she balked at agreeing to a substitute group of Lucias as well, Bing fired her, their falling-out making still more banner headlines. "Madame Callas is constitutionally unable to fit into any organization not tailored to her own personality," said Bing at his most haughty, while Callas, in more earthy terms, dismissed the Bing production of those Traviatas as "lousy, really lousy."

Eventually, the claws were pulled in, Bing and Callas mended their rather heavily battered fences, and the soprano returned to the Met to more extensive press coverage than before. Even the Tebaldi-Callas feud, which had been blown up out of all proportion by the eager gossip columnists, ended in 1968 when Callas attended Tebaldi's opening night of Adriana Lecouvreur. Bing took her backstage after the performance, and as he later described it, "Miss Tebaldi opened the door and the two sopranos fell into each others arms, crying."

Callas retired from the operatic stage after a final Tosca in 1965, but her legend lives on in recordings, video tapes, the biographies that continue to appear at regular intervals, and even as the leading character in the play Master Class, which author Terrence McNally derived (at least in part) from transcripts of the singer's 1971-72 master classes at the Juilliard School. The play had a greatly successful Broadway revival in 2011, starring Tyne Daly, then transferred in 2012 for an extended run in London.

Lift Every Voice and Sing

Although it sprang from the evil practice of slavery, black music in America has enriched our national heritage beyond measure. In 1781, Thomas Jefferson would write that "in music, the blacks are more generally gifted than the whites, with accurate ears for tune and time." In the early 1800's, many southern plantations had bands of black musicians; by 1867, a book called "Slave Songs of the United States" was published to document the widespread use of work songs, dances tunes and spirituals. With emancipation came a new upswing of interest in this music, and an outpouring of talented musicians to create and perform it. The Jubilee Singers of Fisk University brought choral spirituals to the concert platforms of America and introduced them to European audiences. Pianist-composer Scott Joplin sparked the rise of ragtime; and in the concert world, extraordinary artists like the tenor Roland Hayes, and Hall Johnson, conductor of the legendary choir that bore his name, brought black music to the eager attention of music lovers everywhere.

In 1900, the siblings James Weldon and Rosamond Johnson wrote "Lift Every Voice and Sing", an inspiring piece that quickly became known as the Negro National Anthem. "Lift every voice and sing," the lyric begins, "till earth and heaven ring with the harmonies of liberty." Roland Hayes (1887-1976) went on to prove that a black singer need not restrict his repertory to any one style: the program at his 1917 concert debut included Mozart arias and German as well as the spirituals he referred to as "my songs". His subsequent tours took Hayes to Paris, Vienna, Madrid, and many other European centers, including London, where he sang for King George V and Queen Mary at Buckingham Palace. The pioneering path he blazed has been followed by hundreds of other superb singers, but none more distinctive and influential than the two historic figures we consider next.

Marian Anderson—The Whole World in Her Hands

Marian Anderson was the precise opposite to the stereotypical diva: a woman of gentle demeanor, extraordinary modesty, and noble, spiritual dignity. "Yours is a voice one hears once in a century," said Arturo Toscanini in 1935, when Marian Anderson sang in Salzburg Indeed, she became the most celebrated contralto of the modern age. Her illustrious career spanned 40 years, reaching dizzying heights of musical acclaim even as she triumphed over the ugly depths of racism. In Europe, she was treated like royalty; in her own land, she was led to service entrances and asked to take the freight elevators, even in concert halls that proudly displayed her name on their marquees.

Marian Anderson (1897-1993) was born in Philadelphia, where her father sold coal in the winter and ice during the summer and her mother took in laundry. As a child, she sang in the Union Baptist Church Choir for a congregation that not only recognized her talent but contributed funds so that she could take voice lessons. In 1923, Anderson won a local singing competition, two years later she took first prize in auditions sponsored by the New York Philharmonic, and appeared with that celebrated orchestra before making her Carnegie Hall debut in 1929. Although attendance was nothing like the packed houses she would later command, the *New York Times* wrote that the young singer possessed a vocal talent "beyond the usual endowment of mortals."

Anderson's London debut in 1930 led to a triumphant tour of Europe. Her repertoire combined art songs, arias and African-American spirituals, and she conquered audiences from England to Scandinavia, Central Europe to Russia. Back home, recognition arrived more slowly, but her reputation continued on an ever-upward spiral. Then came an event that would thrust Anderson—however unwillingly—into the national spotlight, and help transform the American social landscape.

Anderson's voice had sung been heard in the nation's capital a number of times, but always in churches or schools. Finally, in 1939, her manager arranged a recital date on Washington's most prestigious concert platform, Constitution Hall. A few weeks before the scheduled date, Anderson learned that the Daughters of the American Revolution, the owners of the theatre, had decided that it would not be seemly to have a Black artist featured on its stage. A storm of outrage arose around the country. First Lady Eleanor Roosevelt promptly resigned from the D.A.R., and Harold Ickes, Secretary of the Interior, invited Anderson to perform in an outdoor Easter Sunday concert at the Lincoln Memorial. Seventy-five thousand people gathered for that recital, while the rest of the country listened on the radio. "I had sensations unlike any I had experienced before," the singer recalled in her autobiography. "The only comparable emotion was the feeling I had had when Maestro Toscanini had appeared in the artists' room in Salzburg. My heart leaped wildly, and I could not talk. I even wondered whether I would be able to sing."

Sing she did, of course, and America had a new cultural icon. In due course, she would indeed sing at Constitution Hall, the outcry having caused the theatre to open its stages to artists of all creeds and races. Another color barrier fell on January 7, 1955, when Marian Anderson became the first featured Black artist at the Metropolitan Opera, singing the role of Ulrica in Verdi's A Masked Ball. "The chance to be a member of the Metropolitan has been a highlight of my life," the contralto wrote. "It has meant much to me and to my people. If I have been privileged to serve as a symbol, I take greater pride from knowing that it has encouraged other singers of my group to realize that the doors everywhere may open increasingly to those who have prepared themselves well. Not everyone can be turned aside from meanness and hatred, but the great majority of Americans is heading in that direction I have a great belief in the future of my people and my country."

The Anderson legend continued to grow even as she began slowing down her arduous performing schedule. President Eisenhower appointed her a delegate to the General Assembly of the United Nations; she sang at President Kennedy's inauguration; and she received the American Medal of Honor from President Johnson. On the occasion of her 75th birthday, Congress passed a resolution to have a special gold medal minted in her name.

In 1991, Marian Anderson received her last standing ovation at Carnegie Hall; not on stage this time, but from one of the loges, when Kathleen Battle dedicated a Rachmaninoff song to her idol and acknowledged the beloved contralto's presence in the hall she had first illumined with her artistry more than 60 years earlier.

Bet You Didn't Know

In the eyes of her countrymen, Marian Anderson was always a goodwill ambassador to the world, but the title was made official in 1957 when the State Department invited her to tour India and the Far East.

Paul Robeson—Here he Stands

"Greatness was his cloak," said Count Basie, and the statement well applies to all aspects of Paul Robeson's life: his athletic prowess, his unforgettable singing, his brilliant acting, his scholarly writings, his unyielding battles for social and racial justice. "It wasn't just his voice which made us all love him," said Pete Seeger. "It was his quality as a person, his courage, his determination, and his not retreating into just being a musician."

The son of a former slave, Robeson (1898-1976) was born in Princeton, New Jersey (1898-1976). He was a two-year football All-American, graduated Rutgers as a Phi Beta Kappa scholar, and became only the second African American to get a law degree from Columbia University. As an actor, he created the role of "The Emperor Jones" in Eugene O'Neill's play (he also starred in two other O'Neill stageworks, All God's Chillun Got Wings and The Hairy Ape) and then—both in London and on Broadway—was hailed as the definitive "Othello".

Bet You Didn't Know

George Jean Nathan, the notoriously ascerbic critic, wrote that Robeson was "one of the most thoroughly eloquent, impressive and convincing actors that I have looked at and listened to in almost twenty years of professional theatre-going," and addinged that the impact of his Othello was that, "of a soul bombarded by thunder and torn by lightning."

As a singer, Robeson brought spirituals to the concert platform, indeed becoming the first recitalist to present a program consisting exclusively of spirituals and secular songs derived from Black slave culture. He later expanded his repertoire to encompass folk songs of many lands (in their original languages), becoming also the first male Black artist to achieve top radio and recording popularity.

In stunning combinations of those singing and acting talents, Robeson starred in Showboat, turning "Ol' Man River" (which had been written especially for him by Jerome Kern and Oscar Hammerstein II) into a permanent fixture of American popular culture, and later appeared in nine other major film features, the first pictures to break the prevailing stereotypes and allow a Black male to be portrayed as a person of strength and dignity.

During the 1950s, when America was consumed with anti-Communist witch-hunts, Robeson's outspoken demands for equal rights, his open support for unpopular causes, and his unwillingness to keep silent on issues deemed embarrassing to the State Department, subjected him to an unprecedented campaign of personal vilification and professional harassment. When a member of the House Un-American Activities Committee referred to Robeson's trips to Russia and asked him why he didn't stay there, his proud answer was typical: "Because my father was a slave, and my people died to build this country and I am going to stay here and have a part of it is just like you. And no fascist-minded people will drive me from it. Is that clear?"

If they couldn't drive Robeson out of the country, they did make sure that he couldn't leave by: illegally withdrawing his passport, then effectively closing down his American career by presuring major concert halls to refuse him access, causing music stores to pull his albums off the shelves, and forcing recording studios to deny him use of their facilities. As Studs Terkel put it, the government tried to make "a non person of Paul Robeson." The campaign was carried to hysterical extremes. His name was stricken from historical records, radio stations dared not play a Robeson song lest their licenses be revoked, and for nearly a decade, his magnificent voice could be heard only in the Black churches of America.

After seemingly endless legal battles, and a gradually changing climate in America, Robeson was vindicated; his passport was returned and his international career resumed. When he appeared in San Francisco, the *Chronicle* reported that "the years have done nothing to the greatest natural basso voice of the present generation. Two sold-out concerts in Carnegie Hall (his first appearances there in 11 years) followed, and on June 1, 1958, he sang what proved to be his final American concert. Appropriately, it was at Mother A.M.E. Zion Church in Harlem, where his brother, the Rev. Benjamin C. Robeson, was pastor. Two months later, he was cheered at his concert return to the Royal Albert Hall in London, and his European triumphs continued in concert as well as with a reprise of Othello in a new production at the Shakespeare Memorial Theatre in Stratford-Upon-Avon.

Becoming ill with a circulatory disease in 1961, Robeson returned home to retire from public life, living quietly with his sister in Philadelphia until his death from a stroke in 1976. "Here I stand", wrote Paul Robeson in 1958. "To achieve the right of full citizenship which is our just demand, we must ever speak and act like free men. Americans who wish for peace among nations—and I believe the vast majority of them do—can join with my people in singing our old-time song: I'm going to lay down my sword and shield, Down by the riverside—Going to study war no more!"

Made in Valhalla

Singing Wagner requires a lot more than a helmet and armor. It requires a full and powerful voice to override the sumptuous orchestrations, and—given the length of the music dramas—the stamina of a marathon runner. In the days when Gable and Garbo were big box office draws, Kirsten Flagstad and Lauritz Melchoir were the Wagnerian headliners, with the peerless Birgit Nilsson following in their dramatic footsteps. Must be something in the Scandinavian diet.

Kirsten Flagstad

Born in Hamar, Norway (1895-1962), Kirsten Flagstad began her vocal training at home. Those early lessons with her mother led to professional studies and a 20-year career in Scandinavia, where she gave many concerts in addition to staged operas and operettas. In 1933, she sang several minor roles at Bayreuth, then hit the Wagnerian jackpot as Sieglinde in Die Walkure, the role in which she then made triumphant debuts at Covent Garden and the Metropolitan Opera. When World War II broke out, many musicians fled Europe for America; Flagstad took the opposite route, leaving the United States in 1941 to return to her husband in Nazi-occupied Norway.

This politically unpopular decision caused much anguish among her fans, and complicated her return to international performances after the war. Art did triumph eventually, Flagstad resuming her career in England and then the USA, where she appeared as Isolde in 1951. Nearing 60, the soprano soon afterwards retired from the operatic stage, though she continued to make recordings, and from 1958 to 1960, served as director of the Norwegian Opera in Oslo. Those fortunate enough to have seen Flagstad as Kundry, Brunnhilde, Elizabeth and other strong Wagnerian women (or to have heard the live Met broadcasts) know the intensity of her portrayals; the rest of us must stay contented with her superb recording legacy.

Lauritz Melchoir

Every Sieglinde must have her Siegmund, every Isolde her Tristan, and for many wonderful years at the Met, these leading men were often forthcoming in the substantial personage of Lauritz Melchoir (1890-1973).

Born in Denmark (1890-1973), the great tenor studied at the Royal Opera School in Copenhagen and made his debut there (as a baritone!) in Pagliacci. He soon learned the error of his singing ways, and re-emerged as a full-blown tenor in Tannhauser, adding Siegmund to his stentorian repertoire for his Covent Garden debut, and Siegfried for his first performances at Bayreuth, both in 1924. Two years later, the Met beckoned, and his triumphal debut, again as Tannhauser, began his long and distinguished career as one of the America's most distinguished artists. He missed only one Met season until his farewell performance as Lohengrin in 1950, after which Melchoir found life after the opera in concerts, a batch of MGM films, and musical comedy. Nonetheless, it is as one of the greatest Heldentenors (literally "heroic tenor") of the 20th century that he is best remembered. As

Francis Robinson expressed it, Melchior and Flagstad "put the Metropolitan back on the gold standard."

Bet You Didn't Know

Another of Melchoir's frequent Wagnerian partners at the Met was Helen Traubel, and every time they appeared together, they would indulge in a little game of "who can hold the high note longer", each valiantly trying to outdo the other without making a shambles of the music. Traubel admitted that the tenor could usually outlast her in direct competition. "He seemed to enjoy turning purple," she said.

During a piano rehearsal of "Tristan" aat the Vienna State Opera, Birgit Nilsson's string of pearls snapped, and conductor Herbert von Karajan helped scoop them up for her. Having apparently exhausted his supply of chivalry, Karajan asked the soprano whther the pearls were stage jewelry or real stuff "bought from your phenomenal fees at La Scala." "Don't worry," Nilsson quickly assured him. "These are cheap pearls, bought from your very ordinary Vienna fees."

Birgit Nilsson

The third of our Scandinavian Wagnerians (though she also sang many other roles superbly) is Birgit Nilsson (1918-2006). "I'm a simple person from the country," she told an interviewer, and indeed she grew up as a farmer's daughter in Sweden and used to milk ten cows a day before getting down to musical business. Singing, however, was always part of the Nilsson story, starting with the songs her mother taught her at age two, and continue at age 23 when she was accepted by the Royal Academy in Stockholm. At that point, she pulled her last weeds, milked her last ten cows, and settled down to serious studies. "I really wanted very much to sing," she said, "a whole new life began…"

Unlike some artists who are worldwide successes in their teens, Nilsson's career unfolded slowly. She sang her first operatic role, Agathe in Weber's Der Freischutz, at age 28 when the original soprano canceled at the last moment, and it was another year (and another cancellation) before she appeared as Verdi's Lady Macbeth . Only then did things start moving. In 1948 she drew her first Wagnerian role, Senta in The Flying Dutchman; a few years later, her Brunnhilde sent up international alerts, and she soon was repeating the part in Munich, Vienna, and the Bayreuth Festival, where she would appear regularly from 1954 until 1970.

Her American operatic debut, again as Brunnhilde, was in San Francisco, and such was her enormous success that her 1959 Met debut (as Isolde) was front-page news. So, was her return to the company 20 years later after a five-year absence, first in a gala performance, then for a series of Elektra performances in the Strauss opera, the first of which occasioned a 30-minute standing ovation.

Bet You Didn't Know

During a piano rehearsal of "Tristan" at the Vienna State Opera, Birgit Nilsson's string of pearls snapped, and conductor Herbert von Karajan helped scoop them up for her. Having apparently exhausted his supply of chivalry, Karajan asked the soprano whther the pearls were stage jewelry or real stuff "bought from your phenomenal fees at La Scala." "Don't worry," Nilsson quickly assured him. "These are cheap pearls, bought from your very ordinary Vienna fees."

Although her repertoire extended to many other dramatic operas, among them *Turandot, Fidelio, Salome* and *Aida,* and she retired from the operatic stage in 1982, Birgit Nilsson is still considered one of the greatest Wagnerian sopranos of all time. The Met staged two different productions of *Tristan und Isolde* especially for her (she also was given new productions at 20 other opera houses around the world), and her Wagner recordings remain as peerless trophies of an exceptional life in music. So does the Birgit Nilsson Scholarship Fund, which the soprano established more than 15 years ago at the Manhattan School of Music to encourage the development of future operatic greats. Her name also lives on in the Birgit Nilsson Prize, which the soprano inaugurated late in her life. The #1 million award—the most generous in the world of classical music—went to the tenor Placido Domingo in 2009; in 2011, at a festive ceremony at the Royal Swedish Opera in Stockholm, King Carl VXI Gustaf presented the prize to conductor Riccardo Muti.

Joan Sutherland—Queen of Bel Canto

"Singing is very simple," said Joan Sutherland (1926-2010). "It's basically breathing, supporting, and projecting." Now we know. Certainly, singing came naturally enough to

Joan. At age three, she would sit on the piano bench and imitate her mother's exercises and songs. "Mother cared nothing for a career," the soprano recalled many years later, "she just loved to sing. Before studying as a soprano, I learnt from her many mezzo arias, and ballads with simple melodies that have a firm place in my heart."

Mrs. Sutherland did not feel that Joan (or any youngster) should have formal lessons before age 18, so she gave her daughter piano lessons instead, and let her sing just for fun—and to entertain family and friends, which the child did on every available occasion. Finally, her 18th birthday at hand, Joan applied to and was accepted by the Sydney Conservatory, where made her debut as Dido in a student production of Purcell's Dido and Aeneas, and also started hanging out every so often with a young piano student named Richard Bonynge. In 1951 she moved to London, where she completed her training at the Royal College of Music, spending time every so often hanging out with Richard Bonynge, who had followed her to England. They were married three years later.

For the next four decades, Sutherland and Bonynge were a devoted team, professionally as well as personally. He conducted most of her performances and recordings, researched long-forgotten roles that suited her voice and temperament, and served her variously as vocal coach, accompanist, and morale-booster.

Bet You Didn't Know

To his great credit, Bonynge was never upset to stand more than a little bit in the tall Sutherland shadow. "Let's face it," he told an interviewer, "I've worked all my life to make her sing well, so why the hell am I going to get into a tizz if she gets more applause than I do? It's the nature of things. Down through the centuries, people remember great prima donnas, not their conductors."

Starting out at the Royal Opera House in the small role of the First Lady in Mozart's The Magic Flute, Sutherland was quite a few years away from her status as the first lady of opera, or "La Stupenda", as her fans would dub her. Larger roles followed that 1952 debut, including Aida, Desdemona, and Eva (in Die Meistersinger), but then, feeling that her talents were not being used to best advantage, Bonynge began steering Sutherland away from dramatic repertory and towards the bel canto heroines that up to then had been the primary province of Maria Callas. Sutherland's voice blossomed in this new territory, expanding to a three-octave range and gaining new and incredible facility in scales, trills, and high-flying coloratura.

It all came together with a 1959 production of Donizetti's Lucia di Lammermoor. Maria Callas herself went backstage to congratulate the new-born star, and Sutherland's Lucia went on to international acclaim at La Scala, the Met, and opera houses everywhere. Dozens of other operatic portrayals—from Mozart to Wagner—along with concert appearances in everything from Handel's Messiah to the Verdi Requiem, established her reputation as one of the most versatile of singers; her 30 starring years on stage made the Sutherland career one of the longest in the modern era. In 1979, Queen Elizabeth placed the soprano's name on the New Year's Honors List, conferring upon her the highest title the crown had to offer: Dame Commander of the British Empire. And so it was Dame Joan Sutherland who into her sixties continued to dazzle audiences with her deep musical understanding and peerless vocal pyrotechnics.

Back home in Sydney, Joan Sutherland said farewell to opera with a 1990 performance of Meyerbeer's Les Huguenots, then settled into comfortable retirement, cooking, gardening, and keeping up with the arts by serving as a competition juror. Through it all, Dame Joan maintained a personal modesty quite at odds with her worldwide celebrity. "I'm just an ordinary human being," she said during the intermission of a televised concert with Luciano Pavarotti, "who has been given a really rather wonderful voice."

Beverly Sills—A Good High

When "Beverly Sills is a Good High" buttons were sold as a fundraiser for the New York City Opera, it was both a witty slogan and an apt description of the irrepressible talents, effervescent personality and lofty accomplishments of this native New Yorker (1929-2007). The child of an insurance salesman from Rumania and a musical mother from Odessa, this operatic diva-to-be began her career as "the most beautiful baby of 1932," singing on the radio under the name of "Bubbles" at the age of three. The next year she joined a Saturday morning kid's show, at seven she sang in a movie, and at 10 was a regular on a radio serial, "Our Gal Sunday." Later came a commercial for Rinso White, a singing stint during the early days of TV, and finally, at the venerable age of 18, her operatic debut as Frasquita in Carmen.

The major turning point in her life came when Sills joined The New York City Opera in 1955, singing Rosalinda in Strauss' Die Fledermaus. From then on, up until her retirement at a 1980 gala in her honor (the last aria she sang that night was Rosalinda's, from Die Fledermaus), Sills was the busiest soprano of that famous company, breaking out of traditional repertory to star in Douglas Moore's The Ballad of Baby Doe and Luigi Nono's avant garde Intolleranza, bringing Handel's Giulio Cesare out of mothballs into modern popularity, and crowning her career with unforgettable portrayals of the three Donizetti

Queens: Maria Stuarda, Anna Bolena, and Elizabeth in Roberto Devereux. It was in another operatic rarity, Rossini's The Siege of Corinth, that Beverly Sills made her La Scala debut in 1969, and in which she took her first bows at the Metropolitan nine years later.

She starred in more standard fare too, of course, including Lucia, Manon, Aida, and all three heroines in The Tales of Hoffmann. She once sang 54 Violettas (in La Traviata) within a little over two months, and her gift for rollicking comedy was well displayed in such favorites as Mozart's Abduction from the Seraglio and Donizetti's Daughter of the Regiment. Hubert Saal, longtime music editor of *Newsweek*, dubbed her "a female Buster Keaton" in those roles, going on to note that "the mainspring of her career has been her belief that opera is drama, not a showcase for beautiful voices. Hers, though, was among the most beautiful. Her range was enormous, all gold at the top and silver at the bottom, combining lightness of texture of lustrous shades of color with great strength. It has been a voice that can raise the roof or break your heart."

Another vital element in the Sills success story was her palpable pleasure in performance. "I found singing such a joyous experience that I couldn't wait to get on the stage," she told her Met Opera colleague Jerome Hines. "This joyfulness, and my need to communicate with people, these are my two strongest points. I've always been a people person. I love people, I like to be with people, so when I got on stage, I was home free."

Bet You Didn't Know

In addition to her opera and concert stints, Beverly Sills was a frequent TV visitor, whether joining Johnny Carson for a comedy sketch, sharing witty conversations with Barbara Walters, or lifting her voice in duet with such other TV notables as Dinah Shore, Danny Kaye, and Miss Piggy.

When Beverly Sills stepped back from performing in 1980, it was not to slip into restful retirement. Even before her last note was sung, she had signed on as general director of New York City Opera, a position that allowed her to bring a raft of superb young American singers into the ranks and pull the company back from near bankruptcy to financial good health. Later, she was a hit on radio talk shows, produced and emceed television specials, undertook a whole series of philanthropic fundraising efforts, and served as Chairman of Lincoln Center for the Performing Arts.

"Beverly Sills has captured with her voice every note of human feeling," said Jimmy Carter at the 1980 ceremonies at which she was awarded the Presidential Medal of Freedom. "She has touched and delighted audiences throughout the world as a performer, as a recording artist, and now as a producer—and of all her arts she is truly a master."

Later Legends

We have only touched on a few of the artists who brought opera—and indeed all music—to glittering new heights in the 20th century. There were so many more, the roster (to focus only on Americans) including such national treasures as Robert Merrill, Jerome Hines, Martina Arroyo, Roberta Peters, Anna Moffo, Grace Bumbry, Jan Peerce, Eleanor Steber, Shirley Verrett, Evelyn Lear, and Thomas Stewart.

Each deserves a separate chapter and more, but since abridge we must, we grudgingly narrow the list down to narrow the list two radiant women who took American artistry around the world and back again.

Leontyne Price

Leontyne Price (1927-) was born in Laurel, Mississippi, at a time when a young black girl had little hope of becoming an opera star. Her father worked at a sawmill while her mother, who possessed a beautiful soprano voice, was a midwife whose earnings helped pay the installments on the family piano. The young Leontyne studied piano, sang at local concerts, and pursued her vocal studies at college, but it was not until she won a scholarship to Juilliard and heard her first opera (Salome at the Met), that she knew she had found her true calling.

When she was cast as Mistress Ford in a Juilliard production of Falstaff, Leontyne Price was then taken off the billing, because it was not deemed appropriate for a black singer to perform the role. Only the personal intervention of Juilliard's president (the renowned composer William Schuman) caused the Opera Theatre staff to reverse its decision. Price went on as originally scheduled, and her rise to fame began with that opening night performance.

In the audience was another famous composer, Virgil Thomson, who promptly invited the young singer to appear in the 1952 revival of his opera Four Saints in Three Acts. A year later, Price's shining voice and dramatic acting abilities came together when she starred as Bess in a production of Gershwin's Porgy and Bess that toured Europe and the United States for two years.

In November of 1954, Leontyne Price gave a brilliant debut recital at New York's Town Hall. A month later, she broke another color barrier, appearing as Tosca in a television production of the Puccini favorite, and when she sang Aida at La Scala, she again made history as the first black woman ever to appear at that famous opera house in Milan.

"My career was simultaneous with the opening up of civil rights," the soprano told author Stephen Lubin in 1973. "Whenever there was any copy about me, what I was as an artist, what I had as ability, got shoveled under because all the attention was on racial connotations." The burden of that responsibility was enormous, and it took its emotional toll. "I didn't even have time to lose my temper." Fortunately, Miss Price was and is a survivor. "As a token Black, I paid my dues," she said. "It's kind of wonderful to be able to concentrate on being a plain singer, without the overwhelming weight of the monkey on your back."

As a singer, though hardly plain, Leontyne Price surmounted all those pressures to become a star, then a superstar, finally a genuine American legend. Her Met debut in 1961 was greeted by a precedent-breaking 42-minute ovation, and she went on to sing Tosca, Manon, Butterfly, and many other important roles, including Cleopatra when the new Metropolitan Opera House opened at Lincoln Center with the world premiere of Samuel Barber's Antony and Cleopatra.

Her radiant voice and impressive stage presence seemed especially apt for Aida, the proud Ethiopian princess, which was her signature role. It was the opera of her San Francisco debut in 1957, and of the performances at the Vienna State Opera (under Herbert von Karajan) that solidified her European career. Not surprisingly, it was also as Aida that Leontyne Price said her operatic farewell, an unforgettable performance telecast live from the Met stage on January 3, 1985. Later that year, President Reagan presented the soprano with the National Medal of Arts.

America's prima donna assoluta has received a vast array of other awards, citations, medals, and honorary doctorates. As Lyndon Johnson said in 1965 when he bestowed upon Leontyne Price the Presidential Medal of Freedom, "Her singing has brought light to her land."

Marilyn Horne—A Life in Music

Is there anything this supremely gifted, enormously popular mezzo has not performed? Marilyn Horne has sung American theatre tunes, Russian lullabies, Italian operas, German art songs, and French Christmas carols. She dubbed the voice part for Dorothy Dandridge in the classic film version of Carmen Jones, recorded American hymns with Tennessee Ernie Ford, sang TV duets with Jim Nabors and Carol Burnett, then popped up singing arias on a couple of "Odd Couple" episodes. Back at the opera, she shared memorable performances with three of the other legendary singers discussed in this chapter, Leontyne Price, Joan Sutherland, and Luciano Pavarotti.

Born in Bradford, Pennsylvania (1929-), Marilyn Horne, nicknamed "Jackie" by her brother, who had planned on having a male sibling, started studying under the guidance of her father, an amateur tenor who sensed future greatness in his daughter and insisted she live up to that potential. "As a kid I sometimes wanted to play, go to the movies, baseball games, anything rather than practice," she recalled in her autobiography, "but my singing came first, and I learned early how to sacrifice. The lessons my dad taught me have stood me in good stead; I know for sure that I wouldn't be singing today if I hadn't stuck to the principles established by my father. Nobody ever handed me anything; I had to study, work, and sing my heart out. I've been lucky too, but you have to take advantage of good fortune, and that I've done."

Important Things to Know

Check your collection, if you have that Horne/Ford album, it's now a collector's item fetching an impressive price.

The path from what the singer called "genteel poverty to genteel riches, choruses to center stage" led Horne through California, where the family moved when she was 11. She continued her studies there, including master classes with Lotte Lehmann at the age of 17, during which the famous singer introducing her protégé to the special joys of lieder. Meanwhile, Horne was earning a living by cutting bootleg records, imitating Peggy Lee one day and singing in a doo-wah chorus the next. But opera continued to exert a special pull, and in 1954, she made her debut in Los Angeles in Smetana's The Bartered Bride.

In these early days, Marilyn Horne sang soprano roles, including a three-year stint with a small opera company in Germany, doing things like Mimi in La Boheme and Minnie in Girl of the Golden West. Gradually, though, she discovered the power of her lower range and her incomparable abilities in the strenuous bel canto repertoire. Maria Callas had re-energized this 18th century Italian vocal style, Joan Sutherland and Richard Bonynge had taken up where she left off, fostering a major revival of interest in a number of long-forgotten operas, and now Marilyn Horne was there to give the movement another jolt of virtuosity. "Through Joan's generosity," says Horne, "I became part of the great chain of bel canto singing.

Bellini's Beatrice di Tenda marked the first of many Sutherland-Horne collaborations to come, among them Bellini's Norma at the Met, and Rossini's Semiramide, both at the Chicago Opera and in concert at Carnegie Hall. But there were other operatic heroines to conquer, and Marilyn Horne did precisely that with Carmen, Tancredi, Amnernis (in Aida), Mignon, and Rosina (in The Barber of Seville). The year 1992, Rossini's bicentennial, kept Horne even busier than usual with opera and concert tributes and recordings, among them an anthology of 22 non-operatic songs, several of them unpublished. "Rossini has been good to me," she said, "I only hope I've been as good for him." Somewhere, no doubt, the composer is yelling "Brava!"

Important Things to Know

The Horne discography lists an astonishing variety of pieces, among them the Grammy-winning "In Concert at the Met" with Leontyne Price; "Il Trovatore" and the Verdi Requiem with Luciano Pavarotti; Beethoven's 9th Symphony, both with the Vienna Philharmonic and the New York Philharmonic; a Christmas album with the Mormon Tabernacle Choir; and more recently, a gorgeous collection of lullabies plus a nifty crossover album, "The Men in My Life," in which she sings operetta and popular songs with four of her distinguished opera colleagues: Jerry Hadley, Thomas Hampson, Samuel Ramey, and Spiro Malas.

As she gradually pulls back from operatic performances, Marilyn Horne was drawn to a new passion: reviving the art song recital. This she did first by by dint of her own sold-out concerts, later by the establishment of a Foundation that seeks out and supports young artists committed to this most intimate form of vocal expression ("In opera I go out to the audience," Horne said, "in recital I bring the audience to me"). She signed on as head of the vocal department at the Music Academy of the West, and continues to give notable master classes all around the country. Her lifelong mission, she admitted, was "to share that gift God gave me and in quest of that one beauty He put me here to find."

The Three Tenors

First there were the Three Kings. Then we thrilled to the escapades of the Three Musketeers and howled at the antics of the Three Stooges, but surely there has never been a marketing coup to compare with the conversion of three opera singers into pop superstars. They are capable of filling sports arenas and earning higher fees in an evening than most toilers in the operatic vineyards will amass in a decade.

Granted that Jose Carreras, Placido Domingo, and Luciano Pavarotti have gorgeous voices, remarkable virtuosity and genial stage presences, but their parlaying of high C's into multiple C-notes has been unparalleled in our time. It has also had the distinctive advantage of introducing opera to enormous numbers of people who before the Three Tenors mania would not have touched Verdi or Puccini with the proverbial ten-foot pole.

We were talking about feuds and fusses a while ago; for years, rumor had it that Domingo and Pavarotti were constantly jockeying for position in the operatic world, each having less than the highest regard for the other. This, it turned out, was another bit of pure press-agentry, with as much real substance as the fabled radio feud of Jack Benny and Fred Allen. Just as both comedians had their own extraordinary gifts and were offstage friends, each tenor has carved out his own slice of operatic greatness, and if alleged jealousies could sell more tickets, so be it. Their appearance on the same stage certainly must have sold a ticket or two to listeners hoping to see some onstage blood-letting, especially with a third "rival" tenor there into the bargain. Instead they found three musical teddy bears, all sweetness, light, and mutual admiration. That, in company with splendid singing, proved to be a pretty heady brew.

The first Three Tenors concert was held in 1990, on the occasion of the World Cup Championship in Rome. On a starlit night, with the full moon rising and Zubin Mehta conducting an orchestra of 200, some 6,000 people crowded into the outdoor arena known as the Baths of Caracalla for what was modestly billed as "the biggest single musical event in history." Four years later, that figure paled into insignificance when the Messrs. Carreras, Domingo, Pavarotti, and Mehta joined forces again in Los Angeles' Dodgers Stadium, this time with the Los Angeles Philharmonic and the L.A. Music Center Chorus filling out the roster. Forget the paltry thousands who filled the stadium: The concert was watched by 1.3 billion viewers worldwide and sold 10 million CDs and videos. In 1996, the Three Tenors launched a worldwide tour, with over 600,000 people in concert attendance and millions more in the TV audience so far.

Bet You Didn't Know

Hoping to hop on the entertainment bandwagon have been all sorts of copycat trios, including The Three Irish Tenors, Three Canadian Tenors, Three Mo' Tenors, and moving into slightly different vocal territory, The Three Sopranos and the Three Countertenors.

Three cheers for all of them, but the unique alchemy of Jose, Placido and Luciano is not likely to be duplicated any time soon.

José Carreras

As a small boy in Barcelona (1946-), José Carreras dreamed of becoming a soccer player, but he also enjoyed spending time at the movies, where one day he saw The Great Caruso. Like Mozart, the prodigy who could reproduce anything at the keyboard after a single hearing, the young Carreras found he could imitate Mario Lanza imitating Caruso with uncanny accuracy. His parents had no special musical aspirations for their son, but they were impressed enough to enroll the 8-year-old lad at the Barcelona Conservatory, and also took him to his first opera, a performance of Verdi's Aida at the Teatro del Liceo. Three years later, José was back in that theatre, on stage as the boy in Manuel de Falla's Le Retablo de Maese Pedro (Master Peter's Puppet Show).

The Barcelona air must be good for the voice, for the city gave birth to a pair of the most beloved sopranos of modern times, Victoria de los Angeles and Montserrat Caballe, and it was the latter artist who heard the young Carreras, encouraged him in his studies, and chose him to play the tenor lead opposite her in Donizetti's Lucrezia Borgia. Thereafter, she frequently requested Carreras as her leading man, their continuing friendship both an inspiration to the young tenor and an important spur to his international career. He came to London in 1971 for a concert performance of Donizetti's Maria Stuarda with Caballe, then won the Verdi Voice Competition in Parma, leading to his opening the 1972 season in that city with La Boheme. Another Puccini favorite, Madame Butterfly was his American debut role; Carreras was soon a regular at New York City Opera, and thereafter at the Met.

La Scala invited Carreras to debut there in 1975, and the tenor's fame took another leap forward when Herbert von Karajan chose him for the Verdi Requiem at the 1976 Salzburg Festival. "Maestro Karajan was like a father to me," Carreras says, recalling later performances of Bizet's "Carmen" and Verdi's "Don Carlos" with the renowned conductor.

Everything seemed to progressing in the best possible way when suddenly the picture darkened. Carreras fell ill on the set of a film version of La Boheme, and the music world was stunned to hear that he had been diagnosed with leukemia. Boundless willpower and medical magic combined to beat the affliction, and when Carreras sang a program of Catalan and Italian folk songs in Barcelona on July 21, 1988, a cheering audience of 150,000, including the Queen of Spain, welcomed him back with an enveloping display of love for his artistry and admiration for his courage.

Four years later, Carreras was back in Barcelona, serving as musical director of the Opening and Closing Ceremonies of the Summer Olympics, and he has continued to sing all over the world raising funds for leukemia research, and establishing the José Carreras International Leukemia Foundation to fight the disease. "You have to fight," he said, "and fight by drawing on all your inner resources. You'll be surprised how great they are."

Bet You Didn't Know

E. Donall Thomas, the doctor whose revolutionary treatment gave Carreras back his life and career, won the 1990 Nobel Prize for Medicine in recognition of his significant achievements in leukemia research.

Placido Domingo

What operetta is to the Viennese, and musical theatre to us in America, the zarzuela is to the Spanish. Placido Domingo (1941-) was born into the special musical world of this opera-operetta hybrid: his parents, Placido Sr. and Pepita Embril, were stars of the most successful zarzuela company in Madrid. Following a 1949 Latin American tour, they decided to remain in Mexico City, founding their own company there and allowing their young son to take on a number of children's parts in their productions. Placido Jr. also loved attending orchestral and stage rehearsals; he hung around the set designers and costume makers and did other odd jobs around the place—he liked to put the scores out on the players' music stands.

His musical talent clear, young Placido started piano lessons, entered the Mexico City Conservatory at age 14, and even after his voice broke, continued to make himself useful around the zarzuela company, playing the piano at rehearsals, and even getting to conduct a little. Gradually, he found himself singing in the company (as a baritone) and later became a veteran trouper, with 185 straight performances as one of Alfred P. Doolittle's cronies in a Spanish-language production of My Fair Lady, followed by another 170 or so in Lehar's popular operetta The Merry Widow.

Perhaps it was this wide range of theatrical experience that helped make Domingo the complete musician. How many other opera singers can you name who are equally at home

Bet You Didn't Know

At 18, Domingo went to try out for the National Opera, and was told by the auditioning committee that he sounded more like a tenor than a baritone. So he sight-read a tenor aria and was signed to his first operatic contract. Wisely, he didn't give up his day jobs: he played piano for a touring ballet company, hosted his own musical show on Mexico's Channel 11, helped train a zarzuela chorus, and recorded backup vocals for Mexican cover versions of American pop hits.

with folk tunes and pop ballads, can accompany themselves at the piano, and are skilled enough conductors to land podium assignments at the Met?

Domingo, meanwhile, had graduated from small to leading roles at the opera, and a performance of Tosca proved pivotal. This was because Nicola Rescigno was in the audience, music director of the Dallas Civic Opera, promptly signed the young tenor for his American debut as Alfredo (opposite Joan Sutherland, no less) in Lucia di Lammermoor.

Feeling the need for more seasoning, and the opportunity for more regular singing work, Domingo joined the Hebrew National Opera company in Tel-Aviv, where got both, racking up nearly 300 performances over the next two and a half years. By 1965 he was back in the United States, singing Don José in Carmen for Washington Opera, and at his New York City Opera debut.

A dramatic debut at the Met followed, when Domingo was called upon—with 35 minutes' notice—to step in for the ailing Franco Corelli in Cilea's Adriana Lecouvreur, and not a season has gone by since 1968 without Domingo on the company's artistic roster, where he has remained. All the while, of course, the tenor found himself in increasing demand elsewhere. The year of his debuts in London and at La Scala was 1969, and one of his proudest moments followed in 1970 when he was invited to sing a solemn mass in the Vatican, attended by Pope Paul VI.

Back at the Met, meanwhile, Domingo was the leading tenor at the Met's opening night productions for three out of the next four years. His formal conducting debut came in 1973 (at his old alma mater, New York City Opera), with further podium opportunities unfolding at the Met in "La Boheme", "Carmen" and "Tosca." His recordings encompass an incredible variety of material, which extends far beyond the operatic borders to everything from folk songs to tangos, zarzuela arias, to movie ballads. All in all, Domingo has taken roles in more than 135 different operas, far more than any other operatic tenor. Like Beverly Sills, he also has eased into administrative duties, acting as artistic advisor to the Los Angeles Music Center, and serving as music director for the World Opera in Seville. His contract as General Director of Washington National Opera ended in 2011, but his contract as head of Los Angeles Opera will continue at least through the 2012-2013 season.

"My life has so far been lucky and happy", Placido Domingo wrote at the age of 40; in the three decades since, we are the lucky and happy ones for having been able to bask in the warmth and brilliance of his musical art.

Luciano Pavarotti

Some people swear that Luciano Pavarotti was even more famous than that other Italian tenor, Enrico Caruso. Perhaps the only role in which he lacked credibility was the commercial where he insisted that nobody recognized him without his American Express card. Thanks to a lifetime in the public eye, complete with TV specials, talk-show interviews, zillions of recordings, and even a Hollywood movie, Pavarotti's distinctive voice and ample figure ("he gleefully thumbs his stomach at the universe," wrote Stephen Rubin) were not likely to escape attention, offstage or on.

Born in Modena, Italy (1935-2007) Pavarotti gained his love of singing from his father, a baker who sang in the local opera house. He had little formal training ("There was conservatory with two teachers," the tenor said, "but they ruined all the voices is Modena, so the city closed it down."). His was a natural gift, though, and it began to be honed by years of singing in church and finally, at age 19, voice lessons with the tenor Arrigo Pola. After winning a singing contest in 1961, Pavarotti made his operatic debut as Rodolfo in La Boheme, making enough of a stir to prompt La Scala to offer him a contract understudying three major roles. It must have been a highly tempting proposition, but in an example of the wisdom that would continue to shape his future career decisions, Pavarotti turned it down, telling the management that he would prefer to wait until he could enter the illustrious house as a star.

Instead, he looked for other performing opportunities, finding one in Dublin, where he sang the Duke in Rigoletto. As good luck would have it, Richard Bonynge was in Ireland, auditioning artists to partner Joan Sutherland on an Australian tour. When he heard Pavarotti, Bonynge knew his search was over. The young tenor got the job, went on the tour and, as he readily admitted later on, learned more from the great soprano than from all of his previous teachers. "He was always feeling Joan's tummy to find out how she breathed," said Bonynge, obviously not the jealous type.

Pavarotti would become Sutherland's close friend and frequent singing partner over the years ("The Big P," the soprano calls him affectionately). Alas, La Boheme remained his "lucky opera," and Rodolfo was the role he chose for his debut performances in Vienna and at Covent Garden in 1963, two years later at La Scala (where he did indeed arrive as a star), San Francisco in 1967, and the Metropolitan in 1968, where his Boheme was chosen as the first live telecast from the Met.

Even with his operatic career in full swing, Pavarotti started making time for recitals, which would henceforth be a prominent feature of his musical life. (On the list: the first-ever recital given on the stage of the Met.) His remarkable range, topped by a spectacular upper register, his smooth, confident style, his infectious, endearing personality, had all combined to make him a welcome guest in concert halls around the world; without question, the Pavarotti magic was not dependent on fancy sets, resplendent costumes or on stage dramatics.

The tenor's recordings and videos could probably fill a small library: His entire stage repertory is available on compact disc, and you'll also find Neapolitan romances, Christmas hymns, operetta songs, and in-concert recitals taped at New York's Carnegie and London's

Royal Albert Halls. If you dig around enough in the LP bins, you may even emerge with the soundtrack of his film Yes, Georgio. Twenty years ago, Gerald Fitzgerald said that "not since Caruso has a tenor from Italy so captured the imagination of music-lovers. Pavarotti has become a fact, an indispensable fact, of our musical life, and from the evidence at hand his momentum has yet to reach full throttle."

In his sixties, Pavarotti stepped back from most of the challenging roles that catapulted him to worldwide fame, and his appearances altogether became fewer and farther between. Nonetheless, his popularity endures, and even today, six years after his death, he remains one of the most recognized performers in the world.

CHAPTER 20

It's Not Over Till the Fat Lady Sings

In This Chapter

> ➤ The beginnings of opera
> ➤ The operas of Rossini and Bellini
> ➤ Donizetti, Verdi, Puccini, and Bizet
> ➤ Combining the opera ingredients

Nowadays the ladies are slimmer, the acting more artful, the sets, costumes, and lighting make full use of modern technologies, but opera today remains what it was nearly 400 years ago: a mixture of words and music, the original multi-media entertainment. .

Opera is the original multimedia entertainment. It involves a fusion of words and music (and often dance); it combines visual drama and vocal melody with orchestral underpinnings, adding sets, costumes and lighting effects to the overall package. Compared to the way it was when opera was born some four hundred years ago, the singing is superior and the acting more artful (at least we like to think so; not too many of us were around in 1600 to check it out). And obviously, the set, costume and lighting designers these days make full and often brilliantly inventive use of every available modern technology.

In the Beginning

Around 1600, a group of Italian poets, singers, scientists, and composers used to hang out at the palace of a Florentine nobleman. They called themselves Camerata (small chamber) and their company included Vincenzo Galilei, father of the celebrated astronomer. During discussions of how to advance the arts in society, they hit upon the idea of emulating the simplicity that supposedly had been the essence of ancient Greek music. Of course, nobody knew what ancient Greek music sounded like; fortunately for them, nobody knew what it didn't sound like either, so there weren't too many quibbles.

One of their first steps was the publication of group of songs by one of their members, a part-time composer named Giulio Caccini. It was called "Nuove musiche" (New Musics), and instead of the polyphonic construction favored by most Renaissance composers, these airs were designed for a single voice with an accompaniment of chords. The next step was pulling together a number of these individual pieces into longer productions called "dramma per musica," or drama through music. These in turn became known as "opera," which in Italian simply means "works."

The first important composer to suggest the heights to which such a fusion of music and drama might rise was Claudio Monteverdi (1567-1643). He greatly enriched the orchestral accompaniments, used harmonic dissonances for expressive purposes, wrote hauntingly

Music Word

Opera, in Italian, is the plural of "opus" and therefore means "works". That, of course, is a broad enough term to take in almost everything, and often that's just what you'll find in opera: solo songs, ensemble numbers, spoken declamations, ballets, orchestral overtures and interludes, special lighting and other stagecraft effects, plus an endless variety of stage action, from wedding ceremonies to murders most foul.

Music Word

Libretto is Italian for "little book," and in the old days, librettos (or libretti to use the proper Italian plural) were bound in booklets and handed out to the audience, since nobody would know what was going on otherwise. Not that they necessarily knew what was going on after reading some of the far-fetched plots, but at least they had a fighting chance.

lovely melodies (they say that hundreds of people were moved to tears by a lament in his opera Arianna), and created the earlier works that still hold the stage today, among them . His most popular works are Orfeo and The Coronation of Poppea.

With that kind of head start, it's no surprise that Italy remained the operatic headquarters of the world, exporting its glories far and wide.

Rossini—Man on the High Cs

a) an over-priced Italian wine, as in Rossini Spumanti

b) a songbird in the rossignol family

c) a prolific Italian opera composer.

If you guessed "c," Si! You're our kind of music lover. Gioacchino Rossini was indeed one of the great early 19th century contributors to the art of Italian opera. "Give me a laundry list," Rossini said, "and I will set it to music." By the time he was thirty eight, he had turned 38 laundry lists — sorry, librettos—into operas, then figuring enough is enough, he quit.

Meanwhile, back in 1792, Gioacchino Rossini leap-yeared into the world on February 29th, 1792. His mother was a singer and his father alternated between being the town trumpeter and the town butcher, so young Gioacchino grew up with a love for opera and all the bologna that goes with it. He sang in an opera at age 11, then made his first attempt at writing one a year later. His exceptional talents really began to take shape after his family

Bet You Didn't Know

Over the next forty years, Rossini turned into a great gourmet, grew very fat, and wrote pieces called "Anchovies", "Radishes", and "Hors d'Oeuvres." He also composed "Profound Sleep with Startled Awakenings" and a "Hygienic Prelude for Morning Use", but no more operas.

moved to— speaking of — Bologna. Rossini never really went in for much formal training, but he did take a few courses at the conservatory, even winning a medal for counterpoint, and writing a cantata that was played at his school's annual ceremonies.

His early operas didn't really go anyplace, but Rossini worked fast when he had a mind to, and churned operas out at astonishing pace: four in 1812, another four in 1813. He went steady with The Italian Girl in Algiers, made a hit with The Turk in Italy, even fooled around with The Barber of Seville. Put those eyebrows back down: those are all opera titles. So are The Thieving Magpie, Tancredi, and La Cenerentola (Cinderella), and the dozens of other works that made Rossini one of the most famous men in Europe. Heads of state from Sweden to Turkey sent him presents, gave him honorary titles, invited him to court, and generally treated him like the (musical) royalty he was.

Rossini's music is often described as bel canto, which simply means "beautiful singing." Unlike Weber, Rossini had no interest in portraying supernatural events, bringing ancient legends to life or infusing his stageworks with nationalistic fervor. His gifts lay in making opera a delicious entertainment. "His melodies have chuckles and sparkles in every bar,"

Bet You Didn't Know

The Sultan of Turkey bestowed the Order of Micham-Ifihar upon Rossini, and the composer liked to wear a ribbon decoration that arrived from the King of Sweden. The Czar of Russian sent along a fancy snuffbox, and in Paris, King Charles named Rossini Inspector General of Singing in France. Poor Rossini never quite knew what to do with that last honor, though he did wander around Paris for a while, studying inspecting the songs of street beggars.

wrote David Ewen. "His effervescent music bubbles like champagne." So let's have a toast to old Gioacchino, a bit of an eccentric perhaps, but an opera composer for the ages.

On February 29, 1868, Rossini gathered friends and family around to celebrate his 19th birthday. He had a been a leap-year baby, remember, and indeed there been only 19 February 29ths since his first one in 1792. On the other hand, he was increasingly troubled by a superstitious fear that something terrible would happen on Friday the 13th. Oddly enough, he was right: Rossini died on November the 13th of that same year. It was a Friday.

Rossini's Works You Need to Know

If you're up to a whole opera, start with The Barber of Seville. It's funny, it has the tongue-twisting "Largo al Factotum" and other great tunes (a few of which were appropriated

Bet You Didn't Know

Rossini could be quite acerbic. One of Meyerbeer's nephews visited Rossini to show him a Funeral March he had written after the death of his uncle's death. "Very nice", Rossini said after scanning the score, "but don't you think it would have been better if you had died and Meyerbeer had written the March?"

by Bugs Bunny) and some marvelous ensemble numbers, and there are many superb recordings to choose among.

Otherwise, get the flavor of his witty and animated music from the marvelous Overtures, including, besides those already mentioned, The Silken Ladder, Semiramide, The Thieving Magpie, and William Tell. Just for fun, sample some of the witty miniatures that Rossini tossed off during his retirement years under the umbrella title Sins of My Old Age. And for moments of inspirational guidance, listen to one of his final works that well atones for any sins Rossini may have committed earlier on: the beautiful Petite Messe Solonelle, which is neither little, nor solemn, just very beautiful. Rossini attached to the score an open letter to God. "Here is my poor little Mass," it says, "done with a little skill, a bit of heart and that's about all. Be Thou blessed, and admit me to Paradise."

Bellini

Vincenzo Bellini, born in 1801, came of age in an era when opera was dominated by its stars, when singers felt free to embellish any music set before them or even to substitute a piece by another composer if the mood so struck them. In a very real sense, the operatic whole was often less than the sum of its parts; the parts, in fact, were what drew audiences to the operas. Bellini tried to transcend the tyranny of the tenor (or the sovereignty of the soprano, if you prefer), but he did so gently rather than with revolutionary ardor; as one of his librettist put it, "he tried to remedy the situation with courage, perseverance and love."

Nonetheless, it was the interest of some of the most famous and popular singers of his day that brought Bellini international fame and a continuing supply of commissions. It was their presence that enticed the audience, and later in the 19th century when singers capable of doing the works justice were in far shorter supply, his works faded from the repertoire. They were not to emerge in significant fashion until a new crop of extraordinary artists, including Renata Scotto and Dame Joan Sutherland, took up their cause in our own time.

Bellini, while attempting to follow in Rossini's operatic footsteps, added a whole new fount of lyricism. Steeped in Italian melody, Bellini developed a style we call "bel canto" (literally beautiful singing), where the voice almost becomes an instrument. Here purity of tone and ease of projection counts for more than dramatic passion; long, lovely phrases give way to brilliant passages of highly ornamented vocal embroidery. The composer was also beset by a melancholy soul, and much of his music, as Wallace Brockway puts it so vividly, has "a hushed, neurotic ecstasy, a kind of gently languorous orgasm in moonlit, bloom-pervaded gardens. Long before Verlaine, it was always crying in Bellini's heart."

Alas, Bellini's heart beat only for a tragically short time: he died after what the coroner called "an acute inflammation of the large intestine" six weeks shy of his 34th birthday, in 1835.

Bellini's Works You Need to Know

You can find several recordings of Bellini's first operatic success, Il Pirato (The Pirate), but better stay with his later, far more popular works, among them:

➤ the sleepwalking beauty of La sonnambula

➤ the revisionist history of I Puritani (The Puritans)

Music Word

Bel Canto. Italian for "beautiful singing", Bel Canto denotes the (primarily Italian) vocal style of the 18th century, with emphasis on beautiful sound and brilliant technique, as opposed to dramatic or emotional expression.

➤ the ardent Shakespearian love of Romeo and Juliet—as portrayed in I Capuletti ed i Montecchi (The Capulets and Montagues)

➤ the most famous of all—Norma, with fearsomely difficult roles for both soprano and mezzosoprano that can be thrilling with the right larynxes at play, fairly disastrous otherwise.

A good way to ease into the full operas listed here (and elsewhere in this chapter) is to get one of many highlight recordings on the market. That way, you get all the best tunes and a couple of hours free into the bargain.

Donizetti

Remember Telemann, who could dash off a fugue as quickly as a normal soul would take to write a letter? Gaetano Donizetti was that way with operas, churning out over seventy of them within a span of three decades. "Writing music is nothing," he said once. "It's the damned rehearsals that are so difficult."

It's a good thing, too, because with Rossini's early retirement and Bellini's early death, Donizetti (1797-1848) pretty well had the operatic field to himself. (At least until Giuseppe Verdi came along and showed everybody how dramatic opera could really be.)

Bet You Didn't Know

"It is easier to sing three Brunnhildes than one Norma," said the soprano Lilli Lehmann, who performed both roles at the Metropolitan Opera around the turn of the century.

The fact that Donizetti was speedy didn't necessarily make his operas good, and the bulk of his work has fallen into not unreasonable obscurity. Heinrich Heine called Donizetti's fertility "not inferior to a rabbit's." Even the gentle, good-natured Mendelssohn took issue with his Italian colleague. "Donizetti's operas may be hissed," he said, "but that doesn't matter as he gets paid all the same and can go about having a good time and writing more trash."

Donizetti, however, knew the pulse of the public, and he could whip off catchy tunes that exalt the glory of the singers' voices even as they caressed listeners' ears. He was especially good at comedies, such as the still delightful La Fille du regiment (The Daughter of the Regiment), and L'Elisir d'amore (The Elixir of Love), but almost any story was grist for the Donizetti mill. Do you like English history? He turned Mary Stuart and Anne Boleyn into Maria Stuarda and Anna Bolena. Want to hiss the villainess? Try Lucrezia Borgia. Enjoy travel? You can follow Donizetti plots to France, Spain, India, and dozens of other spots around the globe.

Although Donizetti was by no means the first composer to insert a mad scene in his operas, he came up with one of the longest (about 14 minutes) and certainly the one most often played out on stage. Once again, thwarted love is the cause, as Lucia di Lammermoor murders her fiancé and pleads insanity with a wild display of vocal virtuosity that, as Herbert Weinstock put it rather sourly, "Only an insane woman would think of singing, but that no insane woman would have the control to sing."

Sadly, life imitated art in Donizetti's case, and the composer played out his own mad scene: his body and mind ravaged by syphilis, he was taken to an asylum in 1846 and died two years later, invalid and insane. Donizetti brought few innovations to his music, nor did his works change the course of operatic history; on the other hand, a handful of his works have been cherished by audiences for 150 years, and that is cause enough to be grateful.

Donizetti's Works You Need to Know

In the opera house, costumes, sets, and other visual trappings help shore up the less

Bet You Didn't Know

The first operatic mad scene appeared in "Nina" (1786), by an opera was first used in 1786, by the Frenchman composer Nicolas Dalayrac, the heroine being a lady to describe Nina, a lady who went crazy for lack of love. The composer He used to spell his name d'Alayrac, by the way, but that didn't seem too smart when the French Revolution came along, so he quietly ditched the "d'" symbol of nobilty. Dalayrac also wrote a bunch of patriotic songs, to make sure everybody knew he was one of the Good Guys.

interesting musical moments, so you might want to start with one of the many collections of Donizetti arias, catching such memorable high points as "Una furtiva lagrima" (A furtive tear) from "The Elixir of Love," and another gorgeous declaration of love "O mio Fernando" in La Favorita. The mad scene and the equally famous sextet will give you a Reader's Digest version of Lucia, and in the aria "Ah, mes amis" (Ah, my friends), the tenor shows off no less than nine high C's to the suitably impressed Daughter of the Regiment.

The complete opera sets are the next step along the Donizetti line, and to those mentioned above, by all means add the cheery comedy of Don Pasquale and the high English tragedy of Anna Bolena (although it is a bit difficult to think of Henry VIII as Enrico).

It was Rossini, tongue firmly in cheek, who said, "How wonderful opera would be if there were no singers." If you want to apply that dictum to Donizetti, there are collections of his opera overtures, and a number of rather quaint chamber pieces that sound like operas for instruments. This includes a Sonata for Violin and Harp, a Trio for Flute, Cello and Piano, and a Concertino for Clarinet and Chamber Orchestra.

Music Word

Aria means "air" or song, but in opera, you're not just whistling Dixie: the term suggests a melody of some complexity and length, often designed to express a particular emotion or to carry forward some element of the plot line.

Verdi

That aphorism about opera being great "except for the singers" has sometimes been attributed to Giuseppe Verdi, and it would make equal sense. Like Rossini, Verdi had more than occasional contretemps with wayward prima-donnas; both saw superb operas turned into opening night fiascos by singers who forgot their parts, lost their voices, or fell through trap doors. Both suffered through productions where soloists cut their music or (even worse) added unwritten roulades, which bludgeoned their most tender arias into athletic displays of vocal bravura.

There are those who say that Verdi got even with his singers by writing extremely difficult music for them. He would cast much of it in an extremely high range, often devising arias where the poor soloist has to sing steadily from beginning to end without so much as a two-bar rest for breath-catching purposes. In his young years as a music critic, George Bernard Shaw turned Verdi to task for having ruined a whole generation of Italian singers. "He wrote so abominably for the human voice," said Shaw, "that the tenors all had goat-bleat (and were proud of it); the baritones had a shattering vibrato and could not, to save their lives, produce a note of any definite pitch; and the sopranos had the tone of a locomotive whistle, without its steadiness."

Music Word

In vocal music, a **roulade** is a series of rapid musical notes inserted into a composition, usually on a single syllable, as a decorative embellishment.

Well, singers must have found a way around those booby-traps because there any number of superb Verdi performers around these days; and do they have great stuff to sing! Verdi's music has such strength and dramatic sweep, and such a limitless fountain of glorious melody, that the best of his works stand among the mightiest creations in opera. Verdi had his weaker pieces, but even they have their moments, and given the roster of unquestioned masterpieces, his batting average is right up there with the best of them.

Bet You Didn't Know

Possibly operating on the if-you-can't-beat-'em-join-'em theory, both Verdi and Rossini married sopranos who had performed in early productions of their operas.

Unlike so many composers, whose early works are resounding duds, Verdi's first opera, Oberto, was a big hit. His second was the resounding dud, an alleged comedy called King for a Day that got so badly hissed by the audience at the premiere that it was withdrawn and never performed again, at least not until 1951, by which time Verdi couldn't really care much about it one way or the other.

Back in 1840, meanwhile, Verdi cared about it so deeply that he tore up all his remaining contracts and swore off writing operas altogether. It took a sneaky trick by the impresario at La Scala to get Verdi back on track. He pushed a libretto into the composer's pocket,

Important Things to Know

Do you enjoy soaring love duets and lively choruses? How about virtuosic soprano arias and heroic outbursts for the tenor, with plots that smack more than faintly of political and social satire? If so, Verdi might be your man, since those qualities and more help give his stageworks their special dramatic power.

figuring that curiosity would get the better of him. Which it did. "What could I do?" Verdi recalled many years later. "One day I did a line, the next day another; now a note, now a phrase……." Within three months, the opera was done, and the resulting production of Nabucco was such a smash hit that Verdi never turned back again. He did, though, swear off comic operas, not tackling another one until at the ripe old age of eighty. He dipped into Shakespeare once again (Otello had been produced eight years earlier) and created his breathlessly exciting and brilliantly witty setting of Falstaff.

Bet You Didn't Know

Richard Strauss, not given to over-praising other composer's works, except Wagner sometimes, referred to Verdi's Falstaff as "the greatest masterpiece of modern Italian music" and "a work of artistic perfection."

In between those two comedies came a barrage of unforgettable dramas, their successes marred only by Verdi's constant battle with the censors. They forced him to change titles, locales, and plot elements. For example, the French King in "Rigoletto" became an Italian Duke and the Swedish King in "A Masked Ball" got converted into a Governor of Boston. (The fact that Boston didn't have a governor, and that not too many folks in Massachusetts ran around with names like Riccardo, Renato, and Silvano, didn't bother the censors in the least.)

And then there were those darn singers, again, like the

soprano who decided to go on her honeymoon just before she was to sing the premiere of Sicilian Vespers. (She didn't get married until a year later, but first things first.) There was another singer who, Verdi said, "Screamed in a way that would have rendered her invaluable as a shepherd in the Pyrenees Mountains."

There was Marianna Barbieri-Nini, who kicked up a fuss before the first performance of Macbeth because Verdi made her rehearse one number 150 times. While the audience was already in its seats, he made her put a cloak over her costume and go out into the foyer for run-through number 151.

And let us not forget Fanny Salvini-Donatelli, who sabotaged the premiere of La Traviata. She took the part of the beautiful, consumptive courtesan even though she was plain and plump. Every time she sang about how she was wasting away, the audience howled with laughter, and when she collapsed at the end of the last act, she sent up an enormous cloud of dust. "The premiere," reported one critic, "marked an epoch in the history of colossal fiascoes."

No matter, Verdi's music would eventually triumph over all, and it continues to do so today. The composer received innumerable awards and honors, and when he died, schools were closed and all Italy mourned the loss of a national hero.

Verdi's Works You Need to Know

Verdi, said the musical historian Paul Henry Lang, "has given us opera which exemplifies the essence of the lyric drama; the transliteration of human emotions from a literary sketch into pure music." Even without Rigoletto's hump, La Traviata's glittering ballroom, the horde of spear-carriers in Aida, the costumes, swordfights, and stage effects that enliven performances in the opera house, Verdi's music stands high in its ability to convey drama on its own terms.

Of his nearly thirty stage operas, nos. 16, 17, and 18 are among the most popular ever written: Rigoletto, Il Trovatore, and La Traviata form an astonishing trilogy. He also had three popular Shakespearian tragedies, Macbeth, Otello, and Falstaff. And where would we be without the Triumphal Scene in Aida?

Other Verdi operas to explore include A Masked Ball, Don Carlos, La Forza del Destino (The Force of Destiny), and I Vespri Siciliani (Sicilian Vespers), and if you're not hung up on a good story, there's the operatically grand Requiem Mass. You can, of course, stay instrumental altogether, dipping into the many fine Overtures and ballet sequences from the operas or, for something a little different, Verdi's only String Quartet.

Bet You Didn't Know

"Aida" was commissioned by the Khedive of Egypt in honor of the opening of the Suez Canal. Verdi couldn't make the premiere, but the Khedive came with his wives. It took three loges to seat them all.

Puccini

"I love small things," said Giacomo Puccini, who then went and wrote ten great big operas. But with that love of intimacy came an urge to communicate large emotions. The music of those small things, he explained, must be "true, full of passion and humanity, and touch the heart." It is this quality of direct and urgent communication that has given enduring life to so many of his operatic characters.

Puccini was born three days before Christmas 1848 in Lucca, Italy, and while many family members were church musicians, none seemed to have ventured much beyond the town walls. Understandably, the musical lucre in Lucca wasn't sufficient for the lad, for he is rumored to have trudged the 13 miles to Pisa just to hear a performance of Verdi's Aida. (Let's hope he didn't have to settle for standing room.)

At the age of 22, Puccini wrote a "Glory Mass" that he used to apply for admission to the Milan Conservatory.

In Milan, Puccini unveiled his first opera, Le Villi, and that was good enough to gain him a commission from the fabled La Scala Opera House in Milan. Puccini was on his way, right? Unfortunately, no. At least not yet. His second opera Edgar laid an egg, and Puccini existed, as so many artistic legends had before him, desperately short of cash and rarely able to vary his diet of onions and beans. "I am sick of this eternal struggle with poverty," he wrote to his brother, while storing up memories for La Boheme.

Puccini's first grand success came in 1893 with Manon Lescaut, the press hailing the composer as "a truly Italian genius, whose song is the song of our artistic sensualism. It caresses us and becomes part of us." Finally, things seemed to be looking up, and Puccini enjoyed a couple of years in the public eye and reverence.

Bet You Didn't Know

Nearly 40 years earlier, the guardians of the gates at the Milan Conservatory, in their infinite wisdom, had rejected the application of another young student named Giuseppe Verdi. His compositional skills were inadequate, the registrar reported, and his piano technique was lacking. By now, fortunately, the Conservatory had a new registrar, so Puccini was accepted.

As always, the press can give fame, and the press can take it away. After the premiere of La Boheme in 1896 (conducted by Arturo Toscanini, no less), one critic summarized his reaction to the opera with the remarkably inaccurate prediction that "Even as it leaves little impression on the minds of the audience, it will leave no great trace upon the history of our lyric theatre." Ouch. What Puccini himself proclaimed "the finest opera I have ever written" grew even more dismal reactions, the distraught composer withdrawing the score after only two nights to escape the hissing audiences. The opera's title? Madame Butterfly, which didn't fly again for another four years.

The operatic floppage was only temporary, of course. As we all know, Boheme and Butterfly were soon rehabilitated in public favor, and remain still among the most loved and often performed operas in the repertory. In fact, their heart-wrenching stories and eternal truths have engendering a number of theatrical children, among them the hit Broadway play M. Butterfly and two long-running musicals, Miss Saigon (Madame Butterfly) and Rent (La Boheme).

Speaking of truths, many of Puccini's operas are in what is called "verismo" style. The Italian word is hard to translate precisely, but truthfulness comes close, or perhaps realism, or what literary folk call "a slice of life." Instead of demons and dragons and netherwordly things that go bump in the night, Puccini wrote about people, facing real problems with real emotions. It's hard to imagine Wagner's Valhalla gang riding through modern Berlin, but the starving writer, musician, painter, and philosopher who can't pay the landlord of their Parisian garret in La Boheme transfer readily to the East Village denizens of Rent.

H.L. Mencken, pressed for a single-phrase description of Puccini's music, called it "silver macaroni, exquisitely tangled." Puccini did indeed combine his inborn gift for soaring Italian melody with high theatrical flair and technical mastery. His operas are sentimental, but proudly, unabashedly so. They sing of real-life emotions with such poignancy and

Music Word

Verismo, deriving from "vero", the Italian word for "true", refers to an opera (or indeed a work of literature) that deals with realistic subjects and people from everyday life (as opposed to the historical dramas and mythological legends favored by so many earlier composers). Mascagni's "Cavalleria Rusticana" (1890), recalling dealing with scenes from peasant life, was one of the first verismo operas; another, coming two years later, was Leoncavallo's "Pagliacci", about carnival people. These two one-acters are so frequently coupled in performances at the Met at other major opera houses around the world, that they are often referred to by their affectionate nicknames, "Cav" and "Pag".

drama that one forgets all notions of stage or plot or production. His music sweeps us off into a very special world, and when the curtain falls, we leave that world with the greatest reluctance.

Puccini's Works You Need to Know

Puccini is probably a newcomer's best introduction to the operatic stage. His approachable plots, logical libretti, and strong sense of theatre help a lot; his soaring arias and brilliant orchestrations don't hurt either. His works invite, rather than intimidate, operatic freshmen, so come on in.

La Boheme, with its fusion of high tragedy and low comedy, is an ideal starting point. Bring an extra handkerchief to Madame Butterfly, prepare to (mentally) hiss the vicious villain in Tosca, and for a touch of exoticism, go to China with Turandot and the closest thing to the Three Stooges in grand opera, her Imperial Ministers Ping, Pang, and Pong. Puccini even wrote a western, wherein an escaping outlaw woos and wins the manager of the Polka Saloon, also known as The Girl of the Golden West.

Bizet

Georges Bizet (1838-1875) grew up in a musical household—his father was a singing teacher, his mother a fine pianist—and his musical talents sprouted early. He was accepted into the Paris Conservatory at the tender age of nine, and while still in his teens collected prizes for his achievements at piano and organ, and his early composition efforts garnered him the prestigious Prix de Rome.

After that, it was pretty much all downhill. He wrote all sorts of piano pieces and a symphony, but nobody played them. He wrote an opera and a mass, and nobody sang them. The works that did get played and sung failed to produce any noticeable audience enthusiasm, nor did they fare any better at the hands of the critics. "M. Bizet is a young musician of incontestable worth who writes detestable music," wrote the man in one Paris paper, describing his latest opus as the "these chromatic meowings of an amorous or frightened cat."

All that changed with Carmen, yes? Well, not exactly. First of all, the rehearsals were a nightmare, with the leading singer demanding constant rewrites of their areas and the women's chorus almost going on strike because they claimed their music was too difficult. Then came the premiere, and all sorts of things went wrong. At one point, the tenor went two tones flat and the Carmen couldn't find her castanets (she finally broke a dish and clacked the pieces together). The audience, shocked to see women smoking on stage and even more dismayed by the violent story, booed and hissed. The critics then proceeded to boo and hiss in print, and though the opera staggered on for another 37 performances, it has to be ranked among the more notable opening night fiascos.

Three months to the day after the premiere, during one of those performaces, at almost precisely the moment when Carmen sees death in the tarot cards, Bizet himself died at the age of 37. He was never to know that his opera would be translated into dozens of languages, and acclaimed in every corner of the world, and considered by later generations to be "the Queen of Operas." On the other hand, he never lived to see his glorious music for Carmen set forth in jazz instrumentals or fitted out with pop lyrics, so just possibly he was ahead of the game after all.

Bizet's Works You Need to Know

Carmen is the big gun, of course, and even if you hate singing, you can enjoy its magnificent melodies in the two "Carmen" Suites for Orchestra, and the dazzling "Carmen Fantasy" for violin and orchestra by the Spanish composer Pablo de Sarasate. There's also a much less well-known Bizet opera called "The Pearl Fishers", which is worth looking into.

Otherwise, look for Bizet's delightful suites of incidental music to "L'Arlesienne", his youthful (and charming) Symphony in C, and the delectable suite called "Jeux d'enfants" (Children's Games), which is available both in piano and orchestral form.

Nobody Said It Would Be Easy

Some operas, like some wines, just don't travel well. If you go to Prague, you'll probably find several Dvořák and Smetana operas on the boards, but only the latter's "Bartered Bride" has crossed the Atlantic with any frequency, mostly on the strength of its sparkling Overture and instrumental dances. Spain is in love with the zarzuela, a kind of cross between grand opera and operetta, but even the ardent championing efforts of such high-profile artists as Placido Domingo have failed to infiltrate any of these very attractive pieces into the American mainstream. Want to hear some great operas by Glinka, Rimsky-Korsakov, Borodin, and other Slavic masters? More of these prouctions have come to the USA in recent years, but for many others, with a few exceptions, such as Moussorgsky's "Boris Godunov" and Tchaikovsky's "Eugene Onegin", you'll either have to track them down to Mother Russia, or wait for visiting Russian companies to bring them to us.

Bet You Didn't Know

One of Leoncavallo's miscellaneous flops was called "Are You There?" since it was premiered in London. Apparently the answer was No.

Going to an opera is a little like enjoying meal at a fine restaurant. You sit down at the table with high expectations—if the ingredients aren't fresh or haven't been prepared by a master chef, if the entree is over-or under-spiced, if the service is slow, even if your favorite waiter is on vacation, you may well make a mental note to try the place down the block next time. Countless operas have been relegated to the dust-bins of history because some part of their complicated makeup didn't quite work. Schubert lavished more and more beautiful melodies on more and more stupid plots, so his operatic efforts came to naught. Other composers were foiled by incomprehensible librettos, or else, even when they had given good ones; the spark of inspiration didn't burn quite brightly enough. After Rossini's "Barber of Seville," nobody wanted to hear Paiseillo's opera of the same title any more, and Puccini's "La Boheme", quickly relegated Leoncavallo's "La Boheme" to dust-gathering on library shelves. How often do you run into Paisiello's "The Barber of Seville," or Leoncavallo's "La Boheme"?

It took Beethoven four Overtures, 11 years, and countless revisions to get "Fidelio" right, and it taught him a lesson: he never wrote another opera. Brahms, Chopin and Liszt were even smarter: they didn't compo

Bet You Didn't Know

When Bizet won the prize that sent him to Rome, he carried with him a sealed of recommendation from one of his teachers to an important Italian composer. What with the glorious sunsets and the pasta and the beautiful Italian women, Bizet never quite got around to contacting the composer or delivering the letter, but finally, just out of curiosity, he tore open the envelope to read the message. "My dear friend," it began. "I would like to introduce to you a pupil of mine, M. Georges Bizet. He is a totally delightful young man, intelligent, well-mannered and very friendly. I am sure you will like him immensely.

P.S. Bizet hasn't got the slightest trace of musical talent."

There were many others who did write operas, of course. In fact, they wrote lots and lots of operas, but only rarely did all of the ingredients mesh perfectly, which is why there are so many composers whom we know almost entirely on the basis of one operatic success. Twenty-five-year old Pietro Mascagni had a smash hit with "Cavalleria Rusticana," then spent the rest of his life in a vain attempt to come up with its equal. Ruggero Leoncavallo wrote the other half of the frequently encountered "Cav-Pag" doubleheader, "Pagliacci," but don't expect to find any of his other dozen other operas at the Met either.

Tchaikovsky doubled that success rate, with both "Eugene Onegin" and "The Queen of Spades" receiving many American productions, but Moussorgsky hit the operatic jackpot only once, with his stunningly dramatic portrayal of the Czar "Boris Godounov." Engelbert Humperdinck (the composer, not the pop singer) might as well have retired from the operatic battlefields after "Hansel and Gretel," ditto Gounod after "Romeo and Juliet," and Saint-Saens after "Samson and Delilah," and Bizet after "Carmen."

Masters They Are

The astonishing thing about many of the composers profiled here—plus Mozart, Wagner and Richard Strauss, whom we discussed in earlier chapters—is that they were able to mine so many gems from the operatic fields. Look down the roster of any opera house in the world, and the great bulk of the repertoire (at least in the U.S.) represents the work of those masters.

CHAPTER 21

Those Dirty Plots and Plans: Dramatic Opera

In This Chapter

➤ Borrowing from the Bard

➤ Opera Plots: Who Did What to Whom

➤ Some popular dramatic operas

When most of us hear the word opera, we think first of great singing, then of the overall theatrical experience: the sets, the costumes, the lighting effects, and the numerous other ways in which opera makes a spectacle of itself. Behind every production, though, lies a story: A plot that theoretically engenders the arias and ensemble numbers which gives the soprano a reasonable excuse for going mad and makes it seem vaguely logical for the tenor to unleash a barrage of high C's.

These stories can be realistic or romantic; they can be set in a smugglers' den or atop Mount Olympus; they can deal with historic or purely fictional characters; but they give the composer a framework upon which to hang his memorable musical moments.

To Borrow or Not To Borrow

Shakespeare, they say, didn't bother coming up with original plots—he just swiped, reworked, and embellished older tales of love, jealousy, and greed from any source that had the potential for good theater. In his own words (from Julius Caesar), he was "a surgeon to old shoes."

Turn about is fair play, of course, wherefore succeeding generations of composers and their librettists had no qualms about borrowing from the Bard:

For instance:

> ➤ Gounod had Romeo and Juliet singing in French.,
>
> ➤ Bellini's balcony scene unfolded in Italian (in "I Capuleti ed I Montecchi")
>
> ➤ the lovers graduated to the streets of New York in Bernstein's West Side Story
>
> ➤ Handel's Julius Caesar got into trouble in Egypt
>
> ➤ Benjamin Britten dreamed up A Midsummer Night's Dream

Important Things to Know

Handel's "Julius Caesar", all but forgotten for a couple of hundred years, not only came roaring back to life in the mid 1960s, but served to catapult Beverly Sills (the Cleopatra of the New York City Opera cast) into the international spotlight. "She trilled the birds off the trees" said the conductor of the evening, Julius Rudel, and in short order, she became one of the most popular, in-demand and famous singers of our time. "I got more than I bargained for," the soprano told a Newsweek interviewer, with her typical sparkly humor. "I expected to be carried out feet first from the City Opera, and that people would think Beverly Sills was a place in California."

> ➤ Macbeth, Othello, and Falstaff raised their operatic voices courtesy of Verdi
>
> ➤ Berlioz found two more B's in "Beatrice and Benedict"
>
> ➤ Samuel Barber's Antony and Cleopatra opened the new Metropolitan Opera House in 1966

A good story is a good story, in other words, and the very fact that the Bard made a narrative effective in theatrical presentation gave composers and librettist a certain confidance that it would work equally well on the operatic stage.

Historical Figures

Truth, they say, is stranger than fiction, and when the most far-fetched coincidences can be justified by pulling out the encyclopedia and showing that they actually happened that way, the concoctors of opera knew that they had latched on to a good thing. And if they had to stretch the truth a bit to make the plot work out right, well you can just put it down to poetic license.

Since fact-based plots have a special appeal, the stage has welcomed everybody from Attila the Hun to Joan of Arc, from Nero to Bluebeard.

Political figures are always good for plots dealing with intrigue, corruption and assassination, wherefore we have such epic dramas as Glinka's A Life for the Tsar and Moussorgsky's towering portrait of the tragic Tsar, Boris Godounov. In Giordano's Andrea Chenier, we meet a poet-victim of the French Revolution, and in Donizetti's Anna Bolena

Bet You Didn't Know

Yes, Bluebeard was indeed based on real life. The legend grew up around the horrible deeds of an actual villain, one Gilles de Rais, who in his younger, saner days, was an officer in Joan of Arc's army. Convicted of murder, sodomy and witchcraft, he was hung (and burned, just to make sure) in 1440.

(Anne Boleyn), one of the wifely victims of Henry VIII. This fascination with history and actual news events has continued to our own day, as witness John Adams' Nixon in China and The Death of Klinghoffer, Ezra Laderman's Marilyn (Monroe), Anthony Davis' "The Life and Times of Malcolm X," Michael Daugherty's "Jackie O," and Jake Heggie's "Dead Man Walking."

Death and Transfiguration

This phrase (the title of a famous tone poem by Richard Strauss) pinpoints one of the elements that can turn pure tragedy into inspiring drama. If the hero's death leads to martyrdom, if the heroine dies knowing that she and her lover will be reunited in Heaven, we ourselves feel some sense of relief and uplift. Their suffering has somehow been exalted, their nobility of character has surmounted the afflictions of earthly existence.

When we think of Lincoln or, closer to our own day, Martin Luther King, and John and Robert Kennedy, it is with sadness that their work remained unfinished, but exhilaration that their passionate lives touched us so deeply. Their brutal deaths put their selfless achievements into even sharper relief, enhanced their status as American heros. So it is in opera, where our empathy with the characters on stage brings us a kind of emotional release; their sufferings and moral triumphs deputize for our own struggles to be better human beings.

Opera thrives on such transfigurations, and one fairly sure way to tell that you've been to a serious (rather than comic) opera is that by the time you're ready to go home, most of the main characters will no longer be amongst the living. They may have suffocated in a pyramid, killed each other in a sword fight, expired from tuberculosis, been shot, stabbed, poisoned, or just plain committed suicide, but they will most assuredly have given up the ghost. Equally certain, though, they will rise from the grave on time for their final curtain calls.

The Plots Thicken

Important Things to Know

Just as Shakespeare's tragedies tend to be more popular than the comedies, the most popular operas "Aida", "Carmen", "Madame Butterfly", etc., are the heartbreakers, the ones where half the audience is sobbing as the final curtain falls. At heart, we're just gluttons for punishment.

So you've decided to go to the opera. Great. Be sure to get there early enough to read the synopsis in the printed program. You probably still won't be able to figure out exactly who's doing what to whom at any given point, but you'll at least have a general idea. It also helps that supertitles are now customary in most American opera houses, meaning that translations of the libretto are available in sync with the unfolding of the arias. Anyway, to give you a bit of a head start, here are the stories behind a few of the more popular operas.

Aida

We go far back in time and to a highly exotic location in Aida: Memphis and Thebes in the era of the Pharaohs. Radames, the captain of the Egyptian guards, is loved by Amneris, the current Pharoah's daughter, but wouldn't you know it, he loves Aida, one of Amneris' slaves, who was captured during a battle with the Ethopians. Don't tell anybody, since nobody on stage knows it yet, but Aida is actually of royal blood too, the daughter of Amonasro, the King of Ethopia. As Act I ends, Radames once again goes forth to face the Ethopian army, emboldened by a sacred sword that will ensure his victory.

The big deal of Act II is the Triumphal Scene, with hordes of trumpeters, warriors, slave girls, and usually a few horses, all greeting Radames, who returns in glorious victory with a new crop of prisoners, among them Aida's father. Finding out about his daughter's infatuation with Radames, Amonasro urges her to persuade Radames to reveal the route of the next Egyptian attack; this she does, and Radames, unable to resist her importunings, gives her the details, only to have his words overheard by the jealous Amneris. The Princess decides that if she can't have Radames, nobody else will either. She calls in the guards, and as Aida flees, Radames is captured and charged with high treason. His sentence: to be buried alive. Instead of making good her escape, however, Aida has secreted herself in the tomb, and after the most touching love duet ever to be sung in the absence of oxygen, Aida and Radames die in each other's arms. Their abiding love, foiled by fate and destroyed by jealousy, will at last have passed through death to life eternal.

La Boheme

In Puccini's day, poets, painters and musicians seeking self-expression were called Bohemians. It is Christmas Eve in Paris, 1830, and the four penniless artists who share a garret in the Latin Quarter are enjoying an unexpected largesse of food and wine courtesy of the musician, Schaunard, who had landed a job playing for a nobleman. His companions are Marcello, a painter, the philosopher Colline, and Rodolfo, a poet who until now has been feeding the stove with pages from his latest opus. Their celebration is rudely interrupted by the landlord, Benoit, demanding his back rent, but the foursome manage to befuddle him with wine and flattery, then decide to continue the party at the Cafe Momus.

Rodolfo stays behind to finish some verses when a knock on the door brings in Mimi, asking for a match to light her candle. Love at first sight on Christmas Eve: what better way to set the scene for the unfolding of tragic destiny? The candle goes out again, she drops her key, and their hands touch as they search for it. After back-to-back arias that are as famous as any in opera—"Che gelida mannina" (how icy your little hand is) and "Mi chiamano Mimi" (my name is Mimi)—Rodolfo and Mimi decide that two can live as pennilessly as one, then leave arm in arm to tell the good news to their friends at the café. Adding spice to the party is the arrival of the flamboyant Musetta, Marcello's old flame, now being escorted by the elderly (and not overly bright) Alcindoro. Musetta, having attracted Marcello's attention with a flashy waltz, sends Alcindoro on a manufactured errand, then waltzes off for another fling with Marcello. The others depart as well, after which the bewildered Alcindoro returns to find that the only thing awaiting him is the restaurant tab.

A few months later, there has been trouble in paradise. Marcello and Musetta have had an angry breakup, Mimi and Rodolfo a more reluctant parting, Rodolfo fearing that Mimi's poor health will be further undermined by the poverty in which they are forced to live. The four Bohemians are together again, trying to lift their lonely spirits with a rowdy dance and mock fight when Musetta bursts in with the news that the gravely ill Mimi has returned to die with her lover. Desperately, they try to save her: Musetta goes to sell her earrings for medicine, Colline to pawn his favorite overcoat, Marcello to summon a doctor. It is all too late. After recalling her ecstatic happiness with Rodolfo, Mimi dies quietly, and the curtain falls on the sobbing Rodolfo who calls out Mimi's name one last time.

Carmen

Bizet's masterpiece is set in Seville in 1820 and has a classic theme: a man torn between innocent love and lethal lust. Don Jose, a corporal in a troop of dragoons, is engaged to the sweet Micaela. One day, though, he meets temptation in the form of a sultry gypsy who works in the local cigarette factory. We all know that smoking can be dangerous to your health, and when Carmen throws him a butt (all right, make it a flower), the trap is sprung. Soon a fight breaks out among the cigarette workers, Carmen is arrested, and guess who is sent to guard her? This time around, Carmen's wiles succeed. She promises to let Don Jose come up and see her sometime (in fact, as soon as possible, at a local inn), and the smitten corporal allows her to escape.

This gets him in hot water with his captain, naturally, and Don Jose has to desert his troop in order to keep his rendezvous with Carmen. A toreador also comes to the inn and is immediately attracted to the gypsy girl, but she being faithful to one man (at a time), pays him no heed (well, maybe a little heed), then runs off with Don Jose to hide.

There's not all that much to do in a smuggler's camp, which is where they end up, so Carmen reads her fortune in the cards. Better she should have stayed with flowers: the death card

Important Things to Know

Carmen isn't the only double-dealer in the operatic book. In Massenet's "Manon", the lovers are arrested for (allegedly) cheating at cards; and when "The Girl of the Golden West" wins the freedom of her lover in a poker game with the Sheriff, she definitely had a couple of aces up her sleeve. Gambling secrets are at the heart (and in the title) of Tchaikovsky's "Queen of Spades", and for more genteel shufflings, there's Samuel Barber's one-acter, "A Hand of Bridge".

appears every time. Meanwhile, that secret hiding place seems to be on every road map in the area, since presently Micaela appears looking for her lover, and the toreador shows up too, looking for Carmen. Don Jose and the toreador start fighting, but the smugglers separate them, and as the bullfighter saunters down the hill singing his famous song, Micaela convinces Don Jose to go home to his dying mother.

Well, you get the picture. Carmen has now pledged her amorous allegiance to the toreador. Don Jose is wildly jealous and—outside the bull ring, where the crowds are cheering the Toreador's exploits—he gives Carmen one last chance to return to him. She disdainfully refuses, throwing the ring he gave her at his feet. Pushed beyond all endurance, Don Jose stabs her to death, then sobs out his love for her as the curtain falls.

Fidelio

Fidelity is certainly the subject of Beethoven's only opera, but the nobility and courage of the faithful wife was closer to the composer's heart, which is why "Leonore" was his preferred title. In any case, the heroine is the wife of Don Florestan, a noble Spaniard who was captured by a political rival, Don Pizarro.

The opera opens in a 17th century fortress near Seville, where Florestan has been languishing in a dungeon for two years. He is rumored to be dead, but Leonore believes otherwise, and disguised as a boy, Fidelio, has wangled a job as assistant jailor at that same prison. Pizarro, having received word that the Minister of the Interior, Don Fernando, is coming on an inspection tour, determines to get rid of the evidence. He orders the jailor, Rocco, to dig a grave for the mysterious prisoner, and on the pretext of easing his workload, Leonore follows Rocco down to the dungeon. There, she realizes that the gaunt, chained man in the cell is indeed her husband, but their reunion is interrupted by mean old Pizarro, who is bound and determined to dispatch his enemy before the Minister arrives.

"First kill his wife!" Leonore cries, and when the shocked Pizarro attempts to accommodate her, she pulls a revolver and holds the villain at bay. You know how the cavalry rides to the rescue in a western? Well, that's exactly what happens here, as a trumpet call announces the arrival of the Minister. Don Fernando, having assessed the truth of the matter, frees Florestan, sends Pizarro off to his justly deserved fate, and releases the other prisoners. Everybody then joins in a chorus of rejoicing and gratitude to Leonore, the faithful wife who has saved them all. Surprise! Here's one grand opera that actually has a happy ending.

Lucia di Lammermoor

The story takes place in Scotland at the end of the 16th century, where the Ravenswood and Lammermoor families have been feuding and fighting. Naturally Lucia, a Lammermoor, has fallen in love with Edgardo, the last of the Ravenswoods. Lucia's brother Enrico wants to solidify his fortunes by marrying his sister off to the wealthy Arturo. And mind you, this all before the curtain goes up! When it does, Enrico finds out about his sister's infatuation with his sworn enemy and Edgardo, while swearing his eternal love for Lucia, figures he'd better hightail it to France until the heat's off. Meanwhile, back in the Lammermoor's castle, Enrico shows Lucia a forged letter Edgardo supposedly wrote to another woman, and the gullible Lucia, never suspecting that her brother is a conniving rat, reluctantly agrees to marry Arturo.

The wedding takes place, and guess who comes to dinner? Yep, it's Edgardo, back from France, furious at Lucia's infidelity and lavishing curses on the entire Ashton family. Edgardo and Enrico start fighting, but are separated and agree to settle things once and for all in a duel at dawn. Back at the wedding party, though, Lucia has gone around the bend, dispatching her new husband with a dagger, then staggering down stairs for the mad scene that the audience has been patiently sitting through the rest of the opera for. With a wild flourish of trills and roulades, she evokes past memories, conjures up ghosts, and generally carries on until she collapses, near death.

The next morning, Edgardo awaits the duel, hoping Enrico will kill him and thus end his misery, but when he receives word that Lucia has died, calling his name, Edgardo decides not to wait for Enrico and stabs himself to death. With nobody left to sing anything else, the curtain falls.

Madame Butterfly

It all started in 1888 with Madame Chrysantheme, a French novel by Pierre Loti, who had spent time in Japan as a naval officer. It arrived on the stage 10 years later as a play by the American David Belasco, and continues today—in its Broadway transformation as Miss Saigon, which as of this writing (2013) is still touring around the USA. For opera lovers, though, the story of Madame Butterfly reached its pinnacle of dramatic poignancy in Puccini's 1904 masterpiece, Madama Butterfly.

A 15-year-old girl named Cio-Cio-San ("Cio-cio" is the Japanese word for butterfly; "San" corresponds to Madame or Mrs.) has fallen in love with a U.S. Navy lieutenant stationed in Nagasaki. The callow young man, named Benjamin Franklin Pinkerton, weds her in a Japanese ceremony, knowing that it is not binding upon him. Sure enough, when his enlistment is up, Pinkerton returns home, with the vague promise of coming back to his bride "Un bel di" (one fine day).

That thought (and the gorgeous aria of that title) sustains Cio-Cio-San and her love child for the next three years, as she looks out to sea and waits in vain for her lover's return. Finally, the sound of a cannon announces the arrival of Pinkerton's ship. Madame Butterfly is ecstatic, but Pinkerton, now stricken with remorse and unable to face Cio-Cio-San, rushes off without seeing her. He has left it to his American wife to tell Mme. Butterfly the real reason behind their return: to take the child back to America. Cio-Cio-San agrees, bids an impassioned farewell to her son, and intoning the inscription on a dagger, "death without honor is better than life with dishonor," she commits ritual hari-kiri, while a bit of "The Star Spangled Banner" sounds in the background.

Rigoletto

We're now in 16th century Mantua, where the Duke is an unscrupulous libertine, and his servant, Rigoletto, is a humpbacked jester, who delights in playing tricks on the nobility at court. One of the nobles levels a furious curses at Rigoletto, while others, deciding on some revengeful trickery of their own, arranged to abduct Gilda, whom they believe to be Rigoletto's mistress.

But that was no mistress, that was his daughter, the light of Rigoletto's life, the young and innocent Gilda.

Unknown to Daddy, Gilda has been courted by the Duke of Mantua, disguised as a student and when the nobles bring the abducted Gilda to him, the Duke takes full advantage of the situation and deflowers her.

When Rigoletto discovers the truth, he vows vengeance on the Duke, going so far as to hire an assassin, Sparafucile, to get rid of the seducer. The scheme they concoct is for Sparafucile's young and decidedly not-so-innocent sister, Maddalena, to entice the Duke into an assignation, where he can be conveniently stabbed to death. The scheme might have worked except that Gilda by now is actually in love with the Duke. The scene is now set for the famous Quartet. Inside the house where the dastardly deed is to be done, the Duke and Maddalena are playfully sparking; outside Rigoletto is trying to convince his daughter of the Duke's treachery.

The denouement is not long in coming. Maddalena, having herself fallen under the Duke's spell, begs her brother to kill the hunchback instead. Being an honorable assassin, Sparafucile refuses to dispose of one of his own clients, but does consent to a substitute murder if a convenient victim should come along. Gilda, who has been eavesdropping all this while, determines to save her lover's life, knocks on the door, and becomes that victim, promptly dispatched by the assassin's knife.

Soon Rigoletto returns, receives the body in a sack, and prepares to savor his revenge by tossing it into the river when he hears the Duke's song coming from the house. In a panic, he tears open the sack, where he finds his daughter with strength enough only to confess that she chose to die for the man she loves and to ask her father's forgiveness. The nobleman's curse (remember the nobleman's curse?) has finally come home to roost.

Important Things to Know

Curses are almost as popular as cards in opera plots, especially since they usually come true. When Santuzza curses her false lover (in Mascagni's Cavalleria Rusticana), you can be pretty sure that he won't survive the duel with the other woman's jealous husband. When Paolo is tricked into joining the Council of Genoa in wishing damnation on the villain in "Simone Boccanegra" (it's Paolo himself, though nobody else knows it yet), you can bet your last lire that he'll be hauled off to the gallows before the final curtain falls. And in Wagner's opera, when Isolde curses herself and Tristan, you don't really have to read the plot synopsis to figure out that several passionate love scenes (and three or four hours) later, the lovers will have to resume their romance in the next world.

Tosca

When Tosca opened in 1887, it was a play by Victorien Sardou (actually titled La Tosca), and the title role of the tempestuous diva was undertaken by no less a theatrical legend than Sarah Bernhardt. Puccini retained the high-tension melodrama in his operatic translation, and the soprano who portrays Floria Tosca must be able to deal with outbursts of piousness and passion and convey furious jealousy one moment and selfless love the next.

The story is set in Rome at the turn of the 19th century, when Napoleon had kings quavering in their royal boots and anyone suspected of Republican tendencies was subject to immediate arrest. A political prisoner has escaped and hides in a chapel of the Church of Sant'Andrea. He is Cesare Angelotti, a consul of the former Roman republic, and a friend of the painter Mario Cavaradossi, who is working on a portrait of the Blessed Virgin at the same church. Hot on the fugitive's trail comes Baron Scarpia, the dreaded chief of police, who is convinced that Cavaradossi has had a hand in the escape, in his spare time, lusts after the Tosca, who is the painter's mistress. Plotting to advance his political fortunes, get rid of his rival, and enjoy Tosca's favors with one evil deed, he arrests Cavaradossi. Even under torture, Cavaradossi will not reveal Angelotti's hiding place, but unable to bear her lover's cries of agony, Tosca finally blurts out the secret. Scarpia sends his men to arrest Angelotti, and pronounces a sentence of death for Cavaradossi.

Scarpia now moves on to the rest of his dastardly plan: he offers to spare her lover's life if Tosca will spend the night with him. She refuses him angrily, then begs for mercy, all to no avail. In despair, she finally agrees to Scarpia's bargain. The Baron seems to orders his henchman to stage a mock execution, then turns to claim his prize. Is he ever in for a shock. "Here is Tosca's kiss!" she cries, stabbing Scarpia with a knife from his own table, cursing him as he dies, then in a moment of remorseful reverence, placing prayer candles around his lifeless body.

At the prison, Tosca tells Cavaradossi of the impending fake execution, warning him to fall when the blank bullets are fired. They sing a final duet, full of love and hope for the future. The soldiers arrive, they fire, Cavaradossi crumples to the ground. Waiting until everyone else has left, Tosca rushes to her lover, only to find that the execution had been all too genuine. She has no time to mourn: the guards burst in to arrest her for Scarpia's murder, but tearing herself away from Cavaradossi's lover's body, Tosca joins her lover in death by hurling herself from the castle ramparts.

Yes, opera has all the passionate throbbing of a romance novel, the tingling suspense of a murder mystery, the intriguing twists and turns of a spy movie, and the assorted other examples of blood and gore that fill the evening news on TV. You even get some pretty terrific music into the bargain.

Coda

For a fascinating glimpse into the way fact and fiction come together on the operatic stage, read George Jellinek's *History Through the Opera Glass*. There are several collections of operatic anecdotes and plot synopses, but most importantly, get to see full productions, which—thanks to Metropolitan Opera's new series of HD, large-screen films, are readily available all over the country. You won't be alone, either: when the Met released Mozart's "Don Giovanni" in 2011, it was seen by an estimated 1.3 million people in the USA and Canada. Two excellent paperback collections by Paul England are *Favorite Operas by Italian and French Composers* and *Favorite Operas by German and Russian Composers*. For a top-notch one-volume paperback survey of opera, including the stories of nearly 90 important stageworks, you won't do better than to latch onto *The Limelight Book of Opera* by Arthur Jacobs and Stanley Sadie.

CHAPTER 22

Comedy in the Buff-a

> ## In This Chapter
>
> ➤ Opera for fun
> ➤ No murders tonight
> ➤ Most popular comic operas and their composers

"Opera Buffa" means it's comedy tonight, as opposed to the gloom and doom situations so prevalent in "serious" opera. (Victor Borge says that it's also called "light opera" because the prima donnas weigh less). Comic operas are not about heroines who murder their brothers while descending into coloratura madness, or heros who foil dastardly plots and expire in a flurry of high C's. Rather, they're about everyday people facing the everyday eventualities of life, like heroines dressing up as their brothers while rising to heights of coloratura, or heroes foiling other dastardly plots while trumpeting their high C's. Hmm, maybe there's not as much difference as we thought.

It Will All Work Out

The main way you can tell it's a comedy is that the main characters are still alive when the curtain falls. No matter how many mistaken identities there were, how many schemes-within-schemes go awry, how often misunderstandings cause boy to lose girl (or vice versa), in the end everything works out for the best. The lovers are reunited, the duped villains slink off to lick their bruised egos, virtue is triumphant and everybody (including the audience) can go home happy.

When the biggies (Mozart, Rossini, et al.) wrote comic operas, the musical values are equal to those found in more weighty productions. It's the plot and some of the slapstick antics on stage that produce the laughter. Some of Mozart's music in "The Marriage of Figaro" is as ravishing as any you'll find in his darker operas, and Wagner didn't lose his flair for drama simply because "Die Meistersinger" (the Master Singer) is officially a comic opera.

When the music is lighter in idiom, when the arias are interlaced with fairly extended dialogue, and the comic intent is more clearly delineated, we have operetta, which is the Italian diminutive of opera. In Germany, such pieces are called Singspiels, because the performers are spieling when they aren't singing. Operettas are usually shorter and more good-natured than their operatic relatives, and often use satire to make their witty points.

When gods and goddesses are evoked, it is not to have them carry on in Valhallan excess, but rather to let them experience the same fussings, foibles and follies that beset us regular mortals. Orpheus played his lute in Greek mythology, but when Offenbach gets through with him, he's dancing the Can-can. Gilbert and Sullivan aimed their barbs at more local targets—models of current major generals, rulers of the Queen's Navee and peers of parliament—while Johann Strauss, with gentler satire, twitted Viennese high society.

Music Word

A singspiel indicates a musical drama, usually lighter in tone and spirit than a full-fledged opera, with spoken dialogue interpolated between the musical numbers. Sometimes, as in Mozart's "The Impressario", there's actually more dialogue than music, but "spielsing" doesn't sound nearly so attractive.

Offenbach—Can-can We Dance?

Jacob Eberst never amounted to much, but when he moved to France and changed his name to Jacques Offenbach, things started looking up. Yes, Offenbach (1819-1880), the prototypical Parisian boulevardier, the composer whom Rossini dubbed "the Mozart of the Champs Elysées," and the man whose melodies were the very pulse and beat of France during the Second Empire, was born and bred in Germany

His French career started when he got a job playing cello in the Opera Orchestra, but his penchant for musical pranks (when he got bored, he'd play only every other note in the score) got him in trouble, and he became a conductor instead. Eventually, he decided to try composing a few pieces himself, and when he sold a couple waltzes, his future path was set. He wrote his first operetta at the age of 20, but the big push came in 1855, when he bought a broken-down old theatre on the Champs Elysees, completely renovated it, and started producing his own stageworks there.

Critics flapped but audiences flipped, and Offenbach really hit his stride, turning out no less than eight operettas that year alone, seven more in each of the next two years, and thereafter keeping up an only slightly slower pace of three or four new productions annually, eventually racking up a total of nearly 100. Occasionally, the censors gave him a hard time when some of the spoofs hit too close to home, but Offenbach generally managed to throw them off the track. One of his favorite dodges was setting his operettas in faraway times or climes, thus seeming to avoid any topical references. The ruse was transparent, much to the added merriment of audiences, but censors aren't a terribly bright lot, and Offenbach rarely got himself into serious difficulties.

Bet You Didn't Know

Offenbach's fame and popularity eventually reached across the Atlantic, so he was invited to the USA to participate in the nation's centennial celebrations in 1876. Ten thousand listeners attended his first concert, and he gave several more to even larger crowds. Normally he conducted his own music exclusively, but one night he also introduced a new piece by the 22-year-old concertmaster of the orchestra. "The march was very good," he told the budding composer. "You ought to write an operetta." "I'll remember that," said the grateful John Philip Sousa.

Like the comedian who wants to play Hamlet, Offenbach was obsessed with the idea of writing a "grand" opera, feeling somehow that he had wasted his life on all those frivolous operettas. The result was Tales of Hoffmann, based on the fantasy stories of E.T.A. Hoffmann, but left unfinished at Offenbach's death. Various completions of the work and reorderings of its story sequences have vied for public favor, but in whatever form it's presented, Tales has had precisely the grand success Offenbach envisioned. Still, his fame rests largely upon the rollicking tunes and witty lampoonery of his operettas.

Offenbach's Works You Need to Know

Tales of Hoffmann is a favorite with opera fans (it includes the ever-popular "Barcarolle"), but for operetta delights, Orpheus in the Underworld, with its rowdy Can-can, is probably the best place to start. The Grand Duchess of Gerolstein has the tune that the U.S. military would later swipe for the Marine Corps Song ("From the Halls of Montezuma…"), and there are vocal gems galore in La Belle Helene (Beautiful Helen) and La Vie Parisienne (Parisian Life).

If you'd rather go rollicking without words, sample one of the many CDs of Offenbach overtures on the market, or better still, enjoy "Gaite Parisienne," Manuel Rosenthal's zesty orchestral wingding that incorporates many of Offenbach's best tunes.

Johann Strauss—The Waltz King

Officially, it's Johann Strauss, Jr., since Papa also was an enormously popular composer of waltzes. In fact, for a while, folks weren't sure which Strauss wore the crown, but if you call Johann Sr. the Father of the Waltz, and Jr. the King, you'll be pretty much on target.

Bet You Didn't Know

When the Nazis realized that the Strauss family was of Jewish origin, there was panic in the propaganda office until somebody came up with the bright idea of forging the parish birth documents. With this definitive, albeit falsified, proof of racial purity in hand, the waltzes were returned to official party favor.

Papa Strauss, meanwhile, wasn't too thrilled about possible competition from his kid. First he tried to stop Johann Jr. from composing at all, and when that didn't work, he tried to sabotage the 19-year-old boy's debut concert in Vienna by sending over a bunch of friends to hiss and boo. That didn't work either, because the young Strauss played with such elegance, and his waltzes were so entrancing, that the audience went wild, cheering, shouting bravos, and demanding repeats of almost every piece. At the end of the concert, Johann Jr. signalled for silence, then offered, as his final encore, his father's most famous waltz, "Lorelei Rhine Echoes." That did it. The crowd tore up the place, friends carried Strauss out into the streets on their shoulders, and from that moment on, there was definitely a new Waltz King in town. As one Viennese reporter put it, "Good evening, Father Strauss. Good morning, Son Strauss."

We were, though, talking about operettas, and for quite a while, Johann Jr. was too busy churning out hundreds of waltzes to worry about them until his wife got into the first act. She convinced Johann that longer works could be fun too, and that nobody would mind if he stuffed them full of waltzes. Strauss' first operetta was produced in 1871, with 14 more following over the next quarter of a century.

Bet You Didn't Know

Strauss never wrote a grand opera, but he conducted the first Vienna performance of the Prelude to Wagner's Tristan and Isolde. Later, Wagner said thank you by conducting Strauss' waltz "Wine, Women and Song" at Bayreuth.

The most famous of Strauss' operettas is Die Fledermaus (The Bat), which Mahler conducted on the stage of the Austrian State Opera, and in more recent years has been a holiday favorite at the Met and other opera houses around the world. But "The Gypsy Baron" still gets around once in a while, and it's always fun to spend a musical Night in Venice. Unlike so many other composers who achieved fame only posthumously, we're pleased to report that in his own lifetime, Strauss was rich, revered, and renowned the world over. That's the way it ought to be.

Strauss' Works You Need to Know

Start with Die Fledermaus, of course, chock full of delicious arias, festive ensemble numbers, and enough mistaken identities to populate three other operettas. (Just about the only character who isn't pretending to be somebody else is Prince Orlovsky, and he's always played by a woman.)

You can pay instrumental homage to some of the other operettas with their highly tuneful Overtures, then head on to some of the literally hundreds of instrumental miniatures. The waltzes top the list, of course, but don't neglect the bouncy polkas, marches, and galops that are as masterful, in their own little way, as any big symphony. It was not without reason that another composer of note, when asked for an autograph, inscribed a lady's fan with the opening bars of Strauss' "Blue Danube" Waltz, then signed it "Alas, not by Johannes Brahms."

Gilbert and Sullivan—Here's a How-De-Do

Sometimes the whole can be far better than the sum of its parts. William Schwenk Gilbert was a successful poet and humorist Arthur Sullivan dreamed of writing operas, oratorios, and symphonies. In fact, he not only dreamed, he actually wrote them, not to mention the enormously popular song "The Lost Chord" and the famous hymn "Onward, Christian Soldiers." Despite their best individual efforts, and not infrequent personal frictions, it was only as the peerless team of Gilbert and Sullivan that their full genius was unleashed.

Bet You Didn't Know

Gilbert could be as wittily ascerbic in life as he was at the writing desk. During rehearsals for "Princess Ida", he had a run-in with one of the singers, who blurted out "Look here, sir, I will not be bullied. I know my lines." "That may be so," Gilbert retorted, "but you don't know mine." Even George Grossmith, one of Gilbert's favorites, who starred in most of the original productions, got his comeuppance that same day. After being forced to repeat the same scene twenty times, Grossmith lost his usual cool and yelled out, "I've rehearsed this confounded business until I feel a perfect fool!" "Excellent", was Gilbert's rejoinder. "Now we can talk on equal terms."

Their first collaboration, Thespis, was a flop (to the extent that except for a few choruses, most of the score has been lost), but four years later, Gilbert and Sullivan came up their first success, Trial by Jury. The producer of that show was Rupert d'Oyly Carte, and when he formed a company specifically to produce any and all works to come from the combined pens of Sullivan and Gilbert, the stage was set for a remarkable parade of smash hits. They raised light opera to new heights of lyric invention and melodic imagination, Gilbert's satirical bent and clever verses inspiring Sullivan to his most insightful musical creations. Starting in 1881 with Patience, their new productions were staged at the Savoy Theatre in London, whence arose the term "Savoy operas" and the designation of Gilbert and Sullivan specialists as Savoyards.

Gilbert and Sullivans' Works You Need to Know

You can't go wrong with any of the famous operettas. The Mikado and Pirates of Pinafore are probably the most popular, but by all means have Patience, greet The Gondoliers, bow to Princess Ida, follow The Yeomen of the Guard to the Tower of London, and polish up the handles on the big front door of H.M.S. Pinafore.

Bet You Didn't Know

Tired of having their works pirated by American companies who didn't pay any royalties, G&S decided to stake their overseas claim by premiering "Pirates of Penzance" in New York. That was in 1879, and more than 100 years later, the show had a new lease on American life, the New York Shakespeare Festival presenting a "dusted-off production", starring Kevin Kline as an unusually klutzy Pirate King, and pop stars Linda Ronstadt and Rex Reed as the young lovers. A smash hit off-Broadway, this new "Pirates" subsequently transferred to Broadway and later fame and glory on TV.

For Sullivan without Gilbert, you can bask in the operetta overtures, or if you feel ambitious, try the Irish Symphony. There's also "Cox and Box," Sullivan's short and charming pre-Gilbert operetta (with lyrics by F.C. Burnand); Gilbert without Sullivan, of course, is more of a literary excursion, though some of his "Bab Ballads" have been imaginatively set to music by the American composer Seymour Barab.

Happily Ever After Plots

In an earlier chapter, we pondered some of the stories that propel operatic heroes and heroines to their untimely doom. Now let's look in on the cheerfully bizarre doings that keep things hopping in a half-dozen of the happy-ending shows you're likely to encounter on stage at the Met and other major opera houses.

The Barber of Seville

On a sunlit Spanish street, old Doctor Bartolo lives with his pretty young ward, Rosina, counting the days until she (and more importantly, her dowry) will be his in marriage. Meanwhile, Count Almaviva also loves the lucky lady and schemes to win her hand, aided by his busybody friend Figaro, who not only serves as the town barber, but is available for useful service as a bloodletter, wigmaker, and writer of romantic letters for the literarily challenged.

Even as Dr. Bartolo is scheming with the music teacher, Don Basilio, to slander Almaviva so he'll have to leave town, Figaro suggests that Almaviva get to see Rosina by disguising himself as a soldier and showing up at Bartolo's house with a billeting order. By Act II, Figaro has concocted a bigger and better conspiracy, wherefore the Count appears at Rosina's door dressed as a cathedral chorister. Don Basilio is sick, he says, offering himself as a worthy substitute, a plot that works like a charm until the perfectly healthy Basilio arrives also. When Bartolo himself returns to the scene of chaos, he kicks everybody out, and announces that he will marry Rosina the very next day.

With all those hours left to concoct further machinations, Figaro arranges to sneak back into the house with the Count, then hoodwinks the notary into converting Bartolo's intended marriage contract into one for Rosina and Almaviva. When he realizes what's happened, the Doctor is outraged, but then contentedly mollified when the Count informs him he can have the dowry after all. Between true love and hard cash, everybody is contented, and the opera can end with a rejoicing chorus.

The Marriage of Figaro

Yes, it's the same Barber of Seville who takes on a more important role in Mozart's opera (he's been promoted to Count Almaviva's valet), while the beautiful Rosina is now the beautiful but neglected Countess. Even though the action takes place several years after the adventures described by Rossini, Mozart's opera was written 30 years earlier, premiering in 1786, 10 years after American independence, and just a short time before French citizens would be giving their aristocracy the heave-ho.

The Beaumarchais play on which The Marriage of Figaro is based, and Mozart's opera itself could hardly be called revolutionary, but underlying the lighthearted plot is shrewd social commentary on both the arrogance of the aristocracy and wisdom of a servant class on the rise.

Figaro is engaged to Susanna, the lady-in-waiting to the Countess, but the Count, tired of being faithful for so long, has been eyeing Susanna with more than casual interest. Back then a valet didn't argue with a Count, so Figaro figures he'd better come up with one of his famous schemes to outwit the dirty old man. Speaking of old men, Dr. Bartolo is still kicking around, in fact, still kicking himself for having let Figaro trick him out of his marriage to Rosina. Finally, he comes up with his own idea for revenge. It seems that Figaro still has an unpaid debt, so he flourishes a contract that, in effect, says that Figaro has to marry Bartolo's housekeeper, Marcellina, in lieu of coming up with the money. That's problem #1.

Problem #2 is that Cherubino, a hot-blooded page, who may look like a cherub, but whose galloping hormones make his actions something less than angelic, has been canned by the Count for making out with the gardener's daughter. The lad begs Susanna to intercede for him with the Countess, since he really loves her (the Countess), will die without her, etc. Rather flattered by his attentions, the Countess and Susanna agree to another of Figaro's wild-eyed schemes, this one involving Cherubino dressing up as a woman to impersonate Susanna in an assignation with the count. The part is sung by a woman in the first place, but that's an acting and costuming problem that we can't be bothered with right now. The Count walks in on the plans, and Cherubino has to hide in a closet, then jump out of the window when Susanna decides to hide in the same closet. This is the type of hilarious scene that only the Marx Brothers could improve on.

Things proceed to get more and more complicated, with Susanna impersonating the Countess, the Countess pretending to be Susanna, Cherubino trying to hug every woman in the place, Barbarina confessing that Figaro is really the love-child she had with Dr. Bartolo, Figaro once again available for marriage to Susanna, and the Count first berating his supposedly errant wife, only to realize the error of his ways, and begging her forgiveness. All that remains is a final chorus of jubilation and reconciliation, and memories of the glorious Mozart music that accompanied all those on-stage shenanigans.

Daughter of the Regiment

Donizetti's comic masterpiece takes place in the Austrian Tyrol, which at the time is being occupied by Napoleon's army. Marie, abandoned as a baby on the field of battle and rescued by Sergeant Sulpice, has grown up as the pet of the regiment, regarding each of the French soldiers as her father. Noting that Marie has grown up to marrying age, Sulpice urges her to choose any man in the regiment. She, however, has her eyes (and heart) set on Tonio, a young Tyrolean peasant who recently saved her from falling off a cliff.

Tonio, unfortunately, has been arrested as a spy, but even after that slight misunderstanding has been cleared up, he is informed by Sulpice that only a member the glorious 21st may aspire to the hand of this Daughter of the Regiment. Tonio isn't the smartest peasant in the world, but he figures a way out of the dilemma: he'll just enlist in the Regiment.

Enter the haughty Marquise de Birkenfeld, who identifies Marie as her nobly born niece, and takes her home. Unhappily and tediously ensconced in the Birkenfeld castle, Marie is taught to dance the minuet, to sing dainty serenades instead of the rowdy camp songs she grew up with, and to learn other niceties appropriate to her lofty new status. Worse, Marie is told that she must marry a man of her own station, and the Marquise has picked out just the fellow for her: the Duke of Crakenthorpe.

Soon Tonio arrives, resplendent in his Regiment uniform, and the Marquise stuns the company by announcing that she is actually Marie's mother. Swayed by Tonio and Marie's obvious love for each other, and possibly goaded slightly by the dirty looks she's been getting from the rest of the regimental soldiers, she relents, and the happy couple are reunited with the full blessings of Mama Marquise and Marie's regimental retinue.

Don Pasquale

Less than three years after the Daughter of the Regiment found her true love, Donizetti unveiled his last great triumph, and a stagework that has lost none of its charm in the intervening century and a half. The plot is hardly of Shakespearian depth, but it does have a certain passing similarity to "The Taming of the Shrew" (or, if you prefer, its Cole Porterization as the Broadway hit "Kiss Me Kate").

Bet You Didn't Know

Donizetti composed 67 operas and had them produced within the span of thirty years. We haven't checked the Guinness Book, but we suspect that's a world's record.

In this case, however, the shrewishness is all part of a scheme worthy of Figaro himself. The plotter-in-chief is Doctor Malatesta, who helps foil the foolishness of Don Pasquale, and to unite the young lovers, Ernesto and Norina, while allowing them to keep the inheritance Pasquale will bestow only if Ernesto agrees to marry somebody else. That's an offer Ernesto can and does refuse, whereupon Dr. Malatesta suggests that Pasquale develop a new heir by taking a bride himself. He even volunteers his sister for the purpose, describing her in such angelic terms that Pasquale can't wait to meet her.

One small difficulty here is that Malatesta doesn't have a sister, so he enlists Norina in the cause, introducing her to Pasquale as Sofronia. The girl makes a big show of being modest and unassuming, assuring Pasquale that she can knit up a sweater as well as cook up a storm. When she removes her veil and the now-panting Pasquale sees that she's beautiful into the bargain, he proposes on the spot. Naturally, Norina/Sofronia accepts him on the same spot, and Malatesta now plays his trump card, shlepping in a cousin who pretends to be a notary who can legalize the marriage vows.

The mock ceremony completed, Norina changes from a lovely Miss Jekyll into a horrendous Mistress Hyde. She bosses Pasquale around, makes impossible demands on him, slaps his face, and announcing that she won't be seen in public with a such a decrepit old man, leaves to spend their wedding night at the theatre with a younger swain (Ernesto, natch). Don Pasquale, until recently so excited about his wedding, now can think only of ways to get rid of the horrible nag who has completely messed up his comfortable way of life.

A few more intrigues remain on the menu, but eventually everybody comes clean. For a while Don Pasquale is understandably put out at the way he's been hoaxed, but at the end he forgives Dr. Malatesta ("You scoundrel," he says, "how can I ever thank you?"), pronounces himself well content to be rid of the shrewish Sofronia, and bestows his blessing on the young lovers.

Gianni Schicchi

A disputed inheritance lies similarly at the heart of the comic opera that forms the last the three one-act operas in Puccini's "Il Trittico," the others being "Il Tabarro" (the cloak), a sordid tale of jealousy and murder, and "Suor Angelica" (Sister Angelica), a portrait of religious repentance and transfiguration."

Unlike so many tragic operas that ends with death, the comedy of "Gianni Schicchi" begins with one. It is Florence in the year 1299, and a gaggle of relatives are moaning over Buoso Donati, one of the richest men in the city, who expired only a few moments before. Their laments give way to serious concerns, however, when the rumor circulates that the deceased had left his large fortune to a monastery. Wildly they search for the will, which is found by one of the cousins, Rinuccio. To the dismay of everyone present, Rinuccio holds the document hostage, announcing he'll only let it be read if his aunt will allow him to marry his beloved Lauretta. Permission had earlier been denied because Lauretta is the daughter of Gianni Schicchi, and Schicchi was considered beneath the family's dignity, having had the ill judgment to be born a peasant.

Impatient and greedy to receive her share of the legacy, his aunt reluctantly agrees to the bargain, and sends one of the children to fetch Lauretta and her father, while everybody else crowds around to read the will. Remember that rumor about the bequest to the monastery? Turns out to be 100% true. The relatives are to get nothing, the monastery everything. What to do? Only the wily Schicchi can save them.

Since nobody outside the room knows that Donati is dead, Schicchi has the corpse removed to the next room, climbs into the bed himself, and imitating the old man's voice, asks that a notary be called to prepare a new will. The cousins are delighted at this shift in the monetary winds, but when the notary arrives and Schicchi (alias the "dying" Donati) dictates the new testament, he leaves only small bits of property to the relatives, proclaiming that the bulk of his fortune should go to his dearly beloved friend ... Gianni Schicchi! The relatives are hysterical, but unable to do anything about it without revealing their own part in the attempted fraud, and as Lauretta and Rinuccio fall into each other's arms, Schicchi takes a big stick and chases the greedy relatives of the house. After all, it's his house now.

Falstaff

As its title indicates, Shakespeare was the source here, "The Merry Wives of Windsor" the primary wherewithall of Boito's libretto, with occasional borrowings from "Henry IV," where the grossly overweight braggart, coward and bumbling lover also appears. At the moment, the aging knight is financially embarrassed, but he still fancies himself irresistible to women, so he writes identical letters to a pair of well-off married women, Alice Ford and Meg Page, hoping that their love and fortunes will improve his situation. Unfortunately for Falstaff, the two ladies meet, show each other the letters—word for word the same except for the names—and determine to give the lazy lover his proper comeuppance.

Bet You Didn't Know

When Verdi's first comic opera failed, the young composer was stung so badly that he never composed another one. At least not until he was a revered old man of 77. He began work on it in some secrecy, not sure he would live to complete it, or that he would be content with the piece if he did. For the next two years, he spent two hours a day at his composing table (he had read that longer periods of work might be dangerous for men of his age). in 1893, several months ahead of his 80th birthday, Verdi's attended the premiere of his final operatic masterpiece, "Falstaff."

Enlisting the aid of Mistress Quickly, Mistress Ford sends word to Falstaff that her husband is insanely jealous, but he's invariably out of the house between two and three in the afternoon, so she could receive him then. Promptly at the appointed hour, the preening Falstaff arrives, only to have Meg Page rush in with the news that Ford has unexpectedly returned. The two women hide Falstaff in a laundry basket, then tip the basket and its contents (one portly baritone) into the Thames.

Being fat has its virtues. Falstaff floats on the water until he is pulled out, and returns, sadder and wiser (and wetter) to his stein of ale at the Garter Inn. There he receives another tantalizing offer from Mistress Ford, apologizing for the mishap and promising to meet him at midnight in the royal park. This time Ford himself is in on the game, but he develops a side scheme of his own. His daughter Nannetta is in love with a handsome young lad named Fenton, but Ford wants her to marry the elderly Dr. Cajus. With everybody coming to the midnight rendezvous in disguise, Ford figures he can use the confusion to wed Cajus to Nannetta before anybody is the wiser. Guess what? Mistress Quickly is the wiser and reports the intrigue to the young lovers.

When midnight strikes, and Falstaff eagerly awaits his romantic interlude, Meg Page suddenly bursts in with a group of "witches" who descend on Falstaff and beat him with their broomsticks. Meanwhile, as a notary administers the vows and Ford blesses the couple he assumes to be his daughter and the old doctor, they throw off their disguises and reveal themselves as the newly married Nannetta and Fenton. Ford, Cajus, and Falstaff are all aghast to find that their best laid plans have been thwarted by the Merry Wives of Windsor, but even they, admitting that "all the world's a jest," eventually have to yield to the general merriment.

Coda

"Laughter is not at all a bad beginning for a friendship," wrote Oscar Wilde, and the same is true for opera. It's nice to leave the theatre having sipped the musical equivalent of sparkling wine, to have smiled at the foibles of the characters on stage (even if, or perhaps precisely because, we recognize some of those same flaws in our own makeup), and to have been serenaded by glorious music without shedding tears for the doomed heroine. In short, as Stephen Sondheim so eloquently proved en route to the Forum, sometimes you just want to have Comedy Tonight!

CHAPTER 23

Richard Wagner - En Route to Valhalla

> ## In This Chapter
>
> ➤ The leitmotif
> ➤ Orchestral Wagner
> ➤ Wagner as a librettist
> ➤ A new style of opera
> ➤ Wagner's operas

Wagner's admirers and detractors pretty much agree that he secretly regarded himself as a god, though some might dispute that secretly part. As Wagner (1813-1833) proved with Wotan and with his other creations, gods are far less than perfect, but they do have the power to influence human destiny. In that respect at least, Wagner did indeed have a promethean influence on the destiny of opera, and the development of music in general.

Name that Leitmotif

The 12-year-old Richard Wagner adored Weber's "Der Freischutz," and from it he began evolving a much more intensive use of the leitmotif (leading motive), the musical concept in which a phrase, repeated through the work, symbolizes a person, place, idea, or emotion. The leitmotif is brilliant in its simplicity, providing musical continuity even as it helps us follow the story. In Wagner's later works, these leitmotifs don't just crop up occasionally or to heighten a particular scene—they are the actual building blocks upon which the entire score is constructed.

Wagner himself described leitmotifs as "basic themes." With just a few notes or a special rhythmic pattern or a harmonic phrase, the composer can evoke a specific image in the listener's mind: the Rhine, Valhalla, religious purity, sensual love. You name it, Wagner themed it. (In her hilarious satire of the Ring, Anna Russell compares the raucous cries of the Valkyrie Brunnhilde to the mortal Brunnhilde's sedate love theme. "Well!" she declares, "Falling in love has certainly taken the ginger out of her!") Leitmotifs lead the listener into the heart of the drama, expressing subtle changes as well as radical transformations, probing the characters' inner lives, displaying their secret desires, recounting their experiences, and tracing their destinies.

Playing the Symphonic Card

Verdi and most of the Italian opera composers were primarily concerned with the voice. For Donizetti and Bellini, the orchestra was one big harpsichord, supporting, enhancing, but essentially accompanying the singers. Verdi expanded the orchestral equation, allotting it a more significant role in the operatic scheme of things, but it remained for Wagner to give the orchestra nearly equal voice in his music dramas.

Beyond the overtures, interludes, and ballet sequences, you'll find very few symphonic recordings of Italian opera. Orchestral Wagner, on the other hand, is represented on hundreds of CDs, and excerpts make frequent appearances at symphonic concerts. Tristan and Isolde, for instance, declare their love and breathe their last breath against a passionate symphonic reflection that can perfectly well stand alone (and often does in concert). It's also why you'll recognize the Ride of the Valkyries without a single "Ho-Yo-to-ho!" Human voices and orchestral instruments take equal roles in the unfolding Wagnerian landscape, and their combination is part of what gives his music dramas unique intensity and scope.

The vivid orchestral writing also makes Wagner very difficult to sing, especially if one has to be on stage for the better part of five hours.

Bet You Didn't Know

Many early listeners, as well as many other composers, found Wagner's operas very difficult to sit through. "Wagner is clearly mad," wrote Berlioz, while Auber pronounced Wagner "Berlioz minus the melody." Richard Strauss complained about "the hideous discords that would kill a cat," Tchaikovsky grumbled that "the interminably long dialogues fatigues the nerves to the upmost degree," and another famous Russian composer, Mili Balakirev, put it more simply: "After Lohengrin," he wrote to a friend, "I had a splitting headache." Oscar Wilde, on the other hand, was took a more conciliatory path. "I like Wagner's music better than anybody's," he said. "It is so loud that one can talk the whole time without people hearing what one says."

Hit and Myth

Unlike most opera composers, Wagner was his own librettist, and a pretty darn good one, if he said so himself. Which he did. Often. He wanted his music "fertilized by poetry," and he took inspiration from German literature, history, and mythology, seeking eternal truths in the legends of his own land.

The Germanic gods, creations of the cold North, are dark and somber compared to their carefree Greek counterparts, and therefore perfectly suited to the philosophical, political, social, and economic upheavals of Europe in the mid-19th century. Wagner not only studied these gods, but devoured the works of such German cultural icons as Hegel, Neitzche, and Schopenhauer. His operas don't simply tell this story or that, they explore the most universal themes of human existence; as a result, it is not just in musical circles that their concepts, philosophical messages, and allegorical symbols have been debated for generations. George Bernard Shaw, for one, was convinced that the Ring expressed social criticism, with the gold representing the curse of capitalism. When Walther, the hero of Die Meistersinger, bursts into a passionate hymn to the spring, he's not just picking flowers; the music symbolizes the rebirth of German national traditions. Wagner, in other words, did not so much exalt German legend as transcend it, creating his own myths in the process.

Die Meisterworks

Wagner's early operas were minor events, as he imitated earlier composers and searched for his own musical way. Rienzi, in 1840, was still conceived in the French grand opera style, but the distinctive Wagnerian sound is already at hand. Thereafter, it was all hits, no misses. For 40 years, from The Flying Dutchman (1842) through Parsifal (1882), each succeeding work increased Wagner's fame and heightened his influence. Each was a pivotal achievement, distinctive in form, musically and dramatically powerful, and an opera destined to remain firmly established on the stages of the world.

Tannhauser

In 13th century Germany, troubadours used to gather for song contests (more on this when we get to the section "Die Meistersinger"), and quite likely one of the participants at the Wartburg Competition of 1210 was a minstrel called Tannhauser (some of whose verses, including a "Song of Repentance," survived into modern times). Some 300 years later, a legend grew up in Germany about the Venusberg, a hill where Venus, the goddess of love, held court, enticing men by her beauty, then destroying their souls. Wagner combined fact and fantasy in his opera, set against a backdrop of courtly life in medieval times.

As the scene opens to a celebration of pagan sensuality, Tannhauser is lying with his head in Venus' lap, trying to work up the nerve to tell her that he's had enough of immortal lovemaking and wants to see how things are going back on Earth. Venus tries in vain to dissuade him from this foolish enterprise, but Tannhauser prevails, and returned to the real world, is reunited with the Landgrave (ruler) Hermann, his friend Wolfram von Eschenbach, and sundry other noblemen-minstrels who are gathered at the Wartburg castle. He also looks up an old flame, the Landgrave's niece, Elizabeth, who still loves him, but with somewhat mixed feelings, since he hasn't been around for quite a while.

Bet You Didn't Know

According to the Romans, Venus wore a magic girdle that enabled her to arouse love in others. This didn't sit too well with her husband, Vulcan (the god of fire), who started throwing thunderbolts when he found out that Venus was having a thing with Mars (it was a boy). Venus also hung out with Adonis a lot, and had another child with Achises, while poor Vulcan wound up as the patron god of cuckolds.

Love, meanwhile, is the theme of the song contest, and if Elizabeth wonders where Tannhauser's been, she finds out when he unleashes a hymn to sensual love in the name of Venus. Since everybody else has been singing the praises of love in its purest, most sacred form, the outraged nobles draw their swords and prepare to puncture the pagan. Suddenly Elizabeth intervenes; though she has been wounded by love, she begs Christian forgiveness for Tannhauser. Moved by her noble action, the Landgrave relents, allowing Tannhauser to escape death if he seeks absolution for his sins from the Pope. Since that's an offer he can't refuse (much as he would like to, we suspect), Tannhauser catches the next pilgrimage to Rome.

Months later, Tannhauser straggles back to the castle, exhausted and despairing, since his request has been denied, the Pope declaring that absolution would be as unlikely as his walking staff bursting into flower. Resigned to eternal damnation, Tannhauser calls out for Venus, until Wolfram reveals that Elizabeth has died after months of praying for Tannhauser's soul. The repentant Tannhauser interrupts the funeral procession and dies, embracing Elizabeth's body. The Pilgrims announce a miracle, the Pope's staff has blossomed, and Tannhauser has indeed been redeemed by love and faith.

Lohengrin

One of the many meanings of the word "chivalry" is "the spirit or character of the ideal knight." One of Wagner's many obsessions was depicting this idealistic spirit and character. He tried it first in "Tannhauser," and continued the quest with "Lohengrin," both in the medieval setting and its overall theme of sacrifice and redemption. Wagner, incidentally, reserved those chivalric instincts for his operatic characters. In his private life, he was a liar, a cheat, a vicious anti-Semite, and generally a nasty piece of work.

Anyway, back to thoughts of nobler things, among them a batch of nobles in the dukedom of Brabant (near Antwerp, Belguium) in the first half of the 10th century. The group includes Count Telramund and his wife Ortrud, who among other things, are liars, cheats, and generally nasty pieces of work. Telramund starts out by accusing Elsa, the daughter of the Duke of Brabant, of murdering her brother to gain access to the throne. Elsa recalls a dream wherein a champion will appear to defend her, and sure enough, a knight in shining armor arrives on a boat drawn by a white swan. He declares himself to be Elsa's defender, on condition that she never ask his name nor where he comes from.

The knight conquers Telramund in a duel, but spares his life. Mistake number one, since Telramund and Ortrud immediately slink off to plan their revenge. The next day is the wedding of Elsa and the Knight (they don't believe in long engagements), but even as the bridal procession prepares to enter the church, Ortrud accuses the mysterious champion of having defeated her husband by sorcery, while Telramund himself demands that the knight reveal his identity. The knight refuses. Only to Elsa will he be obliged to reveal the truth, and then only if she breaks her vowe and requests it. In the wedding chamber, Elsa is overcome with doubts, and cannot refrain from putting the fateful question to him. Telramund breaks in with four cronies to kill the Knight (his mistake number one) but the Knight dispatches him instead, announcing that he will yield to Elsa's desire and reveal his secret, but only in the presence of the nobles, and at the same spot where he had first appeared.

I am Lohengrin, he finally tells the assemblage, the son of Parsifal (the old man would later get a whole Wagner opera to himself) and a Knight of the Holy Grail.

Bet You Didn't Know

Being a Knight of the Holy Grail meant that he was a member of a brotherhood of chaste heroes who serve as protectors of the sacred chalice from which Jesus drank at the Last Supper. Religious scholars maintain that the Grail was not the chalice out of which He drank, but the platter off which He ate. Still, it's Wagner's opera, so a Chalice it is.

These knights are granted superhuman powers when defending innocent people, but once their secret is revealed, they must return to their sanctuary. Since Elsa demanded that knowledge, Lohengrin's spell is broken, and even as she tries to talk him out of leaving, the swan appears. With evil glee, Ortrud reveals that the swan is none other than Elsa's brother Gottfried, whom Ortrud herself had transformed by witchcraft. When Lohengrin kneels in prayer, the swan disappears and Gottfried steps out of the river; as the knight departs, the boat now drawn by a dove of peace, Elsa falls lifeless into her brother's arms.

Tristan and Isolde

With Tristan und Isolde, Wagner broke entirely with operatic traditions of the past. There are no arias, no set pieces, no formal ensemble numbers, just "endless melody" (Wagner's own term) and interwoven leitmotifs conceived within a symphonic texture.

Tristan was a Knight of King Arthur's Round Table, who slew dragons, wrote poems, hunted wild boar, saved maidens in distress, and did all the other things that Knights were supposed to do. Then he happened to drink a teeny tiny bit of love potion ... But we're getting ahead of ourselves.

As the opera opens, Tristan is bringing the Princess Isolde from Ireland to Cornwall, where she will become the wife of Tristan's uncle, the aging King Marke. This was not their first meeting, however. Tristan had killed Isolde's fiance in battle, and overcoming her own desire for revenge, Isolde had nursed the wounded Tristan back to health. Now, anger wells up in her again, since the marriage to Marke is decidedly against her will, and she orders her servant Brangane (who happens to be a sorceress on the side) to prepare poison drinks for Tristan and herself. Brangane can't bring herself to do this, so she substitutes a love potion for the poison (the vessel with the pestle?) and instead of death, it is passion that binds Tristan and Isolde together.

Potion or no potion, Isolde married King Marke during the intermission, and Act 2 begins in the castle garden on a clear summer night. Summer nights and love potions are an irresistible combination, so while the King is off hunting, Tristan and Isolde surrender to their passion, not even noticing the daylight rising around them. They awaken to be confronted by the King and his henchman, Melot. The King condemns Tristan to exile, but Melot hungers for blood and challenges Tristan to a duel. Tristan deliberately lowers his guard and allows himself to be wounded. Taken to his father's castle, and lying near death, Tristan hears that Isolde is coming to be with him. As her ship approaches, he tears off his bandages and rises to meet her, only to fall and die in her arms. The King arrives, having learned about the love potion and ready to allow the lovers to reunite, but it is too late, Isolde sings her final lament (the exquisite "Liebestod" or Love Death) before falling across the body of her beloved.

Die Meistersinger

Remember the troubadours and their song contest? Back in those days "Son of Tannhauser" or "Tannhauser II" wouldn't have passed muster, so Wagner moved his new story about troubadours and their song contest to the 16th century and called it Die Meistersinger. He again took one of its main characters—the poet-cobbler Hans Sachs—from German history, and he called the whole thing a comedy, although the critics were not especially amused. "Its horrendous caterwauling," said one of them, "could not be surpassed even if all the organ grinders of Berlin were locked up in the same room, each playing a different waltz."

Never mind. The Overture to Die Meistersinger remains one of the most famous and oft-recorded of all Wagnerian excerpts, and its majestic tones presaging the pomp and ceremony of the Mastersingers convocation. As the familiar strains fade, the curtain rises on Nuremberg around 1550, where the young knight Walther von Stolzing is in love with Eva Pogner, the goldsmith's daughter. Eva returns his affection, but her father has other plans: he has promised to marry her to the winner of the Mastersingers' competition on the following day. Walther decides to enter the contest, but he is not too hopeful: it normally takes years to work your way up from apprentice to full master's status, and besides, the competition has all sorts of complicated rules and regulations that put outsiders at a considerable disadvantage.

At the preliminary hearings, Walther sings a romantic ode to spring, impressing Hans Sachs with its honesty and originality. But leading the pedantic Sixtus Beckmesser is another suitor for Eva's hand, who takes extravagant note of Walther's "mistakes" (i.e., variations from the niggling regulations), and tries to convince everyone that Walther is an unfit candidate.

In Act II, Walther and Eva have confessed their love to Hans Sachs, as well as their plans to elope. When Beckmesser comes around to serenade Eva, she gets her maid, Maddalena, to impersonate her. Beckmesser's attempted love song is thwarted by Sachs, who constantly interrupts it with hammerings on his last, and when Maddalena's fiance witnesses the scene, he naturally assumes that Beckmesser's song is aimed at his intended, and gives him a good thrashing. In all the confusion, Eva and Walther figure that it's a good time to get away, but Sachs wisely stops them.

The next day, in Sach's workshop, Walther tells the cobbler of a glorious song that came to him

Bet You Didn't Know

In the original libretto, the pompous Beckmesser character was named Hans Lick, causing one famous anti-Wagner critic to stalk out of the room at an early reading. His name was Eduard Hanslick.

in a dream. Sachs copies down the first two verses (Walther improvises the third verse when Eva arrives). When Beckmesser shows up, though, he filches the stanzas that the cobbler had notated, and the clever Sachs gives him permission to use it as his own. This he does, producing such ugly sounds, and messing up the texts so badly that he becomes the center of ridicule. Desperately, he lashes out at Sachs, who reveals the truth, and invites Walther to present the noble love song in proper form. This he does in the celebrated "Prize Song," the piece and its composer are hailed by the assemblage, and in an appropriately happy ending (we told you this was a comic opera), the songwriter gets the girl of his dreams.

Parsifal

Remember Lohengrin and his miraculous powers as a Knight of the Holy Grail? If not, please go back and read that part of the chapter again, so we don't have to explain all the stuff again. Don't worry. We'll wait for you.

OK, Parsifal, as we started saying, takes place in and around the castle of Monsalvat in the Pyrenees, where resides the Holy Grail. The Knights sworn to guard it, when they're not sallying forth doing Good Deeds and protecting the innocent, are bound by vows of purity in mind and spirit. King Amfortas has fallen from this high estate, having set out to storm the castle of the magician Klingsor but instead found himself seduced by one of the sirens Klingsor kept around the place for just such eventualities. What's worse, Amfortas had been carrying the sacred spear that had been thrust into Christ's side during the Crucifixion, and when Klingsor wrested it from him, Amfortas received a wound that has never healed. He has tried every balm and remedy he can find, but the word is out that he can only be cured by a touch of the same spear that wounded him, and further, that the spear can only be regained by an innocent, completely naive hero, a "Pure Fool."

In comes a lad, who killed one of the swans, not realizing that the guardians of the Grail held all animals sacred. Chastised by Gurnemanz, one of the Knights, the boy destroys his bow and arrow in penitence, and when questioned, says that he has been raised in the wilderness and knows nothing of the world, not even his own name. Suspecting that here might be the Pure Fool destined to heal Amfortas, Gurnemanz leads him to the castle to witness the solemn ritual of displaying the Grail for adoration by the Knights. The youth watches in silence, understanding nothing of the proceedings, and is driven from the castle.

Soon he has wandered into the enchanted gardens of Klingsor's castle, and meets some of the sirens who tease, taunt, and try to seduce him, this time without success. Klingsor, though, is ready with his ultimate weapon, and sends out Kundry. She is a kind of double agent, an ugly messenger when she serves the pious knights, but a supernaturally beautiful maiden when in the magician's employ. Initially reluctant to lead the naive youth into sin, Kundry eventually rises to the challenge, reminding Parsifal, for that is his name, of his mother's love, and how it can be recaptured in her. Then she kisses him. That much of a fool Parsifal isn't; finally realizing what's going on, he pushes her away, and Kundry, not used to rejection, calls on Klingsor to take action. The magician obligingly hurls Amfortas' spear at Parsifal, but miraculously, the weapon stops in mid-air. The lad seizes it, and the enchantments are broken, with only Kundry left lying on the ground.

As time passes, Gurnemanz finds Kundry near the mountain of the Grail and revives her. Parsifal arrives in full armor, which Amfortas asks him to remove because it is Good Friday. Recognizing Parsifal, Gurnemanz tells him that the Knights of the Grail have despaired ever since Amfortas, anguished and tormented by the still-bleeding wound, has been unable to celebrate the ritual of the Grail. Indeed, the King's father, Titurel, has died of grief. When Parsifal enters the castle to attend Titurel's funeral, he finds Amfortas and heals his wound by touching it with the sacred spear. Parsifal is then anointed King of the Grail in his place, unveiling and renewing the ritual of the Holy Grail. A white dove appears in the sky, hovering over the castle, while Kundry, penitent and free at last from Klingsor's enchantment, is forgiven for her sins and redeemed in death.

With This Ring

For more than a quarter of a century, with time out for writing other operas, songs, and instrumental pieces, Wagner worked on the mighty epic that we know as the Ring Cycle. Calling it a wonderwork, Franz Liszt said, "The Ring of the Niebelung overtops and commands our whole art-epoch even as Mont Blanc does our other mountains." It was an apt comment, even allowing for a certain family prejudice (Wagner had run off with Liszt's daughter, had three children by her, and married her. In that order).

The crowning glory of Wagner's creative life fused elements of mythology, symbolism, poetry, and philosophy. It brought the leitmotif system into its most intricate and effective usage, and exploded the confining boundaries of the operatic stage. In terms of length, complexity, grandeur of design, and sheer intensity of emotional expression, the four Ring operas are unparalleled in the history of the art. Musically, they contain pages of breathtaking beauty and overwhelming power; dramatically (to quote the composer's grandson, Wieland Wagner) they comprise "a crime story and chiller of the first order— blood, murder, and sex, with more surprise and suspense than a James Bond thriller."

The genesis of the Ring operas is a fascinating story in itself. Intrigued by various legends and folk sagas of German and Scandinavian extraction, Wagner fashioned a libretto in 1848 called Siegfried's Death. Three years later, realizing that the subject was too expansive for a single opera, he wrote another dramatic poem to preface it, called The Young Siegfried. Eventually, Young Siegfried, minus the adjective, became the third Ring opera; Siegfried's Death, now dubbed Götterdämmerung (Twilight of the Gods), the fourth. Still later, Wagner decided that the lineage of his hero needed further elucidation, so he wrote Die Walküre

(The Valkyries) to precede the other two. Finally, he prepared the text of Das Rheingold (The Rhine Gold), describing it as a "preliminary evening" to the trilogy.

The librettos, in other words, were written in inverse order, and all four were complete before a single note of music was put on paper. Taken together, said Wagner with his usual modesty, they formed "the greatest poem in the world." This already herculean accomplishment behind him, Wagner began writing the music in 1853, this time tackling the operas in proper sequence. Das Rheingold was finished in mid-1854, Die Walküre in the spring of 1856. The next year saw the completion of the first act of "Siegfried" and part of the second, when inspirations called in other directions. "When will we see each other again?" was the pensive question Wagner penciled into the orchestra score at the point he left off.

For eight years, Wagner dealt with other musical matters, most notably Tristan and Die Meistersinger; then, as if he had never left it, he plunged back into the Ring. Siegfried was completed in February of 1871, and the last musical T of Götterdämmerung was crossed on November 21, 1874.

Das Rheingold

The story of the Rhine gold begins (where else?) at the bottom of the Rhine, where it is being guarded by three Rhine Maidens: Woglinde, Wellgunde, and (our dentist's favorite) Flosshilde. When Alberich, a Niebelung (member of a race of dwarfs), emerges from his murky cavern, they decide to have some Rhinemaidenly fun with him, teasing and tormenting him, but ultimately letting slip the fact that their gold can be fashioned into a ring that grants its bearer ultimate power, provided he renounces love. Alberich, only too happy with such a bargain, curses love, seizes the ring, and heads off to rule the world.

Meanwhile, back on land, the giants Fafner and Fasolt have finished building Valhalla, the magnificent new castle-home of Wotan, king of the gods, his wife Fricka, and their immortal courtiers. Wotan may rule the gods, but he has all-too-human frailties. He had promised the giants that their builders' fee would be Freia, goddess of beauty and youth, but true to his character (or lack of it) he reneges. The giants are none too pleased, as you might imagine, but the resulting row is interrupted by the arrival of Loge, the god of Fire, who brings news of Alberich's theft of the gold and the immense wealth and power he has thus acquired.

Forget Freia! The giants decide that the Rheingold would be a better reward anyway, and Wotan goes with Loge to Niebelheim (the land of the Niebelungs). You really don't want to know all the gory details. Suffice it to say that Wotan and Loge trick Alberich into giving up the gold, and the ring he has forged from it, so Alberich puts a terrible curse on the ring, crying out that it will bring misfortune to anyone who takes possession of it. No sooner does Wotan entrust the ring to the giants than they quarrel, and Fafner kills Fasolt. The malediction has begun to work.

Meanwhile, Wotan is getting edgy about not moving into his new home, and annoyed that Valhalla is surrounded by a fearful mist. To the rescue comes Donner, the God of Thunder, who sets a great storm crashing; in its wake, the clouds are dispelled and the castle stands glistening in the late afternoon sunshine. A huge rainbow bridge stretches out to it, and ignoring the wails of the Rhine maidens below, the gods proceed on their impressive journey home.

Die Walküre

Since the events described in Das Rheingold, Wotan has been busy, fathering nine warrior maidens called Valkyries (he's married to Fricka, but the Valkyries' mother is Erda. Don't ask.) He also has sired brother and sister twins, Siegmund and Sieglinde, with an earth woman. The idea was that the Valkyries can bring fallen heroes back to Valhalla to form an army for the gods' defense, while the earthly offspring can use various means to salve Wotan's conscience not available to the god himself. Well, it's as a good an excuse as any.

Anyway, the opera opens with a wounded Siegmund, pursued by enemies, seeking shelter in a forest hut belonging to Hunding and his wife Sieglinde. Siegmund and Sieglinde are immediately drawn to each other (without realizing their relationship, since the twins had been separated at birth.) When Hunding comes home and learns that Siegmund is an enemy of his clan, he tells the visitor that he will obey the rules of hospitality and provide him with shelter for the night. Mortal combat, however, must follow on the morrow.

Sieglinde doesn't like that idea at all, so first of all she puts a sleeping potion into her husband's drink. Then she shows Siegmund a sword that a mysterious traveler (Wotan in disguise, if you must know) had embedded so deeply within the trunk of an ash tree that only the greatest and strongest of warriors could pull it out. With a mighty effort, Siegmund lifts the sword from its resting place, naming it "Nothung" (born of necessity). Further discussions, not to mention passionate declarations of love, finally reveal that they are indeed brother and sister, but nothing can dampen their ardor now, and they run off together into the night.

Bet You Didn't Know

Singing a long and demanding Wagnerian role is a test of stamina for any artist, and the intense concentration involveds sometimes has to find a release. When the manager of the Met came to Maria Jeritza's dressing room in between acts of a "Die Walküre" performance (she was the Sieglinde that night), he found the great soprano, still in full costume and makeup, turning somersaults.

Hunding may not be the smartest guy in the forest, but when he wakes up, minus sword and wife, he begins to smell a rat, and sets off in hot pursuit of the lovers. Back in Valhalla, meanwhile, Wotan commands Brunnhilde, the most beloved of his Valkyrie daughters, to defend Siegmund against the vengeful Hunding. Unfortunately Fricka, goddess of marriage (not that her own union with Wotan is going any too smoothly), will have none of this incestuous adultery, and demands that Siegmund be killed instead. Wotan, it turns out, can stand up to anything but his wife, so he reluctantly gives in, and changes his instructions to Brunnhilde. The Valkyrie tells Siegmund of his impending fate, inviting him to join the other heros in the palace guard at Valhalla, but he declares that, rather than abandon Sieglinde, he is ready to kill both himself and her. Deeply moved, Brunnhilde resolves to protect them both.

As the duel begins, Brunnhilde uses her shield to safeguard Siegmund, but suddenly Wotan appears, his spear shattering Siegmund's sword. Hunding kills the now-defenseless Siegmund, and Wotan takes his own revenge by striking down Hunding. In all the tumult, Brunnhilde sweeps up the pieces of the sword and helps Sieglinde escape. She will give birth to a great hero, Brunnhilde tells her, who will be named Siegfried, and will one day reforge Nothung into a sword of universal victory.

Wotan is furious as only a thwarted god (and disobeyed father) can be. His pronounces his punishment: Brunnhilde will lose her immortal Valkyrie status, and go into a deep sleep until a man shall find her and take her as his wife. Her sundry requests for mercy falling on deaf ears, Brunnhilde finally begs her father at least to set up some sort of protective device, so that only a true hero would be able to reach her. To this Wotan agrees. He covers Brunnhilde with his shield, then summons Loge (remember Loge?) ordering the god of Fire to surround the sleeping Valkyrie-that-was with a magic circle of flame that only a fearless hero could penetrate. With a last look back at his wayward offspring, Wotan disappears beyond the flames.

Bet You Didn't Know

Another famous Wagnerian soprano, Olive Fremstad, was reclining on her rock, when she realized that the "magic fire" was not coming from the planned burst of steam jets, but was actually spurting forth out with some kind of vile-smelling smoke. She stayed quietly as long as she could, but then called out to the stagehands, her powerful voice reaching half the house as well, "If you don't shut off this stink, I'm leaving right now!" They did, she didn't, and the opera ended right on schedule.

Siegfried

Once again, a lot has happened between operas, and by the time the third section of the Ring opens, Sieglinde has died giving birth to Siegfried. He has been raised by Mime (pronounced Mee-meh), another Niebelung—Alberich's brother, as a matter of fact—who can't wait for the child to grow up big and strong enough to kill Fafner, the giant who now has the Ring. The sneaky Mime plans then to do away with Siegfried, and keep the treasure for himself.

Knowing that Siegfried will need a powerful weapon, Mime has been trying to reforge Nothung from the fragments Sieglinde left behind. Nothung doing. He can only come up with inferior copies, that the already strong Siegfried breaks like so many matchsticks. While Siegfried is out, the Wanderer enters. He looks a lot like Wotan, but what does Mime know? They trade riddles, then the Wanderer leaves with the prophecy that only he who knows no fear can reforge the sword, and the dire warning that Mime will die at the hands of that fearless mortal.

When Siegfried reappears, Mime tries to forestall Wotan's prophecy by frightening the warrior with terrifying stories of the dragon who guards the treasure (i.e., Fafner). Siegfried pays him no heed, and reforges the enchanted sword himself, while Mime cooks up a poison potion for use on Siegfried once the dragon is dead.

Outside Fafner's cave, Mime's brother Alberich is keeping an anxious watch when the Wanderer arrives. A little smarter than his sibling, Alberich recognizes Wotan, and boasts how in short order, the dragon will be slain and the treasure his. Wotan, in turn, predicts that Mime will try to use the strength of a young hero to get the treasure for himself. As morning dawns, Siegfried listens with wonder to the forest rustlings and the songs of birds. But then it's on to business.

He sounds a horn call to waken Fafner, they fight, and the dragon is slain. While withdrawing his sword, though, Siegfried is splashed with some of the dragon's blood. Suddenly, he can understand the language of the forest bird, which first alerts him to the Ring and other treasures hidden in the cave, and then warns him of Mime's impending treachery. Forewarned, and forearmed (with Nothung), Siegfried dispatches Mime in short order, and sits down to see if the little birdie has any more information for him. She has. This time, she tells him about the beautiful Brunnhilde, and even leads him to the rock where the maiden is sleeping within a circle of fire.

At the foot of the mountain, Wotan summons the earth goddess Erda, who, fairly put out at being wakened from a happy sleep, offers a veiled prophecy that the gods will die, the ring will be returned to the Rhine maidens, and the world will be freed from Alberich's curse. At this point, you can either go home, since you know how the story will come out, or stick around for the rest of this opera and all of the next.

Assuming you're still with us, we can wrap up the third Ring story fairly quickly. When Siegfried appears, Wotan attempts to bar his way, but Siegfried shatters his spear with his sword (even as Wotan had shattered Siegmund's sword with his spear back in opera number two), and the king of the gods slinks off, hoping to rebuild his shattered spear and thereby regain his powers. As the fearless Siegfried reaches the summit of the mountain, he passes unharmed through the ring of fire, and as the flames die away, he awakens Brunnhilde with a kiss. After the obligatory love duet, they embrace passionately as the curtain falls.

Götterdämmerung

It is dawn of the next day. Three Norns (fates) are weaving the rope of destiny, when suddenly the thread tears. The end of the gods is imminent. Brunnhilde and Siegfried enter singing of their love, but also of separation, since the hero must go forth in search of further adventures. They trade gifts (he gives her the Ring, she gives him her horse, which had been sleeping on the same rock all those years, and is presumably well rested by now). He sets off for the kingdom of the Gibichungs. Not that he's the jealous type or anything, but he leaves Brunnhilde behind the same old circle of fire, knowing that no other man can reach her.

Bet You Didn't Know

When Arturo Toscanini came to the Metropolitan Opera in 1908, his first rehearsal at the house was of "Götterdämmerung". Soon afterwards, a delegation of orchestral players stormed into the office of the new general manager, Giulio Gatti-Casazza, complaining about the foul names the conductor had hurled at them. What sort of foul names, Gatti wondered. Reluctantly, the players repeated the insulting words, whereupon the manager let out a loud laugh. "You think that's bad," he said; "you should hear what he calls me!"

Pay attention now, because this gets complicated. The Lord of the Gibichungs is Gunther, who's the half-brother of Hagen, who's the son of Alberich, the Niebelung who started the whole megillah in the first place. They hatch a nifty plot to enhance their fortunes, by which scheme Gunther would marry Brunnhilde while Gutrune hooks up with Siegfried. There are a couple of hitches to this plan, among them the love Brunnhilde and Siegfried have for each other and the fact that only Siegfried can penetrate that ring of fire to fetch her out. The solution: another love potion, like the one that sizzled Tristan and Isolde. Siegfried drinks it, develops an instant passion for Gutrune, and goes (disguised as Gunther) to bring back Brunnhilde.

When Brunnhilde realizes what's going on, she angrily accuses her lover of betrayal, but his mind still dulled by the potion, Siegfried denies everything. Brunnhilde, unable to reconcile her conflicting emotions of love, despair, hatred, and jealousy, reveals to Hagen that the one vulnerable part of Siegfried's body is his back. So guess where Hagen sticks his spear?

Hagen also kills Gunther, while he's at it, and as Siegfried's companions somberly place him on his shield and carry him off into the mists, the orchestra throbs out the overpoweringly poignant Funeral Music. The truth finally known to all, Brunnhilde orders a great funeral pyre built for the slain hero, and as the flames burn ever more fiercely, she plunges into its midst to join her beloved Siegfried. The Rhine overflows, putting out the local fire and drawing Hagen to his death beneath its swirling waters. Gleefully, the Rhine Maidens hold aloft the Ring, at long last returned to its rightful place, but in the distance, the fire's glow appears again, this time consuming Valhalla and ending the reign of the gods. As Anna Russell wryly notes, "After nineteen and one half hours, you're back exactly where you started—and at those prices!"

Coda

The problems of casting and originally staging this mighty cycle were bewildering in their profusion (amongst other disasters, the set builder sent the dragon to Beirut instead of Bayreuth), but the premieres went off on schedule on four successive nights in August of 1876. The occasion was, for Wagner, a simultaneous moment of jubilation and despair. On one hand, here was his dream come true—his colossal set of operas produced in a modern new theatre especially created to display them. On the other hand—there was the vicious sniping of the critics, which led to poor attendance at the subsequent performances and a huge financial loss for the entire project.

Poetic Justice

Wagner's day would come, of course, and when it did, the nay-sayers were swept under the rug of history. As the French composer Camille Saint-Saens put it with prophetic eloquence, "Here we have the theatre of the future. A thousand critics, each writing a thousand lines a day for ten years, would injure these works about as much as a child's breath would go towards overthrowing the pyramids of Egypt."

CHAPTER 24

Let Us Pray

> ## In This Chapter
>
> ➤ More than monastery music
> ➤ The ordinary and the proper
> ➤ Requiems and oratorios
> ➤ Motets, hymns, and psalms

In the 1960s and 70s, when churches began presenting rock sermons and folk masses, some of the faithful were horrified at this presumed sacrilege. The history of religious music, though, followed the same evolutionary pattern as secular music, which is why Handel's Messiah, say, sounds very different from Brahms' German Requiem. Monophony gave way to polyphony in church as well as court, and music for prayer was influenced by the same social, political, and philosophical climates that help shape the creation of worldly compositions.

There were many line-crossings within religious music too. On the surface, Masses are Catholic and hymns are Protestant, but you couldn't count on it. The Oxford Movement of the 19th century sought to bring back traditional Latin chants into Church of England services, while the magnificent Mass in B Minor, perhaps the most famous of all the Catholic masses, was the creation of the devoutly Lutheran Johann Sebastian Bach.

Chants of a Lifetime

It's easy enough to recognize the unique character of Gregorian chant, even if the CD doesn't have a picture of a monk on it. The hypnotic effect of those unaccompanied voices has one visualizing a stone-walled monastery, with a well-tended garden and hooded figures moving silently through long, austere hallways.

Gregorian Chant, often called plainsong or plainchant, is named for Pope Gregory I (c. 540-604), who collected and codified various melodies, designating them for specific aspects of Roman Catholic liturgical services. He also established the first singing school in Rome (schola cantorum), where these chants were taught. They are monophonic, meaning that their melodies flow without regular accented rhythms, abrupt variations in volume, or instrumental accompaniment of any sort.

The original development of chants is a matter of speculation, since the earliest extant collections date from around 900. There are more than 500 chants in those early books, however. Most of them were designed for portions of the Mass and while they continued to be faithfully reproduced in volumes throughout the middle ages, new chants were added as well. In almost all cases, the melody was created to enhance the text—either moving one note per syllable, or proceeding as a melisma, with a single syllable set to a series of notes.

Everything Old is New Again

In the 1990s, a CD titled "Chant", which indeed had a solemn monk pictured on the cover, was an unlikely and unexpected smash hit, sharing the best-seller status with such not-quite-so-early music artists as Bruce Springsteen, Madonna, and the Cranberries. "Chant II" was another big success, and today you'll find dozens of Gregorian Chant albums for sale on the internet.

Important Things to Know

Among many other examples of brilliantly marketed albums of medieval and other early vocal music that nonetheless have high artistic value and integrity are those by the women who call themselves The Anonymous Four (if you promise not to tell anybody, their names are Susan Hellauer, Ruth Cunningham, Marsha Genensky, and Jacqueline Homer-Kwiatek; or if you prefer to bask in the glow of performances by the spiritual descendants of the original chanters, sample the CD collections by the Benedictine Monks of Santa Domingo de Silos (one of them has a photo of five monks on the cover). Luxembourg, the Carmelite Prior Choir, or the Gregorian Choir of Paris.

Much the same thing happened with baroque music in the 1950s when, after decades of obscurity, Vivaldi came rushing back to high visibility and enormous popularity, his coattails dragging all manner of lesser contemporaries along for the commercial ride.

Classical Indian music zoomed to sudden Western popularity in the 1960s, and today, opera seems to be more popular than ever, with younger audiences flocking to works of John Adams, Philip Glass, and other contemporary composers. Is there a pattern here? Maybe so: Each generation discovers something "new" that has actually been around for centuries.

The proponents of New Age music gave a modern twist to the ancient chants, attempting to duplicate their mystical, reflective, calming effects, but ignoring the sacred soul that lay at their heart. No matter: the ersatz quality of so many New Age creations may well have encouraged listeners to go back to the source, and thus explain the resurgent popularity of Gregorian Chant.

Mass Appeal

The original chants, as we said, were designed to fit into the solemn ritual of the Catholic Mass, and as polyphony entered the tonal picture, the Mass continued to dominate sacred composition. This became, as *Groves Dictionary* tells us, "one of the seminal forms of European art music." Indeed, the texts of the mass have given inspiration to composers of every era and stylistic persuasion.

The Extraordinary, but Not Proper, Ordinary

The rites of the mass have evolved along with the music, but essentially they are divided into the Ordinary and the Proper. The Proper contains Introductions, Alleluias, and sequences chosen for selected occasions, such as Communion. Most composers, however, have ideas from or been drawn to the texts of the five unvarying sections of the Ordinary: Kyrie, Gloria, Credo, Sanctus, and Agnus Dei.

Music Word

"**Cantus**" in Latin means song or melody, and "**firmus**" translates as just what it sounds like: firm or steady. A cantus firmus refers to the main or given primary melody (often borrowed from other religious pieces or secular songs) upon which a composer builds a more complicated piece by the addition of contrasting themes.

For centuries, the music of both ordinary and proper consisted of a chant melody, called the cantus firmus (fixed song) followed by one created in polyphonic style. By the 15th century, composers were venturing beyond the piece-by-piece method and creating fully polyphonic Ordinary masses to those same texts. By the time of Palestrina in the 16th century, it was no longer unusual for composers to write complete masses. Nor was it uncommon for them to borrow themes from other sources, including bawdy songs (though obviously taking care not to import the lyrics as well). A popular French secular ballad called "L'Homme Arme" (The Armed Man) pops up in at least thirty Renaissance masses, among them Palestrina's masterpiece "Missa Papae Marcelli", dedicated to the Pope Marcellus.

Getting back to the five sections of the Ordinary: the text of the Kyrie is "Lord have mercy upon us; Christ have mercy upon us". Then follows the familiar hymn of praise, "Gloria in excelsis Deo" (Glory be to God on high). The Credo is a confession of faith: "I believe in one God, the omnipotent Father"; the Sanctus simply says, "Holy, Holy, Holy" before proceeding to the often jubilant "Hosanna in excelsis" (Praise in the Highest) and the Benediction: "Blessed is He who cometh in the name of the Lord." The final section, often the most touchingly beautiful, is the prayer for peace to Agnus Dei ("Lamb of God who taketh away the sins of the world."

Requiem: Rest in Peace

Another important form of the mass is the Requiem, titled for its introductory text "Requiem aeternam dona eis Domine" (Give them eternal rest, O Lord"). Since its function is to mourn the departed, the Requiem normally omits the jubilant Gloria and Credo parts of the Ordinary, replacing them with psalm verses and a new segment titled "Dies Irae" (Day of Judgement).

The oldest polyphonic requiem (that has come down to us) was written by the Flemish composer Johannes Ockeghem (c. 1410-1497). More than forty polyphonic requiems survive from the 16th century, and from the 17th on, there were hundreds; The most famous being the uncompleted final work of Mozart, and the elaborate, grandiose Requiems in full-blown Romantic style by Berlioz and Verdi.

Bet You Didn't Know

The far more gentle "A German Requiem" by Brahms caused something of a scandal when it was first sung—precisely because it was set in German, not Latin, and also set Biblical texts on the themes of death and mourning, rather than the prescribed words of the Mass. (The Brahms is a Requiem all right, in other words, but it's not a Requiem Mass).

In the 20th century, France's Fauré and Durufle and England's John Rutter, are among the composers who have given us Requiem Masses of astonishing beauty. While the English master Benjamin Britten (in his "War Requiem") and America's own Leonard Bernstein (in "Mass") follow Brahms' lead by combining the Latin texts of the mass with other poetic expressions.

Oratorio: Hallelujah Handel

Even if it often gives rise to music primarily conceived for concert or theatrical performance, the text of the mass was intended for religious ritual. The oratorio takes a different path to purity: without any pretense to liturgy, it tells a Biblical or other sacred story. In this it is related to opera, and indeed the musical style of oratorios tend to mirror that of operas created during the same period. Operas, of course, carry forward the drama with sets, costumes and stage action; oratorios are content to convey their musical and moral messages through the fusion of words and music alone.

Music Word

An **oratorio** is essentially an opera without acting, a dramatic and extended setting of a spiritualreligious text (often taken from the Bible) for chorus, soloists and orchestra. In the 20th century, a number of composers have devised oratorios on inspirational, though not specifically religious themes, such as Prokofiev's "On Guard for Peace", Shostakovich's "Song of the Forests" and Sir Michael Tippett's "A Child of Our Time."

The Oratorio traces its origin to the informal meetings or "spiritual exercises" of the "Congregazione dell'Oratorio" founded in Rome before 1600 by Filippo Neri. The name comes from the oratory (prayer hall) in which the meetings were held, and where Neri organized sacred plays with choral episodes. The music (as it tends to do), helped emphasize the religious lessons, while attracting people to the organization and spreading its membership to other cities. For this Neri was canonized, the first musician to achieve sainthood.

A century later, oratorio was well established as a musical genre throughout Europe, flourishing both as Oratorio Latino, sung in Latin, and Oratorio Volgare, sung in Italian with a sermon inserted between its two sections. Outside of Italy, the latter functioned primarily as a Lenten substitute for opera in Vienna and other Roman Catholic courts. By the middle of the 17th century, though, a German oratorio style had developed, using that language and accepted in Lutheran services. Heinrich Schutz wrote a Christmas Oratorio in 1665, and Bach combined six Cantatas in an oratorio to be performed on successive days from Christmas to Epiphany.

Handel imported the oratorio style to England, incorporating elements from the English masque and anthem, and fitting out all sorts of Biblical stories with virtuosic solos and robust choruses. Indeed, the oratorio reached its peak with Handel: Few composers thereafter would devote so much of their creative energies to the form; no later oratorio has ever matched the worldwide popularity of *Messiah*.

Bet You Didn't Know

When *Messiah* was premiered in London in 1743, one of Handel's English friends complimented the composer on the "splendid entertainment" he had provided the listeners. "My lord," Handel replied, "I should be very sorry indeed if I had only entertained them. My intention was to make them better."

No way, of course, does this mean that the oratorio was all washed up. Masterworks in the form continued to appear in every succeeding generation. After hearing Handel oratorios during his visits to London, Haydn went home and wrote *The Creation* and *The Seasons*. London called again to Mendelssohn and he obliged with *St. Paul* and *Elijah*, while Berlioz' *L'enfance du Christ* and Liszt's *Christus* gave further evidence that the oratorio was alive and well in the romantic era. In the 20th century, Honegger's *King David*, Walton's *Belshazzar's Feast*, and Stravinsky's *The Flood* have all found wide audiences. For those who have sat through the *Hallelujah Chorus* once too often, let's not forget *"Oedipus Tex," "The Seasonings,"* and several other hilarious oratorio spoofs by P.D.Q. Bach (alias Peter Schickele).

Motet 6

For nearly six centuries, from the Middle Ages through the baroque era, the motet was one of the most frequently encountered musical forms, reigning with equal distinction in and out of the church. The term is derived from "mot" ("word" in French), although in earlier forms of the language, the term could also signify a verse or stanza. Originally, an unaccompanied choral song, the motet grew in complexity with added vocal lines, and it later developed instrumental partnerships. Secular motets were often written in French, expressing the joys and tribulations of love and battle (or vice versa), while the religious motet more often used Latin texts and were found within the context of church services. Later, these would concepts would be combined, the music fitted to bilingual texts.

Music Word

A **motet** is a type of sacred choral composition for church use, usually in Latin, though the words are not specifically part of the liturgy. It has the same purpose in Roman Catholic services as the Anthem does (with English texts) in the Anglican tradition.

Guillaume Dufay (c.1400-1440) a singer in the Papal Choir in Rome, and another composer who used "L'homme arme" in a Mass, created three-part song motets, but by the next generation, five or six parts had become the standard. Josquin des Pres (c.1450-1521) combined flowing melody and imitative counterpoint to add harmonic variety and provide more vivid interpretations of the texts.

Tomas Luis de Victoria in Spain, Thomas Tallis in England, Hans Leo Hassler in Germany, and the aforementioned Giovanni Palestrina in Italy were among the many other masters who added immeasurably to the art and artistry of the motet. In France, birthplace of the form, grand motets, many of them psalm settings for soloists, chorus and orchestra by Lully, Charpentier, Lalande, and others, formed an imposing repertory for the King's Chapel. For quieter moments, there was the "petit (or little) motet," with just two or three voices and continuo accompaniment.

Bet You Didn't Know

Josquin is often referred to by his given name only, and it's a good thing too, since literally dozens of spellings of his surname (Desprez, Depret, Del Prato, etc. etc.) have come down to us.

After 1750, the motet was gradually dethroned as a major musical force, and although Mozart, Schubert, Liszt, Mendelssohn, and Bruckner all created Latin motets, and Brahms contributed several in the German Protestant tradition, its use remained occasional and rather specialized. In the 19th century, Nicolas Slonimsky assured us, "The few composers who stubbornly cultivated it, particularly in Germany, did so more out of reverence for its Gothic past than out of inner imperative."

Hymn: Praise the Lord

Although songs in adoration of God have been discovered from as early as 200 A.D., and Latin hymns emerged toward the end of the fourth century, the word is most commonly applied to the vernacular pieces that came into use with the Reformation. (There were also Homeric and other early hymns that were paeans to pagan gods and ancient heroes, but they need not detain us in this highly reverent chapter).

In Christian worship, the early hymns were monophonic; gradually contrapuntal voices were added, and in the 15th century, polyphonic settings became a regular feature of the Vespers. Sixteenth-century hymns tended to have four-part settings; later the vocal bass was doubled by the organ, and various combinations of voices, including solos, came into common usage.

Important Things to Know

When Professor Higgiens sings his "Hymn to Him" in "My Fair Lady", he's indulging in a double pun, since a hymn is the generic name for songs in praise of God (i.e., Him with a capital H), while the good Professor uses it to heap praise upon the—as he sees it—highly superior intelligence, wit, and wisdom of the entire male gender.

The vernacular hymn remains an integral part of Lutheran worship. The Anglican Church adapted many Lutheran hymns in the 16th century (among them "A Mighty Fortress is Our God," supposed to have been written by Martin Luther himself), but the English Reformation then drifted to Calvinism, which opposed hymns in liturgical services. Puritans, you'll recall, considered singing (along with most other pleasurable activities) an act of the devil, so for some two centuries, English parish church music was essentially restricted to the psalms (see below). It remained so until the 18th century, when nonconformists like John Wesley returned hymns and anthems to a central feature of English church services, new music was commissioned, and parishes even began providing hymnbooks for the congregation to follow.

American hymns evolved from several sources, including the chordal English styles, but also incorporating gospel influences from the 19th century revival movement that reflected traditions of white and African-American evangelical churches. Spirituals were (and are) often sung in Black churches as well, but they are essentially folk songs with religious themes, rather than church music *per se*. On the other hand, the spirituals are among the greatest treasures of American music, welcomed in concert halls around the world in equal partnership to the masterful songs of Schubert or Brahms.

Psalm Readings

From the Greek word meaning "plucking." psalms are prayerful Biblical poems sung with instrumental accompaniment. The Bible tells us that King David not only wrote psalms, but played them on his lyre; in the ancient Hebrew temples, they were chanted daily by the Levites. In early Christian psalmody, the music was interspersed with readings, later a number of the psalms were incorporated into Gregorian chants.

Congregational psalm singing became part of Protestant worship in the 16th century, the texts translated into the language of the country, and paraphrased in metrical verses that simplified group singing. Italian and Spanish psalmody tended to be more elaborate in texture, while in northern Europe, psalms were given freer form by Josquin and his contemporaries, many of them probably intended for performance outside the church.

After 1600, simple psalm singing continued in the reformed churches, while more ambitious settings were usually reserved for motets and anthems. There's one in every crowd, though: The Dutch master Jan Pieterzoon Sweelinck (1562-1621) set all 153 psalms in simple versions for three to eight voices (in French).

In later eras, most psalm settings have been designed for concert rather than churchly use, the more notable 20th century examples including Zoltan Kodaly's "Psalmus Hungaricus", Igor Stravinsky's "Symphony of Psalms" and Leonard Bernstein's "Chichester Psalms". There are also individual Psalm settings by Ives, Cowell, Vaughan Williams, and many others.

Index